JEWS IN THE JAPANESE MIND

OTHER BOOKS BY THE AUTHORS

By David G. Goodman

In English:

Long, Long Autumn Nights: Selected Poems of Oguma Hideo, 1901–1940
(Winner of the 1990 Columbia University Translation Center Award)

Five Plays by Kishida Kunio

Japanese Drama and Culture in the 1960s: The Return of the Gods

Land of Volcanic Ash

After Apocalypse: Four Japanese Plays of Hiroshima and Nagasaki

In Japanese:

Hashiru [*Running*]

Fujisan mieta—Satoh Makoto ni okeru kakumei no engeki
[*Mount Fuji Perceived: The Revolutionary Theatre of Satoh Makoto*]

Isuraeru—koe to kao [*Israel: Voices and Faces*]

Tōbōshi [*My Escapology*]

By Masanori Miyazawa (in Japanese):

Yudayajinron-kō: Nihon ni okeru rongi no tsuiseki [*Theories Concerning the Jews: An Investigation into Debates in Japan*]

Nihonjin no Yudaya-Isuraeru ninshiki [*Japanese Attitudes Toward the Jews and Israel*]

Nihon ni okeru Yudaya-Isuraeru rongi bunken mokuroku, 1877-1988 [*Japanese Debates on the Jews and Israel, 1877-1988: A Bibliography*]

Hokubei Nihonjin Kirisutokyō undō-shi [*A History of Japanese-Christian Movements in North America*]

Niijima Jō: kindai Nihon no senkakusha [*Niijima Jō: Pioneer of Modern Japan*]

JEWS IN THE
JAPANESE MIND

The History and Uses of a Cultural Stereotype

David G. Goodman
Masanori Miyazawa

THE FREE PRESS
New York   London   Toronto   Sydney   Tokyo   Singapore

The Free Press
A Division of Simon & Schuster Inc.
866 Third Avenue, New York, N.Y. 10022

Printed in the United States of America

printing number
1 2 3 4 5 6 7 8 9 10

Library of Congress Cataloging-in-Publication Data

Goodman, David G.
    Jews in the Japanese mind: the history and uses of a cultural stereotype/ David G. Goodman, Masanori Miyazawa.
       p. cm.
    Includes bibliographical references and index.
    ISBN 0-02-912482-4
    1. Antisemitism—Japan—History. 2. Jews—Public opinion.
3. Public opinion—Japan. 4. Japan–Ethnic relations.
I. Miyazawa, Masanori. II. Title.
DS146.J3G66 1995
305.892 ' 4 ' 052—dc20   94-27093
                                           CIP

For Yael and Kai
D.G.G.

To the memory of Ken Sugawara
M.M.

Comprehension . . . means the unpremeditated, attentive facing up to, and resisting of, reality—whatever it may be or might have been.

—Hannah Arendt, *The Origins of Totalitarianism*

It is perhaps hard to accept that scholarly study, and all the time and energy which that implies, can appropriately be lavished on a ludicrous fantasy. . . . Yet it is a great mistake to suppose that the only writers who matter are those whom the educated in their saner moments can take seriously. There exists a subterranean world where pathological fantasies disguised as ideas are churned out by crooks and half-educated fanatics for the benefit of the ignorant and superstitious. There are times when this underworld emerges from the depths and suddenly fascinates, captures, and dominates multitudes of usually sane and responsible people, who thereupon take leave of sanity and responsibility. And it occasionally happens that this underworld becomes a political power and changes the course of history.

—Norman Cohn, *Warrant for Genocide*

CONTENTS

•

ACKNOWLEDGMENTS

My first debt of gratitude is to my coauthor, Masanori Miyazawa, whose work I first encountered in 1974. Miyazawa had been studying Japanese attitudes toward Jews for more than a decade, originally under the guidance of the Dōshisha University historian Ken Sugawara, and had published his first article on the subject in 1963. I became so interested that I later sought him out, and we became friends. This book is the product of our continuing dialogue.

There has naturally been a division of labor in preparing this volume. Miyazawa did much of the initial basic research, and the text incorporates translations and adaptations of substantial portions of his published work. I have supplemented his contribution with research of my own in both English and Japanese sources. I organized and wrote the book, and the voice is mine.

This volume had its immediate genesis in the papers Miyazawa and I delivered at a symposium titled "Japan and the Jews: Past, Present, and Future" held at the Japan Society in New York on April 10 and 11, 1989. Jonathan Rosenbaum, the Director of the Maurice Greenberg Center for Judaic Studies at the University of Hartford, conceived the conference, which he and I organized with financial support from the Anti-Defamation League of B'nai B'rith, the American Jewish Committee, and the Greenberg Center.

The University of Illinois has been generous in supporting this project. I spent the 1988–89 academic year as an associate in the university's Center for Advanced Study. The first draft of the manuscript was completed during the fall semester of 1992, while I was a fellow in the university's Program for the Study of Cultural Values and Ethics. The Program in Arms Control, Disarmament, and International Security (ACDIS) supplied research assistants and the opportunity to publish an early version of chapters seven and eight in its *Occasional Papers* series. Summer support was provided by International Programs and Studies in the form of a William and Flora Hewlett International Summer Research Grant. My appointment as a University Scholar in 1992 also buoyed my spirits.

I have been aided over the years by four able research assistants: Nobuo Horiuchi, Megumi Inoue, Wakako Kusumoto, and Laurie Wesselhoff. Mamiko Nakamura, librarian for the University of Illinois's Japanese collection, helped me solve numerous research problems. Marcia Shelton helped prepare the bibliography.

Numerous friends and colleagues have kept me abreast of pertinent developments with a steady stream of clippings and advisories that otherwise would have escaped my notice. I am especially grateful to Frank Joseph Shulman, Michael Schudrich, Harold Solomon, Mark Schreiber, Neil Sandberg, Kenneth Jacobson, and J. Thomas Rimer for their help in this regard. Richard Minear, James Shapiro, and Betsey Scheiner shared work-in-progress with me. Kevin Doak helped focus my attention on the problem of ethnic nationalism. Boris Katz shared his experience as a youth growing up in Shanghai. John Dower, whose book *War Without Mercy: Race and Power in the Pacific War* I find exemplary, commiserated with me about the difficulty of

•

writing about a subject of this kind and supplied some of the illustrations that appear in these pages. Colleagues at the University of Illinois, especially David Desser, Fred Jaher, Cynthia Peterson, David Plath, Timothy Van Laar, and William Schoedel, gave me invaluable advice and criticism.

I am particularly grateful to those who took the time to read and comment on early drafts of the manuscript. David Biale, Tom Havens, Maureen Kassel, Herb Passin, Ron Toby, Michael Shapiro, and Ben-Ami Shillony gave me constructive feedback at various stages of the book's development. The students in my fall 1993 seminar— Howard Browning, Diana Brummer, Brian Feldges, Linda Keck, Paul Kent Oakley, and Lori Sussman—read and responded sensitively to the penultimate draft.

I would like to thank my agent, Agnes Birnbaum, who believed in this project, and my editor, Adam Bellow, who helped bring it to fruition.

Finally, I wish to thank my children, Yael and Kai, for their perseverance, and my wife, the writer Kazuko Fujimoto, for being my unfailing compass these twenty-six years.

—DAVID G. GOODMAN

With the exception of the Japanese authors of English-language publications, Japanese names in the text and notes appear in the Japanese order, surname first.

JEWS IN THE JAPANESE MIND

I

WHAT THE JAPANESE THINK OF JEWS AND WHY ANYONE SHOULD CARE

ON MARCH 12, 1987, the *New York Times* reported that flagrantly antisemitic books had become sensational best-sellers in Japan. The most popular were two volumes by a Christian fundamentalist preacher named Uno Masami, who claimed, among other things, that the United States was a "Jewish nation" ruled by a clandestine Jewish "shadow government." Jews controlled all the major banks, media, and business corporations in America, Uno asserted, including IBM, General Motors, Ford, Chrysler, Standard Oil, Exxon, and AT&T. He denied the Holocaust, defended Hitler, and claimed that an international Jewish conspiracy was manipulating world economic and political events to destroy Japan.[1]

By April 1987, the two books Uno published in 1986 had sold a combined total of 1.1 million copies, and he was receiving consider-

1

able media attention.[a] His theories were cited as a plausible explanation for Japan's economic woes by Japan's most widely read daily newspaper, the *Yomiuri shimbun;* and he was invited to address a Constitution Day rally sponsored by a conservative faction of the ruling Liberal Democratic Party headed by former Prime Minister Kishi Nobusuke.[2]

Uno's books and the interest they generated were part of a larger phenomenon. Eighty-two books with the word "Jew" in the title were in circulation in 1987, and virtually every major bookstore in Japan had a "Jewish corner" to display the many volumes that were in demand. Titles like *The Jewish Plot to Control the World, The Expert Way of Reading the Jewish Protocols,* and *The Secret of Jewish Power That Moves the World,* authored respectively by a Shintō priest, a university professor, and a senior parliamentarian, were prominently displayed.[3]

These books were lent credibility by the mass media. On December 27, 1987, TV Tokyo (*Terebi Tōkyō*) broadcast nationally in prime time a thirty-minute program that depicted the activities of an "international Jewish capitalist," showed President Ronald Reagan in the Oval Office of the White House discussing U.S. policy toward "Jewish Capital," and portrayed Judaism as a belief in sunspots and the prophecies of Nostradamus.[b] Japan's major newspapers, including the *Asahi, Yomiuri,* and *Nihon keizai (Nikkei),* routinely carried lurid advertisements for blatantly antisemitic books, and, when challenged, retorted angrily that they saw nothing objectionable in doing so.[4]

Emboldened by this media acceptance, antisemitic rhetoric became increasingly prominent in popular Japanese political discourse in the

---

[a] Sales figures from an advertisement by the publisher, Tokuma shoten, in the *Yomiuri shimbun*, April 6, 1987. Tokuma gave the *New York Times* a combined sales figure of 650,000 for the previous month.

[b] Titled "An Introduction to the Japanese Economy," the program was based on Ishinomori Shōtarō, *Nihon keizai nyūmon* [An Introduction to the Japanese Economy], 4 vols. (Nihon keizai shimbunsha, 1986–88). It was an animated version of volume 2, chapter 4, pp. 215–76. The first volume of this work (which does not contain the offensive material) has been translated into English and published by the University of California Press. See Shōtarō Ishinomori, *Japan, Inc.: An Introduction to Japanese Economics (The Comic Book)* (Berkeley: University of California Press, 1988).

•

late 1980s and early 1990s. Stories charging that Jews surreptitiously manipulate American politics and the American economy appeared regularly in mass-circulation magazines. In its July 10, 1992, edition, *Weekly Post* (circulation 688,000) warned that "the Jews" had engineered a recent precipitous drop in the Japanese stock market and were "poised to destroy the Japanese economy whenever they desire." In its December 5, 1992, edition, *Weekly Gendai* (circulation 527,000) quoted interviews with Japanese academics and other "authorities," charging that "the Jewish mass media, which include *The New York Times*, *The Washington Post*, ABC, CBS, and others" had "manipulated public opinion poll results in order to consciously raise the mood [of support] for Clinton." It characterized the president-elect as a Jewish "robot" who had sold out American foreign policy to the Zionist lobby; and it asserted that the new administration would be unfriendly, because it was a "Jewish dummy government" and the Jews were hostile to Japan. "The ultimate aim of the Zionists is to cause disarray in Japanese society," the foreign policy analyst Takahashi Masatake was quoted as saying; and Yajima Kinji, an oft-cited, retired professor of economics, asserted that "to create confusion and then exploit it for their own profit is the standard operating procedure of international Jewish capital."[5]

This antisemitic rhetoric took concrete political form during the July 1992 upper house Diet elections, when the Global Restoration Party (*Chikyū ishin tō*) fielded candidates on a platform that promised to "smite the traitors who are selling out Holy Japan to the diabolical Jewish cult." Each weekend in 1993, as many as 3,500 bright crimson handbills emblazoned with swastikas, accusing Jews and Freemasons of plotting to destroy Japan, were posted around Tokyo and its environs.[6]

More than anecdotal evidence documents the prevalence of negative stereotypes of Jews in Japan. A survey commissioned by the Anti-Defamation League of B'nai B'rith (ADL) in 1988 found that "in the area of personal traits, Jews tended to be seen by large pluralities as unfriendly and greedy. Small margins also saw them as unclean and deceitful." The survey found that Jews were seen as inferior to Christians and Buddhists in virtually all categories and

•

defined as unattractive types along with Muslims, Arabs, and blacks. The state of Israel "ranked at or near the low point in perceptions held of its trustworthiness, commitment to peace, straightforwardness in business dealings, generosity to other nations, and level of economic advancement." Significantly, the survey found that the college-educated, affluent, and younger respondents were more likely to harbor such negative views than others.[7c]

Moreover, negative attitudes toward Jews in Japan are nothing new. College students in a 1962 survey ranked Jews tenth of twelve ethnic groups when asked about their sense of attraction toward the groups and their willingness to marry into them. Only Africans and Koreans ranked lower than Jews, and the author of the survey noted that Jews had consistently been ranked near the bottom in such polls since before the war.[d] In a similar survey conducted in 1963, students

---

[c] The survey, "Anti-Semitism in Japan: A Survey Research Study," was designed by Potomac Associates, a Washington consulting firm, and was authored by William Watts. It was conducted in November 1988 by the Nippon Research Center, an affiliate of Gallup International Research Institutes, and collected data through direct interviews with 1,365 Japanese adults eighteen years of age and older.

[d] The author of the survey, Akita Kiyoshi, collates the data as follows:

TWELVE ETHNIC GROUPS RANKED BY PREFERENCE

Before the China Incident (1937): Japanese-Germans-Italians-Koreans-Americans-English-French-Indians-Chinese-Africans-Jews-Russians.

After the China Incident (1937): Japanese-Germans-Italians-Koreans-Indians-Americans-French-Chinese-English-Africans-Jews-Russians.

Immediate Postwar (1946): Japanese-Americans-Germans/French-English-Italians/Chinese*-Indians-Russians-Jews-Africans-Koreans.

May 1962: Japanese-Americans-English-French-Germans-Italians-Indians-Russians-Chinese-Jews-Africans-Koreans.

[* A slash (/) indicates identical rank.]

In his analysis, Akita explains the students' low ranking of Jews by suggesting that they had been influenced by the prejudice, discrimination, and oppression the Jews had experienced in Europe. He notes that Europeans had frequently exploited the Jews as scapegoats to resolve internal social and political conflicts and had promoted negative stereotypes for their own political purposes. "As a result, because of inaccurate information and propaganda," he writes, "distorted beliefs about the Jews have been disseminated and perpetuated." Why should this have affected the Japanese? "Not only is it rare for Japanese to speak directly with Jews or see them," Akita explains, "it is virtually impossible for them to distinguish Jews from other foreigners. The fact that this sort of prejudice is held by Japanese results from the fact that Jews have been the historical scapegoats of other peoples and because inaccurate information regarding them has been planted deeply in the psyche of the people of Japan."

asked to characterize twelve ethnic groups by selecting from twenty-four pairs of adjectives consistently chose negative modifiers to describe Jews; and when ostensibly positive choices were made—"complex," "clever," "restless," and "wealthy"—the implications were not clear. Jews were most often described as "unhappy," "complex," "dark," "clever," "unsociable," and "hard," which contrasted sharply with the positive description of Japanese, who were considered "clever," "large," "complex," "excellent," "good," and "conservative."[c]

Despite the undeniable prevalence of negative stereotypes, however, Japanese attitudes toward Jews are by no means uniformly hostile. In 1971, the Japanese bought more than a million copies of a sympathetic nationalist treatise titled *The Japanese and the Jews*, making it the best-selling book of the year. By 1987 it had sold more than

---

See Akita Kiyoshi, "Nihon no ichi-daigakusei no minzoku kanjō" [The Ethnic Feelings of Students at One Japanese University], *Jinmongaku* (published by the Jinmon gakkai of Dōshisha University, Kyoto, Japan), no. 70.

[c] In the following data, the numbers refer to the ranking of Jews on a continuum between two adjectives; the higher the number, the stronger the latter image and vice-versa.

FACTOR GROUP 1: FACTORS INVOLVING SUBJECTIVE JUDGMENTS
Happy-Unhappy, 11; Cleanly-Uncleanly, 8; Bright-Dark, 12; Wealthy-Poor, 6; Beautiful-Ugly, 9; Excellent-Petty, 8; Sociable-Unsociable, 10; White-Black, 7; Free-Stiff, 11; Sweet-Smelling–Ill-Smelling, 8; Good-Bad, 8; Kindly-Cruel, 7; Reliable-Unreliable, 8; Clever-Foolish, 4.

FACTOR GROUP 2: SEX-LINKED FACTORS
Manly-Womanly, 7; Brave-Timid, 9; Strong-Weak, 9; Positive-Passive, 8; Large-Small, 10; Dry-Wet, 10.

FACTOR GROUP 3: FACTORS RELATING TO STATES OF BEING
Calm-Restless, 5; Soft-Hard, 10; Complex-Simple, 2.

FACTOR GROUP 4: POLITICAL FACTORS
Progressive-Conservative, 7.

Akita Kiyoshi, "SD-hō kara mita Nihon no ichi-daigaku gakusei no minzoku henken" [Racial Prejudice Among the Students of One Japanese University as Determined on the Basis of Semantic Differentials], *Jinmongaku* (Dōshisha University), no. 104, pp. 10–11.

Another survey confirms Akita's findings. Konno Toshihiko inquired about "outstanding peoples, nations, and races" and found that, while two out of the twelve groups surveyed ranked Jews first and second, overall respondents ranked Jews fifth or below. (Konno Toshihiko, *Bunmei no kaosu—sabetsu, henken* [Civilization in Chaos: Discrimination, Prejudice] (Yachiyo shuppan, 1980), p. 102.

●

three million copies—one for every forty Japanese.[8f] Anne Frank's *Diary of a Young Girl* has sold over four million copies in Japan, more than in any other country except the United States. So beloved is Anne Frank in Japan that the first Japanese company to market sanitary napkins designed especially for Japanese women called itself Anne Co., Ltd., and it sold its product under the brand name "Anne's Day" (*Anne no hi*), which quickly became a euphemism for menstruation in Japan. *Fiddler on the Roof* remains the longest-running musical in Japanese history. Japanese audiences empathize with Tevye the Milkman (as portrayed by the veteran actor Morishige Hisaya) and commiserate with his struggle to maintain traditional values in a changing world.

Some Japanese identify themselves as Jews. The well-known anthropologist Yamaguchi Masao fancies himself "the Jew among the Japanese." Fujita Den, a highly successful businessman who owns a 50 percent share in the Japanese McDonald's franchise and 20 percent of the Japanese Toys "R" Us chain, proudly proclaims himself "a Ginza Jew."[g] And the young novelist Shimada Masahiko has explored the idea of becoming a Jew in his short story, "A Callow Fellow of Jewish Descent."[9]

Theories that identify the Japanese and Jewish peoples also abound, and much "evidence" is evinced of their prehistoric ties. King Solomon's mines are said to have been unearthed at Mount Tsurugi on

---

[f] For a book to have proportionate popularity in the United States, it would have to sell 6.25 million copies.

[g] The *New York Times* quotes Fujita as follows:

> Business people in and out of Japan call me a "Ginza Jew." I am satisfied with that and even call myself a "Ginza Jew." I am proud of being Japanese, but as a businessman I am happy being known as a Jew. Now Jews from around the world call me a "Ginza Jew," too, and treat me like an insider. They treat me differently than gentiles. The title of "Ginza Jew" is invaluable to me in doing business with Jewish traders who control business life in many countries.
>
> Nonetheless, there is no shortage of examples of how I was laughed at, stepped on and insulted by Jews. But I endured these insults just like the Jews have endured all their hardships.
>
> > [Fujita Den, *Yudaya no shōhō* (The Jewish Way of Doing Business), quoted in "Den Fujita, Japan's Mr. Joint-Venture," *New York Times*, March 22, 1992.]

•

the island of Shikoku. A stone engraved with Hebrew letters is reported to have been discovered on the isle of Awaji. The village of Shingō in Aomori prefecture is identified as the site of the grave of Jesus, who is reported to have migrated to Japan after his brother James was mistakenly crucified in his place.[10h]

These legends have been given credence by some intellectuals and fascinate the Japanese reading public. In his 1959 essay on the people of Shiga prefecture, northeast of Osaka, the journalist Ōya Sōichi (1900–1970), after whom a coveted prize for nonfiction writing is named, repeats a theory linking the parsimonious people of the prefecture to the Jews.[i] The prominent novelist Kita Morio, several of whose works have been translated into English, also offers a theory that identifies the Jews with the long-nosed mythical creatures known in Japan as *tengu*.[j] In March 1987, the popular monthly *History Reader*

---

[h] The association of Shingō with Jesus derives from the association of the former name of the village, Herai, with the Japanese word for Hebrew, "Heburai." For a recent report on Shingō, see "Newest Testament: Japan is the Land of the Rising Son," *The Wall Street Journal*, October 1, 1993.

[i] "Long, long ago, after Jerusalem had been occupied by Titus," Ōya writes, "the Jews split into seven groups and were dispersed around the world. Of these, the destinations of six are historically recorded, but the whereabouts of the seventh remains unknown. It is said that this group drifted to Japan and became the people of Ōmi [the ancient name for Shiga prefecture]." Other Jews arrived on board European trading ships and settled in the region in the sixteenth century, Ōya relates, and then he says, "In terms of appearance, there are . . . quite a few Ōmi people who have hook noses like Jews. I have also heard that, when a certain Jewish merchant visited the home of an Ōmi trader in Tokyo to buy goods, he was astonished to discover that the symbols they used in their transactions were identical. It is possible that Ōmi merchants' total devotion to money may have inspired such stories." Ōya Sōichi, *Nihon no jinbutsu kōmyaku* [Mining Japan's People] (Bungei shunjūsha, 1959), p. 281.

[j] "I learned that there is a document in the Butsugen temple in Izu known as 'The Tengu's Apology,' " Kita writes. "[A local historian] Kikuchi Banka has studied this document. According to Mr. Kikuchi, 'Like Japanese mountain ascetics, *tengu* dress like travelers who traverse steep mountains, and their headgear is shaped the same as Jewish phylacteries. In addition, their noses are hooked like the Jews. My intuition is that *tengu* were Jews who migrated to China and Japan in ancient times. There are documents that state that the whereabouts of the most pious of the twelve tribes of the Jews is unknown. Judaism is a religion that worships the sun, and the etymology of "Zion" is "the place where the sun shines." ' In fact, ample research has been done both in Japan and abroad to identify the Ainu with the Jews. As evidence, [researchers] point out many similarities in language and customs." Kita Morio, *Dokutoru Manbou konchū-ki* [Dr. Manbou's Entomology], (Chūō kōron sha, 1961), pp. 88–89.

●

(circulation 180,000) carried ninety pages of essays debating Japan's Jewish roots and ran nine pages of color photographs purporting to depict remnants of ancient Jewish settlements in Japan.[11]

This interest, both hostile and sympathetic, has developed without a visible Jewish presence in Japan. Only about a thousand Jews (mostly businesspeople, students, and diplomats) reside in Japan today, and just 1 percent of respondents in the 1988 ADL survey averred ever having met one. Although small numbers of Jews have lived in Japan since around 1860, the most salient thing about them is that they have been virtually invisible *as Jews* to the Japanese. With few exceptions, they have interacted with Japanese society as nationals of their country of origin and not as Jews. Even Israelis are not immediately identified as Jews in Japan.

Japanese show little interest in Jewish institutions, which in any event do little to encourage dialogue. The synagogues in Tokyo and Kobe exist as centers of Jewish religious, social, and cultural life and have little contact with the society around them. Unlike Christian churches, which actively proselytize and stress the importance of involvement with the Japanese population (indeed, most Japanese churches are entirely Japanese), Jewish institutions generally do not invite Japanese interest or participation. Historically, the Jewish Community Center (JCC) in Tokyo has had no programs to educate Japanese about Jews and Judaism, nor has it maintained continuing links with Japanese scholars and others interested in Jewish subjects.[k] The Israeli Embassy has sponsored numerous cultural programs, but these have been modest, and there has been weak coordination with the larger Jewish community, which has been reticent to become involved with Israeli politics and reluctant to risk making itself the target of terrorist attacks.[l]

The Ainu are a Caucasian people thought to have been among the earliest inhabitants of Japan. Through the course of Japanese history, they were forced progressively northward, and today their remnants live primarily in northern Hokkaido.

[k] This situation is changing, as a Jewish cultural center designed to serve the Japanese public is scheduled to open in the JCC in 1994.

[l] It should be remembered that three Japanese participated in the terrorist attack on Tel Aviv's Lod Airport in 1972, leaving twenty-four dead and seventy-six wounded. Fears of attack by Japanese terrorists have thus not been without foundation.

•

A handful of individual Jews have exercised direct influence on Japanese attitudes. The most influential of these was Jacob Schiff, a financier with the New York investment firm of Kuhn, Loeb and Company, who went out of his way to underwrite loans the Japanese government needed to prosecute the Russo-Japanese War of 1904–05. Schiff was outraged at the czarist regime for its persecution of the Jews and sympathetic with the Japanese underdog in the conflict. Japanese leaders were naturally grateful, and Schiff's intercession became well known in Japan. His fame lent a degree of credibility to the myth of Jewish control over the world economy, but it also influenced Japanese policymakers during World War II, who remembered Japan's debt to Schiff and resisted Nazi pressure to harm the Jews under their control.[12]

In recent years, Marvin Tokayer got to know Japanese scholars of Jewish studies while he was rabbi in Tokyo during the 1970s, and with Japanese ghostwriters he published twelve successful books in Japanese on aspects of Jewish culture.[13] Jack Halpern, another prolific writer, has authored books in Japanese, edited a Japanese-English dictionary, and was last reported to be working on a Japanese translation of the Talmud.[14m] These individuals have indeed had some impact on Japanese impressions of Jews, but overall, direct Jewish influence has been inconsequential.[n]

---

[m] *Jerusalem Report* of August 22, 1991, wrote, "In December 1990, Halpern began assembling a team of translators and computer specialists, creating the first-ever trilingual (Hebrew/Aramaic-English-Japanese) computer database and assembling an extensive library.

"Halpern was born in Germany in 1946 to Holocaust survivors. He studied in yeshivahs in Brooklyn and Brazil, and lived in Israel. He and his Israeli-born wife moved to Japan in 1973 to study Japanese.

"He has subsequently published 13 books in Japanese, including two on Jewish humor; another is on 'The Jewish Mind and the Japanese Mind.' He gives an average of eight lectures a month to Japanese audiences, discussing Jewish history and the Talmud, and gets letters requesting copies of the Talmud in Japanese.

"[Halpern] expects the Talmud project to take at least 15 years. 'That's an optimistic estimate,' he says." Excerpted in *Points East* (A publication of the Sin-Judaic Institute) 7, no. 1 (March 1992), 8.

[n] My own work can be included in this list as well. See David G. Goodman, *Tōbōshi* [My Escapology], (Shōbunsha, 1976); *Isuraeru—koe to kao* [Israel: Voices and Faces], (Asahi shimbunsha, 1979); and *Hashiru* [Running] (Iwanami shoten, 1989).

•

What direct contact with Jews and Jewish culture the Japanese have had has probably done as much to confuse as to enlighten them.° It is obvious to Japanese intellectuals that Jews from Marx to Freud, Arnold Schoenberg to Claude Lévi-Strauss have made an important contribution to modern Western culture; businesspeople and other travelers meet Jewish lawyers and financiers abroad and realize that Jews exercise an influence over the international economy that is sometimes disproportionate to their numbers. Because this is the case, the self-defensive tendency of Jews to alternately portray themselves as a small, powerless people and a political and financial powerhouse naturally bewilders Japanese observers.[15] The conflicting self-images offered up in the translated novels of Jewish-American and Israeli authors like I. B. Singer, Philip Roth, and Amos Oz, ranging from the elegiac to the self-lacerating, augment this confusion. And works of popular spy fiction by both Jewish and non-Jewish writers that describe the sinister prowess of the Israeli secret service, the Mossad, like John le Carré's *The Little Drummer Girl*, Warren Kiefer's *The Pontius Pilate Papers*, and Amos Aricha and Eli Landau's *Phoenix*, further complicate the picture.

That Japanese observers are bewildered by Jews is therefore, to a degree, understandable. That Japanese without any direct experience of Jews have developed rich fantasies about them is also less anomalous than it may seem. Jews were prohibited from living in England for four hundred years, from 1290 to 1656, but that did not prevent the English from cultivating vivid myths about them.[16] More recently (and with horrible irony), the belief in a menacing Jewish conspiracy has persisted in eastern Europe despite the fact that virtually the entire Jewish population was exterminated in the Holocaust.[17] That the Japanese have speculated about Jews on the basis of incomplete,

---

° A case in point is the intense reaction Japanese press officer Satō Masaki received when he asked at a *New York Times* dinner in 1987 how many Jewish editors were employed at the *Times* and why the paper carried so many "Jewish" stories. Satō's questions were tactless and displayed astounding naïveté, but they were probably not malicious, and the intense reaction he received bewildered Japanese observers, who failed to understand what he had done wrong. See *New York Magazine*, April 27, 1987, p. 13; and *Yomiuri shimbun*, April 26, 1987.

•

inaccurate, and contradictory evidence is therefore a curious but not unprecedented phenomenon.

Various attempts have been made to account for the intensity of Japanese interest in Jews, and particularly to explain the persistent, chimerical belief in a global Jewish conspiracy bent on destroying Japan, which is the way we will define antisemitism in these pages.[P] Many writers have traced Japanese fascination with the Jews and Japanese antisemitism back to Japan's World War II alliance with Nazi Germany.[18] A few have found it rooted more profoundly in Japanese history.[19] Others have stressed the function of antisemitism in contemporary Japan as a sublimated expression of anti-American and antidemocratic sentiment.[20] All these explanations are correct to a degree, but none accounts for the diversity, continuity, intensity, and specific content of Japanese interest in the Jews.

The fact is that over the course of the past hundred years, the Japanese have produced enough writing on the Jews to fill a small

---

[P] "Chimerical hostility to Jews" is Gavin Langmuir's definition of antisemitism. By it he means hostility based on "assertions that attribute with certitude to outgroups characteristics that have never been empirically observed." Assertions by Japanese authors that attribute to Jews a global conspiracy to destroy Japan constitute "chimerical hostility" and thus antisemitism in Langmuir's (and our) definition.

Langmuir distinguishes "chimerical" hostility, which he regards as the only "true" antisemitism, from "realistic" and "xenophobic" hostility, both of which embody some "kernel of truth." "Realistic assertions about outgroups," Langmuir writes, "are propositions that utilize the information available about an outgroup and are based on the same assumptions about the nature of groups and the effect of membership on individuals as those used to understand the ingroup and its reference groups and their members. Xenophobic assertions are propositions that grammatically attribute a socially menacing conduct to an outgroup and all its members but are empirically based only on the conduct of a historical minority of the members; they neglect other, unthreatening, characteristics of the outgroup; and they do not acknowledge that there are great differences between the individuals who compose the outgroup as there are between the individuals who compose the ingroup."

See Gavin I. Langmuir, *Toward a Definition of Antisemitism* (Berkeley: University of California Press, 1990), p. 328.

See also "Imaginary Devils," in Ben-Ami Shillony, *Politics and Culture in Wartime Japan* (New York: Oxford University Press, 1981), pp. 156–71.

Since antisemitism as we are defining it has nothing to do with Jews, much less "Semites," we will neither hyphenate nor capitalize the term.

•

library.[q] This book is about that writing and the images of the Jews it contains. It is *not* about Jews or about the Jewish experience in the Far East; nor, while it touches on them, is it a history of actual Japanese-Jewish relations.[21] This book is about the Japanese construct of the Jews, its origins, evolution, and meaning.

Over the course of Japan's modern history, various constituencies have used images of the Jews for their particular purposes. The Japanese construct of the Jews thus developed over time by a gradual process of accretion and instantiates the major themes of modern Japanese history. In the nineteenth century, even before they were aware of the existence of Jews per se, Japanese xenophobes warned of a conspiracy by the adherents of an "occult religion" ("proto-Jews," from our perspective) to destroy Japan. In the early twentieth century, to establish a degree of parity for themselves with the white Christian world, Japanese Christians utilized the notion of Jewish "chosenness" to create a series of distinctly Japanese theologies. During the war, even as it resisted Nazi demands to destroy the Jews in its power, the Japanese government actively exploited antisemitic ideas to control thought and suppress dissent within Japan. In the postwar period, as the facts of the Holocaust became known, many Japanese relieved their sense of war guilt by identifying with the Jews, the quintessential victims of the war. In the 1970s and 1980s, Japanese leftists affirmed their solidarity with the Third World by denying the peoplehood of the Jews and labeling Israel a "Nazi state." And in the late 1980s and early 1990s, ethnic nationalist demagogues and hack writers culled the reservoir of accumulated Jewish imagery to express their revulsion with America's multiethnic democracy and to purvey their dreams of an idyllic, "monoracial" Japan.

The way the Japanese have understood the Jews has had political and intellectual consequences. The polemics against the adherents of a menacing "occult religion" formulated by nineteenth-century xenophobes helped undermine the Tokugawa regime and contributed to

---

[q] Miyazawa's bibliography, covering the years 1877 to 1988, contains more than 5,500 items. See Miyazawa Masanori, *Nihon ni okeru Yudaya-Isuraeru rongi bunken mokuroku, 1877–1988* [A Bibliography of Debates in Japan on Israel and the Jews, 1877–1988] (Shinsensha, 1990).

the creation of the modern Japanese state. The divine connection to the Jewish people intuited by Japanese Christians influenced the development of Japanese religion in the modern period, and through such international evangelists as Sun Myung Moon, the Korean founder of the Unification Church, who studied in Japan between 1938 and 1946, affected world culture as well. Antisemitism has not been used in Japan to persecute Jews, but it has been used to persecute domestic dissidents, especially during the war. In the postwar period, identification with Jews facilitated Japan's recovery by assuaging the Japanese people's debilitating sense of war guilt. During the 1970s and 1980s, the left-wing denial of Jewish peoplehood supplied the rationale for the attack by Japanese terrorists on Tel Aviv's Lod Airport in 1972 and justified Japan's decision to condone the infamous United Nations General Assembly resolution equating Zionism with racism in 1975. Left-wing anti-Zionism also helped justify the first open foreign policy rift between the United States and Japan in the postwar period, which came in 1973–74 over Middle East policy. The calumnies and distortions of Japanese antisemites exacerbated tensions among Japan, Israel, and the United States in the late 1980s. And, during the Gulf War, accumulated Japanese confusions about Jews and about Israel's legitimacy contributed to Japan's inability to formulate a timely, coherent policy response to the conflict.

The concept of the Jews in Japan today is thus a composite of the images that have been employed by diverse social groups over the course of modern Japanese history to serve their various ideological, psychological, and political purposes.[r] These ideas have had a discernible impact on Japanese political and intellectual life. The overarching point of this study is therefore that Japanese ideas about Jews are a logical outgrowth of Japanese cultural experience and that by

---

[r] The Japanese construct of the Jews resembles what Edward Said has called "Orientalism," the West's evolving ideas, images, and fantasies about the Middle East, which, Said has argued, fulfilled certain psychological and ideological needs for Westerners but had little or nothing to do with the Middle East and its people, and in fact impeded true understanding. The Japanese concept of Jews is a kind of reverse Orientalism, a construction of the Jews by the Japanese that has little or nothing to do with Jews per se but reifies a particular Japanese cultural history. See Edward W. Said, *Orientalism* (New York: Vintage, 1979).

•

understanding them we gain unique insight into the workings of modern Japan. This challanges the widely held myth that Japan is a uniquely secular society, innocent of and unconcerned with religious matters. Given the manifold evidence to the contrary, this myth is, to say the least, a non sequitur.[5]

This book therefore aims to do three things. Its immediate purpose is to describe and trace the development of Japanese ideas about Jews, to explain the twin phenomena of antisemitism and philosemitism in a country that has practically no Jewish population. The book's second purpose is to show how Japanese ideas about Jews, which are relatively insignificant taken in isolation, relate to and reflect the

---

[5] The most prominent and influential proponent of this myth was the Harvard University professor and former United States ambassador to Japan, Edwin O. Reischauer. See, for example, the chapter on religion in his *The Japanese Today* (Cambridge, Mass.: Harvard University Press, 1988), esp. p. 215, where, after acknowledging that 70 to 80 percent of Japanese belong to one or more religious bodies, and that "the lives of most Japanese are intertwined with religious observances—shrine festivals, 'god shelves' and Buddhist altars in the homes, and Shinto or Christian marriages, Buddhist funerals, and other religious rites of passage," he concludes surprisingly, "Clearly religion in contemporary Japan is not central to society and culture."

There are three reasons for Reischauer's minimization of the role of religion in Japanese culture. The first is an excessively narrow concept of religion. The second has to do with the general American aversion in the postwar period to recognizing a relationship between religion and politics. Reischauer generalizes this aversion to Japan. For recent discussions of this tendency in America, see Gary Wills, *Under God: Religion and American Politics* (New York: Simon and Schuster, 1990); and Stephen L. Carter, *The Culture of Disbelief: How American Law and Politics Trivialize Religious Devotion* (New York: Basic Books, 1993).

The third reason has to do with the relationship between this tendency in American thought, Cold War ideology, and the orthodox theory of modern Japanese historical development, which Reischauer articulated most clearly and forcefully. To rehabilitate Japan quickly after World War II as an anti-Communist bulwark, it was necessary to depict the war as an aberration in Japan's otherwise steady development toward its self-realization as a liberal democracy, which had now resumed. The extraordinarily gruesome war that Japan had just fought as a "Holy War" (*seisen*) in the name of a divine emperor had to be redefined as the aberrant stratagem of a small group of fanatics and not the natural (albeit extreme) expression of a Japanese culture in which religion played a major part. Reischauer and his Cold War view of Japan therefore minimized the role of religion in Japanese culture and politics, and his theory has been accepted all but universally, not least in Japan, where it has helped to obscure the intellectual origins of Japan's ruling conservative elite. For an analysis of Reischauer's historiography, see John W. Dower, "E. H. Norman and the Uses of History," in John W. Dower, ed., *Origins of the Modern Japanese State: Selected Writings of E. H. Norman* (New York: Pantheon, 1975), pp. 44–52.

•

major intellectual and political currents of their time. The third purpose is to explore the political and intellectual implications of Japanese ideas about Jews for our understanding of the quality and potential of contemporary Japanese culture.

The antisemite Uno Masami got it almost right in 1986, when he titled one of his best-selling books *If You Understand the Jews, You Will Understand Japan*. By understanding Japanese thinking about the Jews, we do indeed better understand modern Japan, its development, its character, and its future promise.

●

II

MOMOTARŌ AS ANTISEMITE

The Cultural Roots of Japanese Images of Jews

JAPANESE ATTITUDES TOWARD Jews are rooted deeply in Japanese culture. Even before they were clearly aware of the existence of the Jewish people, the Japanese had certain ways of relating to foreigners that conditioned the way they would eventually conceive Jews in their imagination.

Throughout history, foreigners have been regarded with alternating awe and contempt in Japan, as beneficent gods and threatening demons. So significant has this ambivalence been that it evolved as a major feature of Japanese religion, which has been especially concerned with the invocation, propitiation, and exorcism of deities. Those deities have often been conceived as "visitors from afar" (*marebito* or *marōdo*) who would arrive from abroad, be entertained until they could bestow their blessings (or at least do no harm), and then be ushered away or driven off. In diverse configurations, this basic pattern has constituted the core of Japanese religious ritual. Secularized and aestheticized, it became the foundation of traditional Japanese theater forms like Nō and Kabuki; and its influence continues to be felt in Japanese culture today. Japanese attitudes toward Jews have followed this basic pattern, imagining them as visitors from afar who are to be idealized and maligned, propitiated and expelled depending on the fluctuating needs of Japan.[1]

Another feature of Japanese culture that has affected the way the Japanese have conceived of Jews is the way various groups have historically manipulated the images of foreigners in accordance with their particular political, psychological, and social agendas. For a millennium, Japanese intellectuals conducted a monologue about China that constantly invoked the image and the authority of the Chinese but had virtually nothing to do with them.[2] From the eighth to the eighteenth century, even as they idealized Chinese civilization and borrowed freely from it, Japanese writers systematically invoked the otherness of China, using it as a foil to define their unique Japaneseness.[a] In the seventeenth century, during the final stage of this monologue, Japanese political thinkers went so far as to usurp China's identity as the "Central Kingdom" (*Chūgoku* or *Chūka*), claiming its mantle of cultural supremacy for themselves.[3b] The Japanese common people have regularly invoked antic images of foreigners—especially Koreans and Okinawans—as counterimages against which to test their unique identity. During the Tokugawa period (1600–1868), the governing regime consciously orchestrated foreign relations to enhance its legitimacy and

---

[a] This practice is not unique to Japan, and Jews have also employed it. Jewish relations with Greek civilization are an example. The Israeli historian of Japan Ben-Ami Shillony has compared the Japanese and the Jews in this regard, describing them as "successful outsiders" who have been able to benefit from contact with other, more powerful civilizations without succumbing to them. See Ben-Ami Shillony, *The Jews and the Japanese: The Successful Outsiders* (Rutland, Vt.: Tuttle, 1991).

[b] Perhaps predictably, Japanese debates about the Jews have also culminated in attempts to appropriate Jewish identity. See especially the discussion of *The Japanese and the Jews* in chapter 6. For a revealing video presentation of the Japanese proclivity to appropriate for themselves the identities of others, see "The Japanese Version," produced and directed by Louis Alvarez and Andrew Kolker (New York: Center for New American Media, 1991).

•

prestige, purposefully exploiting the pageantry of international diplomacy for its own political ends.[4] Twentieth-century Japanese discussions of the Jews have followed this basic pattern: they have been conducted for the most part as a solipsistic monologue to clarify Japanese identity without reference to Jews; and they have culminated in a variety of attempts to usurp Jewish identity.

An example of the way general cultural patterns have shaped Japanese perceptions of Jews is the way the legend of Momotarō, probably the best-loved folk tale in Japan, was applied to Jews during World War II. The legend goes that Momotarō, the pure "Peach Boy," emerged from a giant peach found floating down a river by a childless old couple. The miraculous child grew rapidly into a warrior of extraordinary strength and wisdom, maturing just in time to defend his homeland against alien intruders from Demons' Island. Momotarō vanquished the demons, returning triumphantly with their treasure and their pledge of eternal fealty to Japan. During World War II, Japanese ideologues frequently likened the conflict to Momotarō's struggle, depicting it as a battle to the death between pure Japan and encroaching foreign demons. The Jews were depicted as being among the most formidable demons menacing Japan, and the imaginary duel between pristine Japan and demonic Jews (foremost among whom was the non-Jewish Franklin Delano Roosevelt) was described in copious words and pictures.[5]

Japanese attitudes toward Jews have inevitably been conditioned by general Japanese attitudes toward foreigners, but there are more specific antecedents to modern Japanese attitudes toward Jews than these common cultural patterns. Well before the introduction of European antisemitism to Japan, for example, Japanese xenophobes had already developed a theory that the adherents of an alien "occult religion" ("proto-Jews," from our perspective) had mounted a global conspiracy to destroy them.

In the early nineteenth century, Japan faced a dual crisis. The external challenge posed by the West is the most frequently remarked dimension of this crisis. In 1842, the British defeated China in the Opium War, reducing it to semicolonial status through a system of unequal treaties. This event profoundly shocked Japanese leaders, who had been confident of their ability "to repel the barbarians" by force of arms. In order to avoid suffering the same humiliation as China, Japanese leaders concluded that Japan would have to adopt Western military and industrial technologies, as well as the ideas and modes of social organization that went along with them, and this decision precipitated Japan's modern transformation.

Antedating Japan's response to the Western threat and shaping it, however, was Japan's ongoing response to another, perhaps more basic crisis, a spiritual crisis within. Driving Japanese history and conditioning Japan's perceptions of the West from the late eighteenth century onward was this profound sense of spiritual crisis, a fear that Japan was in danger of imminent moral collapse.

Xenophobia was one of the defense mechanisms employed to deal with this crisis. It sought to use threats from abroad, both real and imagined, to galvanize the Japanese spiritually and intellectually. The self-defensive xenophobia of the early nineteenth century set the pattern for all subsequent anti-foreign thought in Japan, including anti-semitism.[6]

The spiritual crisis of the turn of the nineteenth century was precipitated by the atrophy and attenuation of the religious ideas and institutions that had governed Japanese spirituality for centuries. Buddhism in particular, which had defined the Japanese paradigms of life and death for more than a millennium, had been in decline for two hundred years.[7] So reviled and debilitated was the venerable religion that by the 1860s one Buddhist cleric was predicting an Imperial Rescript that would eradicate Buddhism in five to seven years;[8] and by the 1870s, two-thirds of the Buddhist temples that had existed in Tokugawa Japan had been destroyed by government-sanctioned violence.[c]

---

[c] Meiji University professor Tamamuro Fumio has estimated that of the two hundred and thirty thousand to two hundred and fifty thousand temples that existed during the

At the same time, Neo-Confucianism, which was the dominant strain in Tokugawa intellectual life, had proven too rationalistic to provide satisfying answers to life's ultimate questions; and Christianity, which had been proscribed since the 1630s, continued to be the target of vehement attack. Only Shinto, the indigenous "Way of the Gods," which promoted reverence for the emperor and the Japanese pantheon, was in the ascendant, advocated by the same nativist thinkers who condemned the other religions as pernicious alien creeds.

Symptoms of the spiritual crisis were everywhere. Numerous messianic and healing cults were founded during the early nineteenth century, including the Kurozumi, Konkō, and Tenri sects. These "new religions" (shinkō shūkyō), many of which still exist today, emerged because of the pervasive sense of spiritual disorder among the common people.[9] Mass rioting with distinctly religious overtones was also a frequent occurrence, culminating in numerous outbreaks of popular violence in the decade leading up to the Meiji Restoration of 1868. In 1866 alone, at least 106 peasant uprisings occurred, many infused with utopian calls for "world renewal" (yonaoshi).[10] Antinomianism in the form of transvestite and hysterical, trancelike behavior was common, bespeaking the widespread belief that a world was ending, that the old rules no longer applied, and that an apocalyptic "end of days" was near at hand.[11]

Japanese intellectuals were well aware of this spiritual crisis and the dangers it posed for Japan. In his New Theses (Shinron) of 1825, for example, Aizawa Seishisai (1781–1863) argued that what he called

---

Tokugawa period, less than seventy-five thousand remained after the mid-1870s. Tamamuro announced these findings at the Meiji Studies Conference sponsored by the Edwin O. Reischauer Institute of Japanese Studies at Harvard University on May 8, 1994. For an earlier version of Tamamuro's findings, see Tamamuro Fumio, "Shinbutsu bunri to haibutsu kishaku no jittai," Rekishi kōron, no. 96 (November 1983).

Buddhism was officially disestablished beginning with the shinbutsu hanzen-rei of 1868, which separated Buddhist from Shinto deities and ended the symbiotic relationship between the two religions that had existed for more than a thousand years. All temple lands were confiscated by government order in 1871, and all Buddhist ceremonies performed in the imperial household were abolished. For a brief description of these events, see Joseph M. Kitagawa, Religion in Japanese History (New York: Columbia University Press, 1966), pp. 199–203. For the definitive discussion in English, see James Edward Ketelaar, Of Heretics and Martyrs in Meiji Japan: Buddhism and Its Persecution (Princeton: Princeton University Press, 1990).

•

Japan's "spiritual void" made the country susceptible to ideological subversion and thus constituted its greatest weakness.[12] Writing fifteen years before the Opium War of 1840, Aizawa still believed that Japan could deal successfully with any military threat from abroad, and the danger of ideological subversion and cultural subjugation rather than the military and economic threat posed by the West was therefore uppermost in his mind.[13]

Aizawa's *New Theses* was one of the most influential nationalist treatises produced in the nineteenth century. Taken up and implemented by Meiji leaders, many of its proposals reverberated into the twentieth century.[14] To fill its "spiritual void," Aizawa believed that Japan required a unified system of religious belief. He therefore proposed that the state assume centralized control of all Shinto shrines, which in fact it did in establishing the system of State Shinto following the Restoration.[15] Aizawa next proposed that the state establish an emperor-centered state religion, modeled after what he anachronistically took to be the relationship between church and state in the West; and he formulated the idea of a unique "National Polity" or *Kokutai*, which was enshrined in such seminal documents as the Imperial Rescript on Education[d] and which eventually provided the founda-

---

[d] The text of the Imperial Rescript on Education, which became the catechism for all Japanese schoolchildren through the end of World War II, runs as follows:

Know ye, Our subjects:

Our Imperial Ancestors have founded Our Empire on a basis broad and everlasting, and have deeply and firmly implanted virtue; Our subjects ever united in loyalty and filial piety have from generation to generation illustrated the beauty thereof. This is the glory of the fundamental character of Our Empire, and herein also lies the source of Our education. Ye, Our subjects, be filial to your parents, affectionate to your brothers and sisters; as husbands and wives be harmonious, as friends true; bear yourselves in modesty and moderation; extend your benevolence to all; pursue learning and cultivate arts, and thereby develop intellectual faculties and perfect moral powers; furthermore, advance public good and promote common interests; always respect the Constitution and observe the laws; should emergency arise, offer yourselves courageously to the State; and thus guard and maintain the prosperity of Our Imperial Throne coeval with heaven and earth. So shall ye not only be Our good and faithful subjects, but render illustrious the best traditions of your forefathers.

The Way here set forth is indeed the teaching bequeathed by Our Imperial Ancestors, to be observed alike by Their Descendants and the subjects, infal-

tion for Japan's ultranationalist ideology of World War II.[c] Finally, and most pertinently, Aizawa's terror of "occult religions" (*yōkyō*) and the polemical strategies he developed to deal with this fear established the basic pattern for many types of Japanese xenophobia in the modern period, including antisemitism.

Little is known of Aizawa's background. His family was of humble origin (his distant ancestor Aizawa Sōbei had been responsible for snaring small birds to feed to his lord's falcons) and had attained samurai status only in his father's generation. The alarmist tone of Aizawa's writing may be laid in part to his need to overcome the handicap of his family background, for in the rigid Tokugawa social order it prevented him from participating directly in the formulation of government policy. Sounding alarms of a threat from abroad made it easier for Aizawa to receive a hearing from those in power.[16]

Aizawa believed that what differentiated the West from Japan was its unity of belief. He was aware of Christianity from the accumulated polemical literature that had been penned against it since it was first introduced to Japan by Francis Xavier in 1549.[17] The shared belief in

---

lible for all ages and true in all places. It is Our wish to lay it to heart in all reverence, in common with you, Our subjects, that we may all attain to the same virtue.

[Tsunoda et al., eds., *Sources of Japanese Tradition*, vol. 2, pp. 139-40.]

For a thorough analysis, see Carol Gluck, *Japan's Modern Myths: Ideology in the Late Meiji Period* (Princeton: Princeton University Press, 985), especially chapter 5.

[c] Wakabayashi explains the relationship between the idea of *kokutai* and Christianity as follows: "Aizawa argued that the secret of Western strength lay in Christianity, a state cult that Western leaders propagated to cultivate voluntary allegiance both in their own peoples and in those they colonized overseas. Aizawa called the popular unity and allegiance so cultivated *kokutai*, 'the essence of a nation,' (and by extension, 'what is essential to make a people into a nation'). . . . But in *New Theses* his use of *kokutai* also connoted 'the unity of religion and government' (*saisei itchi*) used by a ruler to create spiritual unity and integration among his subjects. . . . [Aizawa] derived this idea of *kokutai* in large part from a knowledge of Christianity and the West. His studies of world geography and foreign affairs convinced him that Western leaders had attained *kokutai* better than the bakufu [Japan's feudal government]. . . . In *New Theses* Aizawa covertly argued that bakufu leaders must imitate Western methods of government by using the emperor to conduct a Japanese state religion designed to win the same type of national unity and mass loyalty that Western leaders had captured through Christianity." Wakabayashi, *Anti-Foreignism and Western Learning in Early-Modern Japan*, pp. 13–14.

Christianity, he concluded, gave the West an extraordinary power, which it employed to subvert foreign peoples. "The barbarians employ occult religions and other mysterious doctrines to seduce foreign peoples into their fold," he warned. "Should the barbarians win our commoners over to their cause, their paucity of numbers would become a great multitude."[18]

In Aizawa's mind, the threat posed by the West was categorically, even ontologically, different from anything Japan had previously encountered. "In times past, even the worst spreaders of sedition were fellow-nationals working from within," he wrote. "But the Western barbarians are different.

> They all believe in the same religion, Christianity, which they use to annex territories. Wherever they go, they destroy native houses of worship, deceive the local peoples, and seize those lands. These barbarians will settle for nothing less than subjugating the rulers of all nations and conscripting all peoples into their ranks. And they are becoming aggressive. Having overthrown the native regimes on Luzon and Java, they turned their predatory eyes on our Divine Realm. They instigated insurrections in Kyūshū using the same methods as on Luzon and Java.[19]

In Aizawa's view, Japan had been able to escape the fate suffered by other Asian nations because of "the ability of our enlightened emperor to see through their schemes and vanquish the barbarians." However, the threat had now become imminent and palpable. The Western barbarians, who "for hundreds of years . . . have desired and resolved to subvert enemy nations through their occult religion and thus conquer the whole world," were on Japan's doorstep.[20]

Aizawa regarded Christianity as the key to the Western threat. He was very explicit about his fear of ideological subversion and his conviction that trade was merely the initial stage in the West's long-range plan to subjugate Japan.

> [Christianity] is a truly evil and base religion, barely worth discussing. But its main doctrines are simple to grasp and well-contrived; [the

•

Western barbarians] can easily deceive stupid commoners with it. Using clever words and subtle phrases, they would have commoners
believe that to deceive Heaven is to revere it, and that to destroy the
Way is needed for ethical understanding....

Whenever they seek to take over a country, they employ the same
method. By trading with that nation, they learn about its geography
and defenses. If these be weak, they dispatch troops to invade the
nation; if strong, they propagate Christianity to subvert it from within.
Once our people's hearts and minds are captivated by Christianity, they
will greet the barbarian host with open arms, and we would be powerless to stop them.... Barbarian armies seek only plunder, but do so
in the name of their god. They employ this tactic in all lands they annex
or conquer.[21]

Aizawa's fear of Christianity led him to advocate rejecting everything Western:

All Western goods, medicines, woolens, and the like, must be burned
on sight—the sale or use of imported articles must be absolutely for-
bidden. Commoners must be made to despise foreigners as they would
despise dogs and goats, to hate the barbarians as they would hate wild
boars and wolves.[22]

Xenophobe though he was, Aizawa was also a realist. One of the
few Japanese who had personally interrogated a foreigner, he was
well informed about world affairs for his time.[23] When it eventually
became clear that the Westerners were too strong to be simply driven
away, he revised his views and became a proponent of opening Japan
to the West. Despite his fear that Japan would be subverted, he
argued that the nation should adopt Western learning and turn it to
its own use.[24] But this had some of the consequences Aizawa had
predicted, for Japan's adoption of Western technology did inevitably
lead to the acceptance of Western ideas and values, which transformed Japanese culture. Notwithstanding their prescience in this
respect, Aizawa's arguments against Christianity nevertheless consti-

tuted an "ideology of hatred" that stands as the archetype of anti-Christian, and subsequent antisemitic, thought.[25f]

Anti-Christian polemics were not restricted to nativist thinkers like Aizawa. Ukai Tetsujō (1814–91) was a prominent Pure Land Buddhist priest who served as the seventy-fifth abbot of the renowned Chion'in temple in Kyoto. He vehemently opposed Christianity and in 1869 became the leader of the Organization of United Buddhist Sects (*Shoshū dōtoku kaimei*), which opposed the alien religion and promoted Buddhism as the antidote to its pernicious teachings.[g] Ukai's *On Understanding and Rejecting Heresy* [*Hekija kanken-roku*], written in 1861 under the pen name Kiyū Dōjin, is the most famous of his anti-Christian tracts.

Like Aizawa, Ukai had some knowledge of Christianity, but his understanding was colored by a profound loathing. Ridiculing Christian beliefs and practices, he wrote in an almost Biblical cadence,

---

[f] A landmark for pre-Restoration, anti-Christian polemics was the *Collection of Anti-Christian Writings* [*Haiya-shū*] begun by the Mito domain (with which Aizawa was affiliated) in 1855. The *Collection* consisted of two parts. The first part, a facsimile edition of Chinese anti-Christian polemics from the Ming dynasty (1368–1644), was completed in 1856. The second part was a compilation of Japanese anti-Christian literature completed in 1860. The former was particularly important, for it remained a sourcebook of anti-Christian arguments into the Meiji period. In fact, in this respect, the book played much the same role as *The Protocols of the Elders of Zion* in later anti-Jewish polemics. The irony is that the *Collection* and *The Protocols*, both of which attained the status of nationalist bibles in Japan, were themselves imported from abroad. See Itō Tasaburō, "Bakumatsu ni okeru Yaso-kyō haigeki" [Anti-Christian Polemics of the Late Tokugawa Period], in *Kinsei-shi no kenkyū* [Studies in Early Modern Japanese History] (Yoshikawa kōbunkan, 1981), pp. 287, 291.

[g] Buddhists used anti-Christianity as a means to establish their nationalistic bona fides. Ketelaar translates one of the many letters sent to the newly installed Meiji government and signed by thirty-four prominent Buddhist priests in this organization:

> Buddhism should be used to facilitate the hardening of the hearts of foolish men and women to prevent their being deceived by Protestant or Catholic teachings. If this is done, we priests, with over one thousand years of devotion to our nation, will be able to continue our loyal service. Like trees that stand together in a forest, why is it that the various [Buddhist] sects cannot coordinate and consolidate their teachings? . . . All [Buddhist] sects uphold the Great Teaching of our Imperial Nation; thus, without exception, the teaching of each [Buddhist] sect should be used in the guidance of the people's hearts.

> [Ketelaar, *Of Heretics and Martyrs in Meiji Japan*, p. 98.]

•

They serve Heaven and call it their ancestor.

They say one should suffer in the present life to be happy in the hereafter.

They arrogantly treat nature as if it were their palace.

They disrespect the sun and moon as if they were mere lanterns.

They cast their own ancestors' gods into the vortex and the statues of our gods and Buddhas into the fire.

They treat their fathers as if they were equals.

They respect officials as much as insects.

They steal others' land like dogs or mice.

They slaughter animals as if they were vermin.

They arouse the ignorant with theories of heliocentrism.

They build firearms and battleships and are fond of making war.

They make medicine out of the eyes of the sick and oil out of the blood of the dead.

They say people must be crucified to atone for their sins.

They let blood from the back [flagellation] as a means of confession.

They murder little children and eat them.

They seduce others' wives and indulge in indecency.

They sell poisonous opium, greedily depriving people of the money they need to sustain themselves.

They pervert morality; their lies and lawlessness know no bounds.[26]

Ukai rejected the argument that Christians simply perform harmless charitable works. These were, he asserted, merely "means to lure people into their occult religion." The Christians' ulterior purpose, he argued,

> is to interconnect people's minds and take over the entire world. Their plan is first to convert people's minds and then make them submit. Their tactics are so devious as to be beyond description. . . . In addition, they use money to lure them, so not only the ignorant but even the warrior class fall prey to their heresies.[27]

The notion of a conspiracy to take over the world through intellectual subversion and the idea that international commerce would play a role in subverting the well-educated as well as the ignorant are com-

•

mon to both Ukai's anti-Christian predecessors like Aizawa and to his antisemitic successors.

These tenets of pre-Restoration anti-Christian polemics are iden-tical to the tenets of twentieth-century Japanese antisemitism—only the identity of the "occult religion" changed. This becomes apparent in the work of yet another Tokugawa period xenophobe, Ōhashi Totsuan (1816–62).[28] A Confucian scholar and political activist, Ōhashi wrote the four volumes of his virulently anti-Christian *Comments on Heresy* [*Hekija shōgen*] between 1852 and 1853 and published the work, which was avidly read by young royalist zealots, in 1857. In 1862, Ōhashi himself joined an abortive coup against the Tokugawa regime and died the same year after a brief period of imprisonment.

Ōhashi asserted that Western culture was merely a facade for Chris-tianity. "Anything born in the West," he argued, "even the various arts, is in the final analysis an extension of the occult religion," and he warned that permitting other forms of Western knowledge into Japan while prohibiting Christianity "would sooner or later have the same result."[29] Like Aizawa, he was driven by a sense of nationalist mission. "It is lamentable that no one points out the wickedness of these teach-ings and attacks them; it is deplorable that daily the stream of people flowing toward them grows larger"[30]; and he therefore resolved to "be a thorn in the side of those who indulge themselves in the barbarians' arts of death [and] awaken them from their confusion."[31]

One passage from Ōhashi will suffice to demonstrate the congruity of Tokugawa period anti-Christian polemics and twentieth-century antisemitism. In the following passage, the words "Judaism" and "Jews" have been substituted for the terms "occult religion" and "Western barbarians," respectively. The result is a classical antisemitic harangue.

> Now, the intentions of the [Jews] in promoting trade are roundly to be despised and deeply to be feared. As I have said before, their aims are grounded in the [Judaism] that is their guiding principle. The funda-mental aim of the [Jews] is to annex all countries of the world, to treat them as undifferentiated members of the same world order, and to make their national polities, their institutions, and their religions uni-

form throughout. In order for them to achieve this goal, the [Jews] must first involve themselves in every aspect of life and subvert people's minds. Thus, they first employ sonorous phrases, intoning, "The people of all nations walk the same earth and under the same sky, and as they are brothers, it is God's will that they be compassionate toward one another." So saying, they impress the ignorant, and with even more skillful subterfuges stimulate the mind. Simultaneously, they provide their sympathizers with money and other incentives. That they appeal to the stupid masses in this way goes without saying, but they also lure those with some small powers of discernment into their realm of darkness. Making people respect them is part of their insidious plot. . . . Thus, as time passes, they abscond with the hearts of men and convert the multitudes who flock to them. With even more vulgar trinkets, they offer the necessities of life, and sucking out the marrow of the nation, they sap its inimitable strength. Then waiting for the time when the nation is most vulnerable to conquest, they devour it in a single gulp.[32]

This portrait of the threat posed to Japan by Christianity in the Tokugawa period is identical to the portrait that would be drawn of "The Jewish Peril" in the twentieth century. It stressed five themes, all of which would reappear in antisemitic garb in the 1920s: (1) Japan is threatened by an alien, occult religion. (2) This occult religion is the driving force behind a conspiracy of world conquest and domination. (3) In addition to providing the underlying rationale for the conspiracy to control the world, the occult religion also functions as a means of spiritual subversion in every area of culture. (4) Trade and finance are major tools of the conspiracy. (5) The ultimate aim of the conspiracy is to destroy Japan's national identity and create a single world order controlled by the adherents of the occult religion.

In short, the Japanese had an indigenous theory of a global religious conspiracy to destroy them a hundred years before *The Protocols of the Elders of Zion* was introduced to Japan.

•

The Japanese acquired many of their images of Jews from translated Western literature, but those images were also powerfully mediated by Japanese culture.

In preparing translations of Western literature, Japanese scholars and writers inevitably depended on foreign sources for their definition of unfamiliar terms. Many foreign dictionaries contained derogatory definitions of the word "Jew," like the following from *The Concise Oxford Dictionary of Current English*: "Jew: Person of Hebrew race; extortionate usurer; trader who drives hard bargains."[33] These presumably authoritative definitions necessarily influenced Japanese conceptions and have remained standard in many Japanese reference works to the present day.[h]

The translated literary work that most profoundly affected Japanese images of Jews was *The Merchant of Venice*. The play was the first work by Shakespeare to be performed in Japan, and it remained the most frequently produced Shakespearean drama into the 1970s. While it affected the Japanese image of Jews more profoundly than any other literary work, the success of *The Merchant of Venice* had more to do with the way it mirrored *Japanese* preconceptions, preoccupations, and insecurities, however, than anything to do with Jews.

There is speculation that *The Merchant of Venice* was known in Japan as early as 1695, when it is supposed to have influenced the playwright Chikamatsu Monzaemon, who incorporated the theme of paying off a debt with human flesh in his *Ceremony for the Birth of the Buddha* [*Shaka nyorai tanjōe*], but there is no evidence to substantiate this theory.[34] The first authenticated appearance of the play was in

---

[h] In 1984, Eve Kaplan, a Harvard graduate student, initiated an inquiry into Japanese dictionary definitions of the word "Jew." Her efforts led to the formation of an ad hoc group of foreign businesspeople in Tokyo calling itself the International Committee for Cross Cultural Relations (ICCCR), which found in the late 1980s that two-thirds of the 104 Japanese dictionaries they examined contained derogatory definitions of the word "Jew." Armed with these findings, the ICCCR, the American Jewish Committee's Pacific Rim Institute, and other groups approached Japanese publishers to revise these definitions. See "A Jew Is . . ." *Jewish News: The Bulletin of the Jewish Community* [*of Tokyo*] 10, no. 4 (February 1988), 4–5; Willy Stern, "Japanese Dictionaries Encourage Anti-Semitism," *Japan Times*, October 16, 1988; Jennifer Golub, "Japanese Attitudes Toward Jews" (New York: Pacific Rim Institute of the American Jewish Committee, 1992), pp. 6–7.

1883, when a writer named Inoue Tsutomu translated and adapted it as *The Flesh-Pawning Trial* (*Jinniku shichi-ire saiban*). The work became an instant success, making Shakespeare popular in Japan for the first time.

The Japanese were not unaware of Shakespeare prior to Inoue's translation. Charles Lamb's *Tales from Shakespeare* had appeared in 1868. A quaint rendition of Hamlet's "To be or not to be" soliloquy was carried in *The Japan Punch* in 1874; a three-part series on *Hamlet* had been written by the novelist Kanagaki Robun in 1875; and *The Merchant* itself had been adapted as *The Mysterious Breast-Meat Trial* (*Munaniku kishō*) in 1877. In 1879, *King Lear* appeared in a literary Chinese translation by Wadagaki Kenzō. In 1881–82, Toyama Shōichi rendered *Hamlet* as *The Revenge of the Miraculous Prince* (*Reigen kōshi no adauchi*), and a minor cottage industry developed as Toyama and others churned out translations of famous speeches from the Bard.[35]

But *The Merchant of Venice* was the first work by Shakespeare to capture the Japanese imagination. Inoue's translation (a free rendition replete with references to railroads and steam whistles)[36] was quickly rewritten by Utagawa Bunkai for serialization in the *Ōsaka Asahi shimbun*, where it appeared in April and May 1885. The story was immediately adapted for the Kabuki stage by Katsu Genzō, a disciple of the great Kawatake Mokuami, the leading playwright of the day. Katsu rewrote it with the title *Life as Fragile as Cherry Blossoms, A World of Money* (*Sakura-doki zeni no yononaka*),[37] and the play was performed at the Ebisu-za in Osaka by Nakamura Sōjūrō's troupe that summer.[38]

Life as Fragile as Cherry Blossoms, A World of Money was in every respect a typical Kabuki play.[39] Set in Japan, with all the characters recast as Japanese, the play is stripped of its European identity. Antonio is no longer Venetian, and Shylock (renamed Gohei) is not identified as a Jew. Indeed, Shylock is simply a reincarnation of the archetypal miser character who appears throughout the Kabuki repertory.[40] The play conformed completely to the mindset characteristic of Kabuki, and the principle of "rewarding good and punishing evil" (*kanzen chōaku*), which was de rigueur at the time, was faithfully

●

observed. Thus Gohei/Shylock is a pure villain without the redeeming qualities that make Shakespeare's character a complex and interesting, if not particularly likable, human being.

This Japanese Shylock remained the centerpiece of all productions of the play until the late 1960s. And there were many. Counting the documented productions alone, by 1974, *The Merchant* had been staged fifty-six times, ten times more than the second-place *Hamlet*.[41] The productions became increasingly sophisticated, and the portrayal of the characters became more nuanced as translations and acting techniques improved. But the cumulative effect was to identify Gohei as a Jew—that is, to attribute to the Jews the characteristics of the traditional Japanese miser.

Shylock did not appear as himself in a Japanese production until 1903, when Kawakami Otojirō (1864–1911) staged the trial scene of *The Merchant of Venice* at the Meijiza theater.[i] Kawakami had visited America the previous year and had seen Henry Irving play the role. He was so impressed that he decided to play Shylock himself. Irving personally assisted him in this,[42] but unlike the American actor, who was famous for his sympathetic portrayal, Kawakami played Shylock as a dastardly villain opposite his wife Sada Yakko's lithesome Portia.[43] William Archer wrote of the London performance that Kawakami's Shylock "was, as a whole, what we should call a very clever bit of character-acting; but it had no really tragic quality. At the same time the vividness and crispness of the performance in general deserve a great deal of praise."[44]

The first nominally modern production of *The Merchant* was staged in 1906 by the Literary Arts Society (*Bungei kyōkai*) at the Kabukiza theater. The word *modern* is used here advisedly, because the part of Portia was played by the male actor Doi Shunshō. Like Kawakami's troupe, the Literary Arts Society staged only the trial scene, thus reinforcing the identification of *The Merchant* with the miserly Shylock (the merchant of the title is actually Antonio, not Shylock), and the miserly Shylock with the villainous Jews.

---

[i] Kawakami was an early innovator in the theater who tried to reform Kabuki by introducing colloquial language and welcoming actresses, who had been banned from Japanese theater since 1638, back to the stage.

•

The most significant full-scale production of *The Merchant of Venice* to be staged in the prewar period was mounted by the Tsukiji Little Theater in January 1926. The Tsukiji had been built in 1924 as the first Japanese theater dedicated to the production of modern (i.e., European-style) plays. Translated by Osanai Kaoru and directed by Hijikata Yoshi, the two founders of the theater, the play had an all-star cast, including Susukida Kenji as Shylock and Senda Koreya as Antonio. Generally speaking, though, Shakespeare's works remained the province of English literature scholars and Kabuki actors in the prewar period and received scant attention from the modern theater movement until after World War II.[45]

It was not until the late 1960s that Shylock was portrayed sympathetically in Japan. The timing is significant, for this period was the apex of Japanese sympathy for the Jews. In July 1967, the Kurumiza company produced *The Merchant* in Kyoto. Directed by the playwright and critic Yamazaki Masakazu, the play stressed Shylock's humanity.[46] It was the 1968 production by the Mingei (People's Theater) troupe that truly broke with tradition, however. Directed by Asari Keita from a translation by Fukuda Tsuneari, the production was so intent on redeeming Shylock that one critic suggested ironically that the troupe was trying to perform not *The Merchant of Venice* but *The Jew of Venice*.[47] While critics agreed that veteran actor Takizawa Osamu's portrayal of Shylock was extraordinarily accomplished, they also concurred that he had overwhelmed the other actors and dominated the production to such an extent that the play as a whole did not work.[48] Apparently the translator, Fukuda, was himself dissatisfied, for when he directed his own production in 1973, he stressed the need to achieve a more balanced interpretation.[49]

The Merchant of Venice has had a far-reaching impact on Japanese thinking about Jews. Writing in 1923, Watanabe Minojirō (1869–1924), a reporter for the *Ōsaka mainichi shimbun* who took an early and not unsympathetic interest in the Jews, related, "I received the strong impression that the Jews had always been a despicable race like Shylock, who was best described as stingy, greedy, cruel, cold-blooded, and heartless."[50]

This image has been perpetuated through the Japanese educational system. *The Merchant of Venice* was assigned as a required text and was regularly performed by high school students throughout the postwar period.[j] In the late 1980s, numerous translations of the play were available, including adaptations for primary, junior high, and high school students, and these generally allowed little room for empathy with Shylock, who was depicted as "purely and simply fixated on money and the unhampered operation of his business."[51]

The result of this unrelenting exposure to *The Merchant of Venice* has been to render Shylock one of the defining images of Jews in Japan. *The Merchant* has become a fixture of modern Japanese culture, and knowledge of the text is expected of every literate Japanese. So widely known is the drama that in 1985, Iwai Katsuhito, a prominent economist at Tokyo University, was able to publish a serious and commercially successful study of modern capitalism based entirely on the play.[52]

The irony is, of course, that the Japanese image of Shylock, which has been so influential in shaping Japanese ideas about the Jews, has virtually nothing to do with Jews but mirrors Japan's own cultural history. It is an example of how over time the Japanese have fashioned their own image of the Jews from imported raw materials but for their own cultural purposes.

The initial popularity of *The Merchant of Venice* in Japan had nothing to do with Jews but was a function of contemporary Japanese

---

[j] The Education Ministry–approved texts in which the play is excerpted are too numerous to list. Representative Japanese language texts for junior high school students that use the play include *Kokugo: sōgō hen* (8th grade, 1954), *Chūgaku kokugo* (8th grade, 1962), and *Kokugo seikatsu: bungaku hen* (9th grade, 1952), all published by Nihon shoseki; *Kokugo* (8th grade, 1953) and *Kaiteiban chūgaku hyōjun kokugo* (8th grade, 1956), published by Kyōiku tosho; and *Shinpan hyōjun chūgaku kokugo* (8th grade, 1972) and *Kaitei hyōjun chūgaku kokugo* (8th grade, 1975).

The Ministry of Education told the Pacific Rim Institute of the American Jewish Committee in 1992 that the play was no longer being used in Japanese schools. See Golub, *Japanese Attitudes Toward Jews*, p. 12.

The Merchant of Venice has also been used as a text in public schools and has been the subject of controversy in the United States. *Newsweek* magazine reported in its March 21, 1936, issue, for example, the unsuccessful attempt by "the 27-year-old, dark-complexioned head of the Hackensack synagogue . . . to have the play removed from the school's curriculum." And the *New York Times* of February 22, 1981, reported on a controversy surrounding the airing of a BBC/Time-Life version of the play on the Public Television System (PBS).

preoccupations. During the Meiji period, one scholar has suggested that interest in *The Merchant* derived from a Japanese fascination with courts and trials.[53] The obsession with money and moneylenders that pervaded Meiji Japan seems an even more plausible explanation of its popularity. Moneylending for profit was one of the transgressions of which Buddhism was accused when it was under intense fire in the 1870s.[54] In 1879, Katsu Genzō's mentor Mokuami wrote a play entitled *Men Live in a World Where Money Is All* (*Ningen banji kane no yononaka*) based on E. B. Lytton's story "The Money."[55] Ozaki Kōyō's widely read novel *The Demon Gold* (*Konjiki yasha*), in which one of the central characters is a usurer, appeared as a newspaper serial beginning in 1898. And Mori Ōgai's *The Wild Goose* (*Gan*), in which the heroine is unhappily married to a moneylender, appeared in serial form between 1911 and 1913.[56]

Most compelling of all, however, is James Shapiro's argument that, in manipulating stereotypes of the Jews, Shakespeare had played upon the subliminal anxieties of Elizabethan audiences during a period of cultural transition and crisis. Shapiro argues that the Jews in *The Merchant of Venice* are a "source and site of cultural anxiety" and that the play has continued to fascinate audiences around the world for the past four hundred years not because it concerns Jews as such but because it "give[s] voice to recurrent cultural problems of nation, race, and gender" that affect all people. At the turn of the twentieth century, as the impact of rapid modernization began to be felt, the Japanese were concerned with precisely these issues, and *The Merchant*, particularly the trial scene, with its national/racial tensions, gender confusion, and metaphoric threats of emasculation, undoubtedly appealed to them for this reason.[57]

The period when *The Merchant of Venice* became popular and Shylock's identity was formed was a time of dizzying, disorienting social change in Japan. By the 1890s, it was becoming abundantly clear that early Meiji optimism about an easy harmonization of Japanese culture with Western technology (*wakon yōsai*) had been naive. Society was urbanizing at an astonishing rate. By the mid-1930s, 45 percent of all Japanese lived in cities of 100,000 or more, compared with only 12 percent in 1895. Between 1873 and 1905, the proportion of

•

children attending school rose from about 40 percent of boys and 15 percent of girls to better than 90 percent of children of both sexes. An increasing number of these children continued their education in institutions of higher learning, so that between 1900 and 1920 the number of students enrolled in colleges and universities increased two and a half times, from 39,352 to 99,532.[58]

Japan was changing so rapidly that the only thing holding it together seemed to be the Emperor Meiji. When he died in 1912, the sense of cultural crisis was all but overwhelming.

There was also an increasingly pervasive sense of frustration that, despite their best efforts, the Japanese would never be fully accepted by the West because of their race. The initial period of Japan's modernization coincided with the heyday of scientific racism in Europe and the United States, so the Japanese found themselves frequently reminded that their racial inferiority was, by the lights of Western science, empirically verifiable.[59] Discriminatory laws and regulations implemented in the United States and other countries sustained the view that the Japanese could not expect equal treatment in the international community. Japanese frustration came to a head in the early 1920s, when the United States Supreme Court upheld laws barring Asians from becoming U.S. citizens, and the Exclusion Act of 1924 was passed by Congress.[60]

If national identity and race were issues for the Japanese at this time, so was gender. Henrik Ibsen was the most influential playwright of the day, and works like *A Doll's House* and *Hedda Gabler* became the focal point of calls for women's liberation. The Ibsen Society, composed of the most prominent intellectuals of the period, was founded in 1907; and *A Doll's House*, which had been translated in 1893, was staged to great acclaim in 1911, catapulting Matsui Sumako, who played Nora, to the status of a cultural icon. The Bluestocking Society (*Seitōsha*), which initiated the modern Japanese women's movement, was also founded in 1911.[61]

The popularity of early translations and adaptations of *The Merchant of Venice* was thus due to the preoccupations, anxieties, and insecurities of Japanese culture during the mid- to late Meiji period and not to the fact that Shylock was a Jew. Shylock first appeared

•

before the Japanese as an incarnation of the preexisting miser character in Kabuki; the play became popular because it satisfied a popular taste for works dealing with trials, money, and moneylending; and the trial scene in particular appealed to the profound anxieties the Japanese were experiencing during a period of rapid cultural and social change. In other words, the Shylock whom the Japanese frequently assume to be the quintessential Jew is in fact a reflection of their own modern imagination, and Japanese attitudes toward Jews are thus deeply rooted in the modern, as well as the traditional, Japanese cultural experience.

•

III

GOD'S CHOSEN PEOPLE

<small>Jews in Japanese Christian Theology</small>

UNDER INTENSE DIPLOMATIC pressure, the 250-year-old ban on Christianity was lifted in 1873. By 1880, thirty thousand Japanese had been baptized, and within a few years that number had tripled. Anti-Christian sentiment continued to play an important ideological role, with nationalist ideologues casting Japanese Christians as metaphorical foreigners and contrasting their own true devotion to the nation against the Christians' alien faith, but Christianity nevertheless became a potent intellectual force in late-nineteenth-century Japan.[1]

The appeal of Christianity had less to do with theology than with education. Christian missionaries founded schools and provided the most up-to-date, cosmopolitan education available in Japan at the time. The year after the ban on Christianity ended, both the Methodist Aoyama Gakuin (now Aoyama Gakuin University) and the

Episcopalian St. Paul's School (now Rikkyō University) were established in Tokyo; in 1875, Dōshisha English School (now Dōshisha University) was established in Kyoto by the Amherst-educated Niijima Jō (1843–90). Individual foreign missionaries taught Japan's future leaders. The statesmen Ōkuma Shigenobu and Soejima Taneomi were tutored by the Dutch-born, American-trained Guido Verbeck. Captain L. L. Janes profoundly influenced the lives of thirty-five elite students in western Japan known as the "Kumamoto Band."[2] And William S. Clark, who lectured briefly at the Sapporo Agricultural School, left behind an exhortation that resounds in Japan to this day, "Boys, be ambitious!"

Missionary teachers were regarded as representatives of the superior civilization of the West. Consistent with the mainstream of liberal American Protestantism, they taught a doctrine of social responsibility that emphasized ethics over theology. Their lofty ideals and stoic lifestyle impressed the Japanese greatly.

Although the Christianity taught by missionaries in Meiji Japan tended to be nontheological, the translation of the New Testament completed by American missionaries J. C. Hepburn and S. R. Brown in 1880 ineluctably exposed the Japanese to the panoply of Christian images of the Jews, both positive and negative.[a] Through the New Testament, the Japanese learned of the Jews' election as God's "Chosen People" and of how Christianity claimed to have "superseded" Judaism. They were necessarily exposed to traditional Christian stereotypes of the Jews as legalistic Pharisees, intransigent infidels, and

---

[a] The first Japanese translation of the New Testament was brought to Japan by Francis Xavier, who is said to have carried a Japanese translation of portions of the Gospel According to Matthew with him when he arrived in Kagoshima on August 15, 1549. In about 1613, a Japanese translation of the entire New Testament was published in Kyoto by Roman Catholic missionaries. When contact with the West resumed in the 1850s, American missionaries J. C. Hepburn and S. R. Brown began preparing a Japanese translation of the Bible, and in 1880 their work came to fruition in a complete Japanese translation of the New Testament. Translations by the Baptists and other denominations followed. Recently, in 1987, a joint committee of Protestant and Catholic scholars produced a new, "interconfessional" translation of both the Old and New Testaments. (Executive Committee of The Common Bible Translation, ed., *Seisho: shin kyōdō yaku* [The Bible: The New Interconfessional Translation] (Japan Bible Society, 1987), pp. iii–vi.)

Christ killers, but these did not figure greatly in their evolving image of the Jews.[b] Rather, Japanese images derived principally from the original theologies that Japanese Christians developed for themselves in the early twentieth century.

By the early 1900s, Christian missionaries and imported Christian theology had lost some of their novelty and appeal, and a number of attempts were made to develop an authentically Japanese Christianity. Distinct images of the Jews emerged from these attempts. The most significant of these were the neo-orthodox image of Uchimura Kanzō (1861–1930), who regarded the Jews as historical witnesses to the Gospel; the fundamentalist image of Nakada Jūji (1870–1939), who saw the Jews as mystical saviors whose redemption would ensure the political and military, as well as spiritual, salvation of the Japanese; and the syncretic image of scholars and clergy like Saeki Yoshirō (1871–1965) and Oyabe Zen'ichirō (1867–1941), who conceived of the Jews as sharing a common ancestry with the Japanese and thus legitimizing Japan's divine election as a nation.

All these men were members of the first Meiji generation, and their theologies and images of the Jews were developed in response to the tensions and dilemmas of their time. Born between 1861 and 1871, they were trained in the transitional, hybrid educational system of Meiji Japan, a disconcerting mix of classical Japanese and Western learning. Many of them were educated in Christian academies and seminaries, whose curricula were even more idiosyncratic than mainstream institutions. They were the first Japanese able to travel freely

---

[b] The New Testament contains many unflattering images of the Jews. See, for example, John 8:44, where Jesus says to the Jews who doubt him, "Your father is the devil and you choose to carry out your father's desires. He was a murderer from the beginning, and is not rooted in the truth; there is no truth in him. When he tells a lie he is speaking his own language, for he is a liar and the father of lies." In 1 Thessalonians 2:14–15, Paul refers to "the Jews, who killed the Lord Jesus and the prophets and drove us out, the Jews who are heedless of God's will and enemies of their fellow-men." (Scriptural references here and below are from the New English Bible.)

For a brief account of anti-Jewish references in the Gospels, see Robert S. Wistrich, *Antisemitism: The Longest Hatred* (New York: Pantheon, 1991), pp. 13–16. For a more thorough discussion, see Rosemary Radford Ruether, *Faith and Fratricide: The Theological Roots of Anti-Semitism* (New York: Seabury Press, 1974); and Jules Isaac, *The Teaching of Contempt: Christian Roots of Anti-Semitism*, tr. Helen Weaver (New York: Holt, Rinehart and Winston, 1964).

abroad, and like their best-known contemporaries—literary giants like Mori Ōgai (1862–1922) and Natsume Sōseki (1867–1916)—they were obsessed with how to reconcile their Japanese identity with Western culture. Like the philosophy of the Zen scholar Suzuki Daisetsu (a.k.a. D. T. Suzuki, 1870–1966) and the aesthetics of the art historian and popularizer of the tea ceremony Okakura Kakuzō (a.k.a. Okakura Tenshin, 1862–1913), their theologies were attempts to reformulate and reaffirm the validity of Japanese cultural identity in Western cultural terms.[3]

The theology of Uchimura Kanzō began as an attempt to formulate a Japanese identity in Christian terms, but Western culture interfered as a frustrating impediment to reconciling Christian faith and Japanese identity. As Uchimura phrased it in English in 1925,

> I love two J's and no third; one is Jesus, and the other is Japan.
> I do not know which I love more, Jesus or Japan.
> I am hated by my countrymen for Jesus' sake as *yaso*, and I am disliked
>   by foreign missionaries for Japan's sake as national and narrow.
> No matter; I may lose all my friends, but I cannot lose Jesus and Japan.[4]

Uchimura's attempt to define an authentically Japanese Christianity led him to reject foreign missionary influence. For Uchimura, who was born into a samurai family in Tokyo in 1861 and who had graduated from Amherst College in 1887, foreign influence was detrimental to the development of a truly Japanese Christianity. As he later wrote,

> Japanese Christianity is Christianity received by the Japanese directly
> from God without any intermediary; no more, no less . . . the Spirit of
> Japan inspired by the Almighty is Japanese Christianity. It is free,
> independent, original and creative. . . . Only Japanese Christianity will
> save Japan and the Japanese.[5]

•

Finding ways to articulate this unmediated Christian faith was a task that occupied Uchimura throughout his life. His most famous formulation was what he called "Churchless" (*Mukyōkai*) Christianity. Arguing that "there is no organized church in heaven," Uchimura wrote, "It is God's universe—nature. . . . This is our church. No church, whether in Rome or in London, can approximate it. In this sense, *Mukyōkai* has a church. Only those who have no church as conceived in conventional terms have the true church."[6]

Because it undermined their influence, Uchimura's idea of a Churchless Christianity was unpopular with Western missionaries, but he defended his right to develop an autonomous variety of Christianity that would not be beholden to any Western church or denomination.

> I am blamed by missionaries for upholding Japanese Christianity. . . .
> [But] is not Episcopalianism essentially an English Christianity, Presbyterianism a Scotch Christianity, Lutheranism a German Christianity, and so forth? . . . Paul, a Christian apostle, remained an Hebrew of the Hebrews till the end of his life. Savonarola was an Italian Christian, Luther was a German Christian, and Knox was a Scotch Christian. They were not characterless universal men, but distinctly national, therefore distinctly human, and distinctly Christian.[7]

In 1918, Uchimura wrote an essay in which he distinguished three distinct periods in the evolution of his faith. The first period began when he signed the "Covenant of Believers in Jesus" at the Sapporo Agricultural School in 1877 and was baptized the following year at the age of eighteen.[8] Uchimura "accepted the one and only God for the first time through Christianity" and "was freed from all my superstitions." The second period began in 1886, when, at the age of twenty-six, he was profoundly influenced by Julius Hawley Seelye, the president of Amherst College, and "accepted Christ's atonement on the cross for my sins." The final period, he wrote, began when he became convinced in his late fifties of the imminence of the Second Coming. "It was a revolution, an event of such great moment that it ushered in a new era in my life. . . . Behold, everything has been renewed!"[9] Uchimura's thinking on the Jews developed most clearly during this last period, in the context of his fascination with the Second Coming of Christ in the wake of World War I.

War played a consistently significant role in Uchimura's spiritual development. He had originally supported the Sino-Japanese War of 1894–95 as a "just war," but when the conflict ended and he had time to reflect on its consequences, he resolved to become a pacifist. As an "absolute" pacifist, he joined the socialist thinkers Sakai Toshihiko (1871–1933) and Kōtoku Shūsui (1871–1911) in denouncing the Russo-Japanese War of 1904–05 in the pages of the liberal daily, the *Universal Morning News* (*Yorozu chōhō*); and when the paper's founder and editor, Kuroiwa Ruikō (1862–1920) came out in favor of the war, Uchimura broke with him and began to develop his pacifistic arguments in the pages of *Biblical Studies* (*Seisho no kenkyū*), the journal he had started in 1900. Because he had made the commitment to pacifism earlier, his conversion at the time of the Russo-Japanese War was not from "just-war theorist" to "pacifist," but rather away from secular journalism toward a religious idiom and a clearer definition of himself as a man of the cloth.

The fact that Uchimura was profoundly disturbed by the carnage of World War I and that he tried to deal with it in a religious idiom was thus not surprising. "Why did this great war begin," he demanded, "the most meaningless, evil, tragic war in the history of mankind, threatening to destroy the very foundations of human society?" He later confessed that "For several days after July 31, 1914, my faith was severely tested."[10] Uchimura concluded that peace would not come through human means: "There is nowhere on earth whence peace might arise," he wrote, and out of the depths of his despair, he gradually formulated the belief that peace on earth could be achieved only with the Second Coming of Christ.[11] The prophecy of the Second Coming and the raising of the dead contained in First Thessalonians were the true message of the Bible, he contended[12c]; and, using

---

[c] First Thessalonians 4:13–18 reads, "We wish you not to remain in ignorance, brothers, about those who sleep in death; you should not grieve like the rest of men, who have no hope. We believe that Jesus died and rose again; and so it will be for those who died as Christians; God will bring them to life with Jesus.

the English theological terms, he announced, "I am now a Pre-millennialist (one who believes that the Return will precede the coming of God's Kingdom) and not a Post-millennialist (one who believes that Christ will return only after the coming of God's Kingdom)."[13d]

Earlier in his career, Uchimura had eschewed any such chiliastic assertions. In the summer of 1916, however, in his despair over the war, he underwent a change of heart and declared that only with the Second Coming would peace be achieved. "How foolish was I to devote myself for such a long while to trying to improve the world with my poor abilities," he lamented. "That was not a goal for me to achieve. It will only be achieved by Christ when He comes. . . . The

---

"For this we tell you as the Lord's word: we who are left alive until the Lord comes shall not forestall those who have died; because at the word of command, at the sound of the archangel's voice and God's trumpet-call, the Lord himself will descend from heaven; first the Christian dead will rise, then we who are left alive shall join them, caught up in clouds to meet the Lord in the air. Thus we shall always be with the Lord. Console one another, then, with these words."

[d] "Post-" and "premillennialism" are theological terms that derive from the thought of John Nelson Darby (1800–1882), an Irish theologian who preached widely in North America. Drawing on biblical prophecy, Darby and his followers divided human history into periods, or "dispensations," of which the present was the last before the Second Coming. Two versions of this theory developed in the United States following the Civil War, both based on the anticipation of the coming of "The Millennium," the paradisiacal one thousand years prophesied in Revelation 20:6, "Happy indeed, and one of God's own people, is the man who shares in this first resurrection! Upon such the second death has no claim; but they shall be priests of God and of Christ, and shall reign with him for the thousand years." The first version was "postmillennialism," which suggested that the Millennium, when the Anti-Christ would be defeated and Christianity would reign triumphant, was being achieved in the present age and that Christ would reappear *following* this perfection of society by human hands. "Premillennialism," by contrast, argued that the perfection of the world through human efforts was impossible and that the Second Coming of Christ would therefore have to *precede* the Millennium. See George M. Marsden, *Fundamentalism and American Culture: The Shaping of Twentieth-Century Evangelicalism, 1870–1925* (New York: Oxford University Press, 1980), pp. 46–55. See also Ernest R. Sandeen, *The Roots of Fundamentalism: British and American Millenarianism 1800–1930* (Chicago: University of Chicago Press, 1970), pp. 59–80 and passim.

The mainstream of American Protestant theology is "amillennialist," that is, it does not accept Darby's dispensationalism, nor does it interpret literally the prophecies about the Millennium that fundamentalists stress.

Gary Wills explains the impact of premillennialist theology on contemporary American politics in his *Under God: Religion and American Politics* (New York: Simon and Schuster, 1990).

●

Second Coming is the cardinal truth taught in every word of the New Testament."[14]

Uchimura became obsessed with the Second Coming, and he began to devote all his energies to the propagation of his newly reformulated faith.[e] On January 6, 1918, he delivered the first in a series of "Lectures on Biblical Prophecy" at the Christian Youth Hall in Mitoshiro-chō, Kanda, Tokyo, and for the next eighteen months, he lectured almost continuously on the Second Coming in virtually every major city throughout the country.[15]

Uchimura's image of the Jews hinged on the role he assigned them in the drama of the Second Coming. Like many Christians around the world, he was encouraged by signs that a Jewish homeland would soon be established in Palestine. Indications that the prophecy of the in-gathering of the Jews would be fulfilled appeared to Uchimura as a miraculous portent that the Second Coming was near.

> If Palestine is to be redeemed, then surely the Second Coming will also be realized. Our hopes for the Second Coming have been dashed many times. But the prophecy of the Bible is clear. Like the Jews, we shall rely on the Bible alone. But the knowledge that the redemption of Palestine is nigh can only strengthen our belief in the Second Coming. God will not forget his promise to the Christians, as he has not forgotten his promise to the Jews.[16]

---

[e] Uchimura wrote, for example,

> The Second Coming of Christ—the words are simple enough. But the meaning is profound. The principle is fundamental. The Second Coming is, in one respect, the rebirth of all things. It is the reconstruction of the universe. It is the resurrection of Christians. It is the victory of Justice. It is the Final Judgment. It is the realization of the Rule of the Almighty on earth. The sum of all mankind's hopes, that is the Second Coming of Christ. Thus, if one understands the Second Coming, everything will be understood. Conversely, if one fails to understand the Second Coming, one will understand nothing. In fact, it would be no mistake to say that the Second Coming is the core of Truth. It is no wonder that the Bible pays so much attention to this matter, for it is the point from which all things derive and the ultimate goal to which they aspire.
>
> ["Kirisuto sairin o shinzuru yori kitarishi yo no shisōjō no henka," *Uchimura Kanzō zenshū*, vol. 24, p. 385.]

●

Therefore,

> Twelve million Jews have been provided for us as witnesses to the
> Gospel. When we see the prophecy concerning them being fulfilled, we
> believe all the more firmly in the fulfillment of the great prophecy
> concerning us.[17]

Uchimura's understanding of the role of the Jews in the Second
Coming was essentially historical and rational. For him, the in-
gathering of the Jewish exiles was not a mystical event but God's way
of using history to instruct Christians in the truth of prophecy.

> Israel's destiny is a historical fact over which we have no control. Those
> who have eyes can see for themselves. God often uses historical fact to
> instruct us and reinforce our faith. The facts regarding Israel are a case
> in point. In order to make us believe such incomprehensible realities as
> the Second Coming and the Final Judgment, God has brought the
> destiny of the Jews before us as proof.[18]

In Uchimura's view, it was for this purpose that the Jews had
survived four thousand years of persecution and hardship, remained
faithful to the Old Testament, waited eagerly for the Messiah, and
lived in the hope of future redemption. Even after the fall of the
empires of Assyria, Egypt, Greece, and Rome, Israel alone had remained a great power. "Judging from the number of great men they
have produced relative to their population," Uchimura wrote, "they
are a first-class people."[19]

Uchimura fervently supported the restoration of Palestine to the
Jews. He was overjoyed when Jerusalem was liberated from the Turk-
ish "infidels" and returned to the British in late 1917, and he welcomed the reading of the Balfour Declaration before the British
parliament, saying, "Because of this one great fact, the year 1917 will
forever live in world history."[20] Uchimura ascribed particular significance to the establishment of the Hebrew University in Jerusalem,
which he saw as a step toward the redemption of Palestine and a sign
of the fulfillment of Biblical oracles.[21] "From this point of view, the
return of Israel is a vital issue for the entire world, with immense

implications for the whole human race. It is a historical reality that proves the unerring integrity of God's plan."[22]

Uchimura was hardly alone in his excitement. Christians around the world were elated by the prospect of the return of the Jews to Zion. At the two major prophetic conferences held in the United States in 1918, the major topic of political discussion was the British capture of Jerusalem, an event that for this audience overshadowed everything else the allies did.[23] Uchimura was part of this international trend. "I believe that God's hand is everywhere at work, realizing His astonishing plan. In this sense it is obvious that our faith is no small, personal matter, but an issue of significance for the world and the cosmos."[24]

Uchimura's excursion into millenarian speculation lasted about eighteen months. It was an intense reaction to the events of World War I. After that time, Uchimura returned to his neo-orthodox theology with a study of Paul's Epistle to the Romans, a project he shared with his German contemporary Karl Barth (1886–1968), to whom he might profitably be compared. Just before his death, Uchimura took up the subject of the Second Coming again, but this time he was trying to defend his long silence on the subject, and he criticized some of his contemporaries for their excessive apocalypticism.[25]

Uchimura was one of the most influential Japanese intellectuals of his day. His ideas impressed many future leaders of Japan in the fields of education, journalism, and the arts. Among those who attended his lectures were the economist Yanaihara Tadao (1893–1961), the novelists Shiga Naoya (1883–1971) and Arishima Takeo (1878–1923), and the theater director Osanai Kaoru (1881–1928). Following his essentially historical, rational understanding of the Jews, some of Uchimura's followers, like Yanaihara, became prominent liberal defenders of Zionism and advocates of the right of Jews to national self-determination.

Nakada Jūji (1870–1939), who shared the platform with Uchimura Kanzō at the January 6, 1918, "Lecture on Biblical Prophecy," developed a very different theology and image of the Jews. He was a fundamentalist in whose mind Japan's fate became mystically linked to the redemption of the Jews.

While Uchimura and Nakada were momentarily united by their shared devotion to preaching the Second Coming, there were significant theological differences between them. Consistent with his neo-orthodox approach, Uchimura was opposed to attempts to calculate the timing of the Second Coming. "I am satisfied," he wrote, "with the precious promise given by Christ that He will come to us without fail," and he was unconcerned whether the Advent would take place the following year or at some point in the indefinite future: "We believe that the Second Coming will happen in God's good time."[26] In short, Uchimura understood the promise of a thousand-year reign by Christ symbolically, not literally.

Nakada was a fundamentalist who had a very different purchase on these issues. He employed the categories Arminian and Calvinist to distinguish his beliefs from those of Uchimura.[f]

> Mr. Uchimura has not accepted every aspect of our Pure Gospel. From the theological point of view, Mr. Uchimura is a Calvinist, while I remain an Arminian who believes in Holiness and advocates Christian experimentation. Mr. Uchimura and his followers have not come over

---

[f] "Arminian" refers to the teachings of the Dutch theologian Jacobus Arminius (1560–1609), who reacted to the tenets of orthodox Calvinism. Arminianism is the theological basis for evangelical Christian denominations like Methodism, which stress personal salvation through Christ. In general, the Arminians rejected the orthodox view that God predetermines which individuals will be saved and which will be damned. They argued that salvation depends upon an individual's acceptance or rejection of Christ. The Arminians believed that Christ had died for all persons, not just for the elect, and that forgiveness was contingent only on the individual's acceptance of Christ. Orthodox Calvinists, by contrast, believed that Christ died only for the elect. Arminians believed that it was possible to reject God's grace and that without that possibility human volition would be meaningless; and they believed that it was possible to fall from grace, while theological conservatives believed one could not.

For a more complete description of Arminianism, see John Dillenberger and Claude Welch, *Protestant Christianity*, 2d ed. (New York: Macmillan, 1988), pp. 82–85.

to the side of Holiness, nor have I surrendered to them. However, we share a common belief in premillennialism, and we are in agreement only in underscoring this point. Beyond this one point, I accept no responsibility for the beliefs of Mr. Uchimura and his friends.[27]

The alliance of Uchimura Kanzō and Nakada Jūji in the Second Coming Movement was short-lived. Nakada rationalized it by saying, "In a larger sense, there is no Calvinism or Arminianism in the Second Coming. . . . If all denominations are united in their expectation of the Second Coming, even as they express their differences, those differences will become meaningless, for they will only see the Holiness of God."[28] But the gulf between the two men was deep, and their theologies led them in entirely different directions and to dissimilar images of the Jews. Nakada came to see Japan's national salvation as inextricably intertwined with the national redemption of the Jewish people.

Nakada Jūji was born on October 27, 1870, in the far-north town of Hirosaki, in what is now Aomori prefecture. His father, Heisaku, who had been a samurai of the lowest rank in the Tsugaru domain, died before he was four, and thereafter the Nakada family led a penurious existence.[29]

Unlike Uchimura Kanzō, who was trained in the Congregationalist tradition of Amherst and the Hartford Theological Seminary, Nakada's early understanding of Christianity came through Methodism. There was a strong Methodist presence in Hirosaki centering on the Hirosaki Methodist Church and the Methodist Tōō College (Tōō gijuku, also known as the Daimyo School). In 1888, Nakada entered Tokyo Eiwa Gakkō, the forebear of today's Aoyama Gakuin University, another Methodist institution; but having spent too much time practicing judo, he was forced to withdraw in 1891 without graduating. After leaving school, Nakada worked as a Methodist missionary in Yakumo, a small village in Hokkaido, and subsequently served in other northern communities, including Otaru, Etorofu island, and Ōdate in Akita prefecture.

Nakada left for the United States in 1896 and returned to Japan in September 1898. His trip was precipitated by a crisis of faith caused by the death of his first son and the illness of his wife Katsuko.

In the United States, Nakada studied at the Moody Bible Institute in Chicago. The Moody Bible Institute was founded in 1886 by Dwight Lyman Moody (1837–99), a Horatio Alger figure who rose from humble origins to become the most influential evangelist in America. It taught a uniquely American brand of "individualistic, culture-denying, soul-rescuing Christianity."[30] Among its most important teachings were biblical inerrancy, premillennialism, "holiness," and evangelical activism. The Moody Bible Institute also took an active interest in the Jews and prided itself on being "the first and only school" to have a complete training program for missions to the Jews.[31] Virtually everyone involved with American Protestantism at this time was affected by Moody's ideas, and Nakada Jūji was no exception.[32]

Nakada's encounter with the circle of believers he met at Chicago's Grace Methodist Church was at least as significant as the formal training he received at the Moody Bible Institute. Among those he met were Charles Elmar Cowman (1868–1924) and his wife, Lettie Bird Cowman (1870–1960), who shortly became his partners in his ministry in Japan. The Cowmans introduced Nakada to J. R. Boynton, a well-known Chicago physician who practiced faith healing, and A. M. Hills, who later became president of Pasadena College and through whom Nakada came to be convinced that the true power of Christians lay in their holiness. Nakada had been prepared for these "holiness teachings" by his early exposure to Methodism, and taken together, they formed the core of his subsequent faith.

In 1900, soon after his return to Japan, Nakada left the Methodist Church to found his own mission, the Central Gospel Mission (*Chūō fukuin dendōkan*), in Jinbō-chō, central Tokyo. The building, which housed the Nakadas and the newly arrived Cowmans, served as a Bible school by day and a mission by night. It was, in essence, Nakada's Bible Institute in Tokyo.

After a series of reorganizational efforts, Nakada moved away from ecumenical missionary work in 1917 and founded his own church, the Oriental Missionary Holiness Church (*Tōyō senkyōkai hōrinesu kyōkai*).[g] The church was a sizable organization, amalgamating forty-six preexisting churches, fifty ministers, and four churches without ministers.

The Nakada who shared the platform with Uchimura Kanzō in January 1918 was therefore an American-trained fundamentalist minister with his own sizable church organization. Like his role model, D. L. Moody, whose theology "was ambiguous to the point of seeming not to be theology at all,"[33] Nakada's teachings were less than systematic, but in general, they conformed to the broad outlines of contemporary American fundamentalism,[h] with a

---

[g] By 1903, the Central Gospel Mission had outgrown its quarters. After several moves, it settled into a new building in Kashiwagi, Yodobashi-chō. In 1907, Uchimura Kanzō also moved to Kashiwagi, and by chance, he and Nakada lived within a three-minute walk of each other.

The group led by Nakada now called itself the Oriental Missionary Society (*Tōyō senkyōkai*), and its target was expanded to include all of East Asia. A conflict developed between Cowman and Nakada over leadership of the mission, however, and in 1911 it split into the Oriental Missionary Society led by Cowman and the Japan Holiness Church (*Nihon seikyōdan*) headed by Nakada. Later, the two groups were reconciled, but their relations continued to be strained.

[h] Nakada articulated the major tenets of his beliefs as follows:

THE TRINITY, that is, the Father, Son and the Holy Spirit, are the main overseers (*shukansha*) [of human affairs].

SECTS have no claim on us. Our only affiliation is with God's Church.

DISTINGUISHING US is our quest for salvation, holiness, and healing through faith, as well as the Second Coming of Christ.

OUR TEXT is the single volume of the Old and New Testament. That is all we require.

CHINESE AND KOREANS may come to us to improve themselves, and if they do we will become the center of Oriental Enlightenment.

OTHER CHURCHES may send us novices for training.

SUSTENANCE will be provided by God, since we depend entirely on our faith.

[*Honō no shita* (Tongue of Fire), December 25, 1904; quoted in Yoneda, *Nakada Jūji den*, pp. 136–37.]

In addition, the following policies adapted from the Oriental Missionary Society are also instructive.

• This organization is, as the name indicates, a missionary society. Our purpose is simple: to propagate the complete Gospel, that is, the Foursquare Gospel (salvation, holiness, the Second Coming of Christ, and healing) all over Japan.

•

premillennialist eschatology at the center of his beliefs.[i]

Nakada's thinking on the Jews intensified steadily throughout his career. By the early 1930s, he had come to believe that the Bible contained hidden references to a special relationship between the Japanese and the Jews, and he further became convinced that if Christians understood this special relationship, they would better be able to understand Japan's unique global mission.[34] Nakada described these beliefs in a series of six lectures on "Japan in the Bible" (*Seisho yori mitaru Nippon*) that he delivered at the Yodobashi Holiness Church in November 1932. The lectures were published the following January and went through several reprintings, including an English translation, which appeared in 1933.[35]

In his introduction, Nakada explained that his discovery of a special relationship among the Second Coming, Japan, and the Jews had prompted him to write his book. "I have discovered," he wrote, "that

---

- This organization is viewed in this country as if it were a particular denomination, but in fact it is (in a sense) a cooperative organization of many denominations supported by voluntary contributions from people at different churches in Europe and the United States. . . .
- From the outset, we were determined to concentrate our energies on spreading the Gospel. We did not divide our energies among educational projects, social welfare, or charitable works. . . In light of the urgent state of affairs, it would be foolish to squander our limited resources. We shall focus totally on our first priority: spreading the Gospel.
- We would also like to work inside the Church. . . . How could we sit idly by and not help prepare to meet our Returned Savior? . . . Pitiful as our efforts may be, we shall make whatever preparations are required to go out and support our Lord if that is His will. In this way we shall seek to hasten Our Lord's Second Coming.

  [*Seiketsu no tomo* (Friends of Holiness), January 1917, quoted in Yoneda, *Nakada Jūji den*, pp. 234–35.]

[i] "The Foursquare Gospel, that is, salvation on the cross, sanctification through the activity of the Holy Spirit, God's healing, and the premillennial Return of Jesus Christ" was offered as the basic formulation of faith by the Oriental Missionary Society in a statement issued on October 31, 1917, the four hundredth anniversary of the posting of Martin Luther's "Ninety-Five Theses Against Indulgences," the beginning of the Protestant Reformation. (*Nakada Jūji zenshū*, vol. 7, pp. 78–79.) In Nakada's mind, the four elements of the Gospel did not exist independently but culminated in the Return of Christ, which interrelated new life (spiritual rebirth), holiness (demonstration of the blessing of rebirth), God's healing (the first sign of the rebirth), and the Second Coming (the physical realization of rebirth). (*Nakada Jūji zenshū*, vol. 2, p. 551.)

the Japanese people have an important role to play in the Second Coming, in particular that they are intimately involved with the redemption of the Jewish people, which will accompany the Second Coming, and so I decided to write this book."[36]

Nakada's views on this intimate relationship originated with his insight that the mention of an "angel rising out of the east" in Revelation 7:2 was a reference to Japan.[37j] In fact, according to Nakada, the Bible is replete with references to Japan. In his interpretation, all references to "the rising sun" and "the east," such as Isaiah 41:2 ("Tell me, who raised up that one from the east, one greeted by victory wherever he goes?"), apply to Japan.[k] He wrote that he had reached this conclusion with trepidation after years of study:

> During the last 30 years while travelling all over the world I made a search of the books in the great libraries of many countries to see if I could find anything concerning this Land [of the Rising Sun] but so far I have found none. As I continued my study of prophecy I found that there were prophecies in regard to Japan but I hesitated to make them public as it is such a serious matter and I did not wish to present it before the people as just a matter of uncertainty. I was afraid of having gotten forced meanings or made farfetched and strained interpretations as I ought not to do such a thing with the Holy Scriptures. For a long time I prayed about it but the more I prayed the more God revealed to me the prophecies concerning Japan.[38]

Having thus discovered numerous references to Japan in the Bible, Nakada went on to argue that Japan had been providentially pro-

---

[j] Revelation 7:2–4 reads, "Then I saw another angel rising out of the east, carrying the seal of the living God; and he called aloud to the four angels who had been given the power to ravage land and sea: 'Do no damage to sea or land or trees until we have set the seal of our God upon the foreheads of his servants.' And I heard the number of those who had received the seal. For all the tribes of Israel there were a hundred and forty-four thousand."

[k] Nakada lists several of these references, including Psalms 50:1, 113:3; Isaiah 41:2, 41:25, 43:5, 45:6, 59:19; Ezekiel 43:2; Malachi 1:11; Daniel 11:44; Zechariah 8:7; Matthew 2:1–2, 8:11; Revelation 7:2–3, 16:12. See Bishop Juji Nakada [Nakada Jūji], *Japan in the Bible*, tr. David T. Tsutada (Tokyo: Oriental Missionary Society, Japan Holiness Church Publishing Department, 1933), pp. 133–35.

•

tected by God throughout history, the better to fulfill the special mission He had in store for it. The way the Japanese had successfully repelled Mongol invaders in the late thirteenth century, Japan's isolation from the West, and the Japanese victory in the Russo-Japanese War were, according to Nakada, all preordained by God.[39] It was now incumbent on the Japanese, who had received these abundant blessings, to fulfill their special mission, which they could do most effectively through prayer:

> Now, as never before, it is our privilege and duty to pray conscientiously for the protection of God and His Divine Guidance for our nation that is holding so difficult a stand at heavy odds against the nations of the present world and also pray for the future of our beloved nation. Our deligates [sic, to the League of Nations] are now engaged in hard wordy battles at Geneva; but we have with us the mighty weapon of prayer which is quite unknown to them.
>
> Brethren, should we not as faithful elect Japanese, pray all the more earnestly at these critical times, for our nation that she may fully comprehend and discharge the mission entrusted to her by God?[40]

Nakada became a supporter of Japanese militarism, because he believed the Japanese military was (unbeknownst to itself) serving God's purposes:

> Everyone knows how busily Japan is engaged in military preparations these days but only a few know for what purpose and when these armaments will be utilized: even the people of the Military Departments are doing this unknowingly but in the clear light of the Scriptures we see that these armaments are for the day when they will be used by God to hold back or suppress the four angels while the "servants of our God will be sealed in their foreheads".[1]

---

[1] Nakada continues,

The sealing of the Jews in their foreheads does not seem to mean here to bring them to salvation by the preaching of the Gospel among them, but rather to make them realize that they are the Chosen race of God and that God had promised to Abraham to give them the land of Palestine as their inheritance;

●

The military dimension of Japan's mission was secondary, however, according to Nakada. Japan's primary mission was to pray for the Jews.

> Then what sort of rescuer is he to be who comes up from the East? First, he shall have a special mission entrusted to him to intercede and pray to God for the Jews, and second he shall have the duty of suppressing all the disturbers of the world-peace under the Anti-Christ.[41]

The Japanese had been selected for this special mission because they were innocent of any transgression against God's chosen people. "Do we not see a deep meaning in this," he asked, "that God is going to use mightily this Japanese race that has not harmed the chosen Jews?"[42]

Nakada's image of the "faithful elect Japanese chosen by God for a special mission" functioned as a Christian theological justification for Japanese imperialism. "It seems to me," he wrote, "that God is leading and causing our nation to step further into the continent and be more closely related to continental affairs than ever before and have keener interests in them."[m]

---

it is needless to say that there will, of course, be means for them to wake up inwardly to this fact, but it seems as if God is going to use this race from the rising of the sun as a means from outside for the same purpose.

[Nakada, *Japan in the Bible*, p. 99; *Nakada Jūji zenshū*, vol. 2, p. 131.]
The Scriptural reference is to Revelation 7:2–4. See note above for the text.

[m] Nakada offers the following textual evidence for his conclusion:

Just at this critical moment, a race will be raised up to help from the East; if we turn to the afore quoted texts of Isa. 46, God tells that He will call "a ravenous bird from the east", and this means nothing more than aeroplanes i.e. this race of the east is said here to come for the help of the afflicted people under the Anti-Christ, by means of aeroplanes; further in Isa. 41, we read of the victorious advance of this man from the east towards the west of the continent: this does not refer to any naval victory: I do not mean to flatteringly praise the continental policy of our Military Department at present but I am simply saying what the Word of God declares: and we can easily be convinced of this if we see the past history of Japan under the providence of God; for instance, Korea, a part of the continent has long since become our territory and now Manchuria which became independent and

•

But Nakada's conception of Japan's divine mission extended beyond East Asia, and he scolded the Japanese military for not having attacked Baghdad during World War I:

> I have been told, that England, in her confusion upon seeing Turkey joining the German side, asked Japan to send her army towards Bagdad [*sic*] across the Persian Gulf—this demand Japan did not accept because of the vast distance: had the people of our Military Department had the knowledge of the parts to be played by Japan in the future in these locations, in the light of the Scriptures, they would not have so lightly forsaken such a rare opportunity of obtaining a suitable military base in these regions for our future activities.[43]

Nakada did "not hesitate to declare that sooner or later Japan will certainly withdraw herself from the League of Nations"[44]; and he derided the international body, saying, "Who could expect to bring peace to this world by such human agreements and conventions? But we look for it in the Coming of Christ."[45] For Nakada, Japan was the linchpin that connected the redemption of Israel, the Second Coming of Christ, and the realization of true world peace in the Millennium, and he urged the Japanese to "pray on with this great and glorious vision."[46]

Nakada believed the Holiness Church had a unique role to play in the realization of Japan's divine mission. "If we love our nation and fellow-countrymen," he preached, "we should pray ever more earnestly for the Jews."[47] The Holiness Church had been praying fervently for the salvation of the Jews and had been making monthly contributions on their behalf, and Nakada was convinced God would take notice of these devotions. He was also convinced that the Holiness Church had been able to undertake these acts of charity only because of the guidance of the Holy Spirit. He wrote with great pride that his church had devoted itself to the welfare of the Jews since its

---

separated from China recently cannot go on without our protection and supervision.

    [Nakada, *Japan in the Bible*, p. 90; *Nakada Jūji zenshū*, vol. 2, p. 122.]

•

foundation.[48] "We have only about 20,000 Holiness people in Japan," he wrote, "but how solemn it is when we see these people representing the whole nation in interceding for the Jews."[49] These efforts had gone all but unnoticed and unrewarded, but Nakada was convinced they would hold great significance for Japan in the coming time of tribulation: "God who is merciful even in His wrath will surely remember our remaining nation and people in the coming days because of our present intercessions for His Chosen Race."[50]

By August 1933, eight months after he had published *Japan in the Bible*, Nakada's sense of urgency had intensified to the point where he issued guidelines to his followers, explaining precisely how they should prepare themselves for imminent "rapture" into heaven.[n] In October, he directed his followers to pray for the Jews, preaching that the teachings of Isaiah 25:9 and Romans 11:26 prophesied the salvation of the Jews[o]: "They anticipate, not only the salvation of the individual Jew, but the salvation of the Jews as a nation, so that the kingdom of Israel might be established and the people of Israel

---

[n] Nakada's guidelines were these:

First, pray to Our Lord that He comes; act as if the Second Coming were tomorrow; do not plan projects that will take 10 or 20 years; do not invest in savings or insurance; do not expend large amounts on children's education; do not worry about the problems of marriage, for we shall be raptured and transformed into bodies of glory; regard your clothing, food, and housing as borrowed temporarily; concern yourself in conversation with talk of everlasting life; do not leave savings for future times of hardship; maintain a church only sufficient to keep out the elements and alert each other to the imminent Coming of Christ; pray each morning at five o'clock, "Lord Jesus, come to us!"; preach the Second Coming urgently from the pulpit; be prepared to be persecuted everywhere because of this truth.

["Sashiatari kaiketsu subeki koto" (Problems to Solve at This Moment), in Yoneda, *Nakada Jūji den*, pp. 461–62.]

[o] Isaiah 25:9 reads, "On that day men will say, 'See, this is our God, for whom we have waited to deliver us; this is the Lord for whom we have waited; let us rejoice and exult in his deliverance.' "

Romans 11:26 says, "When that has happened the whole of Israel will be saved, in agreement with the text of Scripture: 'From Zion shall come the Deliverer; he shall remove wickedness from Jacob.' "

•

called a blessing by all nations." The Book of Revelation, he preached, "regards the salvation of the individual, but most of it concerns the salvation of the nations of the world. And it is indisputable that the Jews are central among them."[51] Thus, to Nakada, prayers for the Jews were indispensable for the Second Coming of Christ, and the Japanese would be saved as a people by virtue of such prayers.

Nakada's shift of emphasis away from the salvation of individual souls to collective, national salvation alienated some of his followers.[52] When he threatened to fire five instructors at his Bible Institute if they did not accept his teachings and deliver lectures advocating his beliefs, a crisis ensued. The instructors, all of them Nakada's disciples, accused him of "fascism." They criticized him for asserting that the primary mission of the church was to pray for the Jews and the establishment of a Jewish state and for stressing the salvation of the Japanese nation rather than the salvation of individual souls.[P] Nakada rejected this criticism, and in October 1936, after a long battle, a schism occurred. The church split into two separate churches, both of which took names that in English would be rendered "Holiness Church": *Kiyome kyōkai* led by Nakada, and *Nihon seikyōkai*, the defecting faction.

When in May 1939, shortly before his death, Nakada embraced Dr. Abraham Kaufman, president of the Far Eastern Jewish Council, beneath crossed Japanese and Zionist flags in Tokyo, it was a consummation of the literal identification Nakada had made between the Japanese and Jewish nationalist movements, an identifi-

---

[P] The indictment charged,
  • Bishop Nakada has committed acts and made remarks that disrespect, disregard, and deny the central mission of this church, which is the propagation of the faith and the salvation of souls. These are fascist acts and remarks that ignore the constitution of the Church.
  • Bishop Nakada asserts that the main mission of this Church is prayer for the redemption of the Jewish people and the establishment of their state.
  • Bishop Nakada stresses the salvation of the Japanese people during the time of Tribulation rather than individual salvation.
    [Yoneda, *Nakada Jūji den*, p. 465.]

•

cation that would have serious political consequences for his church during the war.[53]

"I should like to prove that Israelitish blood runs mixed in the Japanese veins and in this we are not without historical evidences," Nakada Jūji wrote in *Japan in the Bible*.[54q] His "evidences" were the common ancestry theories of Saeki Yoshirō and Oyabe Zen'ichirō, exponents of a third Christian theological response to the dilemmas of Japan's modern development, Christian-Shinto syncretism.[55] Unlike the theology of Uchimura Kanzō, which departed only modestly from the framework of Calvinist Protestantism, and Nakada Jūji, who was essentially a fundamentalist in the American mold, common ancestry theory (*dōsoron*), the belief that the Japanese and the Jews are genetically related peoples, was an original Japanese theology that eschewed Western models.

The Japanese are not the only ones to have speculated on a his-

---

[q] Nakada believed that the Japanese were a unique amalgam of the postdiluvian races from whom the Jews are descended; and for him this racial amalgamation was evidence of Divine election.

> The Japanese are an inter-mixture of the three original races i.e. the Shemitic [*sic*], Hamitic, and Japhetic—for the Jews are descendents [*sic*] of Shem, the Hittites, of Ham, and the Ainus, of Japheth. (The Ainus should be classified among the white people as the Aryan or the Caucasian people). Thus, we see here the wonderful amalgamation of all the three races in one Japanese race which can not be found anywhere else: of course, there are places where people of these three different races are living together, for instance, in America, but no other race has ever been the product of a supernatural welding of these three races. Here I again say that the Japanese must be a chosen people charged with a special mission toward the entire world. All the three races were brought in here by what I called "Eastern Adoration" and here they have been happily welded together and made one Japanese race. Should we not then in such a clear light of His Second Coming as we have, respond to the Holy Spirit that is withing [*sic*] us and strive to accomplish the mission charge [*sic*] upon us?

[Nakada, *Japan in the Bible*, pp. 44–45. *Nakada Jūji zenshū*, vol. 2, pp. 75–76.] Shem, Ham, and Japheth were the three sons of Noah from whom all the peoples of the world are said to have descended. See Genesis 7:13.

torical link between the Japanese and Jewish peoples. As recently as 1980, an Israeli named Joseph Eidelberg published *The Japanese and the Ten Lost Tribes of Israel*, in which he compared historical accounts in the Hebrew Bible with Japanese dynastic histories and concluded that the Japanese were descended from the Jews.[r]

The first Japanese-Jewish common ancestry theory was not the brainchild of a Japanese or a Jew but of a Scot named Norman McLeod, who published his *Epitome of the Ancient History of Japan* in 1875. In the preface, McLeod wrote that he had arrived in Japan in 1867, the last year of the Tokugawa regime, and that he intended to produce an illustrated, twelve-volume description of the country similar to Engelbert Kaempfer's famous three-volume chronicle of the

---

[r] Eidelberg's analysis of the Taika (or Taikwa) reform of 645 provides a taste of his perspective. Eidelberg takes issue with virtually all historians of Japan, who agree that the Taika reform "was an application to Japan of the system then in operation in the T'ang empire." (See, for example, George Sansom, *Japan: A Short Cultural History*, revised ed. [New York: Appleton-Century-Crofts, 1962], p. 96.) By contrast, Eidelberg writes,

> The Taikwa reform is usually attributed to a strong Chinese influence over Japan. However, casting a glance at some of the laws implemented during the Taikwa era, one notes that except for the cap-rank system, there were very few Chinese elements in the reform. . . . However, a close examination of the laws promulgated during the Taikwa era reveals that many of them bear a striking resemblance to the Hebrew laws of the Old Testament, and particularly to the body of laws set forth in the Book of Deuteronomy.
>
> [Joseph Eidelberg, *The Japanese and the Ten Lost Tribes of Israel* (Givatayim, Israel: Sycamore Press, 1980), pp. 83–84.]

Eidelberg adduces fewer than three pages of "evidence" to support this revolutionary hypothesis. (Other examples of his argument may be found in Ralph Amelan's review of *The Japanese and the Ten Lost Tribes* in the *Jerusalem Post*, August 8, 1985.)

While Eidelberg shares with Japanese common ancestry theorists a fondness for philology, arguing that certain morphological similarities between the Japanese and Hebrew languages demonstrate a link between the Japanese and the Jews, he cites no Japanese sources, indiscriminately uses examples from biblical Hebrew, modern Hebrew, and even Aramaic, and seems completely unaware of the Japanese literature on Japanese-Jewish common ancestry.

A similar lack of familiarity with Japanese sources characterizes R. Yoshiwara (Roger Ahlberg), *Sumerian and Japanese: A Comparative Language Study* (Chiba, Japan: Japan English Service, 1991). Strictly speaking, this work is not a common ancestry theory, but it does suggest Middle Eastern roots for the Japanese language.

Eidelberg's book was published in Japanese in 1984. See Nakagawa Kazuo, tr., *Yamato minzoku wa Yudayajin datta: shutsu-Ejiputo kara Nihon e no michi* [The Yamato People were Jews: The Road from the Exodus to Japan] (Tama shuppan, 1984).

1690s.[s] McLeod explained that he was publishing the present volume in anticipation of that magnum opus, which would improve upon Kaempfer's work by giving "a more accurate and detailed account of the origin of the Japanese, with a description of their Jewish belongings."[56]

"A stout-hearted, frugal, and religious man who started his career in Scotland in the herring fisheries, and ended up in Japan as an independent missionary,"[57] McLeod and his theories received short shrift in the foreign community. The *Japan Mail* of February 10, 1874, reported, "On Wednesday evening last, Mr. McLeod gave his lecture upon the 'Identity of the Mikado, Miya and Kuge Sama etc. with the Ten Lost Tribes of Israel.' He attracted but a small audience, and did not even contrive to keep them together above a few minutes."[58] His ideas received even less attention among the Japanese, who ignored them for a hundred years.[59]

While there is no evidence that McLeod influenced Japanese common ancestry theorists directly, it seems likely that he and they were the products of the same English tradition of speculation on the fate of the Ten Lost Tribes of Israel. As early as the 1650s, writers in England had debated whether the American Indians were descendants of the Ten Lost Tribes, and that debate continued into the twentieth century.[t] In 1822, Richard Brothers, principal founder of "Anglo-Israelism,"[60] published his *Correct Account of the Invasion of England by the Saxons*, in which he "proved" that the English were descendants of the Ten Lost Tribes.[61] By the turn of the twentieth century, the theory that the English were descendants of the Jews had

---

[s] A German physician attached to the Dutch East India Company, Engelbert Kaempfer lived in the foreign enclave on the island of Deshima in Nagasaki harbor from 1690 to 1693. He was an avid chronicler of Japanese history, geography, and customs.

[t] Brotz writes that a book by Thomas Thorowgood called *Jewes in America, or, Probabilities that the Americans are of that Race* appeared in 1650, which was followed two years later by a book by Hamon L'Estrange the Elder called *Americans No Jewes, or Improbabilities that the Americans Are of That Race*; and that this debate continued until at least 1836. Howard Brotz, *The Black Jews of Harlem: Negro Nationalism and the Dilemmas of Negro Leadership* (New York: Schocken Books, 1970), p. 3. As the source of this information, Brotz cites Cecil Roth, ed., *Magna Bibliotheca Anglo-Judaica: A Bibliographical Guide To Anglo-Jewish History* (London: Jewish Historical Society of England, 1937), sec. B. 17.

•

an estimated two million adherents in England and the United States, and one contemporary authority described the literature on the subject as "enormous."[62] Proponents of Japanese-Jewish common ancestry theory were inspired by this same trend.[u]

Other non-Western societies besides Japan have produced common ancestry theories. As recently as October 1992, the *New York Times* reported on the resurgence of a neo-Christian sect founded early in the twentieth century in South Africa on the basis of such a theology. This black African analogue shares many of the characteristics of Japanese common ancestry theory, including a disillusionment with Western Christianity, nationalism, a vision of an apocalyptic war with the white world, and of course the claim to common ancestry with the Jews.[v]

An American sect, the Black Hebrews, also claims common ancestry with the Jews. In *Black Hebrew Israelites from America to the Promised Land*, Shaleak Ben Yehuda asserts that African Americans are the descendants of the ancient Israelites:

---

[u] While excepting his own theory, Kawamorita Eiji, one of the common ancestry theorists we treat below, states explicitly that Japanese theories of common ancestry were modeled after English speculation on the fate of the Ten Lost Tribes. See Kawamorita Eiji, *Nihon no naka no Yudayajin* [The Jews in Japan], ed. Nakajima Seikan (Tama shuppan, 1990), pp. 4–5.

[v] The *Times* reported,

The Israelites are one of an estimated 3,500 independent churches in South Africa that have either spun off from missionary denominations or sprung up on their own.

"The mainline churches were led by whites from abroad who were very sweet on Sunday—'We are all God's children'—then on Monday to Friday they were involved in making oppressive laws," said the Rev. Kenosi Mofokeng, general secretary of the African Spiritual Churches Association, with 500 member churches. . . .

Enoch Mgijima, who founded the Israelites in 1907, was a lay preacher who left the Wesleyan Methodist Church after an apocalyptic vision of a war between blacks and whites.

His disciples regard themselves as the real children of Israel, descendants of the biblical Jacob. They observe the Sabbath on Saturday and celebrate Passover as their main religious festival, but they are Christians. They hold that Jesus was black. The men shave their heads in sorrow for the oppression of blacks. . . .

["Queenstown Journal: Crucified in the 1920's, Black Sect Rises Again," *The New York Times*, October 6, 1992. (Emphasis added.)]

Our preachment in the pages of this work is to identify the people referred to as Afro-Americans, negroes, blacks, etc., in the United States and other areas of the Western Hemisphere through recorded history and prophecy within the pages of scriptural text that infallibly identifies these people as the biblical descendants of the Hebrew nation from the patriarchs of Abraham, Isaac, and Jacob, and the spiritual heirs of all covenants according to the promise.ʷ

Unlikely as it may seem, the history and theology of the Black Hebrews provide important perspective on the Japanese experience. Black Judaism is one of many responses to the dilemma of black existence in the twentieth century. At least eight black Jewish sects originated in Harlem in the period from 1919 to 1931.⁶³ Howard

---

ʷ Ben Yehuda explains,

In 721 B.C., when the True Nation of Israel left the page of time, their history, identity, and descendants slipped into oblivion. . . .

Since 721 B.C., due to the world conspiracy, the Kings of the earth have merged the history of the True Hebrew Israelite Nation with that of Jewish literature and folklore. The world has since accepted its creation of a pseudo-chosen people and subsequently transplanted them in the Northeastern African Country of Israel, the land which was given according to a divine promise, to the seed of Abraham (through Isaac and Jacob). . . .

It was a prophetic prediction that the Ancient Biblical Hebrew Israelites and their descendants would lose their identity and all knowledge of self and be debased and sidetracked for a prophetic period of 2,500 years.

Through extensive research, the author has uncovered facts which reveal that those commonly called Afro-Americans, Blacks, negroes, etc., are the "children of the Prophets" (Hebrew Israelites).

[Shaleak Ben Yehuda, *Black Hebrew Israelites from America to the Promised Land: The Great International Religious Conspiracy Against the Children of the Prophets* (New York: Vantage Press, 1975), p. 2; unnumbered first two pages of the introduction.]

Ben Yehuda also goes on to blame the Jews for black suffering: "The greatest executor of the ills of the Children of the Prophets is without a shadow of a doubt the socio-religious Jewish community in the United States and Jerusalem. The consequences of the exploitation of our people by this community has dehumanized the Children of the Prophets." (Ben Yehuda, *Black Hebrew Israelites from America to the Promised Land*, p. 109.) Like the theories of many of his Japanese counterparts, Ben Yehuda's visions degenerate into antisemitism.

For a brief but magisterial discussion of black antisemitism, see Henry Louis Gates Jr., "Black Demagogues and Pseudo-Scholars," *New York Times*, July 20, 1992.

•

Brotz points out that seventeenth-century speculation on the fate of the Ten Lost Tribes was an integral part of the Protestantism that became the religious tradition of the slaves, and the view that the Negroes are really the Hebrews of the Bible thus derived from the slaves' own Protestant religious tradition.[64] The appearance of black Judaism in the 1920s was an expression of the same incipient black nationalism and disaffection with Christianity that produced the Black Muslims.[65] And a sociological study of the black Jews found that on average they were better adjusted than their Protestant counterparts and that their Jewish identity moderated their feelings of powerlessness, normlessness, and anomie.[66]

Common ancestry theories are thus not unique to Japan, nor are they without psychological benefits for their adherents. They have been espoused by alienated, marginal, oppressed peoples throughout the world as part of their effort to reject the authority of European Christianity while still laying claim to the empowering heritage of monotheism. As Brotz has written of the black Jews, a presumed link with the Jews and Judaism has offered these peoples a new conception of themselves as nations with a proud past and triumphant future.[x] When they identify with the Jews, their distinctive racial identity ceases to be a liability and becomes a mark of superiority that they believe even white Christians must respect. They express contempt for white culture by rejecting what it holds most sacred; they assert their independence of whites by scorning their moral and religious prin-

---

[x] In this sense, common ancestry theories are a variety of what the anthropologist Ralph Linton has called "rational revivalistic nativism," an attempt to come to terms with an intractable social situation and compensate for the frustrations of a society's members by imagining a past golden age:

> Rational revivalistic nativistic movements are, almost without exception, associated with frustrating situations and are primarily attempts to compensate for the frustrations of the society's members. The elements revived become symbols of a period when the society was free or, in retrospect, happy or great. Their usage is not magical but psychological. By keeping the past in mind, such elements help to re-establish and maintain the self-respect of the group's members in the face of adverse conditions.
>
> [Ralph Linton, "Nativistic Movements," in William A. Lessa and Evon Z. Vogt, eds., *Reader in Comparative Religion: An Anthropological Approach*, 2d ed. (New York: Harper and Row, 1965), p. 501.]

•

ciples even as they lay claim to these principles for themselves.[67] These are precisely the characteristics and goals of Japanese theories of common ancestry with the Jews.

Saeki Yoshirō (1871–1965) was one of the first to formally propose the theory of Japanese-Jewish common ancestry.[y] His "Regarding Uzumasa," an appendix to his monumental *Research into Nestorian Inscriptions in China*, appeared in 1908.[68]

Saeki was a respected scholar. Born on September 15, 1871, in Hiroshima prefecture, he graduated from the law department of what is today Waseda University. After graduation, he traveled to America and Canada, where he studied at the University of Toronto. Saeki was baptized in the Anglican-Episcopal Church of Japan (*Nihon Seikōkai*) in 1890. He became interested in cultural interactions between Asia and the West during the Russo-Japanese War and subsequently devoted himself to a lifelong study of Nestorian Christianity in China. He conducted research in China from 1930 to 1931 and upon his return became a research associate at Tokyo Imperial University. He published his *Study of Nestorianism* (*Keikyō no kenkyū*) in 1935 and *The Nestorian Documents and Relics in China* in 1939. He was granted a doctorate in recognition of this work by Tokyo University in 1941. Between 1943 and 1949, Saeki published a four-volume study of Christianity in China. Notwithstanding his lifelong commitment to Christianity, he was buried in a Buddhist ceremony when he died on June 26, 1965.

In the course of his research, Saeki took an interest in the origins of the Hata clan, a group of continental immigrants who had arrived in Japan in the mid-fifth century. According to Saeki, after thorough research in Japanese sources, he concluded that the Hata clan, who had settled in the western suburbs of Kyoto in a village called Uzu-

---

[y] Others who conducted "research" in this area were figures as diverse as the Byron scholar Kimura Takatarō (1870–1931), the journalist and politician Takegoshi Yosaburō (1865–1950), and the Christian socialist and anarchist Ishikawa Sanshirō (1876–1956). See Sugita Rokuichi, "Shomotsu kara mita Nihon no Yudaya mondai" [Japan's "Jewish Problem" as Seen in Literature] in *Yudaya-shi kenkyū yodan* [Digressions of a Student of Jewish History] (Kyōbunkan, 1962); and "Nihon ni okeru Yudaya rongi no tokui sei" [Idiosyncrasies of Discussions of Jews in Japan] in *Isuraeru-shi zakkō* [A Miscellany of the History of Israel], (Kyōbunkan, 1964).

•

masa, were "not from [the Korean kingdoms of] Silla or Paekche, nor does their name indicate that they were descendants of the First Ch'in Emperor of China,[z] nor were they Chinese." By making "a clod of earth speak volumes," Saeki arrived at the conclusion that the Hata clan could only have been Jewish:

> History books were silent on the question, and for a long time I gazed absently into the skies of Uzumasa. Finally, I was left with no alternative but to go back and look for an explanation in the small Shinto shrine located in the precincts of Uzumasa temple. It is not for lack of historical evidence that the history books are silent. If one is sensitive enough, even a clod of earth speaks volumes. How much more might one learn from a shrine, where the hopes and aspirations of generations are distilled?[69]

The philological arguments Saeki adduces to support this conclusion are too arcane to detail here. Suffice it to say that they are typical of the associative, syncretic logic characteristic of Japanese religious tradition.[70] In a later revision of his article, however, he condensed his ideas in a way that provides a taste of his reasoning: "*Uzu*," he declares, "is a corrupted form of the word 'Ishu,' that is, 'Jesus,' and *masa* derives from 'messiah.' These can thus be none other than a corrupted form of the words 'Iesu-meshia,' that is, 'Jesus, the Messiah' from the Aramaic or the Semitic."[71]

The fact that Saeki concludes that the Hata clan could only have been Jewish from a tortuously derived allusion to "Jesus, the Messiah" indicates the essentially Christian and rather desperate nature of his theory. "Regarding Uzumasa" became the cornerstone of all subsequent Japanese common ancestry theories and set the paradoxical precedent for identifying purportedly ancient Christian sites in Japan as evidence of early Jewish settlements in the country.[72]

In his voluminous *Origin of Japan and the Japanese People* (*Nippon oyobi Nippon kokumin no kigen*, 1929), a second common ancestry

---

[z] Saeki is referring to the fact that the Chinese character used to write "Hata" is also the character for "Ch'in" and can also mean "Chinese."

•

theorist, Oyabe Zen'ichirō (1867–1941), expanded on Saeki's work, arguing that the Japanese and their emperors were descended from the Jews.[aa] He cites the long history of the Japanese, their divine mission, the everlasting nature of their covenant with God, and their tradition of unswerving loyalty to their emperor as evidence that the Japanese were originally Jews:

> It is well-known to Biblical scholars in the West and the world over that approximately three hundred years before the enthronement of the Emperor Jimmu [in 660 B.C.E], two tribes of the Hebrews—Gad, the most valiant, and Manasseh, who were descended from the eldest son of the patriarch—fled eastward carrying the Hebrews' sacred treasures, and to this day their whereabouts remain unknown. A close study of the ancient Hebrews as they are described in the Jewish scriptures reveals an extraordinary number of similarities between our two peoples. The Japanese and the Hebrews are virtually identical, particularly in regard to the pious way in which we observe our religious festivals. These exact correspondences convince me that we are in fact one race.[73]

[aa] Oyabe argues,

> The unbroken line of Japan[ese emperors] did not just emerge from the sea one day. In ancient times, the north-eastern corner of the East Asian continent sank into the sea because of a major upheaval. The area was inundated and became part of the ocean. The land that remained, supported by massive roots, became islands. Ever since, numerous peoples have dreamed their days away in this peaceful ocean basin, making no contribution to civilization whatsoever. However, our ancestors, with three thousand years of culture behind them and blessed by God with a divine mission, migrated to this land and by dint of zealous effort established the Imperial nation of Japan. Unlike the people of the United States in North America, whose ancestors immigrated individually and separately, our ancestors arrived as a mass with a longstanding tradition of fealty to their sovereign and in possession of sacred treasures that were the sign of the ever-lasting covenant that existed between them and their Divine Lord. The nation that was created through the toil shared by sovereign and subject was none other than this Divine Nation, Japan.

> [Oyabe Zen'ichirō, *Nippon oyobi Nippon kokumin no kigen* (Kōseikaku, 1929), pp. 21–22.]

Oyabe employs the same sort of philological argumentation as Saeki. He says, for example, that the origin of the word "mikado" for emperor derives from *mi-* (the honorific prefix) and *Gado* (as Gad is pronounced in Japanese). See pp. 389–90.

•

Oyabe Zen'ichirō was born in 1867 in Akita prefecture in northern Japan.[74] He traveled to America in 1888, where he studied at black institutions, first at the Hampton Institute, then at Howard University, where he transferred in 1890. In 1894, he entered the Yale Divinity School. Baptized in 1895, he worked as a missionary in Hawaii from 1895 until 1897, when he returned to Yale, where he received his doctorate of divinity in 1898. Oyabe chronicled these years in his English autobiography, *A Japanese Robinson Crusoe*.[75]

Oyabe returned to Japan in 1898 and served as minister of the Yokohama Union Church but resigned from the position after only eight months when a fire destroyed the building. In 1899, he traveled to Hokkaido, where he remained for ten years as a missionary to the Ainu. The following year, with the support of prominent politicians like Itagaki Taisuke and Ōkuma Shigenobu, he established the Society for the Education of the Aborigines of Hokkaido (*Hokkaidō dojin kyōikukai*), and he continued to strive for the betterment of the Ainu for the remainder of his life.

In 1924, Oyabe published *Genghis Khan Was Yoshitsune*, in which he argued that the medieval Japanese hero Minamoto-no-Yoshitsune (1159–89), who is generally believed to have died a tragic death at the age of thirty, had not actually perished but had fled to the Asian continent, where he assumed the identity of his Mongolian contemporary, Genghis Khan (1167–1227).[76] *The Origin of Japan and the Japanese People*, which followed in 1929, was also an effort to rectify what Oyabe regarded as the errors in the nationalist ideology of the time. The work was well received, and excerpts were included in government-approved school texts as exemplars of neoclassical Japanese prose.[77] Oyabe taught at Kokugakuin University and other Shinto institutions and died in his home in Tokyo on March 12, 1941.

Oyabe explains his motives for writing *The Origin of Japan and the Japanese People* in the preface. As was true for Saeki, his basic assumption is that Japan is a holy nation. Christianity, he asserts, had been prefigured in Shinto, but the Japanese religion had, for unspecified reasons, failed to keep pace with the times. By studying Christianity, Oyabe says he had hoped to bring Shinto up to date so that it (as the Japanese national expression of Christianity) could become the salvation of all Japanese. "In order to validate my theory that the doctrine of Christianity is the same as our Shinto," he wrote, "I studied theology in the United States; and, desiring to explore the heart of Shinto, I became a lecturer at the Institute of Japanese Classics, Kokugakuin University, and others of the best institutions dedicated to the study of Shinto." Realizing that reforming Shinto would inevitably lead to a confrontation with the emperor system, however, he had turned his attention to less controversial subjects, like the fate of Yoshitsune.[bb]

[bb] Oyabe's own rendition of his career is worth quoting at length:

Despite my poor ability, I wanted to make a profound study of why our Japan is a holy nation, so I spent years collecting materials. I returned from the culturally resplendent West and immediately immersed myself in a desolate Ainu village. I dedicated the prime of my life to the education of these aborigines. As I was doing so, I researched the details of their language and customs, searched for remnants of their primitive cave dwellings, and furthered my research by excavating many ancient stone tools and earthen vessels. In order to validate my theory that the doctrine of Christianity is the same as our Shinto, I studied theology in the United States; and, desiring to explore the heart of Shinto, I became a lecturer at the Institute of Japanese Classics, Kokugakuin University, and others of the best institutions dedicated to the study of Shinto. I also went to Southern China, Korea, the Ryūkyūs, Chishima, as well as Siberia, Manchuria, and Mongolia to search for and to observe any trace of our people from ancient times. All of these experiences have been put to use in this book.

For many years, I yearned to study abroad but was unable to do so because of poverty. At the age of nineteen, however, I made up my mind and boarded a foreign sailing ship. After arriving in New York, possessed of nothing, I spent thirteen years of hardship studying in foreign schools. I spent not a penny from Japan during this time, but nonetheless was able to graduate from Yale University, one of the five best universities in the world. After returning to Japan, I persuaded people both inside and outside the government to establish a school for the poor and innocent Ainu in one of their villages, and for ten years I dedicated myself to their education, all the while supporting myself on my own earnings. Through all these hardships, I came to realize the need to teach the Japanese people Shinto so that they might nurture their faith. However, Shinto as it existed was bound by archaic customs and was unable to keep pace with world progress. I therefore sought to reform Shinto and make it an institution that would benefit both public affairs and private morals. I turned the affairs of the school over to the Hokkaido prefectural office and returned to Tokyo. I spent the next ten years running from one end of the country to the other to accomplish my scheme. During this time, the older and wiser men upon whom

•

Oyabe's theory of Japanese-Jewish common ancestry was thus part of an explicitly syncretic theology that regarded Shinto as the Japanese national expression of Christianity. His goal in studying Christianity was, he says, to enhance Shinto so that it might better serve the Japanese nation.

Oyabe was motivated by a sense of crisis, and by revealing the true origins of the Japanese people he believed he was preparing his compatriots to meet this crisis. "People no longer recall the origin of their sacred nation," Oyabe wrote, "but the world is not always peaceful. When confronted with raging winds and surging waves, the Great Ship of Japan, with eighty million souls on board, can only depend on the strength of true patriots filled with the Japanese spirit to save it. All who call themselves Japanese should nurture this spirit, for without it we are lost."[78]

Like the influential mainstream ultranationalist Ishiwara Kanji (1889–1949) and Oyabe's South African counterparts, Oyabe believed in an imminent apocalyptic confrontation with the white world.[cc] The essence of the Japanese spirit for him as for other common

---

I had relied all passed away. I also realized that any reform such as the one I envisioned could not but impinge upon the Grand Shrine at Ise, the original source of Shinto [and the shrine of the Imperial House]. I therefore abandoned my plan and set out for Manchuria and Mongolia. After about one year, I returned to Japan and set about diligently to correct the image of the noble Yoshitsune that had mistakenly been drawn by historians. Now I have taken up my pen once more to write about the daunting subject of the origins of our Great Japan, which in sum is the present work.

[Oyabe, *Nippon oyobi Nippon kokumin no kigen*, preface, p. 5.]

[cc] Ishiwara Kanji, a general operations officer on the Kwantung Army staff in Manchuria, was one of those responsible for the 1931 Mukden Incident, which marked the beginning of Japan's military involvement in China, and one of the chief architects of Japan's wartime ideology.

Ishiwara believed that a "Final War" between the East, led by Japan, and the West, led by the United States, was inevitable. "This will not be accidental, it will be the product of divine will, the great natural tide of human civilization," he wrote; and he asserted that "Japan must be victorious, not for the sake of her own national interest, but for the salvation of the world."

Ishiwara was profoundly influenced by Nichiren Buddhism, a nationalistic Buddhist sect founded in the thirteenth century. Nichiren Buddhism was the subject of renewed interest in the increasingly nationalistic Japan of the early twentieth century, and at the forefront of this revival was a religious propagandist named Tanaka Chi-

ancestry theorists was Japan's election as God's chosen people, and he was convinced that Japan's divinely determined destiny was to free Asia from the yoke of Western imperialism. He identified the Jews as Asians and condemned European antisemitism as a form of anti-Asian racism. It was Japan's divine mission, he asserted, to eschew such bigotry and bring universal peace and brotherhood to the world.

> I have one thing to say to my fellow Japanese. The hour is late. While the world is at last on the brink of achieving the truth of universal brotherhood, there is a sequence to be followed. First, we Asians must be united, and we [Japanese] as the agents of Heaven must bring peace to hundreds of millions of Asians, teaching them that with us true security lies. That Westerners shun Asians is wrong. For us to follow their example and despise and shun the Jews, who are racially and culturally the same as we, would be equivalent to abandoning our ideals of Greater East Asia and will ineluctably lead Asia into the land of death. Those obstinate bigots who are hostile to innocent Japan stand

---

gaku (1861–1939). Tanaka's followers asserted that "Japan is the Truth of the World, Foundation of Human Salvation, and Finality of the World."

The congruity of Nakada Jūji's premillennialist nationalism, Oyabe's common ancestry chauvinism, and Ishiwara's Buddhist-inspired theory of the "Final World War" (sekai saishū sensō) is obvious. Just as the Christians looked forward to the millennium, Ishiwara believed that "The last war in human history is approaching— Nichiren's 'titanic world conflict, unprecedented in human history'—which will be the gateway to a golden age of human culture, a synthesis of East and West, the last and highest stage of human civilization." The difference was that the Christians were marginal at best, while Ishiwara was a high-ranking army officer with real influence over strategy. Among other positions he held, Ishiwara was a lecturer at the Army Staff College (1925–28); operations officer in Manchuria (1928–32); commander of the Fourth Infantry Regiment (1933–35); and chief of operations, Army General Staff, Tokyo (1935–36). And as Mark Peattie writes, "The theory of the Final War, which joined these two elements [of religious prophecy and military science] in his thought, came to be a basic premise underlying all his major decisions, the departure point for all his subsequent judgments on national policy."

Far from being an aberration, therefore, in a signficant sense, the apocalypticism of common ancestry theorists like Oyabe was typical of its times. While they themselves may have had little political impact, common ancestry theorists participated in, contributed to, and reinforced the intellectual milieu that made the chiliastic ideology of World War II possible. See Mark R. Peattie, *Ishiwara Kanji and Japan's Confrontation with the West* (Princeton: Princeton University Press, 1975), pp. 42, 57–58, 72.

•

in defiance of Providence. That they will be punished is a foregone conclusion. We, the people of the Divine Land, must open our hearts to the Jews and give them our sympathy, for like us they are persecuted without reason. We must guide them to the light, the establishment of a Divine Nation, the ideal of the Hebrews and the mission of Japan, and encourage their cooperation with the ideals of universal brotherhood and unity. This is none other than the sacred teaching of our Imperial ancestors—to unite the entire world under one roof—and it is our expression of filial piety to our forebears and our devotion to God.[79]

Unlike Nakada Jūji, who had identified Japanese nationalism with Zionism and who believed, literally, that the salvation of the Jews would be the salvation of Japan, Oyabe asserted conversely that *Japan* was to be the salvation of *the Jews*. He thus castigated the Jews for having the audacity to pursue their own national ambitions. Japan, he insisted, would fulfill their aspirations for them:

Oh you descendants of the Jews, unaware of Holy Japan standing flawless and exemplary lo these three thousand years! Awake to the blindness of your plan to build a holy nation: it is redundant, like piling roof upon roof. Universal brotherhood and unity have been Japanese national ideals since time immemorial. You have named your goal Zionism. In order to achieve it, you incite the proletariat in every nation, exploit their weaknesses, and advocate communism; you champion anarchism and disturb world peace, turn every nation to republican democracy, and finally seek to control the world by resurrecting your kingdom and establishing divine rule. Were it Heaven's will that you should succeed, it would not wait for your feeble schemes but would accomplish the goal over night, just as by the hand of God the cities of Sodom and Gomorrah were rendered over night a sea of death. Cease your vain strivings, for they are like unto sowing seeds in the dead of winter. . . . Awake to the ultimate truth and entrust everything to the power of Almighty God. Cease your vain propaganda. Build your nation adjoining Japan, in eastern Siberia, on the shores of Lake Baikal. Live in intimate proximity to us. Patiently spread the Word of

God throughout the world. Offer the people of the world, intoxicated with material civilization and utterly confused, the opportunity to come to their senses. Become intermediaries to bring true peace to the world.[80]

For Oyabe, Japanese imperialism was divinely ordained, and the Jews were God's designated instrument to bring the truth of Japanese imperialism to the world.

A third and younger Japanese Christian who shared the syncretic vision of Saeki and Oyabe was Kawamorita Eiji (1891–1960). Kawamorita was a Presbyterian minister who lived most of his life in the United States and produced a monumental, two-volume *Study of Japanese Hebrew Songs* (*Nihon Heburu shiika no kenkyū*), in which he revealed that well-known Japanese folk songs were actually derived from Hebrew.[81]

Kawamorita was born in rural Iwate prefecture and studied theology at the Christian North Japan College (*Tōhoku gakuin*) before emigrating to America in 1920. He earned two doctorates in the United States, one in divinity from the Western Theological Seminary in 1934 and one in Bible from the San Francisco Theological Seminary in 1940. In 1928, he became pastor of the Japanese Presbyterian church in Seattle. At this time, he was also taking courses in Asian studies at the University of Washington. During his career, he served as pastor of many Japanese Christian churches up and down the Pacific coast. In May 1942, Kawamorita's career was interrupted when he was interned with other Japanese and Japanese Americans, first at Tanforan, California, and then, from September 1942, in the relocation camp at Topaz, Utah. After his release in 1945, Kawamorita worked to rebuild Japanese-Christian institutions in California. He died in San Francisco on March 6, 1960.

Kawamorita's *Study of Japanese Hebrew Songs* is an epic effort to discover in modern Japanese remnants of a Hebrew language and poetry that supposedly died out in Japan thirteen hundred years ago. Of his inspiration to undertake the work, Kawamorita wrote, "From the end of 1933, the Spirit of the Lord came unto me repeatedly,

•

occupying my soul and dominating my life with such intensity that I could not ignore it even in my dreams. . . . I am transmitting this prophecy to the world, which I believe to have been entrusted to this humble scholar by God."[82]

Kawamorita distinguished his ideas from those of Oyabe Zen'ichirō, but his work reveals the same syncretic theological impulse.[83] Like Oyabe, Kawamorita reasoned that because Japan was a holy nation and that because God was the source of all holiness, Japan's holiness must derive from God. It followed that Japan's divine emperor could only have been descended from God's chosen people, the Jews. Kawamorita thus wrote of the origins of his *Study*,

> I was led to a clarification of our National Polity [*kokutai meichō*], to wit that our Emperor is the undisputed successor to the eternal throne of the Great King David of Israel, and that without the Emperor System Japan will lose its reason to exist. I announce this to the Japanese public without hesitation and unashamed, before heaven and earth, as one scholar's cry of conscience.[84]

For Kawamorita and other common ancestry theorists, asserting common ancestry with the Jews was a way of simultaneously professing Christianity and affirming Japaneseness. It was, particularly for an expatriate like Kawamorita, a way of resisting total submersion in Western culture.

All three of these common ancestry theorists shared a similar background. They all had a lifelong, professional commitment to Christianity: one (Saeki) became a scholar of Christianity; the other two were ordained Protestant ministers. They were not trained in mainstream Japanese schools but received an unorthodox early education in private Christian seminaries and academies. All of them completed their education in North America. These experiences made them marginal, alienated members of Japanese society; and their nationalistic theology, which asserted that Japan was a holy nation based on its common ancestry with the Jews, was an attempt to reconcile their Christianity with their Japanese identity. Like Uchimura Kan-

zō's Churchless Christianity, common ancestry theory was an attempt
to circumvent Western culture and subvert the authority of Western
missionaries. Sakai Shōgun, another common ancestry theorist whom
we treat below, put it most succinctly and provocatively when he
wrote,

> Japan has leapt from the ignoble position of an isolated island in the Far
> East, nay, a nation of pagans, to the status of a world-class empire
> blessed by God. The right to look down upon the countries of the West
> that profess Christianity is ours. It is high time they discovered that
> Japan is God's sacred repository . . . that Japan is a divine nation with
> no need of their arrogant missionizing.[85dd]

The common ancestry theorists differed from both Uchimura and
Nakada Jūji, however, in their heterodox readiness to ignore the basic
theological and sectarian distinctions that differentiated one religion
from another and to follow instead the links and associations they
intuited through an exegesis of Japanese texts. While Uchimura is
thus best seen as a neo-orthodox Christian comparable to Karl Barth
and Nakada as a fundamentalist akin to D. L. Moody, common
ancestry theorists are best understood as highly original religious
syncretists.

Bizarre as some of their ideas may seem, all three of these theological streams have continued to influence Japanese culture and Japanese conceptions of the Jews to this day. Through evangelists like

---

[dd] Sakai also had the following recommendations to make to Christian missionaries: "If
you truly believe it is your life's mission to enlighten Japan, then I beseech you to
abandon the Star-Spangled Banner, divest yourself of all your worldly possessions,
become naturalized Japanese citizens, and missionize on your own. Poor though we
may be, we Japanese will never allow the righteous to perish by the wayside. Even if
our people were so merciless as to leave you and your families to starve, missionaries
devoted to the propagation of a foreign faith should be ready to accept such an
eventuality without complaint. If you are not prepared to do this, does that not amount
to a confession that you are not wholeheartedly devoted to your mission in Japan?"
Sakai Katsuisa (Shōgun), "Zainichi Beikoku senkyōshi ni ataete tettai o susumu sho"
[Advice to American Missionaries in Japan to Withdraw], in *Yudaya minzoku no daiinbō*
(Naigai shobō, 1924), p. 327.

Sun Myung Moon, the Korean founder of the Unification Church, who was in Japan for an extended period between 1938 and 1946 and who was undoubtedly familiar with them, they influenced the development of Christianity in other Asian countries and elsewhere in the world as well.[ee]

[ee] Sun Myung Moon (b. 1920), founder of the Unification Church, reportedly spent eight years (1938–46) in Japan, originally traveling there as a student of electrical engineering at Tokyo's Waseda University. Almost nothing is known of Moon's experience in Japan, but the period between 1936, when he reports having received his first revelation, and 1946, when he began his public religious mission, corresponds to his stay in Japan; and his subsequent teachings, which stress the Second Coming of Christ and the special role of Korea as the birthplace of the savior, bear a striking resemblance to some of the theological ideas circulating in Japan at the time. If this is indeed the case, Japanese theologies and their attendant attitudes toward Jews have had an influence on the United States and other societies through the activities of the Unification Church and its theology.

This is not to suggest that Unification theology is nothing more than a Korean version of Japanese Christian ideas. Rather, it is the product of a syncretic process similar to that which produced Japanese Christianity; and it seems likely that Japanese Christian ideas were one unacknowledged element in the Korean syncretic blend. See Frederick Sontag, *Sun Myung Moon and the Unification Church* (Nashville: Abingdon, 1977), p. 78; David G. Bromley and Anson D. Shupe Jr., *"Moonies" in America: Cult, Church, and Crusade*, Sage Library of Social Research 92 (Beverly Hills, Calif.: Sage, 1979), pp. 36–37; and George D. Chryssides, *The Advent of Sun Myung Moon: The Origins, Beliefs and Practices of the Unification Church* (New York: St. Martin's Press, 1991), pp. 46–107.

Compare Moon's Unification theology also to the syncretic postwar Japanese theologies discussed in Chapter 6.

•

IV

THE PROTOCOLS OF ULTRANATIONALISM

The Rise of Antisemitism Between the Wars

The Protocols of the Elders of Zion was introduced to Japan during the Siberian Intervention of 1918–22. Frequently reprinted and readily available, this bible of antisemitism profoundly affected Japanese images of the Jews and is widely accepted as authoritative even today.[a]

---

[a] Even when Norman Cohn's definitive exposé of the notorious forgery was translated into Japanese in 1986, the publisher included *The Protocols* (printed on pink paper) as an appendix, and the book was marketed as a version of the classic conspiracy theory. According to the translator, Uchida Tatsuru, a legitimate scholar of modern French philosophy who has also translated several works by the French-Jewish thinker Emanuel Lévinas, the publisher, Dynamic Sellers, bought the translation rights to the book assuming that it treated *The Protocols* favorably, and they included a translation of the tract over his objections. Personal conversation with Uchida Tatsuru. See *Shion kenja no giteisho: Yudayajin sekai seifuku inbō no shinwa* [The Protocols of the Elders of Zion:

The success of the Russian Revolution and the fall of the Romanov dynasty in October 1917 shocked the Japanese government, which immediately began exploring ways to deal with the crisis. The military and the Foreign Ministry favored intervention, regarding the Bolshevik coup as an excuse to establish a Japanese foothold in Siberia; but the *Ōsaka Asahi shimbun*, the *Tōyō keizai shimpō*, and other newspapers campaigned vigorously against such a move. In January 1918, the battleships *Iwami* and *Asahi* were dispatched to Vladivostok. In April, infantry troops began landing. In May, the Japan-China Joint Defense Agreement provided a pretext for deploying troops in northern Manchuria. Japan also made contact with the men waiting in the wings to fill any power vacuum that might develop: Gregorii Semenov, who was preparing to set up a counterrevolutionary government in Trans-Baikalia, Dmitrii Horvat, managing director of the Chinese Eastern Railway, and Peter Derber, who was planning a new government in Vladivostok.

Official word of the intervention came from the Japanese government on August 2. On the third, America announced that it was also intervening, and a joint intervention involving American, Japanese, French, British, Canadian, and Czech forces became a reality. In addition to landing a large contingent at Vladivostok, Japan sent a force from Manchuria to Trans-Baikalia, eventually bringing total Japanese troop strength to more than seventy-two thousand.

Japanese troops remained in Siberia longer than any other force. All the other intervening nations had withdrawn by June 1920, but the Japanese remained. They occupied Khabarovsk and Chita and advanced into Nikolaevsk, establishing puppet governments in various locales and setting the stage for the Nikolaevsk Incident of May 1920.[b] Japanese forces stayed in Siberia until October 1922, when

---

The Myth of a Jewish Plot to Take Over the World], tr. Uchida Tatsuru (Dynamic Sellers, 1986).

[b] The Nikolaevsk Incident involved the killing of some seven hundred Japanese and Russian counterrevolutionary prisoners by Red Russian partisans in May 1920. It led to the Japanese occupation of northern Sakhalin. Formal relations with the Soviet Union were only established in 1925, when Japan withdrew without the compensation it had demanded.

•

criticism both at home and abroad made it impossible to continue the intervention; northern Sakhalin remained in Japanese hands until 1925.[1]

The Protocols of the Elders of Zion was being distributed as required reading to White Russian and Ukrainian troops in Siberia.[2] Japanese soldiers also received copies and took it back with them to Japan, where it helped them explain how the revolution had occurred and why they were powerless to reverse it.[3]

The Protocols of the Elders of Zion ranks with *Mein Kampf* as one of the cardinal texts of modern, political antisemitism.[4] It consists of twenty-four "lectures" in which a member of a fictitious secret Jewish government known as the Elders of Zion expounds on a Jewish plot to take over the world. *The Protocols* was fabricated by the Russian secret police working in France during the Dreyfus Affair, probably in 1897 or 1898, on the basis of earlier fictional sources. It was first published in Russia between 1903 and 1907 but became influential only after the Russian Revolution of 1917, when it was translated and adapted into many languages. The automobile magnate Henry Ford published an English-language version of *The Protocols* titled *The International Jew* in 1920, and this edition subsequently became a staple of Nazi propaganda.[c]

The Protocols purports to document a centuries-old conspiracy by the Jews to take over the world in order to install a Jewish despot. The Elders are supposed to believe that only a despot can rule society effectively and that only coercion ensures social order. The purpose of *The Protocols of the Elders of Zion* is thus to attribute to the Jews a grotesquely dehumanizing conspiracy to take over the world based on a profoundly misanthropic politics.

According to *The Protocols*, in the modern world, where capital is power, the Jewish conspiracy has taken the form of "international Jewish capital." The Jews, *The Protocols* asserts, intend to use the power of capital to destroy the already weakened Gentile states in

---

[c] *The International Jew* was reissued in Japan in August 1993. See Henry Ford, *Kokusai Yudayajin: gendai ni yomigaeru jidōsha-ō henrii fōdo no keikoku* [The International Jew: Automobile Magnate Henry Ford's Undying Warning and Its Relevance Today], ed. and trans. Shima Kōichi (Tokuma shoten, 1993).

•

order to unify the world under their own rule. This is to be accomplished through specific steps. On the surface, the Jews will support liberalism and democratic institutions, but their ulterior motive will be to sow dissension and chaos, which are the inevitable result of pluralism and democracy. Concomitantly, the aristocracy and others capable of exercising true authority will be discredited. Because it will be easy for the Elders to manipulate presidents as puppets, presidential regimes will be favored. Furthermore, industry will be concentrated into giant monopolies, so that it will be possible for the Elders to destroy all non-Jewish fortunes when it suits them.

The Jews will also disrupt international relations and foment incessant wars of attrition to weaken the Gentile states. On the domestic front, the Gentiles will be encouraged to become atheists and indulge in every kind of luxury, license, and depravity. This will be accomplished through liberal education and through the mass media, which will turn the Gentiles into submissive cattle incapable of independent thought.

The Protocols contends that the Jewish conspiracy has already made significant inroads. Legitimate authority has been undermined, economic disorder is chronic, financial manipulations have produced enormous national debts, and public finances have been reduced to hopeless confusion. Soon the Gentile states will be in such chaos and desperation that they will gladly relinquish control to the Elders, who are using their control over the world's vital resources to exacerbate the situation.

The point of all these purported machinations is to realize the Messianic Age, which *The Protocols* defines as the time when the world will be united under Judaism and a Jewish despot. The divinely preordained success of the centuries-old Jewish conspiracy is near at hand, *The Protocols* asserts, but it will be a truly nightmarish world, where social control and social engineering will maintain the appearance of peace, liberty, and justice but where all will in fact be enslaved.

The similarities between *The Protocols of the Elders of Zion* and the anti-Christian polemics of the Tokugawa period are too numerous to go unremarked. The existence of an international, occult religious conspiracy to take over the world, the central role played in the conspiracy by economic forces, the threat of spiritual subversion through manipulation of the ignorant masses, and the mortal peril in which this conspiracy placed righteous monarchies like Japan are all aspects of *The Protocols* that had been prefigured in the anti-Christian arguments of Aizawa Seishisai, Ōhashi Totsuan, and Ukai Tetsujō and that made it palatable and credible to Japanese readers.[d]

One of the first men to introduce *The Protocols* to Japan was Higuchi Tsuyanosuke (1870–1931), who spent thirty-nine months attached to the Japanese Army in Siberia. He was an early graduate of the Russian Orthodox Nikolai Seminary in Tokyo and had studied at the Theological Seminary in St. Petersburg, where he received his divinity degree. Higuchi was hired as a professor of Russian in army schools shortly after the intervention began. Anti-Russian sentiment was running high in Japan, and the Japanese military was placing new emphasis on improving Russian language education among its personnel.

For Higuchi, the Siberian intervention was a high-minded attempt to save the pure Russian people from the clutches of the Jews. The lectures he delivered upon his return from Siberia were filled with a romantic longing for the Czarist past. He mourned the passing of the time-tested ways, the "benevolent" system developed over centuries, and he cursed the forces that had destroyed it: the Bolsheviks and, behind them, the nefarious Jews.

In 1921, Higuchi published his collected lectures under the title *Yudayaka—The Jewish Peril*—thus coining the Japanese term. Using the pen name Kitagami Baiseki, which he took from his birthplace on the Kitagami River, he wrote that he had first become interested in studying the Jewish question while a student in the Russian capital. In a statement issued on the occasion of the publication of *The Jewish Peril*, Kitagami wrote, "As I witnessed the Russian Revolution and

---

[d] Interestingly, *The Protocols* itself drew on earlier anti-Christian literature. Among its sources was a novel written by Eugène Sue in Paris in the 1840s, which attributed a conspiracy for world domination not to the Jews but to the Jesuits. See Robert Wernick, "Don't Look Now—But All Those Plotters Might Be Hiding Under Your Bed," *Smithsonian* (March 1994), p. 113.

•

searched for its underlying cause, it became my humble desire to warn the Japanese people of the Jewish peril threatening us and to do what I could to remove it."[5]

Seen through the distorting lens of *The Protocols*, the Russian Revolution became for Higuchi an example of how a cabal of un-scrupulous Jews had brutalized the innocent Russian people.

> No matter how barbaric and bestial the Russians may be, if the Russian Revolution had been led by Russians, it would not have been as brutal as it was. At least there is no example of such brutality in the 900-year history of Russia. The suspicion therefore arises that some dark force was behind the brutality, that the devil himself was directing the rev-olution. But when one learns that the leaders of the communist regime are all Jewish and then reads through the plans of the Jewish conspir-acy, everything becomes clear.[6]

The first complete Japanese translation of *The Protocols of the Elders of Zion* was produced in 1924 by Hō Kōshi, the pen name of Yasue Norihiro (a.k.a. Yasue Senkō, 1888–1950), under the title *Behind the World Revolution (Sekai kakumei no rimen)*. Yasue had been a member of the first class of students sent by the army to study Russian at the Tokyo School of Foreign Languages, and from 1918 to 1920 he was assigned to the headquarters of the Fifth Army in Siberia. In 1921 he was dispatched by the General Staff Office to Palestine to inves-tigate the Jewish question, and in 1938 he became head of the Intel-ligence Bureau of the Kwantung Army in Dairen. During World War II, Yasue was the top expert on Jewish affairs within the Japa-nese Army.

The way *The Protocols* related to the forces of nationalist xeno-phobia and syncretic Christian theology is most clearly displayed in the career of Sakai Katsuisa (popularly known as Sakai Shōgun, 1870–1939), who was dispatched to Siberia during the Siberian in-tervention as a Russian-language interpreter. Born in rural Yamagata prefecture in 1870, Sakai was a contemporary of Saeki Yoshirō and Oyabe Zen'ichirō. He was baptized in 1888, and after graduating from the missionary North Japan College, traveled to America in

●

1898, where, like Nakada Jūji, he studied at the Moody Bible Institute. He returned to Japan in 1902 and served in the Japanese Army during the Russo-Japanese War of 1904–05, where he presumably acquired his Russian-language skills.

Sakai began his career as a Christian minister in January 1906, immediately after the Russo-Japanese War, when he founded the Society for the Glorification of God (*Sanbi shōrei-kai*). He showed early syncretic tendencies, sponsoring worship services at Mt. Fuji. In 1915, he renamed his organization the Japan Glorification Corps (*Nihon sanbi-dan*); and in June 1917, he changed the name again to the National Faith Promulgation Corps (*Kokkyō senmei-dan*). These name changes indicate the increasingly nationalistic character of Sakai's thought.

Sakai was originally pro-American, democratic, and pacifistic.[7] After his experience in Siberia, however, his writing took a sharp rightward turn; and in 1924, he published three books that promoted his new ultraconservative views: *The Jewish Plot to Conquer the World* (February), *The Great Jewish Conspiracy* (March), and *The Jews and the Reality of the World* (April).[8] As can be gathered from the titles, all were antisemitic tracts based on *The Protocols of the Elders of Zion*. "I sense," Sakai wrote in *The Great Jewish Conspiracy*, "that [the Jews'] evil grasp will shortly extend itself to our Imperial nation and even encroach upon the Imperial family itself," and he declared it his solemn duty to prevent this from happening.[9]

What was the nature of the Jews' "evil grasp"? For Sakai, all ideologies that threatened imperial Japan "from the *red* of Bolshevism to the *white* of Democracy" were "Jewish." "Recent trends like universal [manhood] suffrage, women's suffrage, and other such tendencies should not befoul the mouths of loyal Imperial subjects," he wrote. "What is more, universal suffrage is the first step toward republicanism!"[10] Sakai's invective was aimed at Britain and America as well as at the Bolsheviks, but apart from this dollop of anti-American, anti-British animosity, there is little to distinguish his ideas from the Jewish Peril theory of Higuchi Tsuyanosuke.

Notwithstanding his clearly antisemitic message, Sakai also devoted many approving pages to the Jews' return to Zion. "The rebuilding of Zion is not merely the ambition of the Jews but a mission from God. Their movement is thus not an invasion but a revival. They should attack proudly, their flag unfurled!"[11] So enthusiastic was Sakai about the Jews' return to Palestine that in 1928 he wrote a letter to the Zionist organization in England asking for a loan of £2,000 on the basis of his Zionist credentials.[e]

Sakai's enthusiasm for Zionism was linked to his unique religious vision. His practice, he says, was "to first rely on passages from the Bible, second to seek out the facts, and then to judge with the eyes of faith"[12]; and throughout his work, he uses Biblical references to find mystical links between Japan and the Jews. It is hard not to be impressed by his ingenuity, and then he arrives at this startling intuition: "I am thus convinced that Japan is the remnant of King David's kingdom."[13]

> I . . . believe beyond the shadow of a doubt that the original identity of Imperial Japan was the Kingdom of Israel. What do I mean by this? That the Kingdom of Israel, which continued the lineage of Adam, ancestor of all humanity, for fifty-five generations and possessed of a history of 4,300 years, was in fact established by the same Divine Decree that created Japan; that it is descended from the same celestial family as our Emperors; and that it regards the same Three Sacred Regalia as national treasures.[14]

Why had the identity of Japan and Israel been concealed for so long? Basing himself implicitly on the conspiracy theory of *The Protocols of the Elders of Zion*, Sakai concluded that this was part of God's plan to enable them to clandestinely establish their power throughout the world. Despite appearances, Jewish power had never actually waned, Sakai argues. Rather, in the covert form of the international

---

[e] The letter was discovered by the Waseda University historian Kobayashi Masayuki during his 1962 trip to Israel. Kobayashi wrote, "A proponent of antisemitism claiming to be a Japanese Zionist asked for £2,000 [from English Jews] in 1928. (There are eight letters written in English in one archive. The correspondence came to an end when he asked for a large sum of money from the British Zionist authorities)." See Kobayashi Masayuki, "Yudaya ryokō memo yori" [From Notes Taken on a Jewish Trip], in *Yudaya-Isuraeru kenkyū*, No. 3 (1964).

Jewish conspiracy and, simultaneously, embodied in Imperial Japan, it had flourished without interruption throughout history. Anticipating Oyabe Zen'ichirō, Sakai asserted that the Japanese were God's *original* chosen people and the Jews were descended from the Japanese. The ultimate success of Zionism was assured, Sakai was convinced, because of its link with Japan:

> Two thousand six hundred years ago . . . Israel came to a tragic end through exceedingly complex and profound causes and entered the ranks of the decimated nations. That decimation was not for lack of national power, however, but was paradoxically to enable Israel to develop on a global scale. Insofar as they are descendants of Japan's Unbroken Imperial Line, the Jews should not continue in their ruined state for a single day longer. That is why . . . God has roused through prophecy the people of the decimated nation of Israel, the Jews most particularly, and secretly moved His kingdom to Japan. Thus, although the Kingdom of Israel has feigned ruin in order to accomplish its goal of development on a global scale, there has not been a single day when it has not thrived as Imperial Japan. Imperial Japan was established simultaneously with the destruction of the Kingdom of Israel, and both nations commonly embody the essence of the National Polity that derives from the Unbroken Line of Imperial Sovereigns. What is even more remarkable is that the Kingdom of Israel was buried in the dustheap in recent times, while Japan was hidden in obscurity in ancient times. . . . Thus, the first half of Israel's history is known while the latter half is lacking; and Japan's modern history has been astonishing while its early history is lost. By connecting the two, do we not realize a grand nation that extends from the past through the present and into future, unifying history from alpha to omega? Is not such a linkage in fact the way to realize for the first time a kingdom of our Unbroken Line of Emperors that will have worldwide legitimacy?[15]

Culling *The Protocols of the Elders of Zion*, the Christian syncretist Sakai reasoned that when God's son Jesus, God's people the Jews, and God's nation Japan came together, Zion would for the first time

•

achieve global hegemony, and the "kingdom of Zion will emerge as the premier, unparalleled, and singular Utopia."[16] He was convinced that the simultaneous ascent of the Jews and Japan would lead to their rapprochement and that the return of the Jews to Palestine should be greeted with celebration as the fulfillment of prophecy and the first step toward the realization of a Judeo-Japanese "Empire of Zion."

Sakai's fundamentalist advocacy of Zionism did little to mitigate his terror of Jewish power, however, for he believed that the Jews were ignorant of their common mission with Japan. Despite their kinship with the Japanese, in Sakai's mind the Jews still posed a dire threat to the well-being of the country.

> Today the world is a battlefield. Japan is under attack by savage external threats and internal confusion. What we should fear most is not cannonballs but ideological deviation, not battleships but conspiracy. Like the Jews, I am an advocate of the restoration of Divine Rule and a Zionist. Nevertheless, I do not wish their conspiracy to succeed anywhere in Japan or for it to contaminate our Imperial Land, for I believe that Imperial Japan has no need of their conspiracy and in fact is in a position to enlighten them.
>
> However, since the people of Japan have not yet roused themselves from their infatuation with foreign cultures, the black hand of the [Jews'] great conspiracy has already begun to invade their thinking.[17]

All the liberal ideas that abounded in Japan in the early twenties during what is known as the period of Taishō democracy were, for Sakai, manifestations of the Jewish menace. Sakai believed that a reconciliation between the Japanese and the Jews would be possible only after all these "Jewish" ideas had been swept from the country. He thus issued the following warnings:

> As long as [the Jews] regard us as their enemy, then so be it. We shall defend our nation against its enemies lest its future be threatened. I therefore hasten to warn all patriotic Japanese: so long as Japan contents itself with lapping up the leftovers of the West and views Westerniza-

tion as the be-all and end-all of things, then the Jews will despise our Empire and treat it with the same contempt in which they hold the Western monarchies.[18]

My urgent duty, therefore, is to alert the people of this country to regard the Jews as their enemy and to warn them against falling victim to their schemes.[19]

Once we have forced the enemy [Jews] into retreat, we can teach them the Divine origin of the Japanese Empire, and after that we can cooperate with them in perfecting Divine Rule over all the earth.[20]

In order to make manifest the mystical relationship that Sakai believed existed sub rosa between the Japanese and the Jews, he planned to establish a "Society for Japanese-Israelism" (*Nichiyu kyō-kai*).[21] It was not until 1932 that this organization was actually established, but in the meantime, Sakai traveled to Palestine with Yasue Norihiro, translator of *The Protocols*, to investigate Jewish issues. In 1936, he founded "Mystical Japan" (*Shinpi-no-Nipponsha*), an organization that published a journal by the same name. In the journal, Sakai stressed the divinity of a Japan dedicated to establishing "the Kingdom of the Japanese Emperor over all the earth," and he began mass-producing texts missionizing for his mystical religion.

Sakai's image of the Jews was the culmination of the process of accretion that had begun more than a century earlier. It combined strains of indigenous xenophobia, Christian theology, and the antisemitic conspiracy theory of *The Protocols of the Elders of Zion* to produce the image of the Jews that Japanese ideologues would exploit during World War II.

In the 1920s, the ideas of Higuchi Tsuyanosuke, Yasue Norihiro, and Sakai Shōgun constituted a minority ideology at best. Moreover, they were opposed by conscientious critics from both the liberal and conservative camps. The most vocal liberal critic was Yoshino Sakuzō

(1878–1933), a professor in the law department of Tokyo Imperial University and an early advocate of democracy in Japan. In a far-sighted essay published in June 1921, Yoshino wrote of the conspiracy theories being introduced by the military men returning from Siberia: "When I saw that today influential people are attempting to resist new ideas with this sort of ludicrous gimmick, I began to worry about the potential retarding effect on our culture, and I realized that I could not remain silent." He accurately described *The Protocols of the Elders of Zion* as "a forgery based on Westerners' traditional prejudice against Freemasons and Jews created to incite a hatred of Bolshevism"; he correctly identified *The Protocols* as a reactionary work intended to galvanize the right wing against the forces of liberalism, progress, and peace; and he argued that it was inconceivable that Jews would write anything so patently contrary to their own interests.[22] On the conservative side, Mitsukawa Kametarō, who differed with Yoshino on many other issues, concurred with him on the subject of Jewish conspiracy theory, which he denounced in *The Delusion of the Jewish Peril*, which he published in 1929.[23]

By World War II, however, antisemitism had become a ubiquitous part of Japanese ultranationalist rhetoric. The growth of antisemitism from the idiosyncratic ideology of a few extremists in the 1920s to an integral part of ultranationalist ideology in the 1940s was not an aberration but a logical extension of previous trends.

The liberal experiments of Taishō democracy in the early 1920s gave way to an increasingly conservative politics in the late 1920s and early 1930s. The Peace Preservation Law of 1925, which had been passed to mollify conservatives angered by the enactment of universal male suffrage that year, was amended in 1928 to permit the death penalty for "thought crimes." The law, which prohibited organizations or movements that advocated changing Japan's emperor-centered theocracy, the *Kokutai*, was the basis for the extensive apparatus of thought control that shaped Japanese intellectual life through World War II.

Worsening economic conditions in the late 1920s also strengthened military and right-wing forces, who urged the government to adopt a more hard-line foreign policy and a more aggressive pursuit of

Japan's vital interests on the Asian continent. The Manchurian incident of September 1931 was the first realization of these aims. Over the objections of the civilian government, Japanese military forces occupied portions of northern China, leading to the creation of the puppet kingdom of Manchukuo in February 1932. A year later, in February 1933, Japan withdrew from the League of Nations, which had condemned its aggression in China. Increasingly alienated from the West, Japan drew closer to Germany, which was also being isolated diplomatically.

Given their subsequent alliance with Nazi Germany, it is easy to assume that the Japanese took an early interest in Nazism, which represented a movement of conservative reaction similar to what was happening in Japan. Japanese interest in Nazism, however, was decidedly lukewarm. Journalists were much more concerned with domestic affairs and with the implications for domestic politics of the Manchurian incident. The Japanese media dutifully reported that the Nazis had become the largest political party in Germany with their victory in the German elections of July 21, 1932, but they devoted the most space to the tenth Olympic games in Los Angeles.[24] The Japanese performed extremely well in the games, so the enthusiasm was understandable.[f]

It was not until 1933 that Japan turned its attention from the Olympics to Geneva.[25] The first Hitler cabinet was born in January of that year. Japan withdrew from the League of Nations in February, followed by Germany, which withdrew in October. The Japanese greeted Matsuoka Yōsuke, their chief delegate to the league, like a conquering hero upon his return from Geneva.

Bound by their shared anti-Communism and isolated in international society, Japan and Germany drew closer together. In 1936, the Anti-Comintern Pact was concluded between Germany and Japan. In

---

[f] Nanbu Chūhei won a gold medal in the hop-step-and-jump; Nishida Shūhei performed well in field events, placing second in the pole vault; in water sports, Japan won impressive victories in five out of six events (the 400-meter free style was the exception); Nishi Takeichi placed first in the steeplechase; and the Japanese team won second place in hockey despite the fact that this was the first year Japan had competed in the event.

•

September 1940, Japan formally joined the Axis with Italy and Germany by signing the Tripartite Pact. The more Japan became psychologically dependent on its German ally, the more voices extolling Hitler and Germany came to dominate Japanese intellectual life.

These developments vindicated the antisemitic commentators spawned in Siberia, who had long warned of the Jewish Peril. Now they were joined by a new contingent who argued that, as a matter of pragmatic politics, Japan should demonstrate its solidarity with Germany by making antisemitism a national policy. In both cases, the antisemites interpreted the news of the persecution of the Jews in Germany not as barbarism but as a vindication of their views. Hitler's words and deeds were taken as proof of the reality of the Jewish menace.

The views of these antisemites notwithstanding, there was still considerable skepticism in Japan about Hitler's racial policies during the early 1930s. Much of the reporting on Germany remained clearly anti-Nazi, particularly among liberals, despite intensifying censorship. An editorial published in the *Asahi shimbun* on January 31, 1933, for example, commented on Hitler's appointment as chancellor of Germany but touched only briefly on the Jewish Problem.

> Extermination of the Jews is a representative slogan of the National Socialist Party, and it is a fact that in July 1932 the National Socialists submitted a bill to the Prussian Diet, proposing to confiscate all land owned by Jews. There can be little doubt that Hitler's accession to power will cause considerable alarm among the Jews.

A day later, in its "Vox Populi, Vox Dei" (*Tensei jingo*) column, the *Asahi* dismissed Nazi threats against the Jews as political sloganeering. "When they achieve power," wrote the *Asahi*, "all political parties try to avoid making good on their campaign promises. This will be the case with Nazi pledges to oppress the Jews. It will be no simple matter to root out Jewish intellectual and economic power."

Upon learning of the actual persecution of the Jews following the general election of March 5, 1933, however, the *Asahi* severely criticized the Nazi regime.

•

The policy of repression adopted by the German authorities is an outrage, leading them to extreme measures impossible to condone in normal human terms. When the Germans carry out in the twentieth century atrocities that can only be likened to those committed by the First Chinese Emperor 2,200 years ago, we are left aghast.[g] Einstein and Haber have contributed more to the greatness of Germany than a hundred Hitlers. Whether it is better to improve the standing of one's people through international cooperation or through xenophobic nationalism is a question we need not answer here. Suffice it to say that Germany may yet fall victim to its own policies and come to rue the day it adopted them.[26]

On the same day that this editorial appeared, the *Asahi* further criticized the irrationality and inhumanity of German attempts to expunge Jewish blood in its "Vox Populi, Vox Dei" column, comparing it again to the first emperor's atrocities.

The tone of the news articles published at this time was consistent with these editorials. There were articles that reported that protests had taken place against Germany in various sectors of Japanese society; some articles discussed trends among Jews in various countries and related growing opposition to Hitler; other articles described critically and in detail the Nazis' continuing persecution of the Jews; still others criticized Germany because of the deleterious effect events in that country were having on the rest of Europe.

Almost without exception, Japanese newspapers were critical of the Nazi regime in 1933. An editorial in the *Asahi* of July 4, 1933, for example, discussed how growing concern over the Nazis had come to dominate the political situation in Europe; and another *Asahi* editorial pointed out on November 14, 1933, how the results of the German general election had precipitated a crisis in governments throughout

---

[g] The first emperor of China (*Shih Huang-ti*) unified China in 221 B.C.E. Regarding the classics as subversive to state power, he set his deputy Li Ssu about destroying them in 213. Only utilitarian books were spared; all others were destroyed. One thousand scholars were buried alive, and others were punished by banishment and death. The short-lived dynasty ended in 207 and has since become a symbol of barbarism in China and Japan.

●

Europe. Newspapers related how virtually all candidates in the German election had been members of the Nazi Party and how a current of fear was running through the population (November 10). The *Asahi* simply noted matter-of-factly that "at least on the surface the results were an expression of absolute support for the Hitler regime" (November 14). Nowhere do the newspapers take an active, pro-Nazi stance.

This critical trend dominated Japan's intellectual monthlies as well. Among the prominent intellectuals who spoke out against the Nazis in the pages of the *Central Review* (*Chūō kōron*) were the critic and literary scholar Katsumoto Seiichirō (1899–1967); the liberal critic and former editor of the *Japan Times*, Baba Tsunego (1875–1956); the Christian social activist Kagawa Toyohiko (1888–1960); and the economist and reformist governor of Tokyo in the late 1960s, Minobe Ryōkichi (1904–84). Essays by the Tokyo Imperial University philosophy professor Kuwaki Gen'yoku (1874–1946) and the American-educated pragmatist thinker Hoashi Riichirō (1881–1963) appeared in the small but influential *Collected Lectures on Morals* (*Teiyū rinrikai rinri kōenshū*).[27h]

Liberal Japanese intellectuals wrote a clear but limited critique of the new Nazi regime. The reports by Katsumoto, Minobe, and others accurately described the March 5, 1933, elections, the vicious attacks on Jews that followed the Nazi victory, and the way these attacks developed into a nationally orchestrated campaign of violence against Communists, workers, and others. Despite the clear perceptions of these writers, however, they clearly underestimated Nazi power, and this limited their critique. They operated on the assumption that the Nazi leadership was essentially friendly to big capital and that therefore it was inconceivable that it would attack Jewish capitalists. Minobe interpreted the persecution of the Jews as a simple expedient, for

---

[h] The full translation of the title of this magazine would be "Collected Lectures on Morals from the Morals Society of 1897." *Teiyū* is the designation of the year 1897 according to the Chinese zodiac, presumably the year in which the society was founded. It began publication in 1900 and continued, with some changes in the title, until 1949. The magazine corresponded in influence and stature to the present day *Shisō* [Thought], a prestigious monthly published by Iwanami shoten.

●

example, and he asserted that "this kind of ostentatious child's play isn't going to affect the big Jewish concerns in the least."[28]

Liberal writers also overestimated the ability of anti-Nazi forces to respond to the National Socialist challenge. They were not so naive as to think that the Nazis could be toppled by simple political intrigue, but they argued that "considerable time will be required before [the opposition] is totally overwhelmed by the Nazis, and there will undoubtedly be a major collision between the two before the ultimate outcome is determined."[29]

These writers thus seriously underestimated the power of Hitler and his minions—but that, of course, was hardly an error unique to them. Many German intellectuals also believed that Hitler would not last six weeks and that his inability to govern would be the end of the Nazis.[30]

Liberal Japanese journalists were also convinced that it was in the area of economic policy that the Nazis would be judged. Nazi economic policies had brought Germany to the brink of disaster, they argued, and when that fact became apparent, the Nazi dictatorship would collapse. "When that happens," Minobe predicted, "resistance among the German people, especially the SS, will come to a head."[31] In somewhat different terms, Baba Tsunego suggested that it was unlikely that the German people would fail to resist the Nazis when it became clear that they could not make good on their promises of reform. He therefore regarded Hitler as a short-lived aberration. Baba argued that even if there was some basis for the German hostility to the Jews, to base national policy on a philosophy of racist bigotry was to return to an age of barbarism.[32] Baba apparently believed that while Nazi methods would have no chance of success in a normal society, economic hardships had drawn out the pent-up rage of the lower classes in German society, making the Nazi phenomenon possible.

The maniacal character of Nazism was clearly beyond the capacity of Japanese intellectuals to comprehend fully, but their miscalculations notwithstanding, they reported on the Nazi movement in detail, and they were fully capable of recognizing and criticizing its barbarism. In 1933–34, Japanese liberals had not yet relinquished the floor to the Nazi sycophants.

Jews were not the only ones persecuted by the Nazis, of course. Many non-Jewish anti-Nazi scholars and intellectuals were expelled from the country, their property confiscated, their books burned. Recognizing that culture itself was being threatened, Kuwaki Gen'yoku condemned Nazi policies and argued that they would destroy the German nation.[33] To Hoashi Riichirō, the infantile belief that such policies would extirpate the non-German spirit and unify the German race was simply pathetic. "The goose-stepping Germans are kicking themselves in the head and marching headlong toward the destruction of German culture," he warned. "Spengler's *The Decline of the West* ought to be retitled, *The Decline of Germany*, for the drift toward racist nationalism is simply self-destructive."[34]

Japanese views of Hitler and the Nazis changed rapidly after 1935, but that makes Yanaihara Tadao's 1937 critique all the more noteworthy. A professor of economics at Tokyo Imperial University, Yanaihara (1893–1961) later served as president of the institution from 1951 to 1957. He was a Christian (a disciple of Uchimura Kanzō), a socialist, and a perceptive critic of Japan's colonial policies. As early as 1923, he had supported Zionism as a progressive, noncapitalist, nonexploitative colonial movement. "The Jews are often spoken of as cold-blooded usurers or conspirators out to capsize the world," he wrote, "but one look at their constructive ideals and activities in the Zionist movement should dispel all such misconceptions."[35]

Yanaihara's understanding of the Nazis was acute. He pointed out that Nazism was a reactionary movement against socialism and Communism, that the persecution of the Jews was a fundamental Nazi policy, and that abrogation of the Versailles Treaty and rejection of the World War I settlement were the Nazis' top priority. None of these policies, Yanaihara argued, was in Japan's interests. He noted that while England, the United States, and France also rejected Communism, they were not sympathetic to Japan's participation in the Anti-Comintern Pact, regarding it as an expression of Japanese sympathy for Nazism, and he criticized the Nazi-like character of Japan's leadership.[36]

Another such perspicacious critic was the independent journalist Kiyosawa Kiyoshi (1890–1945), who died in prison shortly before the end of the war.[37] In 1937, Kiyosawa was reporting from Germany, where he originally took up the problem of Nazi power by asking, "not why Hitler is popular, but *is* Hitler popular?" As Hitler's dominance became indisputable, however, he was forced to ask the "why" question. His conclusion was that Nazism was in essence a religious movement and was thus impervious to logical analysis. "Even those who are critical [of the Nazis]," he had to admit, "must recognize their power to get things done, which derives from their youth and enthusiasm, and that at present they have the support of the masses." Kiyosawa regarded the persecution of the Jews and the struggle with the Christian church as symbolic of this intolerant religious movement, and he seems to have despaired that anything could be done until the movement burned itself out.[38]

The clear-sightedness of these critics notwithstanding, by the late 1930s, the flood of Nazi literature into Japan had become irresistible. Hitler's *Mein Kampf* was translated in 1937, Alfred Rosenberg's *The Myth of the Twentieth Century* appeared in 1938, and the rest of the Nazi canon followed. Alfred Stosz's 1934 book, *The War Between the Jews and Japan*, also appeared in Japanese in 1938. Legitimized by these works, discussions of "The Jewish Menace" took on a new prestige and authority.[39]

Domestic Japanese publications about Jews proliferated rapidly in this environment. In addition to general interest magazines, which had always carried articles on Jewish subjects, specialized Jewish periodicals also began to appear. *Studies in the World's Secret Powers* (*Kokusai himitsuryoku no kenkyū*), issued on an irregular basis, first appeared in 1936, published by the Association for International Political and Economic Studies (*Kokusai seikei gakkai*), a paragovernmental organization affiliated with the Foreign Ministry. Each issue of the magazine ran a minimum of 288 pages and on occasion reached 437 pages. On its title page it carried the words "Handle With Care," and for added effect, from the second issue, the words "Top Secret" were also printed on its cover.

The successor to this organ was *Jewish Studies* (*Yudaya kenkyū*), which began monthly publication in May 1941. The journal boasted subscribers throughout the country, and universities had *Jewish Studies* clubs on their campuses. Numerous ultranationalist publications also appeared and continued to publish throughout the war, providing a further venue for Japan's antisemites. The monthly *Anti-Communist Report* (*Hankyō jōhō*), published by the International Anti-Communist League (*Kokusai hankyō renmei*), which was founded in April 1937, was an example of such an ultranationalist-antisemitic publication.

Yonemoto Sanji offers a glimpse of how Japanese attitudes had changed. In the introduction to his 1943 translation of Walther Brewitz's antisemitic *Four Thousand Years of Jewish History*, Yonemoto wrote,

> We are all aware to some extent of the role the Jews played in modern history, particularly in the French and Bolshevik revolutions, but when we consider the traitorous Jews who stabbed Germany in the back during the dark days at the end of the World War and in its aftermath, we cannot but approve Germany's policies toward them today.[40]

That the Jews were traitors had become common knowledge. Yonemoto was thus able to dismiss "criticism of Nazi 'barbarism' " as nothing more than "ludicrous liberal sentimentalism." "The richness of Nazi politics and the sophistication of the German people," he wrote, "are evident in the way they have responded to the Jewish problem, which requires of them at least the degree of historical knowledge Brewitz presents in this book."[41]

Another author, Hazumi Ichirō, typified the growing Japanese adulation of Hitler. The Führer, he wrote, was "confronting all challenges free of prejudice, cool as ice, visionary, and totally uninhibited." Hazumi "respectfully submitted" that Hitler had "taken it upon himself to act as the savior of mankind, liberating humanity from mean-spirited Jewish liberalism and democracy. I am absolutely convinced that he possesses the magnanimity of a god."[42]

The German government also promoted antisemitic "research" in Japan, and Japanese organizations collaborated in these efforts. The European Studies Society (*Ōshū jijō kenkyū kai*), which was supported by the German embassy, performed anti-British, anti-Communist, and antisemitic propaganda functions for the Germans, and the Japanese-German Culture Society (*Nichidoku bunka kyōkai*) also contributed.

The effect of this proliferation of antisemitic materials was augmented by the silencing of dissent. In January 1936, existing wire services were merged into the Dōmei news agency, a public corporation that was directed from the Cabinet Information Bureau and that became the sole official source of national and international news. Between 1937 and 1939, local dailies in most prefectures were consolidated into a single regional paper; and between 1936 and late 1939, the number of periodicals was cut by police censors in Tokyo by one-third. Liberal academics like Yanaihara Tadao and Kawai Eijirō (1891–1944), also an economist at Tokyo Imperial University, were hounded from their professorships and their writings were proscribed.[43] Commentators who had earlier provided broad-minded perspective on questions of Japanese foreign policy as well as Jewish issues like Katsumoto Seiichirō, Baba Tsunego, and Kiyosawa Kiyoshi were silenced. Liberal monthlies like the venerable *Chūō kōron*, which had begun publishing in 1887, and *Kaizō*, the voice of 1920s liberalism, were subjected to intense censorship before being forced out of publication completely in July 1944.

In short, antisemitism became an integral part of Japan's wartime ideology during the country's general descent into ultranationalist irrationalism in the 1930s. It did not go unopposed but was strenuously criticized by both conservative and liberal commentators. Japanese wartime antisemitism was an extension and amplification of xenophobic ideas that had been developing in Japan for a century. The role of Nazism was to legitimize and reinforce these ideas, not to create them.

●

While it legitimated the ideas of existing antisemites, Nazi influence also encouraged other intellectuals with no antisemitic background to adopt an antisemitic stance. This change can be observed in the careers of two intellectuals, Nunokawa Magoichi (?–1944), a professor at Meiji Gakuin College and an adviser to the Ministry of Agriculture and Commerce; and Kuroda Reiji (1890–1937), an early leftist radical who became an outspoken right-wing journalist in the 1930s.

Nunokawa, who published under the pen names Nunokawa Seien and Yamagata Tōkon, was a scholar of broad interests, conversant in a wide range of subjects, including philosophy, sociology, and ethnology. At the end of World War I, he was traveling in Europe and witnessed the Russian Revolution firsthand. His initial contact with Jews apparently came at this time. In the mid-1920s, he became the editor of *Collected Lectures on Morals* and immediately began publishing in its pages.[44]

When Nunokawa wrote on Jewish issues during the 1920s, he did so from a general cultural perspective, attempting to grasp Jewish character as a product of the Jews' struggle for survival. His tone was respectful and sympathetic.

> The Jewish character is above all the product of history. Inwardly, they are characterized by the fervent desire to protect their racial purity and their unique religious beliefs; outwardly, they are characterized by their efforts to maintain their communal identity in competition with others and to resist the persecution and abuse inflicted upon them. Many peoples have been persecuted and abused throughout history, but the Jews are a rare example of a people that has persevered, learned from their experience, and used it to survive.[45]

According to Nunokawa, the Jews had been persecuted and abused everywhere they went, but they had persevered and, never having lost

•

their sense of themselves as a great people, projected an aura of mastery over the world in both its material and spiritual dimensions. They had given birth to Christ, whose teachings informed European civilization; produced the financiers who controlled the world economy; promulgated socialism, the religion of the downtrodden; and given rise to great leaders in every field, from politicians and military officers to scientists and musicians. Nunokawa argued that these accomplishments had not resulted from persecution but because the Jews were "a people with an inextinguishable inner light, a passion and principles, who have been forged and cultured over time." They were, in short, exemplary in the history of world civilization.

At first glance, the Jews would appear to be promoting the contradictory doctrines of capitalism and socialism. In Nunokawa's view, however, these were both products of the same spirit of resistance to the regnant powers of the time. Capitalism aimed at achieving victory for the Jews by manipulating the world's finances; socialism sought the same goal by improving the lot of the underprivileged. The relationship between the weak and the strong was not immutable, and the history of modern Europe was in fact the history of the enfranchisement of the dispossessed, so Nunokawa asserted that these activities of the Jews were beneficial.

On the other hand, Nunokawa held the Jews partially responsible for their identity as pariahs. "They, unfortunately, lack refinement of character and are cold and unfeeling," he wrote. Furthermore, the psychological dynamic at work in the relationship between the weak and the strong

> is in general such that when the weak are not in revolt they are fawning, when they are not jealous they are cunning, and they are forever succumbing to discontent and despair. There are those among them who would act craftily and stoop to flattery, those who are anxious to sell themselves to the highest bidder. We should not necessarily view this behavior as contemptible but rather understand it as the unavoidable strategy of those who strive for intimacy with power in order to survive.[46]

Nunokawa argued that in contrast to the many peoples throughout history who had followed patterns of surrender and extinction or
resistance and defeat, the Jews exemplified a pattern of degradation
and rebirth. He was deeply impressed that through their experience
they had "acquired a power that is almost intimidating."[47]

Nunokawa learned first from his study of the Jews that there
was insight to be gained from a comparison of the Japanese and
Jewish experience. From his understanding of the power dynamics
of Jewish survival, he made policy recommendations to the government and demands on the social movements of the time. In the
never-never land of Jewish theorizing, his approach was a relatively
constructive attempt to develop a theory of culture based on the
Jewish experience.

The tenuousness of Nunokawa's understanding of the Jews is also
obvious, however, and in 1938, when debates over the Jews were
being reconstituted in the atmosphere of "spiritual mobilization" for
war, Nunokawa joined the antisemitic camp.

Nunokawa was an acquaintance of Wakamiya Unosuke (187?–
1938), an advocate of antisemitism since the 1920s. As a child, Wakamiya had trained as a Zen acolyte. He had spent ten difficult years
studying in the United States and England, and from 1921 to 1932, he
taught sociology at Keio University, a prestigious private institution.
Wakamiya also served as the editor of two newspapers at the time, the
Nihon and *Chūō shimbun*. In a July 1938 article written on the occasion of Wakamiya's death, Nunokawa praised Wakamiya's antisemitism as being twenty years ahead of its time. "After twenty years, I
have finally awakened to the correctness of Wakamiya's views. How
foolish are those, if such there be, who even now refuse to acknowledge his foresight. All those who mourn his passing should carry on
his pioneering work and deepen their appreciation as a tribute to his
memory."[48]

The major nationalist intellectual issue of the day was *Kokutai
meichō*—"clarifying" Japan's unique emperor-centered theocracy.[i]

---

[i] The most important attempt to "clarify" the national polity was *Kokutai no hongi*,
published by the Ministry of Education on March 30, 1937. By March 1943, this work

Like innumerable others, Nunokawa engaged this issue. He distinguished between thought that promoted Japan's unique national polity and "thought that should be expunged and rooted out." The latter was "the radical variety that stands in opposition to our national polity, obscures our constitution, harms public peace, and destroys social order. It is, in short, the very thought against which the Tripartite Pact was devised as a defense."[49] In a succession of articles, Nunokawa refined this view, attributing all evil thought to the Jews. "I feel constrained to point out," he wrote, "that the evil root of these 'dangerous ideas' is intimately related to the thought and action of the Jewish people."[50] By contrast, the thought Nunokawa argued should be encouraged was, tautologically, "of the variety appropriate to enhancing the spiritual life of the people by enhancing Japan's unique culture and to manifesting the pure and virtuous idea of our nation."[51] In these pronouncements, Nunokawa's former ideas about the Jews were transmogrified into antisemitic cant. He had become a devoted ideologue, overwhelmed by burgeoning ultranationalism and full of praise for Japan's ally Germany.

Nunokawa was affiliated with the Association for International Political and Economic Studies from the time of its inception in 1936. He became editor of *Jewish Studies* when it began publishing in 1941, and he joined the association's board of directors in 1942. Nunokawa believed that these activities put him "in the forefront of intellectual life."[52]

Five short years earlier, *Collected Lectures on Morals* had published criticism of the Nazis by Kuwaki Gen'yoku and Hoashi Riichirō. From the time of the Anti-Comintern Pact (1936), however, it became to all intents and purposes an antisemitic organ. Thus, even the most sophisticated elements of Japanese journalism degenerated into apologists for the status quo. Nunokawa Magoichi's conversion to antisemitism was indicative of the general degeneration of Japanese intellectual life in the prewar years.

---

of nationalist Shinto fundamentalism had sold more than 1.9 million copies. (Robert King Hall, ed., John Owen Gauntlett, tr., *Kokutai no Hongi: Cardinal Principles of the National Entity of Japan* [Newton, Mass.: Crofton, 1974], p. 10.)

•

Kuroda Reiji represents a different pattern of conversion to antisemitism. A leftist intellectual in the 1920s, he abandoned Marxism in the 1930s to become a nationalist admirer of Hitler. His about-face was one version of a widespread pattern of intellectual apostasy on the left known as *tenkō* (literally, "changing course").

Kuroda was a founding member of the *Shinjinkai*, or New Man Society, one of the most significant and influential left-wing groups in prewar Japan.[53] The society was founded in December 1918, just a year after the Russian Revolution, by students and former students at Tokyo Imperial University. Its program called for the emancipation of humankind and the reform of Japan:

> 1—We will cooperate with and seek to accelerate the new tide which is moving toward the liberation of Man, which is the prevailing tendency of world culture.
> 2—We will join the movement for the rational reconstruction of contemporary Japan.[54]

Members of the New Man Society went on to become leaders of Japan's left-wing movement. Among them were Akamatsu Katsumaro (1894–1955) and Sano Manabu (1892–1953), who helped found the Japanese Communist Party; and Nakano Shigeharu (1902–79), a leading poet and social critic. The group published a journal, *Democracy* (*Demokurashii*), which was later renamed *Pioneer* (*Senku*), *Comrades* (*Dōhō*), and *The People* (*Narōdo*), reflecting the increasing influence of Soviet Communism on the movement. The society continued to function until April 1928, when it was ordered to disband by the university; and it dissolved completely in November 1929 after struggling for a time underground.

Two of the New Man Society's principal mentors were Yoshino Sakuzō and Asō Hisashi (1891–1940), a labor leader and two-term member of the Diet. Kuroda Reiji came to the New Man Society through the Thursday Club (*Mokuyōkai*), so named because it met on Thursdays in Asō's home to study social issues, particularly the Russian Revolution. Kuroda joined the Thursday Club because he shared Asō's interest in the Soviet Union. After his graduation from the economics department at Tokyo Imperial University in 1916, Kuroda had gone to work for the East Asian Economic Research Bureau, which was connected to the South Manchurian Railway Company, and he thus had access to the latest information on developments in the USSR.

Kuroda's real name was Okanoe Morimichi. The pseudonym Kuroda Reiji was concocted from the Japanese pronunciation of "Kropotkin" and "Lenin" and testified to his original ideological commitments. Kuroda never discussed his background, and little is known of his origins, but he was clearly an idealistic but alienated young man. He was from a poor family and had had to work his way through school. With an elite education, he developed a cosmopolitan orientation to the world; he became alienated from his family and village communities and, by extension, the quasi-familial nation Japan.[55] Henry D. Smith has written that Kuroda "was a genuine eccentric, a master of several languages, ranging from Russian to Malay, who expressed his contempt of traditional Japanese ways by eating potatoes and wearing Russian worker's garb."[56]

This alienated, idealistic, and cosmopolitan young man did an ideological volte-face in the early 1930s to embrace Japanese nationalism. In doing so, he was part of the larger phenomenon of Marxist apostasy known as *tenkō* that affected many members of the left, particularly the idealistic former members of the New Man Society. In fact, it was Sano Manabu, whom Kuroda had introduced to the Thursday Society, who was one of the initiators of the *tenkō* phenomenon.

On June 10, 1933, Sano and Nabeyama Sadachika (1901–79), both members of the Japanese Communist Party Central Committee, publicly renounced their allegiance to the Party and declared their fealty to the emperor.[j] The effect of this turnabout was overwhelming,

---

[j] Their statement recanting their beliefs reads in part:

    Those events of national significance that have confronted our people since the Manchurian Incident [1931] . . . have awakened the Japanese consciousness inherent in all of us, communist or not. We are proud of the history of the Japanese people, who, as a great independent nation, have substantially contributed to the development of mankind and we have come to believe in their

leading to mass defections from the left. "Within a month," writes Tsurumi Shunsuke, "30 per cent of the unconvicted [political] detainees (415 out of 1,370) and 34 per cent of the convicts (133 out of 393) had defected. By the end of three years, 74 per cent (324 out of 438) of the convicts defected."[57]

Tenkō has been a particularly troubling issue in Japanese intellectual history.[58] Beginning in the 1920s, Marxism was virtually synonymous with social science in Japan, that is, with the systematic analysis of society against a broad historical background, and to turn one's back on it was therefore to abandon the effort to deal rationally with the world.[59k] That Japanese intellectuals rejected Marxism and embraced irrational nationalism with such alacrity and in such numbers in the 1930s became a major problem for postwar Japanese thinkers as they tried to redefine their role and come to terms with the legacy of the war.[60]

---

superior quality. The critical world political situation, particularly the war situation facing Japan, has aroused our national consciousness.

The imperial system of Japan, unlike tsarism, has never been a system of exploitation and suppression. The imperial household has been an expression of national unity; it has reduced class violence within the country, bringing equilibrium to social life and ensuring a smooth transition from one class to another at times of social change. . . . The overwhelming majority of the people respect and identify with the imperial family. The Japanese people have the sense of being a great kinship group, of which the imperial family is the head. . . . With the slogan 'Overthrow the Imperial System,' the Communist Party flouts the feelings of the people and for this reason is alienated from them.

The Comintern has very little understanding of the historical traditions, peculiarities of social life, and psychological features of the Japanese nation. It cannot understand them. It has steered Japan toward a theory of class struggle based on European experience, not on Japanese peculiarities.

[George M. Beckmann and Genji Okubo, *The Japanese Communist Party, 1922–1945* (Stanford: Stanford University Press, 1969), p. 246.]

[k] The intellectual historian Fujita Shōzō has stressed the intimate relationship between Marxism/Communism and modern Japanese intellectual life: "In every case, one of the prerequisites to *tenkō* was the existence of an attitude of spiritual autonomy [*shutaiteki na seishin taido*]. The thing that first engendered such a spirit in modern Japan and thus made possible the modern intellectual history of this country was clearly, in both its productive and counterproductive aspects, Communism." Fujita Shōzō, "Shōwa hachinen o chūshin to suru tenkō no jōkyō" [The Situation of Tenkō Circa 1933] in Shisō no kagaku kenkyūkai, ed., *Tenkō*, vol. 1 (Heibonsha, 1959), p. 35.

●

In Kuroda Reiji's *tenkō*, the abandonment of Marxism and the embrace of nationalism was precipitated by his encounter with Adolf Hitler. Serving as a foreign correspondent in Germany, Kuroda "developed a limitless fascination with both the German *Weltanschauung* and their actual nationalist movement."[61] In 1931, he interviewed Hitler at Nazi headquarters in Munich and was completely smitten by him.[62] By 1936, when his book *Der Führer Hitler* was published, he had become a devoted admirer of the German dictator.[63]

Kuroda simultaneously became a virulent antisemite. He first expressed his view of the Jews in his 1936 *Study of the Dreyfus Affair,*[64] which departed dramatically from the sympathetic portrayal drawn in the series of articles published six years earlier by the popular novelist Osaragi Jirō (1897–1973).[65] By 1937, when he began to serialize "The Scandal of the Panama Canal: A Prime Example of Jewish Duplicity" in *Studies in the World's Secret Powers*, Kuroda's conversion to Nazi-style antisemitism was unmistakable. He wrote,

> I have become convinced that in order for a race to realize its unique culture and national destiny, it must attack and destroy Judaism in all its forms, both seen and unseen. My point is that this insight is equally applicable to Japan.[66]

His purpose in writing, Kuroda continued, was to reveal to his readers how "the Jews, 'devils dispatched to destroy human civilization,' are insanely dancing their diabolical dance, laughter pealing from their lips."[67] Kuroda urged that "even in Japan, where no ghettos exist, each one of us must actively disgorge the Semitic worldview that has lodged itself in our breast."[68]

For Kuroda, antisemitism was the necessary concomitant to Japan's alliance with Germany and therefore to its survival.

> Japan has offered its hand in friendship to Germany, a nation of antisemites, and so it is only natural that we must also study the Jewish problem. Since in my view this agreement [the Anti-Comintern Pact] has no meaning unless people understand the true nature of the Jews,

•

I regard this as an ideal opportunity to inform the general public that the Anti-Comintern Pact is of necessity a matter of antisemitism.[69]

Kuroda Reiji had traveled 180 degrees from his original alienation from Japan to an enthusiastic embrace of its "unique national polity," from cosmopolitan Marxism to xenophobic nationalism, from the liberalism of Yoshino Sakuzō to Nazi-style antisemitism. His transformation was part of the mass defection of left-wing intellectuals in the 1930s and a prime example of how antisemitism developed in the context of modern Japanese intellectual history.

•

V

JEWS AS THE ENEMY

THE FUNCTION OF ANTISEMITISM IN WARTIME JAPAN

BY THE BEGINNING OF World War II, antisemitism had become an integral part of Japanese ultranationalist rhetoric. "The Jews are the curse of mankind," inveighed the dean of Japan's nationalist writers, Tokutomi Iichirō, in his *Citizen's Reader for Certain Victory*. "Under the guise of democracy they wield their plutocratic hegemony in the United States. American democracy has become a Jewish den."[1] It was against this "evil and ugly plutocracy" that Japan was fighting, Tokutomi claimed.[2]

Tokutomi's diatribe was not an isolated deviation in wartime propaganda but part of what the historian John Dower has identified as "an outburst of anti-Jewish race hate" that was particularly strong during the early years of the war.[3] This antisemitism was not used to persecute Jews, nor was it by any means central to Japan's wartime

106

ideology, but it did influence the way the Japanese viewed the war and was employed by the government on the home front to silence dissent and enforce ideological conformity.

Writing in late 1939, the conservative commentator Itō Ken spoke for an increasing number of Japanese when he asserted that the world war was actually a war against the Jews. In Itō's view, Japan and Germany were engaged in a single struggle on their respective fronts to thwart a common Jewish enemy, and Japan's true purpose was to expunge Jewish influence from Asia. "Japan must tread calmly and deliberately," he intoned, "for the small steps Japan takes are giant strides for Asia."[4]

Atago Hokuzan, a professor at Tōhoku Imperial University, carried Itō's reasoning a step further.[5] Japan's mission was not simply to rescue Asia but to redeem all humankind from the Jews. "The degree to which countries retain a democratic character is precisely the degree to which they are subject to the Jewish dictatorship," Atago argued. "The extent to which the so-called fascist countries are totalitarian and espouse ethnic nationalism [minzokushugi] is precisely the extent to which they have thrown off the Jewish yoke." "Only Holy Japan," Atago declared, "remains to strike down the Jews and save Mankind."[6]

Writing in Collected Lectures on Morals, Kumamoto Arihisa described this titanic struggle between Japan and the Jews in the classic terms of the time, as a conflict between old and new world views. "The Jewish economic monopolism that resides in the philosophies of liberalism and capitalism and seeks to conquer the world through the power of money" was the outdated world view, while ethnic nationalism and the totalitarianism of the Axis were the wave of the future. Victory was assured to the latter, Kumamoto assured his readers, because Britain was on the brink of collapse and the Jew-controlled United States was mongrelized and unstable.[7]

These antisemitic interpretations of the war were disseminated by Japan's major newspapers. Antisemitic rhetoric and opinion began to appear in their pages as early as 1938. Following Germany's annexation of Austria in March of that year, the Asahi shimbun wrote that all that remained to be done was to reform traffic regulations, do

JEWS IN THE JAPANESE MIND

away with the Austrian flag, and "clean out the Jews" (March 16). When Franklin Roosevelt protested the events of *Kristallnacht*, the *Mainichi* supported Germany.[a] Using intentionally vulgar language, it wrote on November 17, "It is none of America's business whether the Germans choose to boil the Jews or fry them in oil"; and it defended German newspapers against the criticism leveled at them by British reporters. "How in heaven's name," it demanded, "can the German government be held accountable for spontaneous acts of revenge against the Jews by the German people!"

The Japanese government controlled the press during the war, but while it strictly censored everything that was published, it did nothing to discourage antisemitism.[b] Takeda Seigo, author of a 1944 book titled *Newspapers and the Jews*, defined Japan's newspapers as "a weapon of war to destroy the Anglo-American-Jewish enemy"; and he expressed his "profound hope that our newspapers and news agencies will valiantly charge forward toward victory in the ideological war against Anglo-American-Jewish thought."[8] Among other functions, Takeda saw it as the role of Japan's newspapers "to completely expunge Anglo-American-Jewish influence" and "join forces with the news organs of our ally Germany to launch a frontal assault on the journalistic plots of the Anglo-American-Jewish foe."[9]

All of Japan's major newspapers carried antisemitic articles. The *Yomiuri* ran stories blaming "war fever" (*sensō kaze*) on the Jews and claiming that Commodore Matthew Perry had spearheaded a Jewish invasion of Japan.[10] It even featured articles on the theme of "The Inhuman Machinations of the Jewish Vampires."[11] The *Asahi* carried an article by Navy Lt. Fukui Shinzō urging people to beware of the

---

[a] *Kristallnacht*, "The Night of Broken Glass," was November 9–10, 1938, when hundreds of synagogues and Jewish businesses in Germany were damaged or destroyed, and 30,000 Jews were arrested and sent to the concentration camps of Dachau, Buchenwald, and Sachsenhausen.

[b] Control was exercised through the Cabinet Information Bureau (*Naikaku jōhōbu*), which was created in September 1937 and upgraded to an Information Board (*Naikaku jōhōkyoku*) in December 1940, resulting in a sharp curtailment of the news reaching the Japanese people. Another mechanism of control was the Newspaper Council (*Nihon shimbunkai*), which had the power to blackball any reporter whose views it disliked. See Thomas R. H. Havens, *Valley of Darkness: The Japanese People and World War Two* (New York: Norton, 1978), pp. 62–63.

Jewish influence that threatened to undermine scientific thought.[12]

Of all the major dailies, however, the *Mainichi* was the most enthusiastic promoter of Nazi ideology. Beginning in 1938, the *Mainichi* used the visit to Japan by members of the Hitler Youth Movement to celebrate its special relationship with Germany. The paper lauded the activities of the Hitler Youth in daily accounts; and on the occasion of their visit to its head office, the paper reported that "all the employees of the newspaper, from the management on down, welcomed the guests with open arms."[13] They went on to congratulate themselves on the fact that the leader of the group, a Mr. Schultz, had recognized the *Mainichi*'s importance. In the autumn of the same year (1938), the *Mainichi* sponsored a "Greater Germany Exhibit," to which it appointed Foreign Minister Ribbentrop and Minister of Public Enlightenment and Propaganda Goebbels as advisers. The *Mainichi* announced that it had sought the direct participation of the German government to underscore the authoritative character of the exhibit.[14]

The *Mainichi* actively promoted antisemitism throughout the war. In July 1942, it sponsored a "Symposium on the Jewish Problem and the International Ideological War." In March 1943, it organized a series of lectures and an exhibit on "The Jews and International Secret Societies." In July of the same year it also cosponsored a symposium on "the Jewish Problem" held by the Association for International Political and Economic Studies.

In individual articles, too, the *Mainichi* continuously promoted an antisemitic interpretation of the war. On March 6, 1943, for example, it ran an article on "The Jews, Rulers of America"; on July 29, it proposed in an editorial that the bombing of Rome had been the result of a Jewish conspiracy; on September 12, it suggested that a Jewish plot had been responsible for Italy's surrender; and on April 3, 1944, it wrote that Pietro Badoglio's declaration of war on Germany was brought about through the influence of British and American Jews on their brethren in Italy.

In sum, by the 1940s, antisemitism had become an integral part of ultranationalist thought actively disseminated and promoted by Japan's major newspapers with the approval of the Japanese government. It reached every corner of the country. So pervasive had it become that the highly respected liberal historian Irokawa Daikichi later recalled with admirable candor the following entry he made in his diary while a student at one of Japan's premier high schools.

> Stalin, Chiang K'ai-shek, Roosevelt, and Churchill are all puppets of International Jewry; the roots of their strategy lie in secret Jewish organizations of Jewish military industrialists, international business-men, finance capitalists, the members of secret societies, speculators, and the like; Hitler and the Nazis are the saviors of mankind for combating them. . . . Japan has also been victimized by the Jews, who initiated the present war. Any Japanese with an ounce of sense knows that we are not imperialists. . . . Our theory of "eight corners of the world under one roof" [*Hakkō ichiu*] is far greater, more introspective, and sublime than the theory of "the absolute superiority of the German *Volk*." . . . Hitler is the hero of the century, an agent of Nietzsche, the savior of Western civilization, and anything but an imperialist![15 c, d]

Japanese wartime antisemitism was not used to persecute Jews, but that does not mean it had no consequences. Early on, the government

---

[c] The historian Saitō Takashi also recalled in similar fashion, "During the war, all the knowledge we had about Europe and America was what we could glean from our Western history and world geography textbooks. Books describing 'the Jewish global conspiracy' and 'the Masonic threat' were available, and our knowledge was so poor that we readily believed the theories they presented." Saitō Takashi, "Rekishi to no deai," *UP*, September 1975.

For recollections by other legitimate Japanese intellectuals of wartime antisemitic indoctrination, see Kimura Hiroshi, "Yudayajin-netsu ni toritsukarete" [Taken Captive by the Jewish Fever], *Shokun*, January 1971; and Mizuta Hiroshi, "Issatsu no hon: 137" [One Book: 137], *Asahi shimbun*, October 13, 1963.

[d] Chinese intellectuals held similar views of the Jews at this time. Frank Dikötter notes, "Contempt for the Jews [among Chinese intellectuals], and even a feeling of hatred towards them, remained vivid for decades. Wu Zelin, an outstanding anthropologist active in the 1930s, recently recalled that he and his colleagues used to find the Jews 'laughable, despicable, pitiable, admirable, enviable, and hateful.' " Frank Dikötter, *The Discourse of Race in Modern China* (Stanford: Stanford University Press, 1992), p. 114.

歴史読本 増刊 臨時 '87-3

特集 世界 謎のユダヤ

第一部 ユダヤの世界戦略 《議定書》神話の成立

継体王朝はユダヤ系王朝か
騎馬民族とユダヤ
第二部 日本とユダヤ 秦族はユダヤか
日本とユダヤは同祖か

●特別企画 ユダヤ有名人事典

The Japanese image of Jews is a composite that has evolved over the course of two hundred years. This cover from the March 1987 special issue of *History Reader*, a widely read monthly for amateur historians, devoted to "The Jews: Enigma of the World," captures well the various elements that make up the Japanese view. The inscrutable rabbinic face looks out over the Empire State Building and the earth, symbols of a presumed Jewish global hegemony. The desert, hazy in the background, represents Israel. The blank scroll and six-pointed star are meant to indicate the Jewish canon and Zionism. At the bottom right, the *torii* gate signifies the persistent theory that the Japanese and the Jews are related peoples. (*Shinjinbutsu Ōraisha*)

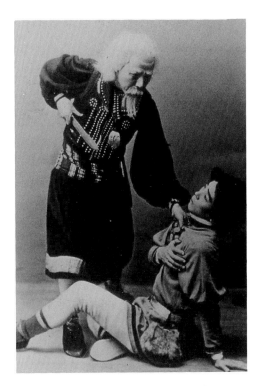

First adapted for the stage in 1885, *The Merchant of Venice* is the most frequently performed Shakespearean drama in modern Japan. It has especially fascinated Japanese audiences, who have seen their own insecurities reflected in its themes of racial and religious conflict, threatened emasculation, and gender confusion. In the path-breaking 1903 production (left), Kawakami Otojirō's Shylock threatens Antonio, played by Fujisawa Asajirō. In the all-male 1911 production (below), Tōgi Tetteki in the role of Shylock menaces a kneeling Antonio while Doi Shun-shō in the role of Portia (at left) commands him to stop. *(Tsubo-uchi Memorial Theatre Museum, Waseda University)*

Japanese Christian theologians found the concept of Jewish "chosenness" useful as they struggled to reconcile their Japanese identity with their Christian faith. The neo-orthodox Uchimura Kanzō and the fundamentalist Nakada Jūji (above left, center and left) saw the successes of the Zionist movement after World War I as a sign that the promise of the Second Coming of Christ would soon be fulfilled. Syncretists like Saeki Yoshirō (above right), Oyabe Zen'ichirō (shown standing next to a seated Ainu chieftain, below left), and Sakai Shōgun (below right) reasoned that since the Japanese were God's chosen people, they must necessarily be related to the Jews. This close identification gave rise to widely varying attitudes, ranging from philosemitic idealization to antisemitic abuse.

Antisemitic imagery abounded during World War II, but Japanese antisemitism was used to justify the war and suppress domestic dissidents, not to persecute Jews. In the above cartoon, titled "Rays of Enlightenment Illuminate the World," the Rising Sun disperses Japan's enemies, including the Americans, British, Chinese, and Dutch (labeled A, B, C, and D). The "J" on the crown flying from the American's head signifies "Jews." Left, a caricature wearing a dunce cap inscribed with a Star of David and labeled "Jew" is perched on the Statue of Liberty, inflating a star-spangled balloon that signifies the inflated profits Jews were supposed to be making from the war. Other burdens the "Grieving Statue of Liberty" must bear include (clockwise from top) a demonic FDR who wields the banner of democracy in one hand and the club of dictatorship in the other, the self-indulgence of a group of revelers, the public's helpless bondage to the warmongers, and the lack of discipline among striking workers. Both cartoons are from the January 1942 issue of *Manga* magazine.

Wartime antisemitism built upon traditional Japanese attitudes toward foreigners. In these cartoons, the legend of the pure "Peach Boy," Momotarō, is given an antisemitic twist. At left, Momotarō drives out Franklin Delano Roosevelt, who is cast in the role of the horned demon. Below, FDR, who wears a Star of David around his neck, is revealed to be a Jew. He clutches a bag of money and quakes before Momotarō's threatening sword as airplanes and ships fall from an upturned tray that bears the title "Arms Dealer." "Don't act so surprised," the caption reads, "you're the one who opened this war bazaar, after all!" Both cartoons are from the February 1942 issue of *Manga* magazine.

Pacifism became the cornerstone of Japan's postwar identity, and many Japanese sought ways to ensure that their country would never again tread the path of militarism. Museums like the Kyoto Museum for World Peace at Ritsumeikan University were established to educate visitors about the evils of war. The exhibit above displays concentration camp uniforms and explains the fate of European Jewry as an integral part of World War II. *(Kyoto Museum for World Peace, Ritsumeikan University)* At the same time, however, the view that the Jews threaten Japan's national security persisted and was promoted by extremists on both the left and the right. The diagram below, from an article by Hirose Takashi in *Sapio*, a newsmagazine published by a major publishing firm, purports to chart the Rothschilds' global domination of financial institutions, the media, military affairs, and politics. Hirose is a member of the leftist "Committee for Palestinian and Jewish Studies" and the author of the introductory essay in their 1986 volume, *The Jews: Merchants of Diamonds and Death*.

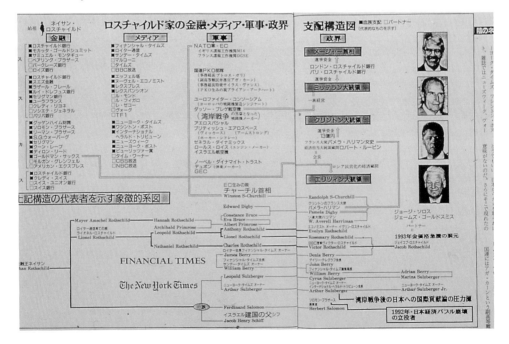

There was a marked recrudescence of anti-semitic thought and rhetoric in Japan in the mid-1980s. The covers of Yamakage Moto-hisa's *The Jewish Plot to Control the World* (above left) and Yajima Kinji's *The Expert Way to Read the Jewish Protocols* (above right)—published in 1985 and 1986 respectively—accurately reflect the principal tenet of this resurgence, which was that Japan stood in mortal danger from an international Jewish conspiracy out to destroy it. Although Yamakage is a little-known Shinto priest, Yajima is an internationally known professor of economics who was quoted twice by *Time* magazine in 1987. At right: the cover of the Korean translation of Uno Masami's 1986 book, *If You Understand the Jews, You Will Understand the World*. Uno has distinguished himself by his alliances with antisemitic demagogues and Holocaust deniers in other countries. Given Japan's general stature as a cultural pacesetter in Asia, it is perhaps inevitable that Japanese stereotypes of Jews should have been exported to other Asian countries.

At least as problematic as antisemitic books themselves are the garish ads all the major Japanese dailies carry for them. With circulations approaching ten million, these newspapers routinely deliver flagrantly antisemitic imagery and rhetoric to virtually every Japanese home. Above, a one-third-page advertisement for the pseudonymous Jacob Morgan's *Get Japan, The Last Enemy: The Jewish Protocols for World Domination* that appeared in the *Nihon keizai shimbun* on July 27, 1993. The legend at the top reads, "The Jewish Protocols for World Domination." In the center are the front and back of the ¥5000 bill, with arrows pointing to "Jewish" designs that the ad says insult the Emperor and the Japanese people. A handbill distributed by the League of National Socialists in 1992

(right) invites people to a lecture commemorating the 103rd anniversary of Adolf Hitler's birth. The flier demands that foreigners be expelled from Japan and decries recent political scandals. Political turmoil and the worst economic recession in the postwar era have given new impetus to xenophobic ethnic nationalism, leading to the establishment of overtly antisemitic organizations, including a political party.

arrived at a policy of self-interested neutrality toward the Jewish population under its control. Such a policy was judged to best serve Japan's war aims, and those who deviated from it were punished. This policy was amoral and by no means "pro-Jewish," for at the same time, the Japanese government also actively promoted antisemitism within Japan as a means to control domestic thought and justify the war.

Japan's basic policy toward Jews was formulated by Army Minister Itagaki Seishirō (1885–1948) and officially adopted on December 6, 1938, by the Five Ministers Conference (*Goshō kaigi*), the highest policy-making body in the Japanese government, consisting of the prime minister, foreign minister, and the ministers of the army, navy, and treasury. After a preamble that declared Japan's commitment to the principle of racial equality, that noted the need to attract international capital to the empire, and that stressed the need to avoid antagonizing the United States, the conference adopted the following three principles:

1—Jews living in Japan, Manchuria, and China are to be treated fairly and in the same manner as other foreign nationals. No special effort to expel them is to be made.

2—Jews entering Japan, Manchuria, and China are to be dealt with on the basis of existing immigration policies pertaining to other foreigners.

3—No special effort to attract Jews to Japan, Manchuria, or China is to be made. However, exceptions may be made for businessmen and technicians with utility value for Japan.[16]

The Japanese government formulated this policy in 1938 for two reasons. First, following the signing of the Anti-Comintern Pact with Germany in 1936, Nazi intelligence operatives were stationed in Japan and began promoting Germany's antisemitic program. At the same time, a growing number of Jewish refugees were coming under Japanese control. By March 1938, twenty thousand Jews had crossed the Soviet Union and were seeking refuge in Japan's puppet kingdom, Manchukuo. Other Jewish refugees were making their way to Shanghai by boat. By May 1941, as many as six thousand Jews had passed through the Japanese port of Kobe on their way to various third-country destinations.[e] While only a handful of Jews remained in Japan when war broke out with the United States in December 1941, the Jewish population of Japanese-controlled Shanghai swelled to eighteen thousand.[17] The government required some basic policy to deal with these two issues.

Many articles describing the arrival and life of the Jewish refugees in Japan appeared in the Japanese press. Even as they insinuated the risks of allowing such a large number of "dangerous conspirators" into Japan, the newspaper accounts were not entirely unsympathetic.[18] Read today, they give the strong impression that the refugees were treated humanely and with consideration by their Japanese hosts, an impression borne out by the testimony of the refugees themselves.[19]

The government's basic policy toward the Jews did not change during the war. It was confirmed by Foreign Minister Arita Hachirō at a meeting of the budgetary subcommittee of the House of Peers on February 27, 1939. And at a private banquet on December 31, 1940, new Foreign Minister Matsuoka Yōsuke told a group of Jewish businesspeople, "I am the man responsible for the alliance with Hitler, but nowhere have I promised that we would carry out his antisemitic policies in Japan. This is not simply my personal opinion, it is the position of Japan, and I have no compunction about announcing it to the world."[20]

Japanese officials acted in accordance with this policy. In Harbin, Higuchi Kiichirō (1888–1970), the head of military intelligence from August 1937 to July 1938, made the decision to admit Jewish refugees to Manchukuo. The Germans, in the person of the German ambassador, protested this decision to the Foreign Ministry. The Foreign

---

[e] Inuzuka Kiyoko reports that between July 1, 1940, and April 15, 1941, 2,797 Jews had passed through Kobe, and 1,591 remained in the city. (Inuzuka Kiyoko, *Kaigun Inuzuka kikan no kiroku: Yudaya mondai to Nippon no kōsaku* [Records of the Navy's Inuzuka Operation: The Jewish Problem and Japan's Maneuvers], (Nihon kōgyō shimbunsha, 1982), pp. 276–77.)

The Jewish community of Kobe, which numbered approximately fifty families, established the Kobe Jewish Community (known as "Kobe Jewcom," from the cable address) in July 1940, and with the help of the Joint Distribution Committee in New York City, helped the refugees find housing, get visas, and depart for their ultimate destinations.

•

Ministry forwarded a copy of the German protest to the headquarters of the Kwantung Army in Manchuria, where Higuchi was asked to explain his action to Tōjō Hideki, then chief-of-staff. Higuchi responded,

> So long as German policy applies only within that country's borders, I would not criticize it. To do so would be inappropriate. However, when the Germans are unable to solve a problem within their own borders and impose it on others, then they should be prepared to accept criticism from the countries and the peoples upon whom they impose. . . . I am all for amicable relations between Japan and Germany, but Japan is not a dependent of Germany, nor do I believe that Manchukuo is a dependent of Japan, so I question seriously the attitude of Germany, the Japanese Foreign Ministry, and the Japanese Army Ministry who question me in connection with the legitimate workings of Manchukuo's foreign policy carried on in accordance with my personal advice.[21]

Tōjō agreed with Higuchi and reported this to the Army Ministry. The German protest ended without discernible effect.

Jews in Shanghai were essentially hostages during the war, and it is doubtful whether life under the Japanese was quite as idyllic as former Japanese officials claimed self-servingly afterwards,[22] but there can be no denying that all the Jews who spent the war years in Shanghai survived the conflict in relative tranquillity. Seven yeshivahs operated in Shanghai throughout the war, educating three hundred scholars. In 1943, a ghetto was established and movement was restricted, but this "ghetto" was nothing like its European counterparts. There was enough food, and cultural life continued. The Zionist Organization of Shanghai (ZOS) and the youth movement, Betar, continued to function; and a Jewish journal, *Our Life* (*Unzer Lebn*), was published in Yiddish, Russian, and English.[23] One former resident of Shanghai recorded her profound gratitude toward her Japanese captors for providing a safe haven for her and other Jews in a poem written in 1991. Her sentiments are widely shared.

•

Reading and hearing lately about Shanghai

Has me praying to Adonai

That credit be given, to whom it is due—

To make people feel proud anew;

For saving us from awful mayhem,

Almost inflicted by Shanghai Nazis, to please them.

   Divulging the rescuers, should be a breeze,

   By now everybody knows, those were the Japanese.

   Who were friendly towards us Jews,

   At the time, when "hate" made the news.

   Yes everyone! We were spared the way,

   The six million went, in that dramatic play.

We were "free" people in a strange land,

Some, equally working with Chinese hand in hand.

There were also hard times, loved ones, losses too.

Nevertheless, we stuck together like glue.

Regardless of people complaining about life in camp,

Compared to extermination, "Shanghai was Paradise"—somewhat damp![24]

In fact, Shanghai ultimately became home to more Jewish refugees (twenty-five thousand) than Canada, Australia, New Zealand, South Africa, and India combined.

While the Japanese government was implementing this pragmatic policy abroad, however, it was also exploiting antisemitism at home to enforce ideological conformity. Its prominence can be judged from the frequent mention it received in the thought-control publications of the Home Ministry's Police Bureau: the monthly *Special Higher Police Report* (*Tokkō geppō*) and the annual *Status of Social Movements* (*Shakai undō no jōkyō*). Within the Foreign Ministry, the Second Section of the Research Department (*Chōsabu dainika*) was the unit principally responsible for dealing with the Jewish issue. The Association for International Political and Economic Studies, which published the antisemitic *Jewish Studies*, was affiliated with this unit. Shiratori Toshio (1887–1949), ambassador to Italy from December

•

1938 to late 1940 and one of the principal architects of the Tripartite Pact, was the most prominent Foreign Ministry official to act as liaison between the ministry and the association.[25]

The way the government manipulated the image of the Jews for thought control purposes (and was in turn manipulated by it) can be illustrated with three examples: the suppression of the Holiness Churches, the selective acceptance of common ancestry theories by official antisemites, and the use of antisemitism as a litmus test to browbeat and intimidate government ministers.

On June 26, 1942, ninety-six members of the three branches of the Holiness Church founded by Nakada Jūji were arrested and imprisoned for "thought crimes." Additional arrests were made in February and April of the following year, bringing the total number of detainees to 111. Of this number, more than half were prosecuted; 19 were sentenced to jail terms, and several died in prison.

The reason for this crackdown was that the theology of the Holiness Church violated the draconian Peace Preservation Law, which permitted the death penalty for certain thought crimes. As the indictment read,

> With the outbreak of the Great Pacific War, the so-called apocalyptic believers [shūmatsu kyōto] arrived at the erroneous conviction that, to wit, "At long last the overture to Armageddon has begun, the Final Judgment, when every nation on earth and the entire human race shall be judged. At long last the time for the construction of God's Kingdom on earth through the Second Coming of Jesus Christ is drawing near." They abruptly developed an active and aggressive campaign to propagate their beliefs, and they began to spread their atrocious and pernicious doctrines.[26]

These beliefs were considered "atrocious and pernicious" because they

not only deny our National Polity and are unrepentant in their profa-
nation of the Great Shrine [of Ise], but they also regard the Jews as
"God's Chosen People" and delude themselves with visions of recon-
structing a Jewish state. . . . Finally, they preach the heresy that the
purpose of the Great Pacific War is to construct a Jewish state, which
distorts and obscures the significance of our Holy War. They are se-
ditious elements susceptible to exploitation by our enemies and a great
obstacle to the prosecution of the war.[27]

It is inconceivable that Nakada Jūji's nationalistic fundamentalism
constituted a meaningful political threat to the Japanese state. Nevertheless, on April 7, 1943, all three branches of the Holiness Church
were suppressed as a peril to the war effort.[f]

Despite their small membership and vulnerability, the Holiness
Churches, along with Uchimura Kanzō's Churchless Christianity
movement and the Jehovah's Witnesses, clung to their independent
beliefs and resisted official repression. By contrast, the mainstream
Christian churches accepted the official ideology; they were concessive
to government policies and cooperated in the suppression of dissident
elements; and their leaders were not above espousing antisemitic ideas.

In 1941, most of the Protestant churches in Japan were consolidated into a single organization called the United Church of Christ in
Japan (*Nihon Kirisutokyōdan*). Tomita Mitsuru (1883–1961), the leader
of the United Church of Christ in Japan, rationalized the need to
"rework" the "pernicious doctrines" of the Holiness Churches because of the subversive threat they posed. "From our point of view,"
he wrote, "it is the followers more than the leaders who are most
strongly attached to these pernicious doctrines, and many of them
cannot extricate themselves from them, so we are fearful that they

---

[f] The breakdown of the June detainees was as follows: *Nihon seikyōkai*, 41; *Kiyome
kyōkai*, 44; *Tōyō senkyōkai kiyome kyōkai*, 11. Of these, 33 were prosecuted. See Wada
Yōichi et al., eds., *Tokkō shiryō ni yoru senji-ka no Kirisuto-kyō undō* [The Christian
Movement in Wartime Japan As Seen in the Records of the Special Higher Police], vol.
2 (Shinkyō shuppansha, 1972), pp. 243–48. Information regarding the 1943 detainees
may be found in volume 3, pp. 127–28.

•

may hold secret meetings among themselves, and we wish to be particularly cautious in this regard." Accusing the Holiness believers of confusing religion and politics, an ironic indictment considering the source, he attributed their transgressions to their "low intellectual level and lack of Biblical and theological understanding." Tomita said he felt personally responsible as head of all Protestant denominations in Japan, but he expressed the strong conviction that valuable lessons could be learned from the experience. He pledged "to assemble the clergy in each region and retrain them in the single approved set of religious doctrines" lest similar deviations recur in the future.[28]

Tomita's views were restated even more trenchantly by Matsuyama Tsunejirō (1884–1961), treasurer of the United Church of Christ in Japan.

> I think it was appropriate to ban their churches, since they preached doctrines that stood in opposition to our National Polity. It is a grievous error for Christians to preach the Second Coming of Christ in Japan. In the final analysis, I believe that this was a fortuitous incident for Christianity in this country, because as a result the United Church of Christ in Japan has achieved total unity, and we have begun the process of establishing a truly Japanese Christianity. All of this, I believe, is the result of the Providential work of God's hand.[29]

In August 1943, Matsuyama gave a lecture entitled "The Problems of Christianity Today" in which he presented an even more explicit criticism of the Holiness Churches and distinguished "Japanese Christianity" from the "Judaized" Christianity of the Western democracies. Patterning himself after *Fundamentals of Our National Polity* (*Kokutai no hongi*), the official expression of ultranationalist ideology published by the Ministry of Education in 1937, Matsuyama recognized "the eternal and changeless character of Imperial rule" and stated his belief that Christianity in Japan should develop "within those limits." "Christianity, too, has national boundaries, and there is nothing wrong with acknowledging that fact. For the Judaized Christianity of the United States and Britain, democracy may be appropriate, but Christianity in Japan must center on our Imperial Family, revere our ancestors, and worship our gods."[g]

In June 1943, with the impetus from the suppression of the Holiness Churches, the Society for the Study of Greater East Asian Christianity (*Daitōa Kirisutokyō kenkyūkai*) was established and undertook a "reformation" of Christianity in Asia. Aware that the Holiness Churches had violated the Peace Preservation Law by their involvement with the Jewish question, Wataze Tsuneyoshi (1867–1944), the managing director of the former Union Church, approached Japan's leading antisemitic and ultranationalist ideologues to curry their support.[h] Wataze's aim in organizing the society was explicitly antisemitic.

> I have long been interested in the Jewish Problem, and as a result of my reading of works by those associated with the Association for International Political and Economic Studies and works by individual authorities on the Jewish problem like Lieutenant General Shiōden, as well as through an examination of publications relating to the organization and history of the Holiness churches, I came to the realization that the thought and beliefs of the Holiness adherents were a skillful blending of the Jew-Zionists' theory of world domination with Christian millenarianism, asserting Jewish domination of the world, and, in addition, promoting the primacy of the Jews on the basis of the idea that Jewish domination of the world was the only truth, and that they had violated their Japanese patriotic duty with these beliefs. I am aghast, but at the same time I cannot help but sympathize with those who unwittingly fell victim to the evil Jew-Zionist conspiracy to dominate the world. . . .

---

[g] Matsuyama continued, "Japanese Christianity must become the leader of Christianity throughout Asia and must subsume the ailing regions of China and the South Pacific, establishing an Asian Christian Alliance at the earliest possible date." Matsuyama's lecture was, in short, the ideology of the Greater East Asia Co-Prosperity Sphere in Christian garb. Wada Yōichi et al., eds., *Tokkō shiryō ni yoru senji-ka no Kirisuto-kyō undō* [The Christian Movement in Wartime Japan As Seen in the Records of the Special Higher Police], vol. 3 (Shinkyō shuppansha, 1972), pp. 62–66.

[h] Among those he approached were Tokutomi Iichirō (a.k.a. Tokutomi Sohō, 1863–1957), Doihara Kenji (1883–1948, an army general, executed as a Class A war criminal after the war), and Amō (Amau) Eiji (1887–1968, the director of the intelligence agency).

•

It is an undeniable fact that today's Anglo-American Christianity was
devised to serve the purposes of the Jew-Zionist plot to take over the
world and dominate its thought, and the belief in the Second Coming
of Christ, which holds the apocalyptic view that Christ will reappear to
rule the world, can be considered a representative idea of this sort. At
present, virtually all Protestant churches in Japan accept Anglo-
American theology unconditionally, having been trained by American
and British ministers, so it is an undeniable fact that they have unwit-
tingly become the active tool of the Jew-Zionists. Our urgent mission
today, when our Emperor in his exalted wisdom has commanded us to
destroy America and Britain, is to expunge Anglo-American-Jewish
thought from the Christians responsible for our portion of the ideological spectrum. . . . I have therefore reached the conclusion that, unless we create an organization that can induce the Japanese Christian
community to reflect on itself and extirpate Anglo-American-Jewish
thought, that is, unless we begin a movement of reform, there can be
no hope of reforming Christianity in Japan.[30]

On June 27, 1943, the Society for the Study of Greater East Asian
Christianity held a "Lecture Meeting to Eradicate the Evil Ideology of
Anglo-American-Jewish Thought and to Declare the Establishment
of a Christianity for Great Japan" at which Wataze spoke. A proc-
lamation was adopted stating: "We dedicate ourselves to reject the
Anglo-American-Jewish ideas masquerading as Christianity, to expunge its evil thought, to realize the true essence of Christianity, and
with it to contribute to the Great Mission of Imperial Japan."[i]

---

[i] In addition, the following proposals were also adopted.
- We resolve to expunge the evil Anglo-American-Jewish thought that persists
  in our church, smash the British, Americans, and Jews intellectually, and, on
  the basis of a realization of the true nature of Christianity, establish a Christianity for Great Japan and thus promote the spirit of self-sacrifice and
  loyalty.
- We perceive a brilliant future on the road ahead and resolve to dedicate
  ourselves to pioneering efforts through our missionary work.
- We resolve to eradicate the poison of Anglo-American-Jewish thought that
  has been spread among the peoples of Greater East Asia and to develop a
  genuine Christianity.

•

It was truly ironic that the Holiness Churches, which under Nakada's leadership had inclined so precipitously toward nationalism and had taken upon themselves the exaltation of the Imperial institution, were in the end suppressed for denying Japan's unique National Polity. For them, it must have seemed a totally incomprehensible charge trumped up by the state for unfathomable reasons.[31] Especially for those who had broken with Nakada and established other churches because they could not abide his teachings on the Second Coming, government suppression must have come as a bolt out of the blue.

If the Japanese government chose to suppress the Holiness Churches because of Nakada Jūji's teachings that the Japanese were descended from the Jews and that Japan's salvation would come through the redemption of the Jewish people, it actively promoted other varieties of common ancestry theory through the Association for International Political and Economic Studies, which it funded through the Foreign Ministry.

The attorney Tadai Shirōji lectured before the association on "The Relationship Between Our Culture in the Age of the Gods and Jewish Thought" (*Waga jindai bunka to Yudaya shisō to no kankei ni tsuite*), and the text of his presentation was published in the October-November 1942 issue of *Jewish Studies*. Masuda Masao, a founder of the association and one of the foremost proponents of antisemitism in wartime Japan, also became a devotee of common ancestry theory. Masuda wrote that "Jewish culture developed diabolically as a counterfeit expression of Japanese Sun Goddess culture":

> No country has a more profound relationship with the Jews than Japan. The relationship can be traced back to ancient times.... What is known as Judaism today is actually a counterfeit religion forged by Jewish priests who dressed up the Satanic god Yahweh in the garb of

---

• We, together with the Christians from our allies of the Axis, resolve to examine the new mission of Christianity, to aid in the ethical enlightenment of the human race, and to contribute to their spiritual improvement.
  [Wada Yōichi et al., eds., *Tokkō shiryō ni yoru senji-ka no Kirisuto-kyō undō*, vol. 3, p. 60.]

the Sumerian sun god and other gods. . . . On the basis of research into folk religion, archaeology, philology, and folklore we are convinced that, in point of historical fact, the Sumerians were one branch of the divine Japanese race. (Note: The claim of the Jews that the Japanese are descended from them is the grossest kind of Jewish drivel and an expression of their ignorance. There are many examples of Jewish sacred rituals that were derived from the Sumerians. I intend to discuss these in more detail when I refute the fundamental errors in Oyabe Zen'ichirō's *The Origin of Japan and the Japanese People*, which have long misled the public). Thus, what is known as Jewish culture developed diabolically as a counterfeit expression of Japanese Sun Goddess culture, and from this point of view also, the relationship between the two is significant.[32]

Masuda argued that only from this unique Japanese point of view could the real Jewish problem be understood and measures taken against it.

The proof of his thesis, Masuda argued abstrusely, lay in "the ancient records of the *Kojiki* and *Nihon shoki*, particularly in the accounts of the Age of the Gods," but "these can only be properly interpreted by those versed in issues of the spirit world." That indeed was the mission of the Association for International Political and Economic Studies, and Masuda was "convinced that this war will end and the world will be saved when we understand these issues correctly and formulate correct policies to address them."[33]

Developing his point, Masuda asserted with apocalyptic panache,

Since accurate versions of the ancient legends and documents have been lost, destroyed, or distorted, it would seem to be impossible to know the essential nature of the Age of the Gods, . . . but there is ample evidence that our Emperor did in fact rule the world before the great transmutation of the earth. . . . This great war corresponds precisely to that event, and, as then, when the cave where the Sun Goddess had concealed herself was opened, once the world is united under the Emperor, it will be reborn in His Divine Light. That is why the Emperor is the true messiah of the world and why this Great War is a restoration of the world.[34]

•

In another issue of *Jewish Studies*, Kubota Michiatsu fulminated against common ancestry theories, which he denounced as "a conspiracy to convince the Japanese to become pro-Jewish," but his criticism was aimed ad hominem at Oyabe Zen'ichirō and Sakai Shōgun and did not condemn the theories as such. "We must by all means discriminate clearly [between them]," he cautioned, "in conformity with the research being done on the Age of the Gods."[35]

In other words, while the common ancestry theory of Nakada Jūji was condemned and suppressed by the authorities because it challenged nationalist orthodoxy, Masuda Masao's inverted version of the theory, claiming that the Jews were counterfeit Japanese, enjoyed government support because it was consistent with that orthodoxy.

Antisemitism proved to be a doubled-edged sword, however. At the height of the war, the legitimacy of antisemitism had become so well established that ideologues were able to use it to browbeat government ministers. On January 26, 1944, for example, Shiōden Nobutaka (a.k.a. Fujiwara Nobutaka, 1879–1962), a retired army lieutenant general and member of the Imperial Diet, challenged the government's policy toward the Jews during a parliamentary session. Shiōden was a popular politician who had run in the final Diet election of the war in April 1942 on an antisemitic platform and polled more votes than any other candidate in the country. Several officials responded to Shiōden's questions, and their responses are instructive, because they illustrate the acceptance of antisemitic mythology at the highest levels of government, and because they show the very tenuous familiarity of government officials with the actual details of antisemitic thought. The responses also reveal how the notion of "proper place" was used to reconcile antisemitism with Japan's stated policy of equality among the races.[36]

After acknowledging that the Jewish problem was global in nature and had to be handled carefully, Home Minister Andō Kisaburō made the following statement, in which he distinguished between what he said was the legitimate need to end racial discrimination and the pernicious doctrine of "indiscriminate equality":

•

The abolition of racial discrimination does not mean indiscriminate equality [*musabetsu byōdō*], but in a world where discrimination exists, Japan helps each people take its proper place and allows them a comfortable life. . . . Thus, as the Honorable Mr. Shiōden has just said, when the government calls for the abolition of racial discrimination, this should not be construed as a call for indiscriminate equality. Rather, recognizing that [a form of] discrimination exists within the founding ideals of Japan itself and recognizing, moreover, that legitimate differences do exist between people, it is Japan's policy to find for each people its proper place and allow them to pursue happiness in a stable environment. Our purpose, to put it another way, is to realize coexistence and coprosperity.

Education Minister Okabe Nagakage responded,

I agree with you [Mr. Shiōden] completely that the Jewish problem is an exceedingly important issue. It seems to me that the Japanese have not given the Jewish problem enough thought in the past. I was not aware of your testimony in the previous session, but as I have just instructed my deputy, I want to look into this matter. As a matter of fact, it seems to me that this is more than a question of a particular ethnic group and must be taken up as a matter of Japanese ideology, so I will do everything possible to respond to your expectations.

Amō Eiji, head of the Cabinet Information Board, said,

This war is not simply a military conflict; the war of ideas is also an extremely important part of it. As you have pointed out, Jewish thought, Freemasonry, and Internationalism continue to exist and thrive. We are doing our utmost in our work to study these ideological problems carefully, and we are responding with careful scrutiny to developments as they arise.

In these exchanges, Shiōden succeeded in forcing cabinet ministers to acknowledge the legitimacy of antisemitism and to affirm his own

•

position as a leading antisemitic authority, but he did not succeed in forcing the reconsideration of government policy toward the Jews that he ostensibly sought. The real significance of antisemitism in wartime Japan, therefore, was its usefulness in formulating and maintaining Japanese nationalist ideology and not in facilitating the persecution of Jews.

Within nationalist discourse, there were three basic positions on the Jews. All three were based on an acceptance of antisemitic myths about Jewish power. The idealist position was espoused by Koyama Takeo, who sought to enlist Jewish power to build the Japanese empire. He was opposed by Shiōden Nobutaka, who countered that the Jews were so overwhelmingly powerful that any role given them would expose the empire to mortal danger from within. The third position was taken by Inuzuka Koreshige, a practical, results-oriented nationalist who, as the official directly responsible for the Jews of Shanghai from 1939 to 1942, had to reconcile the demands of nationalist ideology with the clear policy directives of the Japanese government.

In his 1941 book *East Asia and the Jewish Problem*, Koyama, a self-styled "Jewish specialist," described the tradition of tolerance that he asserted was the foundation of Japan's Imperial Way.

> From its inception in ancient times, the Yamato Race has always treated with love and understanding those peoples who have submitted to us, and we have never abused or harmed them in any way. History proves that we who are descended from the gods have always incorporated other peoples and immigrants, have assimilated them in harmony, and have never done anything to evoke racial rivalry or strife. This is none other than a manifestation of the Imperial Way, the essence of which is the great ideal of universal human brotherhood under the aegis of Japan which has informed our nation since its birth.[37]

Koyama argued that European-style antisemitism was inappropriate for Japan and that the Jews should be dealt with in accordance with this principle of universal brotherhood under the emperor—*hakkō ichiu*, literally "the eight corners of the world under one (Japanese) roof."

Koyama argued further that applying Japan's founding ideals was the most practical course of action. He pointed out that it would be extremely difficult to establish a "New Order in East Asia" (*Tōa shinchitsujo*) by force of arms alone and that Japan's real problem was therefore to elicit the cooperation of the various peoples under its control. "We must make them understand through a faithful application of the Imperial Way that Japan is truly a nation to be trusted and that the Yamato Race is truly worthy of their allegiance as the leading race."[38] Koyama believed this policy had to be applied equally to the Jews of East Asia, for although their numbers were infinitesimal, "not only do they control global financial empires that have amassed enormous power in China, but they are closely related to world Jewry, which exercises untold covert power in the political, financial, and journalistic spheres of the Western nations, so the treatment they receive in Japan and in East Asia will have no small impact in the international realm."[39]

Jews had already made a contribution to Japan's development, Koyama asserted. He noted Jacob Schiff's financial support during the Russo-Japanese war, but he also pointed out that Jews figured prominently among Japan's foreign business partners and that Jewish businesspeople living in Japan had helped open markets for Japanese goods in the Middle East and Africa. Japan was, if anything, in the Jews' debt, he wrote. Koyama thus concluded that, "as in the case of other peoples, to manage [the Jews] and convince them to ally themselves with us should be the guiding policy of our nation, which has taken upon itself the heavy responsibility of prosecuting the war in China and rebuilding Asia."[40]

In Koyama's idealistic formulation, this did not imply exploitation. "The aim of the Imperial Way must be the harmonious blending of all peoples and the elicitation of the mutual cooperation that wells up spontaneously from within them." "The usefulness of the Jews to Japan," he argued, "should only be considered in terms of the 'cooperation' that they offer freely as the situation requires because they understand the tradition of Japan's Imperial Way, believe that Imperial Japan is truly a nation to be trusted, and accept the Yamato Race as leaders deserving their allegiance."[41]

With respect to Jewish refugees, Koyama acknowledged that it was politically impractical for Japan to simply harbor Jews who had escaped from its ally Germany, but he also argued that

> as Japanese, we should begin with a clean slate in our relations with [the Jews], and we must reject hand-me-down antisemitism in the Western mold. No, rather, to the greatest extent possible, we should treat them humanely and in that way display the essence of Japanese morality, which is the Imperial Way of universal brotherhood. This is our prerogative, and the desires of our allies Germany and Italy are irrelevant in this regard.[42]

In short, Koyama Takeo explicitly rejected Nazi-style antisemitism. His conception of how to deal with the Jews was formulated according to the ideals of Japanese imperialism.[43]

In contrast to Koyama, Shiōden Nobutaka adamantly opposed any role for the Jews in the Japanese empire, and he denounced the notion as "a scandal against the Imperial State."

Shiōden Nobutaka's fascination with the Jewish question dated from his encounter with *Les Juifs et la Guerre* by André Spire, which he read during World War I, while he was a young Japanese Army officer attached to the French Army. Stimulated by Spire's book, he went on to read hundreds of antisemitic tracts from France, Germany, Russia, England, and the United States. Shiōden later stressed that his introduction to the Jewish problem was not the result of anti-Bolshevism, but he was also attached to the Army Intelligence Bureau in Vladivostok and Harbin during the Siberian intervention, and there can be little doubt that he deepened his Jewish "research" while he was there.

Shiōden was a true believer in the emperor system who provides a clear link between the xenophobic nationalism of the nineteenth century and Japanese antisemitism during World War II. As early as 1925, in his *Studies on the Jewish People*, he had depicted Japan as engaged in a struggle to protect its unique national polity from the predations of the Jews. The emperor system, according to Shiōden, "was built on the great ideal that has endured unerring and infallible for thousands of years: the unique and unrivalled Imperial Institution of Japan, its *Kokutai*."[44] The Japanese emperor was a god incarnate (*arahito-gami*), the embodiment of justice and righteousness, who differed fundamentally from other earthly rulers, who merely governed territory. In Shiōden's view, to protect this emperor from the Jews was "not only to serve Japan but all the nations of the world"; and this, he argued, was "the perfect and flawless mission of the Yamato Race."[45]

Shiōden related this emperor-centered ethnic nationalism to antisemitism and Nazism. In July 1939, following a visit to Nazi Germany, he wrote proudly to the Nazi publication *Der Stürmer*,

> I am pleased to inform you that copious information and material collected during my journey in Germany has now been translated into Japanese by experts. This will contribute to the enlightenment of the Japanese about the Jewish plan for world-domination.[46]

In Shiōden's Nazi-influenced version of events, the Jews had attacked Germany and Italy, their two greatest enemies and the greatest barriers to their goal of world domination, but this Jewish aggression had failed, succeeding only in driving Germany and Italy together in an alliance against them. Stymied in Europe, Shiōden argued, the Jews had

> now deviously imported to Japan, which is woefully ignorant of the Jewish problem, the notion that they might be useful to us. But having planted an explosive charge in the centers of civilian and military power at the heart of Imperial politics, economics, foreign policy, and military affairs, they would allow themselves to be used only up to a point where they can best detonate their bombshell.[47]

•

In other words, according to Shiōden, the notion of using the Jews for the benefit of the Japanese empire was itself a Jewish plot. He thus urged,

> In its efforts to solve this critical Jewish problem, the government should not simply swallow whole the conclusions of a few government researchers and the imprecations of the Jews, who bow low and seek to become a Trojan horse in our midst, but consult broadly the views of civilian scholars and develop a resolute national policy with which to confront the current situation.[48]

And he warned ominously,

> If the government should make light of these various plots and misjudge the situation, and if they fall into the "solution" that the Jews and Freemasons desire, then how will they ever make amends to the Imperial Ancestors, to the hundred million of their countrymen, or to the valiant spirits of those who gave their lives in this great endeavor, their survivors, and the countless brave soldiers who lost limbs and were disabled because of their blunder?[49]

Shiōden similarly rejected any suggestion that the Japanese should have sympathy for the Jewish refugees. "These are people passing through the Orient on their way to their paradise, America, blown by the winds of a world war that erupted because of the movement to create a world state that their leaders plotted."[50]

Occupying the middle position between Koyama Takeo and Shiōden Nobutaka on the gamut of nationalist discourse about the Jews was Navy Captain Inuzuka Koreshige (a.k.a. Utsunomiya Kiyo, 1890–1965). Inuzuka was an officially recognized antisemite who lectured and published widely on "The Jewish Menace." He had first been exposed to antisemitism in 1920, during the Siberian intervention, and he attributed his "insight" into the Jewish problem to his experience there.[j] In January 1932, he lectured to sailors on the bat-

---

[j] "I realized in 1920, during the Siberian Intervention," Inuzuka later wrote, "that

tleship *Fuji* on "The Roots of Evil Ideas"; and in April of the same year, he spoke to naval cadets at Yokosuka on "The Secret Purposes of the Jewish Societies and the Reality of the Global Anti-Imperial Revolution." Both lectures were published and circulated as "secret documents" by the Education Bureau (*Kyōikukyoku*) of the Navy Ministry and were subsequently reprinted in the same "secret" format by the Criminal Affairs Bureau (*Keijikyoku*) of the Ministry of Justice.[51, 52]

Inuzuka was also practical, however. In February 1938, he appeared at a seminar sponsored by the Cabinet Information Bureau, where he delivered a lecture entitled "On Freemasonry" and made the following recommendations regarding Japan's Jewish policy.

> First, we require a permanent organization for early warning and surveillance . . . Second, our fundamental policy must naturally conform to national policy and national priorities, be fair and equitable, comprehensive, and in the spirit of the principle of universal brotherhood under the Emperor [*hakkō ichiu*]. But third, it is necessary to point out that past *empirical evidence* reveals many cases in which the *shortest way* to subjugate the calculating, self-serving Jews was to be prepared to *sternly chastise* them in the short term. Any police or paragovernmental organization that would implement this policy must be absolutely and permanently prepared for such an eventuality. Without such preparedness, *we will be perpetually threatened by their ideological and economic warfare*, and we will *constantly be required to resort to military force*, thus putting ourselves at a disadvantage.[53] (Emphasis in the original.)

This pronouncement combines the ideological idealism of Koyama Takeo with the profound terror of the Jews characteristic of Shiōden Nobutaka. In the final analysis, however, it offers a practical prescrip-

---

behind the Russian Revolution was the terrifying Jewish Problem, and I have spent the last twenty years, since the London Naval Conference and my stay in Paris, actively studying this subject." From the jacket of *Yudaya mondai to Nihon* [The Jewish Problem and Japan] (Naigai shobō, 1939). Inuzuka wrote this book under his nom de plume, Utsunomiya Kiyo.

tion for Japanese bureaucrats dealing directly with Jews. Inuzuka's prescription was to preempt Jewish power lest it threaten Japan and force the Japanese to resort to force to suppress the Jews. This was the formulation that guided him during his tenure in Shanghai.

Inuzuka was above all a fervent Japanese nationalist. After the war he denied that he had ever been an antisemite, but he never denied being an extreme chauvinist, a true believer in Japan's divine mission.[k] His convictions are obvious in numerous documents, including his 1939 "Letter to the Leaders of the Jews." Echoing earlier writers like Oyabe Zen'ichirō and Sakai Shōgun, he urged the Jews to submit to Imperial Japan for their own good:

> As an impartial third party and as the leaders of Asia, we [Japanese] recognize that the main reason you Jews have been condemned to the sad fate of wandering down to the present day is the guiding spirit of your race [minzoku shidō seishin] that your leaders chose for you 2,000 years ago out of concern for the dark road that lay ahead when your country was destroyed. We hear your explanations and we have studied your appeals against the delusion of a "Jewish Peril," against totalitarianism, and your desperate defense of liberalism. However, the facts of [your behavior during] the China Incident have confirmed our above stated convictions about you. Consequently, today, when you have no other permanent paradise outside of Asia, if you truly care about the future of your people and wish to live and work in peace, then as one Asian people, you should actively support and contribute to the Holy

---

[k] In the years following her husband's death in 1965, Inuzuka Kiyoko worked tirelessly to establish his reputation as a friend of the Jews. In a five-hundred-page book and numerous articles, she attempted to demonstrate that her husband had always had the best interests of the Jews at heart. Within the context of Japan's entirely legitimate war aims in China, she argued, her husband had sought to exploit the Jews for the good of the Japanese empire. This was a much more benign approach than the one taken by Shiōden Nobutaka, Inuzuka's rival in the army, who, she claims, advocated the extermination of the Jews. (Inuzuka, Kaigun Inuzuka kikan no kiroku, p. 81.) That Japanese imperialism and aggression in China, which Inuzuka supported unequivocally, were not necessarily in the best interests of the Jews (or of the Chinese for that matter!) is an idea Mrs. Inuzuka does not consider. See also "Watakushi ga mita han-Yudaya undō" [My Recollections of the Antisemitic Movement] (Zenbō, August-September 1987), pp. 58–63 and 38–41, respectively.

•

War of Sacred Japan, which is ruled over by a god incarnate who seeks
to implement the ideal of universal brotherhood and provide a place for
all peoples under Japan's protection. So long as you are unwilling to
commit yourselves as one of the foundation stones of this Asian renaissance, you can hardly expect us to change our perception of you [as
rootless, wandering pariahs].[54]

I am convinced that the only road left open to you is to submit and
pledge your allegiance to Japan.[55]

Inuzuka decided early on that following their expulsion from
Europe, the Jews would have no alternative but to live in East Asia,
"the land of their forefathers." "In the final analysis," he argued, "the
Jews, who are Asiatics, will have no choice but to live under the
guidance of Japan."[56] Inuzuka conceived of this phenomenon as
"the return to Asia of Jewish Asiatics," and, echoing the common
ancestry theorists, he characterized this as "a return of the Jewish
people, who were estranged from the leadership of Japan in primeval
times." Inuzuka explained Jewish reluctance to cast their lot with
Japan by "their lack of research on Japan, particularly their lack of
understanding of the Japanese Spirit, and their misjudgment of the
nature of Japanese peoplehood." According to Inuzuka, the way to
deal with this problem was "to teach them these things in real terms
through our own loyal and patriotic behavior, and to enlighten them
through the establishment of Japanese studies and the explanation of
ancient Japanese cultural history. As a result, until they become aware
of their past errors and submit to us, we have the responsibility as the
builders of the new East Asia to be unstinting in our efforts [to
convert them]."[57]

Inuzuka put his nationalist conception in its clearest form in his
"Letter to the Leaders of the Jews":

Your people have a history of less than 5,600 years. As it is clearly stated
in the standard history of the *Chronicles of Japan* [*Nihon shoki*], the Age
of the Gods, with which the history of Japan commences, lasted more
than 1,790,000 years. . . . The very Principle of Creation is embodied in

•

the Japanese National Polity; it has been communicated through our blood and is expressed in the flower of the Japanese spirit.... In contrast to the Yamato Race, who are flourishing in concert with the universe through our all-encompassing character, the fact that you Jews who pride yourselves on your own superiority have had no country of your own for 2,000 years demonstrates that the guiding spirit of your race runs counter to the spirit of the universe. Moreover, today, when the cultures of all the peoples of Asia are being encompassed and assimilated and given eternal life by Japan, there is something about your situation that especially moves us who are the beneficiaries of these blessings.... If you would only change your understanding of Japan, you too could submit and benefit from the great spirit of Japanese universal brotherhood.[58]

Inuzuka's position was updated and sanitized in the 1970s by his wife Kiyoko, who had served as his secretary in Shanghai and who claimed to have ghost-written many of his antisemitic tracts.[59] Her rephrasing, however, only confirmed the unrepentantly chauvinistic character of her husband's thought. "We offered the Jews," she wrote, "refuge as Jews under Japan's protection based on the principle of racial equality, without ethnic prejudice and out of respect for the unique character of the Jewish people. However, we required that they understand Japan and cooperate in the construction of the New Order in Asia."[60]

Inuzuka's desire to harness Jewish power was constrained by government policy. In July 1939, he coauthored a ninety-page "Joint Report on the Jews in Shanghai" (*Shanghai ni okeru Yudaya kankei chōsa gōdō hōkoku*) with army Col. Yasue Norihiro and the Japanese consul in Shanghai, Ishiguro Shirō. The report ranged over a broad variety of topics, including "Concrete Policies for Using Jewish Power in China to Influence American Popular Opinion and the Far Eastern Policy of the United States as well as Advisers to the U.S. President to Become Either Pro-Japanese or Neutral" and "Research and Survey Regarding Attracting Jewish Capital." The report also contained a version of a proposal to create a Jewish settlement in Manchuria or China proper for at least thirty thousand Jewish refugees. In earlier

•

versions, Inuzuka had apparently projected a figure as high as three hundred thousand.[61] Oyabe Zen'ichirō had made a similar proposal as early as 1929.[62] In either case, the notion of creating a Jewish enclave in China was a logical consequence of the overestimation of Jewish power in nationalist ideology that derived from *The Protocols of the Elders of Zion*. It ran directly counter to the government's decision against making special overtures to the Jews, however, and was never adopted as government policy.[63,1]

In the final analysis, what most clearly distinguished Inuzuka from Koyama Takeo and Shiōden Nobutaka was that Inuzuka's Jewish fantasies were constrained and guided by Japanese government policy. Otherwise, he was a nationalist ideologue like his fellows, decisively influenced by antisemitic myths about Jewish power.

There was a final Japanese attitude toward Jews during the war that should be mentioned in conclusion: the commonsense altruism of Sugihara Chiune (a.k.a. Sugihara Senpo, 1900–1986), the Japanese consul in Kovno (Kaunas), Lithuania, in 1940. Ignoring Foreign Ministry cables ordering him to desist, Sugihara issued as many as six thousand transit visas to Jews fleeing the Nazis in the summer of that year. The visas, which enabled the refugees to traverse the Soviet Union and travel on to third countries through Japan, were issued on the basis of the fiction that the bearers were destined for the Caribbean island of Curaçao, which required no entry visa. Those who, after their arrival in Japan, could find no third country to take them

---

[1] Inuzuka's call for the Jews to make a home in the Japanese empire is the basis for what Marvin Tokayer and Mary Swartz have called the "Fugu Plan." The name derives from a statement Inuzuka made in January 1939 likening the Jews to the blowfish (*fugu*), a seafood delicacy that can be fatal if prepared incorrectly. (Inuzuka's statement is quoted in Kranzler, *Japanese, Nazis and Jews: The Jewish Refugee Community of Shanghai, 1938–1945*, p. 169, from Kase, "Nihon no naka no Yudayajin," p. 242.) The idea was that if Japan manipulated the Jews correctly, they would serve Japan's interests; if they were mistreated, they would be deadly. The Japanese government never pursued such a plan. See Marvin Tokayer and Mary Swartz, *The Fugu Plan* (New York: Paddington Press, 1979).

•

remained in Kobe until they were transferred to Shanghai, where they spent the duration of the war.

Sugihara's actions were an expression of the same simple decency that many Japanese showed to Jewish refugees during their sojourn in Japan. It stood in stark contrast to the self-interested chauvinism of approved ideologues like Koyama, Shiōden, and Inuzuka; and it ran directly counter to the explicit government policy against affording Jews any special treatment. The government took a dim view of Sugihara's altruistic insubordination, which it punished by transferring him from his post in Kovno and eventually dismissing him from the foreign service.[64]

VI

IDENTIFICATION AND DENIAL

THE USES OF THE JEWS IN THE POSTWAR PERIOD

THE JAPANESE LOST the war. It had been a fifteen-year struggle of incalculable cruelty. The Japanese initiated it at Mukden, Manchuria, on September 18, 1931. Its merciless carnage stretched through their withdrawal from the League of Nations in 1933, the beginning of full-scale war with China and the Rape of Nanking in 1937, the attack on Pearl Harbor in 1941, the Bataan Death March in 1942, and the slaughter of civilians in Manila in 1945.[a] By the time the war ended,

---

[a] "Japanese fighting men added to the carnage [in Manila] by murdering, raping, beating, or burning hapless Filipino civilians caught within their lines. About 100,000 Filipino civilians died in the battle for Manila—almost six times the number of soldiers killed on both sides. . . . Of all Allied cities, only Warsaw suffered greater damage during the war than Manila." Ronald H. Spector, *Eagle Against the Sun: The American War with Japan* (New York: Vintage, 1985), p. 524.

at least ten million Chinese were dead and 60 million left homeless. Four million Indonesians were either killed by the Japanese or died of hunger, disease, or lack of medical attention; and other Asian countries suffered similar losses.[1]

The Japanese also suffered. By the time they surrendered on August 15, 1945, between 2.5 and 3 million Japanese were dead, about half of them civilians. Japanese cities were in ruin, laid waste by Allied bombing attacks, which left vast plains of rubble punctuated only by phantom plumbing fixtures (the only things that did not burn) protruding from the earth. The Japanese economy was devastated, functioning at one-quarter of its previous capacity. Almost 9 million Japanese had to be repatriated from abroad, 5.5 million demobilized soldiers and 3.25 million civilians.[2]

Japanese suffering was real but not unsurpassed. Japanese casualties were less than half the combined German military and civilian total, and one-seventh of the approximately twenty million Soviet citizens who perished. Even the highest estimates put the number of Japanese dead at fewer than half the number of Jewish noncombatants slaughtered in the Holocaust.

Understandably, coming to terms with the legacy of the war was the major preoccupation of the Japanese during the postwar period. Overwhelmed by what had befallen them, and to a lesser extent sickened by what they had done, the Japanese resolved to transform themselves and their society. With a rapidity and earnestness that impressed all observers, not least the occupying American forces, the Japanese followed the advice of the Christian socialist Kagawa Toyohiko and converted themselves from "100 million balls of fire" (*ichioku hinotama*) into "100 million penitents" (*ichiokunin no sōzange*).[b]

This transformation process affected all aspects of Japanese life and society. Intellectual leadership passed from the conservative right, whose emperor-centered nationalism had brought Japan to the brink

---

[b] Kagawa was not the only one calling for penitence. See, for example, Tanabe Hajime, *Zangedō to shite no tetsugaku* [Philosophy as Metanoetics] written during the war in 1944. The work has been translated into English by Yoshinori Takeuchi (Berkeley: University of California Press, 1986).

•

of extinction, to the leftist and liberal leaders who had criticized Nazism and opposed ultranationalism. Left-wing intellectuals flourished during the early Occupation, when they were encouraged by Occupation officials as the best alternative to Japan's conservative leadership, and they continued to dominate Japanese culture throughout the postwar period.

In political and economic life, too, Japan turned its attention away from overseas expansion to domestic economic recovery and development. The conservative politician Yoshida Shigeru (1878–1967), who led Japan during much of the early postwar period, serving five terms as prime minister between 1946 and 1954, rejected right-wing calls for rearmament and made economic development the nation's highest priority. Yoshida made the crucial decision to abandon the military ambitions that had been the centerpiece of Japanese foreign policy for decades and to place Japan under the U.S. nuclear umbrella. He thus sacrificed a degree of Japan's political autonomy but freed the nation to pursue unfettered its commercial concerns. Yoshida's policies, which later came to be known as the Yoshida Doctrine, reflected less idealism than a hardheaded assessment of Japan's needs and possibilities in the Cold War world.

In general, the Japanese reacted to the defeat in three ways. The first was remorse. A broad spectrum of humanists from the center to the left sincerely regretted what Japan had done and welcomed the democratic reforms instituted by the Occupation. Even the Japanese Communist Party (JCP) embraced the Occupation, vowing in early 1946 to forswear violent revolution and become a "lovable" political movement. Parliamentarianism and humanism became the watchwords of the left from the JCP on down, and Japanese intellectuals formed what the renowned political scientist Maruyama Masao (1914–   ) has called a "community of contrition" (*kaikon kyōdōtai*).[3]

The second reaction was metamorphosis. Yoshida Shigeru and other conservative politicians, many of whom had served in wartime cabinets, transformed themselves into "liberal democrats" overnight because they were realists, not idealists. They espoused demilitarization, democratization, and alliance with the United States because they believed they could best achieve their nationalist goal of maximizing Japanese power through these policies.

The transformation of former conservatives into postwar democrats was aided by the advent of the Cold War and the abrupt change in Occupation policies known as the "Reverse Course." In 1948, to meet the challenges of the incipient Cold War, the Occupation deemphasized its previous commitment to reform Japanese society and made its first priority the creation of a strong Japan that could serve as a bulwark against Communism. As part of this new policy, Occupation authorities rehabilitated numerous wartime nationalists whom they had previously purged. The most conspicuous beneficiary of this reversal was Kishi Nobusuke (1896–1987), who had held wartime cabinet positions from 1941 to 1944 and had been detained as a Class A war criminal after the defeat. Kishi went on to become Japanese prime minister from 1957 to 1960.

The symbolic culmination of this process of conservative transformation came in 1955, when the Liberal Democratic Party (LDP) was founded, institutionalizing the metamorphosis of authoritarian conservatives into "liberal democrats." So successful was this metamorphosis that the LDP went on to control Japanese politics for the next thirty-eight years.

The third reaction was popular reformulation. Despite Japan's aggressive role in precipitating and prosecuting the war, the Japanese people increasingly came to view it as a kind of natural disaster that had befallen them and themselves as the innocent, passive victims of a catastrophe whose causes were imponderable and beyond their control.[4] The August 1945 atomic bombing of Hiroshima, in which the Japanese were indeed victims, increasingly came to be viewed as a synecdoche for the entire Japanese war experience.

Each of these three reactions to the war—remorse, metamorphosis, and reformulation—produced an associated set of attitudes and images of Jews. Liberals sought to fashion a new, realistic, and objective image of Jews. Conservatives used the same alchemy that transformed them from wartime nationalists into liberal democrats to camouflage and obfuscate their history of antisemitism and to transform themselves into "friends of the Jews." And the people at large

•

came more and more to identify with the Jews, whom they regarded as the quintessential victims of the war.

In sum, the postwar period was a time of authentic change in Japanese society, but it was also a time of continuity. Despite a significant improvement in Japanese understanding of the Jews, prewar images survived, frequently camouflaged and transformed, but nevertheless intact.

As soon as the war ended, Japanese attitudes toward the Jews changed precipitously. The historically based, liberal attitudes of Japanese intellectuals ranging from Uchimura Kanzō, Yoshino Sakuzō, and Yanaihara Tadao to the liberal critics of Nazism in the 1930s, Kuwaki Gen'yoku, Hoashi Riichirō, and others came to the fore.

The advent of the new era was signaled by the Protestant theologian Ariga Tetsutarō (1899–1977), a scholar and thinker trained at the University of Chicago, Columbia University, and the Union Theological Seminary. Ariga taught at Dōshisha University during the war and became professor at Kyoto University in 1948, where he served as dean of the faculty of literature from 1960 to 1962. In the candid introduction to his 1946 translation of Leo Baeck's *The Essence of Judaism*, Ariga repudiated Japanese antisemitism and called for a new, objective appreciation of the Jews and Judaism.

> Heretofore, knowledge about the Jews in Japan has been provided primarily by Christians and antisemites. . . . To Christians, the Jews are the "People of the Old Testament," the faithless ones who abandoned Christ and who were in turn abandoned by him. One wonders, however, whether Jews themselves would be prepared to accept such a definition without objection. That they would hardly be willing to accept the representations of the antisemites goes without saying.
>
> The antisemites . . . have constructed a false image of the Jews. They have frequently ignored the distinction between Judaism and Christianity. For the most part, they have been the puppets of the

antisemitic movement in Germany. To be freed from this perverted image of the Jews is not only necessary for the sake of Judaism but for the sake of the Japanese as well, and now is the time for this liberation to occur.[5]

Liberals regarded the war as a disaster produced by the particular character of Japanese society and culture. Maruyama Masao wrote of Japanese "fascism," treating Japanese and Nazi aggression as the product of distinctive but related political systems.[6]

This forthright attitude toward the war and the quest to understand its roots was reflected in the 1956 introduction to Viktor Frankl's *Man's Search for Meaning*, written by the editors at Misuzu, the book's publisher. They reacted to Frankl's revelations of the Nazi genocide with a sense of recognition, moral outrage, and personal responsibility.

> When we reflect on the currents of modern history that commence with Japan's invasion of Manchuria in 1931, there are two events that are so monstrous that they make one ashamed to be human. These events took place in the context of war, but they relate to Japan's domestic politics and the character of the Japanese people more profoundly than to war. They are, moreover, events that force us to reassess fundamentally what it means to be human.

The Misuzu editors clearly identified Japanese war crimes with their German counterparts.

> The first event was the Rape of Nanking in 1937, when Japanese forces, after occupying Nanking, pillaged, burned, tortured, and raped the innocent citizens of Nanking and in the process murdered an estimated 200,000 people. . . .
>
> The second was the organized mass slaughter perpetrated in the concentration camps, the implementation of Nazi ideology, between 1940 and 1945. This mass murder was not the result of some primitive impulse or a momentary loss of control, but an organized, highly efficient, premeditated attempt by the Nazi state to implement a coldly

•

calculated plan of diabolical inhumanity. . . . At Auschwitz alone, three million lives were lost, and figures for the total number of dead range from eight to twelve million. This amounts to between one-tenth and one-seventh of the entire population of Japan.

Never before in the history of the human race has evil been organized in this way, nor has it produced results on such a massive scale. There can be no doubt that these epoch-making events will forever live in the human memory.

Finally, the Misuzu editors argued that the Japanese should endeavor to understand the Holocaust to better appreciate their own war experience and prevent its recurrence.

What follows is a translation of Professor Frankl's *Ein Psycholog erlebt das Konzentrationslager*, his account of how he as a Jew was imprisoned in Auschwitz and miraculously survived. As the author himself states, this is an attempt to understand man in extreme situations, and the dignity that derives from his profound understanding of human psychology is at least some small redemption for the tragic reality. . . .

In the process of editing this book, we asked ourselves whether it was really necessary to acquaint ourselves with these unspeakable horrors. But demands for an objective understanding of what happened answered our question. We would like to believe that for reflective people "knowledge is transcendence." And through our own everyday political convictions, we hope to preclude the future recurrence of this kind of tragedy.[7]

Many serious books about the Jews and Israel were written by Japanese authors in the 1950s. Among these were Okakura Koshirō's Marxist *Tales of Palestine* and Takebayashi Fumiko's popular *Gestapo—The Untold Story of How the Jews Fought the Beast of the Century*, both of which appeared in 1950. In 1954, *Israel* was included in a photographic series published by the influential Iwanami publishing firm. In 1957, *The Middle East* by the leftist writer Kai Shizuma and *Israel: Focus of International Struggle* by the mainstream scholar Sugita Rokuichi appeared. The influential series of essays by

●

the liberal humanist Takeyama Michio titled "The Collapse of the Human Spirit: On the Nazi Mass Murder of the Jews" also began appearing in November 1957.[8]

Along with these Japanese works, numerous books about Jews were translated from European languages. Anne Frank's *Diary of a Young Girl* was published in Japan in 1952, the same year it appeared in the United States. In 1956, in addition to Frankl's *Man's Search for Meaning*, Jean-Paul Sartre's *Anti-Semite and Jew* was published and had an extraordinary impact. Elie Cohen's *Human Behavior in the Concentration Camps* and Lord Russell of Liverpool's *The Scourge of the Swastika* appeared in 1957.[9c]

Films enhanced Japanese understanding of the Holocaust as well. Movies about the Holocaust, including. *The Thirteen Steps (Der Nürnberger Prozess)*, *Mein Kampf*, *Night and Fog (Nuit et Brouillard)*, and Frédéric Rossif's *The Witnesses (Le Temps du Ghetto)*, were successfully screened in commercial theaters.

Serious scholarship on Jewish life and history had been virtually nonexistent in Japan before 1945. A very limited amount of material had been produced incidentally by scholars in the course of their work on other subjects. Kemuyama Sentarō (1877–1954), a lecturer on European history at Waseda University, for example, wrote a two-part article about antisemitism and Zionism in the May and June 1905 issues of *The Central Review*. The article was the first introduction the Japanese received to the oppression of Jews in Russia, the Kishinev pogrom, and the Zionist movement.[10] Other prewar scholars who treated Jewish subjects early on were Chō Hisayoshi (1880–1971) and Sugawara Ken (1889–1976).

Scholars of European history who touched on Jewish themes in the postwar period included Murase Okio (1913–), who published widely on modern German history and Nazism; Hidemura Kinji (1912–), an authority on the conflict between Hellenism and Judaism in the ancient world; Handa Motoo (1915–77), an authority on early Chris-

---

[c] The works of Anne Frank, Victor Frankl, and Sartre were originally published in 1947; Cohen's book was published in 1953 and Russell's in 1954.

tianity; and Doi Masaoki (1924–), who wrote on the historical Jesus and on the Spartacus revolt.

With the foundation of the Japan Association for Jewish Studies (*Nihon Isuraeru-bunka kenkyūkai*) in 1960 by historians Kobayashi Masayuki, Sugita Rokuichi, and others, the study of Jewish history and civilization came into its own in Japan. The association took a highly critical attitude toward previous Japanese thinking about the Jews and stated its views unequivocally in its founding "Prospectus," which it issued in September 1960 and reprints in every issue of its journal, *Studies on Jewish Life and Culture.*[11]

> Publications on the Jews that have appeared [in Japan] in such profusion over the past forty years, including some very recent ones, have combined anti- and philosemitic attitudes in a bizarre melange. It is incumbent upon us to point out that these publications have been all but totally devoid of a basic knowledge of their subject and have been characterized instead by irrational argumentation, antihistoricism, and an aberrant politics based on a form of fanatical racism.

Also criticizing philosemitic expressions of sympathy for the state of Israel based on theories of common ancestry, the association's Prospectus continued, "We who seek to relate to the Jews and Israel on an entirely different basis [from these theorists] look forward to sharing the results of careful, objective research and to giving these scholarly findings a social expression as well." The association sought "to disassociate itself from [previous Jewish studies] and create an organization that will treat those debates and that [antisemitic] movement as the subject of scholarly examination, analysis, and criticism."

Taken together, these developments—the emergence of well-informed journalists and scholars from across the ideological spectrum, the translation and acceptance of Jewish literature, and the establishment of a serious scholarly organization for Jewish studies—constituted a substantial and permanent break with the past.

•

Two controversies illustrate the serious and responsible way many Japanese intellectuals related to the Holocaust and the survival of the Jewish people. The first was the Japanese debate over *The Deputy*, (*Das Stellvertreter*), the 1963 play by the German dramatist Rolf Hochhuth that sparked one of the most furious controversies in the history of world drama. The second was the debate over Israel's conduct of the Eichmann trial in 1961 and 1962.

Hochhuth's play *The Deputy* is a bitter indictment of the behavior of Pope Pius XII and the Roman Catholic Church during the Holocaust. The main protagonist is a young priest named Riccardo Fontana, who accuses the pope of criminal negligence because he is silent in the face of the genocide of the Jews. "A deputy of Christ who sees these things and nonetheless permits reasons of state to seal his lips— wastes even one day in thought, hesitates even for an hour to lift his anguished voice in one anathema to chill the blood of every last man on earth—that Pope is . . . a criminal."[12]

Fontana's accusations fall on deaf ears, however, and, powerless to change the policy of the Holy See, he ultimately dons the yellow star himself and departs for Auschwitz, there to stand with the Jews, the victims. This, he believes, is where Christians, and above all the pope, belong. "Since the Pope, although only a man, can actually represent God on earth, I . . . a poor priest . . . if need be . . . can also represent the Pope—*there* where the Pope ought to be standing today."[13]

Hochhuth's searing indictment precipitated a maelstrom of protest and counterprotest. So extensive was the debate that the theater scholar Eric Bentley collected representative examples of the criticism in a 250-page volume,[14] and at least two major studies of Vatican diplomacy appeared in the wake of the controversy.[15]

The international debate over *The Deputy* extended to Japan. Even before the Japanese translation appeared in 1964, critics discussed the play in numerous articles.[16] A public debate over the pope's wartime

•

responsibility ensued and gradually developed into a debate over Christianity's responsibility for the Holocaust.

The main combatants in the Japanese debate were Tatsuki Shin, who argued for the pope, and Takeyama Michio, who defended Hochhuth. Tatsuki Shin is the pen name of Ninomiya Nobuchika (1922–), an editor with the *Yomiuri* newspaper who was educated at the Jesuit Sophia University.[17] Takeyama Michio (1903–1984) was a former professor of German literature at Tokyo University, a translator of Nietzsche and Albert Schweitzer, and a well-known novelist.

Takeyama was one of the first Japanese to seriously consider the complex moral issues raised by the Holocaust. In 1948, he had explored Japanese war responsibility in *The Harp of Burma* (*Biruma no tategoto*), a moving antiwar novel about a Japanese soldier in Burma who abandons his national identity and becomes an anonymous Buddhist monk dedicated to praying for the repose of the dead. The novel was translated into English and made into a powerful film.[18] In his series of articles entitled "The Collapse of the Human Spirit: On the Nazi Mass Murder of the Jews" (*Ningen seishin no hōkai*), Takeyama continued his meditation on the war, addressing some of the most painful but unavoidable questions surrounding the Nazi genocide. Takeyama's articles had a far-reaching impact. Among other things, they introduced Alain Resnais's graphic 1955 documentary *Night and Fog* (*Nuit et Brouillard*), precipitating a widespread discussion of the film in Japan even before its belated released in 1961.[d]

Takeyama's central concern was how such heinous crimes could

---

[d] Produced in 1955, Resnais's film caused a sensation worldwide, but Japanese customs authorities repeatedly refused to allow it to enter Japan on the pretext that it was "too brutal." For this reason, it was not until November 1961 that the film had a brief public run. Even then, a total of fifty-seven seconds were cut from the film in six places. (*Asahi shimbun*, evening edition, October 19, 1961, and *Shūkan Asahi*, October 27, 1961.)

Ōshima Nagisa's 1960 film *Night and Fog in Japan* (*Nihon no yoru to kiri*) is widely assumed to have taken its title from Resnais's work. See, for example, David Desser, *Eros Plus Massacre: Introduction to the Japanese New Wave Cinema* (Bloomington: Indiana University Press, 1988), pp. 25–31. However, according to Yokobori Kōji, who served as assistant director of the film, the title actually derives from a novel by Matsumoto Seichō called *Nihon no kuroi kiri* (The Black Fog of Japan). Phone interview with Yokobori Kōji, December 13, 1992.

•

have been committed in Christian countries. He came to the conclusion that Auschwitz was a logical outgrowth of Western civilization, a by-product of its religion and history.[19]

In his debate with Tatsuki Shin, Takeyama traced the origins of the Final Solution to the Christian Scriptures. Given the fact that the Jews posed no military threat to the Nazis and that killing them deprived Germany of their labor, thus hampering the war effort, Takeyama reasoned that the Final Solution could not have been the product of rational calculation but must have been the child of theology. He concluded that the conflict between Judaism and Christianity enshrined in the New Testament and an integral part of the European psyche had erupted into historical reality during the Holocaust. Takeyama argued, in short, that the gas chambers derived from the Gospels.[20]

Writing in *Liberty* (*Jiyū*), the same magazine that carried Takeyama's articles, Tatsuki Shin responded with a defense of the pope. Tatsuki first accused Hochhuth of maliciously twisting the facts. He perceived in Hochhuth's play an insufficient familiarity with the psychological, political, and historical realities of the time, and he accused Hochhuth of both prejudice and a sense of inferiority toward the Catholic Church. Contrary to Hochhuth's assertions, he contended that the pope had in fact resisted Nazism in both word and deed and that there were no grounds for the accusation of nonfeasance. Tatsuki argued that papal power was inherently limited, that no one could have done more than Pope Pius had done, and that a confrontation with the Nazis would only have exacerbated the situation and endangered the lives of Catholics as well as Jews. Tatsuki finally protested that Hochhuth had singled out the Catholic Church for criticism but had ignored the overt collaboration of the Protestant churches.[21]

Takeyama Michio responded to this argument point by point in an article in which he compared the wartime role of the pope and the Japanese emperor, but in the end he threw in the towel, apparently concluding that rational arguments were futile. With more than a touch of irony, he wrote that if guilt was relative and depended simply upon self-perception, then indeed the pope was not guilty because he

•

did not consider himself to be so. "There is no doubt that Pius XII was a man of noble character," he wrote.

> In terms of courage, it is inconceivable that he was the inferior to the King of Denmark [who personally sheltered Jews]. He was not a man to bring shame on the Holy Spirit. That he did not fulfill the responsibilities that we of other faiths might think incumbent upon a man in his position of authority must have derived from his religious beliefs. In his frame of reference, inaction did not constitute a sin. In this sense, the Pope was not culpable.[22]

Takeyama's attitude toward the Jews also differed radically from Tatsuki's. Tatsuki acknowledged that certain passages in the New Testament provided the impetus for religious and social antisemitism throughout the medieval and early modern periods, but he argued that these passages represented "transitional antisemitism, meaningful only until the Jews recognize the Messiah." Tatsuki insisted that "the harsh language used with respect to the Jews in the Gospels is intended to rouse them from their state of delusion"; and he distinguished Christian anti-Judaism from Nazi antisemitism, arguing that Nazi antisemitism, which sought the annihilation of the Jews and not their salvation, "was animated by an entirely different philosophy." He thus rejected any suggestion of a link between the Christian Scriptures and the gas chambers.[23]

Takeyama Michio not only refused to accept Tatsuki's distinction between Christian anti-Judaism and antisemitism, but he eventually came to perceive in Christianity the intellectual roots of fascism and Communism. For him, all three of these "religions" were anathema and he concluded that Christianity was ultimately responsible for the grotesque excesses of the twentieth century. As he wrote in 1973 at the age of seventy, "Fascism, Communism, and the Bible—I would like to stay as far away from these interrelated systems as possible. This trinity has caused me much grief. Out of ignorance, I wasted much of what little time I had on this earth on two of the hoaxes [Christianity and Communism] European civilization has foisted on the world. Now the sun is setting and the true way remains out of reach."[24]

●

Takeyama's poignant conclusion, reached in his twilight years, was that the Holocaust had demonstrated the essential bankruptcy of Western civilization.[e]

The Japanese debate over *The Deputy* was as intricate and probing as debates in other countries. How much it contributed to Japanese understanding of the Jews remains an open question, however. There are no important Jewish characters in *The Deputy*, and while it presents the moral dilemma of Christians during the Holocaust, it does so *in the absence of Jews*.[f] Thus, while it undoubtedly deepened the

---

[e] The controversy did not end there. In 1970, five years after the debate between Takeyama Michio and Tatsuki Shin had ended, the Catholic novelist and future president of the Japan P.E.N. Club, Miura Shumon (1926–), took up Tatsuki's cudgels and criticized Hochhuth, saying that *The Deputy* had been written in the form of a play, but "its real intention was to denounce Pius XII as Hitler's accomplice, and so it should be treated, not as a work of literature, but as propaganda."

> We can sympathize with Hochhuth, who experienced Germany's defeat as a fifteen-year-old member of the Hitler Youth and who saw all the ideals he had been taught by the Nazis collapse. It is only regrettable that when he reached maturity and decided to get to the truth about that dark period, he sought to compensate for the destruction of the sacred dreams of his youth by taking it upon himself to drag what others hold sacred through the mud.

In contrast to Takeyama, who despaired of Christianity because of the Holocaust, Miura castigated the Japanese for being too willing to accept Hochhuth's perspective and reject the religious basis of European civilization. But when Miura reduced World War II to "the sin of all mankind" and asserted that he was "convinced that [the pope] must have been deeply pained and prayed" for the victims of the Holocaust, he committed the same error of overgeneralization as Takeyama, albeit in reverse. Where Takeyama held Christianity responsible for all the evils of twentieth-century Europe, including the Holocaust, Miura exculpated Christianity completely by reducing the whole question of papal responsibility to meaningless generalities and personal opinions.

See Miura Shumon, "Pio XII wa Nachi no dairinin ka?" [Was Pius XII the Deputy of the Nazis?] *Shokun*, September 1971, pp. 228–233.

[f] Robert Skloot writes,

> The murder of Father Fontana at the end of *The Deputy*, a Jew by disposition and desire, underscores the increasingly obvious diminution of the Jewish presence or of positive Jewish images in the plays of Holocaust experience as dramatized by German-language playwrights. . . . *The Deputy* would seem to extend further the diminishment of the individual, and especially the individual Jew, which is the progression [in German-language plays about the Holocaust] I am attempting to trace.
>
> [Robert Skloot, *The Darkness We Carry: The Drama of the Holocaust* (Madison, Wisc.: University of Wisconsin Press, 1988), pp. 101–2.]

•

Japanese appreciation of some of the profound moral dilemmas surrounding the Holocaust, the controversy over *The Deputy* probably
did little to enhance Japanese understanding of the *Jewish* experience
at the heart of the catastrophe.

In contrast to the controversy over *The Deputy*, the Japanese debate
over the Eichmann trial, while frequently critical of Israel, augmented
Japanese understanding of the Jewish Holocaust experience and
marked the apex of Japanese interest in and knowledge of the Jews.[g]

Obersturmbannführer Adolf Eichmann, the Nazi bureaucrat in
charge of administering the Final Solution, was captured by Israeli
secret service agents in a suburb of Buenos Aires on May 11, 1960. His
trial on fifteen counts of war crimes, crimes against the Jewish people,
and crimes against humanity began in Jerusalem on April 11, 1961.
He was found guilty and hanged on May 31, 1962.

The trial was one of the most widely reported news events of the
postwar period. Hannah Arendt, who covered the trial for *The New
Yorker*, for example, collected her dispatches in her probing and controversial book *Eichmann in Jerusalem: A Report on the Banality of
Evil.*[25]

Japanese journalists were also in Jerusalem in force, and the Japanese news media competed to inform their readers and viewers
about the Jews, Nazism, and Israel. Besides representatives of the
diplomatic corps and staff reporters from the major newspapers, distinguished independent writers like Muramatsu Takeshi (1929–),
Kaikō Takeshi (1930–1989), and Inukai Michiko (1921–) were also
dispatched to Jerusalem as special correspondents. Muramatsu, a conservative scholar of French literature who later served as dean of
Tsukuba University, went on to write extensively about the Middle

---

[g] This assessment is tempered somewhat by the results of a survey Miyazawa conducted
in 1962 during the Eichmann trial, when Japanese interest in the Jews was at its peak.
The survey of 250 high school and college students revealed that the knowledge of
young Japanese regarding the Jews and Israel was still extremely tenuous. Nearly a
quarter (24.4 percent) were unaware of the existence of a Jewish state; and of those who
were aware, almost 20 percent could not name it correctly. Only 30.8 percent could
identify Auschwitz; 98.8 percent were unfamiliar with Tel Aviv. Thus, despite the
attention given Jews and Israel in the press and the increasingly widespread availability
of reliable information on these subjects, there remained a considerable degree of
ignorance about Jewish issues in Japan.

●

East. Kaikō subsequently covered the Vietnam War and became Japan's premier war correspondent. Inukai, granddaughter of Prime Minister Inukai Tsuyoshi, who was assassinated by ultranationalists in 1932, pursued a distinguished career as a liberal journalist and humanitarian activist.

Japanese coverage of the Eichmann trial spanned the entire gamut of political opinion. On the issue of jurisdiction, for instance, conservatives agreed with defense counsel Robert Servatius's assertion that the tribunal was a kangaroo court with no right to try the defendant.[26] Left-wing journalists like Kaikō Takeshi, on the other hand, ridiculed Servatius's arguments as "little better than ridiculous."[27]

Between these poles, Muramatsu Takeshi staked out the middle ground. "It seems to me," he wrote, "that ideally speaking this matter should have been taken up by an international tribunal or, failing that, by East or West Germany." But he acknowledged that "outside of Israel no other country or international body has been willing to prosecute [Eichmann]. In view of the fact that no other country has dared to move against him, no one can complain if Israel, which has suffered and sacrificed so much, takes it upon itself to mete out justice." Muramatsu recognized that there may have been no preexisting law against genocide,

> but for one state to plot the extermination of an entire people and to actually carry out that plot has no precedent in history. Because there is no precedent, there is no law; and because there is no law, legal procedures have necessarily been primitive. For the victims and their survivors to arrest their persecutor and place him on trial may bear a surface resemblance to victor's justice, but the two instances are fundamentally different. In this sense, I can sympathize with the Israelis and believe that what they are doing is right.[28]

Inukai Michiko was more idealistic. She argued that "problems of this magnitude, which bear on the survival of the human race, are not problems that individual states or individual peoples should attempt to solve; rather, they should be treated by an organization representing all humanity, composed of representatives of each of the world's nations and peoples." Inukai insisted that Eichmann "should have been tried from the standpoint of humanity," by a supranational organization. In her view, while the United Nations might be weak and imperfect, it nonetheless constituted a supranational, supraethnic organization and was the only body where the influence of national vindictiveness and revenge could be obviated. Consequently, she argued that "Israel should have taken its verdict [to the U.N.] for final disposition."[29]

While Japanese commentators were divided over specific issues like these in the Eichmann trial, they nonetheless shared a sense of outrage at the defendant and a general comprehension of what Israel was trying to accomplish. Even those who were critical of the trial recognized its historical significance. Inukai, for example, believed that if the trial had been conducted as she suggested, it would have provided humanity with a way out of the vicious cycle of persecution and revenge that plagued it; and she believed that, by failing to set this example, the Jews and Israel had squandered an opportunity to show the world that they were indeed God's "Chosen People." Her view echoed Martin Buber, who had warned that executing Eichmann was "a mistake of historical dimensions."[30]

The high expectations of people like Inukai led to a sense of intense disappointment as the trial progressed. The liberal *Asahi shimbun* pleaded, for example, that the trial not be allowed to degenerate into an act of revenge but that it be invested with larger historical significance.[31] "We are not out to save Eichmann's life necessarily," it editorialized, "but will his execution not strengthen the impression that his life was taken in revenge and weaken the historical meaning of the trial? . . . If the point is to underscore the inhumanity of murder, then it is all the more important to forswear execution."[32] Israel's aims, the *Asahi* argued, would not be served by the death sentence but "had already been achieved by the trial itself." In its view, an execution would leave "the bad after-taste of a public lynching." "The vengeful 'tooth-for-a-tooth' [*sic*] attitude only invites the repetition of the vicious cycle of history," it wrote. "If the plaintiff is civilization, as is claimed, then its approach should at least be civilized. Then, at the very least, Israel might have been reevaluated as the dawning of a new age in human affairs."[33]

The *Asahi* "worried that in reality [the execution] will be seen as a primitive, sublegal device to exact 'an eye for an eye.' " If there were concerns about the adequacy of international law or about jurisdiction, "then [the Israelis] should have done more than the law required, not less."[34] It was not enough, in the *Asahi*'s view, to punish Eichmann as the perpetrator of heinous crimes. Rather, the paper urged that attention should have been focused on the all-encompassing mechanism of war that provided the foundation for Eichmann's actions and that was the basis for the real and present danger of nuclear conflagration.

A commentator named Inoue Makoto leveled the most severe criticism of the death sentence, concluding that it placed Israel on a moral par with the Nazis. "The most serious accusation one human being can level against another," he wrote, "is that his crime warrants the penalty of death." In the Eichmann case,

> Judges, none of whom felt his life was in the slightest danger, sat in judgment over a man for more than a year in 121 court sessions and forced another human being to confront the certain prospect of his own death. I can find no more words to defend the Israeli court, which insisted ostentatiously on the legitimacy of the death penalty, than I can for [Eichmann's crimes]. . . . The psychology that would tolerate this kangaroo court is part and parcel of the psychology that makes wars possible. It is the psychology that the taking of human life is justifiable under the right circumstances. In the extreme, it is this diabolical attitude that will lead mankind to destruction.[35]

Inoue argued that Israel should have sent Eichmann back to Argentina and should have enacted a law that would have utterly deprived him of his human rights in Israel henceforth and forever more. "The knowledge that there is a place in the world where one is without human rights would be the heaviest cross for someone like Eichmann to bear," he concluded.[36]

•

Kaikō Takeshi also wondered "if the death penalty was not just another form of terrorism masked as 'Justice.'" He deplored the fact that "in the final analysis, these Hebrews, who have repeated so often that they are the 'Chosen People,' showed no more wisdom than this"; that "they [had] acted like any other people." After some hesitation, Kaikō concluded, "[The Israelis] should have let Eichmann go. They absolutely should have let him live. They should have let him live and released him and allowed him to determine his own fate by his own hand. They should have branded his forehead with a swastika and let him go free."[37]

Muramatsu Takeshi took a more realistic view. While he did not comment directly on the execution, he did not regard "the obvious verdict" as a failure or a mistake. Muramatsu argued instead that the Nazis, who had massacred six million Jews, and Eichmann, who had implemented the Final Solution with efficient precision, should not be viewed as isolated madmen or otherwise exceptional people but as ordinary human beings like ourselves. He suggested that the trial presented an opportunity "to scrutinize the Eichmann in all of us."

> The black nihilism that lurks in the shadows of everything the Nazis did is related to the nihilism that underlies everyday life today, and that is the reason why Nazism was able to become as powerful as it did and why even philosophers like [Martin] Heidegger became enthralled by it. How capable, one wonders, is today's vague humanism of countervailing this kind of power? It seems unlikely that the Nazi political system will ever be resurrected. But the problem of the Nazis will remain. Their ideology and acts are unspeakably grotesque, but their very grotesqueness highlights the problems that confront the modern age. Unless we solve these problems, we will not be able to come to terms with our own war-related problems either.[38]

According to Muramatsu, more than the Hitlers and the Goebbelses, it is the Eichmanns who are unforgivable, for "six million people died at the hands of men who insisted that they were just following orders. In all of human history, there has never been such an outrage."[39]

•

The Eichmann trial provided the Japanese with the most sustained period of concentrated attention on the Jewish experience in Japanese history. The same newspapers that during the war had dutifully toed the antisemitic line, now ran stories like "The New Country, Israel" (*Asahi*); "Israel: A Country We Should Get to Know" (*Asahi Journal*); "Israel: Homeland of 'The Chosen People' " (*Mainichi*); and "From the Mediterranean to Japan" (*Yomiuri*).[40] Japan was developing a nuanced, true-to-life image of the Jews.

The Japanese public seldom heard from unabashed antisemites during the postwar period: they were too thoroughly identified with the discredited ultranationalist ideology of the war to be tolerated. That does not mean they disappeared completely, however. They and their ideas survived, assuming a new "philosemitic" guise.

There were, of course, exceptions to this general rule. Nishitani Misao, whose article "Beware the Jewish Plot!" appeared in March 1954, claimed, for example, that "Japan was defeated by the Jews," and, save for the emperor system, "everything in Japan today, including the constitution, politics, education, and the shape of society itself are the product of one thing and one thing only: the policies of the Jews." These policies, Nishitani argued, "have inflicted greater damage on the Japanese ethnic nation [*minzoku*] than all the deceptions of the Communist movement." All that could be done, he argued, was "to come to the aid of the victims of the war, to work for the return of our countrymen who remain in China and the Soviet Union, and to strive for the freedom of those convicted of war crimes." Nishitani asserted that in this way it would be possible "to draw once again on the well-spring of the Japanese spirit that has been buried" by the war.[41]

Much more common were ex–miliary officers like Inuzuka Koreshige, who, after a period of disgraced isolation, reemerged around 1950 miraculously transformed into "friends of the Jews."

The Japanese surrender of August 15, 1945, found Inuzuka in the

Philippines. He had been reassigned to sea duty and left Shanghai on March 7, 1942, possibly as the result of efforts by the Germans and bloodthirsty Japanese antisemites like Shiōden Nobutaka to remove an obstacle to their efforts to exterminate the Jews in Shanghai.[42] The fact that a ghetto was established after Inuzuka's departure lends credibility to this theory.

Inuzuka was arrested and charged with war crimes. In his own defense he produced a silver cigarette case that had been presented to him by the Union of Orthodox Rabbis of the United States in gratitude for his role in bringing the last one thousand Jewish refugees stranded in Kobe to Shanghai in 1941. The case was engraved with the inscription "In Gratitude and Appreciation for Your Service For The Jewish People."[43] The tactic worked, and Inuzuka was not prosecuted.

Emboldened by the Occupation's Reverse Course and the rehabilitation of wartime nationalists, Inuzuka led other former soldiers and political conservatives in establishing organizations to promote Japanese-Jewish friendship. These organizations included the Society for the Study of Japanese-Jewish Relations (*Nichiyu kankei kenkyūkai*), the Society for Japanese-Jewish Dialogue (*Nichiyu konwakai*), and the Japan-Israel Association (*Nihon-Isuraeru kyōkai*), which Inuzuka founded in 1952. These efforts were welcomed by Jews in Japan and elsewhere who were grateful for Inuzuka's protection in Shanghai and for his support of the newly founded state of Israel.

In the mid-1950s, Inuzuka was confronted with evidence that he had been a prolific antisemitic ideologue before and during the war. Michael Kogan, who had spent his youth in Harbin and returned to live in Japan after the war, had discovered incriminating Foreign Ministry documents in a secondhand bookstore in Tokyo that detailed Inuzuka's activities.[44] Kobayashi Masayuki, a professor of history at Waseda University, also argued forcefully that Inuzuka had always been an unscrupulous and opportunistic nationalist and never a friend of the Jews.[45] As a result, Inuzuka became persona non grata among some Jews and Japanese, but condemnation was far from universal, and he remained president of the Japan-Israel Association until his death in 1965. In 1982, through the efforts of former Tokyo rabbi

Marvin Tokayer and Hebrew University professor Ben-Ami Shillony,
Inuzuka's cigarette case was accepted into the collection of Holocaust
memorabilia at Yad Vashem, the Holocaust memorial in Jerusalem,
and Inuzuka's wartime record of ultranationalism was officially
obscured.[46h]

Inuzuka Koreshige is typical of the transformation and continuity
of wartime nationalism in the postwar period. His survival was made
possible by changing Occupation (and later American) policies, which
minimized the significance of the past ideological misdeeds of its
anti-Communist allies, and by Jews who wanted to recognize the
contribution of those Japanese who, for whatever reason, had helped
save Jewish lives during the Holocaust. Inuzuka thus embodies the
revisionist, amnesiac tendency that has distorted perceptions of Japanese history by ignoring obvious but inconvenient continuities—and
the complicity of Jews and others in perpetuating this tendency.

Mimura Saburō (1904–75) was the theoretician who rationalized
the philosemitic conversion of the long list of men like Inuzuka.
Mimura was a former Communist who had committed *tenkō* in the
1930s and who had been active in the Association for International
Political and Economic Studies during the war. His argument, in
sum, was that any interest taken in the Jews during the war was ipso
facto proof of philosemitism. With the exception of a few extremists
like Shiōden Nobutaka, all Japanese "antisemites" were actually closet
Zionists in Mimura's view. In *Japan and Israel: Enigmas of the World*
(1950) and *Japanese History Seen as the Reverse of the Jewish Problem*
(1953), Mimura systematically recast Japan's leading ethnic nationalists as philosemitic "friends of the Jews."[47i]

---

[h] The cigarette case was assigned Yad Vashem's collection number 2274.

[i] Mimura's list includes military officers like Koiso Kuniaki, Ishiwara Kanji, Hata
Shinji, Yamamoto Eisuke, Yasue Norihiro, Komatsu Junzō, Inuzuka Koreshige, Wa-
tanabe Wataru, Konishi Chihiko, Itagaki Seishirō, Ōkubo Kōichi, and Nishimura
Shigeru; academics like Saeki Yoshirō, Kotsuji Setsuzō, Nakagi Teiichi, Fujisawa
Chikao, Sakon Yoshisuke, Sakai Atsumichi; politicians like Ichijō Sanetaka, Komori
Yūsuke, Kangyū Tsuneo; lawyers like Uzawa Fusaaki, Tadai Shirōji, Nakasato
Yoshimi, Uchida Masami; religious leaders like Nakada Jūji, Kawamorita Eiji, Oyabe
Zen'ichirō, Tsubaki Shin'ichi, Ujitoko Teikan, Numa Yasuyo, Ishii Shikanosuke, Ueni-
shi Masumi; as well as others like Nakayama Tadanao, Teramura Sentarō, Uchida
Bunkichi, Tanaka Seiichi, Hidaka Miho, and Yamane Kikuko.

•

One of the beneficiaries of Mimura's revisionism was Masuda Masao (dates unknown), a founder of the Association for Political and Economic Studies and a vociferous antisemite. Contrary to overwhelming evidence, Mimura asserted that "Mr. Masuda was never an antisemite."

> No later than two or three years prior to the end of the war, [Masuda] had become a complete philosemite. Once he had become versed in the Takenouchi Document[j] and had come to believe in the divine revelation contained in inscriptions from the Age of the Gods (*jindai moji*), there was not so much as a speck of antisemitism in him. He was simply afraid to go against the tide of the domestic situation and was pushed along by the force of inertia. In retrospect he seems almost comical, for he was absolutely in awe of the Jews.

Mimura argued, moreover, that this "philosemitism" was the highest form of Japanese patriotism:

> The philosemitic movement, far from being subversive, was the highest expression of Japanese patriotism, for it was a movement that only

---

[j] *Takenouchi bunken*, also known as the *Takenouchi bunsho* or the *Isohara bunsho*, is an apocryphal document said to be in the possession of the self-proclaimed descendants of Takenouchi Sukune, a semihistorical figure from the third or fourth century C.E. The document is supposed to have been written in the mystical script of the Age of the Gods (*jindai moji*), which its proponents assert existed in Japan prior to the adoption of Chinese characters and which is supposed to have contained the elements of all human languages, including Hebrew, Greek, Egyptian hieroglyphics, Sumerian, the Roman alphabet, Sanskrit, and Chinese. According to these proponents, the Takenouchi Document demonstrates that Japan was the source of all human civilization, unifying within itself all the world's cultures in peace and harmony. Because of a series of primeval natural disasters, however, Japan's power to govern was weakened, and it was forced to relinquish its global hegemony. In the seventh century B.C.E., with the accession of the first emperor, Jimmu, Japan itself was reunited and all the world's great religious leaders, including Moses, the Buddha, Lao-tzu, Confucius, Christ, and Muhammad, are said to have come to Japan to study before returning to their own countries to preach the Way to their respective peoples. The Takenouchi Document continues to be cited by common ancestry theorists and other mystics even today. See, for example, Yamane Kiku, *Kiristo wa Nippon de shinde iru: ishoku kōshō—uchū kōkogaku no genten* [Christ Died in Japan: Sources of Cosmic Archaeology, An Unorthodox Study], (Tama shuppan, 1958).

●

those who believed deeply in the mission of the Japanese ethnic nation
could have undertaken.[48]

Here Mimura construes the common ancestry notion that a link with
the Jews substantiates Japan's claim to divine origins to mean that *any*
interest taken in the Jews was *necessarily* a form of Japanese patriotism
because it was a way of affirming Japan's "holy mission"; and any
affirmation of Japan's holy mission was necessarily a form of
"philosemitism" in Mimura's mind because it was predicated on an
acceptance of the Jews' claim to election as God's chosen people.

According to Mimura, this prewar "philosemitic" movement developed out of a true understanding of the mystical origins of the
world. Because it was based on the special relationship with God
shared by the Japanese and Jewish peoples, it was also "the shortest
route to world peace." In Mimura's words, prewar efforts to relate to
the Jews

> arose out of historical necessity, because of research on the ancient
> world and ethnic cultural history. Moreover, the establishment of
> heaven on earth and the construction of a world of eternal peace are the
> sacred mission assigned to both races. The movement is based on the
> sense of self-awareness and mission shared by the Japanese and the Jews
> that they are the races prepared by God since prehistoric times for this
> task. . . . In other words, the [philosemitic] movement developed out of
> the agreement of the Japanese classics and the Jewish scriptures (the
> Old Testament) regarding the special mission of these peoples and
> upon the common features of their history and culture. The shortest
> route to world peace and the realization of heaven on earth is therefore
> cooperation between the two races based on their common mission and
> self-awareness.[49]

Mimura, who spent the postwar years working as an archivist for
Ōmoto-kyō (literally, "Religion of the Great Fundamentals"), a
world-renewal cult founded in 1892, believed that only those who
shared this mystical conviction of the Jews' racial affinity and common racial mission with Japan could accomplish a true rapproche-

•

ment between the two peoples in the postwar period.[50] All others were opportunists who cynically sought to exploit the Jewish issue. They "profane the spirit of the movement, cause people to misunderstand it, and constitute a great obstacle to the future," he wrote.[51]

Mimura Saburō's intellectual alchemy transformed Japan's wartime antisemites into postwar philosemites. In similar fashion, prewar theological speculation involving the Jews also survived the debacle of defeat and took on a new, philosemitic guise.

A renewed interest in religion was one of the major responses to the sense of emptiness and loss brought on by defeat. By the early 1950s more than 700 new religious movements with more than 375,000 clergy had appeared in Japan.[52] Sects that took an interest in the Jews were a tiny minority, and they were by no means hostile, but their speculations did reproduce in the postwar period the same array of attitudes present in the prewar era.

We have already cited the views of Ariga Tetsutarō, who extended into the postwar period the rationalism of prewar liberal Christianity. Nakada Jūji's fundamentalism survived in the form of the Holy Ecclesia of Jesus (*Sei-Iesukai*), which was established by Ōtsuki Takeji (1906–) in January 1946. Ōtsuki was a follower of Nakada's who had joined the Holiness Church and worked as a missionary in Manchuria and Korea. On January 9, 1938, he had experienced "a baptism of the Holy Spirit," and that experience had provided the impetus for his own revival movement.

The Holy Ecclesia of Jesus continues Nakada's fundamentalist teachings about the special role of the Jews and Israel in the Second Coming. The Ecclesia is Zionistic, maintaining hostels in Kyoto and other cities around Japan called Beit Shalom (House of Peace), where any Israeli can stay free of charge for three days. It also supports a chorus called the *Shinonome* (Dawn) Choir, which performs Hebrew and Japanese songs at Israeli Independence Day celebrations and other events.[53]

An example of a syncretic neo-Christian sect established in the postwar period is the Makuya (Tabernacle) sect, founded in 1948 by a nationalistic Christian named Teshima Ikurō (1910–73). Teshima was originally a devotee of Uchimura Kanzō's Churchless Christianity, but he broke with the movement because of what he regarded as its excessive rationalism.

In the winter of 1948, Teshima had a traumatic dispute with the Occupation authorities in Kyushu, who had ordered the demolition of a local school. Teshima opposed the order, and, fearing reprisals, fled to a cave near Mt. Aso, an active volcano in central Kyushu, to avoid arrest. After a period of intense meditation and prayer, he experienced a revelation from God, which instructed him to befriend the Jews, God's chosen people. When Israel was founded a few weeks later, on May 14, Teshima interpreted it as a sign that the spiritual renewal he sought for Japan was linked to the destiny of the fledgling Jewish state, and he became an ardent Zionist.[54]

As the title of his book *The God of Uzumasa: Hachiman Worship and Nestorian Christianity* reveals, Teshima's nationalistic-Zionist theology is descended from Saeki Yoshirō's common ancestry theory. Teshima amplified Saeki's theory in a variety of ways, adding, for example, new ideas about Hachiman, the Shinto god of war.[55]

The Makuya is best understood, however, as a Japanese form of Pentecostalism.[56] The sect, initially known as the "Original Gospel Movement" (*Genshi fukuin undō*), emphasizes faith healing, glossolalia, and other ecstatic experiences characteristic of Pentecostalism. This has become the dominant dimension of Makuya theology for its fifty thousand to sixty thousand members.[57]

The Makuya sect is best known both in Japan and abroad for its fervent and unconditional Zionism. The sect is legendary in Israel, where its members live, learn Hebrew, participate in Zionist demonstrations, and pray devoutly at the Wailing Wall. In 1967, one Makuya member attracted attention in Japan by volunteering to serve in the Israeli Army during the Six Day War,[58] and Teshima contributed an ambulance to the Lod Airport near Tel Aviv after Japanese gunmen massacred tourists there in 1972. The Makuya sect has produced a Japanese-Hebrew dictionary and translations of Jewish liturgical works, including the Passover Haggadah.

Less well-known outside of Japan are the syncretic theologies of Matsumoto Fumi (dates unknown) and Okusho Kazuo (1921–). Like their predecessors Oyabe Zen'ichirō and Sakai Shōgun, they combine

•

emperor-centered Shinto nationalism, Christian theology, and *The Protocols of the Elders of Zion* to produce their theories.

Matsumoto established the Institute for the Study of World Religions (*Sekai shūkyō kenkyūjo*) at the Myōkōin neo-Buddhist temple at the foot of Mount Fuji. Her 1958 book, *Building the Altar at Mount Fuji* (*Fuji Kaidan'in konryū*) reprints Kubota Eikichi's 1938 translation of *The Protocols of the Elders of Zion*.[59] Kubota's fervent patriotism, Matsumoto wrote, reduced her to tears,[60] and she "decided to utilize the freedoms of speech and religion to include *The Protocols of the Elders of Zion* in [her] work in order to unshroud Japanese history, reveal the truth of the world's religious heritage, and thereby contribute, however modestly, to the cause of world peace."[61] "As a means to accomplish this great end," she wrote, "I will reveal the leaders of the Jews, who, though they are disguised as evildoers, once unmasked will be seen to be the truly righteous, the avatars of true holiness, the embodiment of the mission chosen by God."[62]

Addressing the Jews who established the state of Israel, Matsumoto continued, "As a representative of the Japanese people, I extend our gratitude to you and offer condolences for your years of suffering; I pray that the day will soon arrive when we will be able to join hands in prayer together before the Dharma [Buddhist Law], the Torah, and all the foundations of world religious history."[63]

Using apocryphal inscriptions written in the mystical script known as *jindai moji*[64] to substantiate her argument, Matsumoto "unshrouds history," revealing, among other things, that the mythical Japanese hero Yamato Takeru was descended from Moses and that his child "Christ hints in the Book of Revelation that he ascended the throne as the Emperor Ōjin." Matsumoto also interprets the esoteric meaning of the Lotus Sutra and the secret teachings of Nichiren, but her exegesis is utterly hermetic.

In similar fashion, Okusho Kazuo constructs a comprehensive history of the world based on the apocryphal Takenouchi Document, which he claims to be far older than either the official eighth-century histories of Japan, the *Kojiki* and *Nihon shoki*, or a number of other pre- and postwar ultranationalist sources.[65]

According to Okusho's soteriology, "The Savior of Mankind who will appear in this decadent modern age [*mappō gendai*] will appear on earth with an incomparably more important historical mission than particularistic ethnic and racial saviors of the past like Sakyamuni, Christ, and Mohammed." Like Nakada Jūji, he extrapolates the conclusion that this universal savior will emerge from Japan, "the Land of the Rising Sun, the leading nation of the world [*tokoyokuni no omoya*]," from references to "a small country in the east" in the Buddhist and Christian scriptures. Writing in 1972, Okusho sought to demonstrate not simply that the messiah would appear in Japan but that he would appear in the person of the Japanese emperor.[66]

Okusho develops a highly imaginative, alternative history of Japan according to which Jimmu, the mythical first emperor, who tradition holds ascended the throne in 660 B.C.E., "was actually the 1,169th in the Imperial Lineage." Okusho asserts that Japanese history should therefore be backdated by at least ten thousand years to give Japan its proper place as "the main house and parental nation (Holy Nation) antedating all other nations of the world."[67]

Following the Takenouchi Document, Okusho contends that the Japanese emperor originally ruled the entire world but that political rebellions and natural disasters forced him to relinquish control temporarily. That the emperor was predestined to regain his original global hegemony and reunify the world was foretold in countless sources, Okusho asserts.[68]

But what of the relationship between the Japanese and the Jews? According to Okusho, Moses visited Japan after being appointed "King of the Nations" by the Japanese emperor. Emperor Sujin, who reigned ten generations after Jimmu, dispatched the Three Wise Men to visit the Christ child, and Christ himself visited Japan, "Divine Nation, homeland of his ancestors and his soul," after his crucifixion.[69]

As his predecessors did, Okusho identifies Japan with the Jews because of a shared sense of national mission he imputes to both. He also uses yin-yang theory to demonstrate the complementarity of Japanese and Jewish history, where, as Sakai Shōgun also asserted, the Jews were in the ascendant when Japan was in decline, and vice versa.[70]

●

Thus, in Okusho's view, while both the Japanese and the Jews "are descended from the gods, the Japanese are more precious to Jehovah, who is in fact Kunitokotachi-Ōkami, the founder of Japan, and therefore it is preordained that the savior of the world shall come from Japan. . . . Christ's appearance out of the ranks of the Jews was merely a rehearsal for the appearance of the real messiah from Japan."[71] Giving his argument a racial twist characteristic of common ancestry theories across cultures, Okusho adds, "It is significant that Christ, who appeared out of the ranks of the Jews as the savior for the white people, will emerge from the Japanese Imperial Family when he reappears as the savior of all mankind. . . . Therein lies Heavenly Providence, the Divine Will to Cosmic Unity."[72] On that very day, "the Divine Nation Japan will manifest its essential nature as the Home of All Humanity, the Bulwark of the Nations, and will see Divine Government restored to the world . . . when humanity will be saved and the construction of heaven on earth will be accomplished."[73]

According to Okusho, the atomic bombing of Hiroshima and Nagasaki was intended as a baptism of fire, an expiation of past sins, leading Japan to abandon war and become a nation of culture, a light unto the world. He relates the dropping of the bomb to the opening of the Heavenly Cave in Japanese mythology, when the Sun Goddess emerged from concealment and shed her light upon the world,[74] and he anticipates the imminent "unification of the world under the power of the Emperor," which he predicts "will certainly take place within a few decades, in the twenty-first century."[75] Okusho's theories thus reiterate in the 1970s the view expressed earlier by Masuda Masao that World War II corresponded to "the opening of the Heavenly Cave, for out of the unification of the world under the Emperor will come a world truly illuminated by the light of God."[76]

A final example of a postwar syncretic sect is the Dragon Princess cult founded by Fujita Himiko, who received a divine revelation from the Princess of the Dragon Palace (Ryūgū Otohime) on October 7, 1973, during a visit to the traditional site of the Heavenly Cave in Kumamoto prefecture.[77] In contrast to other syncretic sects, Fujita's theology denies the authority of Japan's imperial family and argues that the Dragon Princess, a Shinto divinity who appears in the legend of

•

Urashima Tarō, a sort of Rip van Winkle character, is the true savior of humankind. Asserting that "Man is human, but woman is divine," the sect advocates female supremacy in the world, identifies the Sun Goddess's brother Susa-no-O with Jehovah, and venerates Jesus Christ.

Fujita's sect also accepts common ancestry theory and is highly nationalistic. She believes in the divine election of the Jews and teaches that the Japanese are descended from the Ten Lost Tribes. Sharing the Jews' election by God, Japan, she believes, is a holy nation and the source of all culture. Contrary to all historical evidence, she asserts that Chinese characters (*kanji*) developed from the Japanese *kana* syllabaries. Japan is thus the alpha and omega of culture and the only logical source for messianic salvation, which will come through the Dragon Princess.

Fujita interprets current events through the prism of her theology. In 1982, after Israel's invasion of Lebanon and shortly before she visited the Jewish state, Fujita updated classical Shinto beliefs to interpret events in the Middle East. The Jews, she argued, were "angry spirits" who haunted the world, and she urged that they be propitiated so that the world could be saved:

> The massacre of refugees in Beirut is a tragedy. Such a tragedy should never occur again, it should be pulled out by its roots. But what are its roots? The angry spirit of Israel has been haunting the world for the last four thousand years. Only when this angry spirit is pacified can mankind be saved.

The survival and metamorphosis of wartime antisemites like Inuzuka Koreshige into philosemites and the transformation of theological ideas to accommodate the realities of defeat, the Holocaust, and the existence of the state of Israel attest to both the dynamism and creativity of Japanese culture and to the persistence of prewar personalities and ideas in the postwar period.

•

The transformation of personalities and ideas that characterized the postwar period created an undercurrent of moral and intellectual ambiguity that intensified as the postwar period wore on. This ambiguity affected virtually every aspect of postwar Japanese intellectual life and acted as an insidious and powerful brake on an honest confrontation with the legacy of war.

Aside from Occupation support, the most important factor making the conservative transformation possible was the unwillingness or inability of the Japanese people at large to accept the basic liberal premise that Japanese and German "fascism" could be equated.[k] The Japanese for the most part refused to see themselves and their wartime record as even remotely comparable to that of Germany. Instead, they emphasized the differences between the two countries and their wartime regimes. The emperor, it was frequently pointed out, was not an omnipotent *Führer* like Hitler; the Japanese did not persecute the Jews as the Germans did; and Japan was the victim of history's first nuclear attack.

One example of this attitude appeared in Asahiro Masatoshi's afterword to the Japanese edition of Wolfgang Scheffler's *The Persecution of the Jews in the Third Reich, 1933–1945*.[78] Asahiro used the horror of the death camps to minimize Japanese wartime misdeeds. The Japanese, he argued, would have been incapable of such cruelty, which they found incomprehensibly alien. He admitted that the Japanese might be capable, in principle and at some point in the indefinite future, of committing atrocities, but somehow to his mind the horrors that accompanied Japan's aggressive fifteen-year war in Asia did not constitute "barbaric acts." To Asahiro's way of thinking, German atrocities against the Jews made whatever Japan did during the war pale by comparison, and on this basis he argued that the Japanese were "exceptionally human."

---

[k]Whether or not the term "fascism" is appropriate to describe Japanese ultranationalism has been the subject of scholarly debate. See, for example, Miles Fletcher, "Intellectuals and Fascism in Early Shōwa Japan" and the rebuttal by Peter Duus and Daniel I. Okimoto, "Fascism and the History of Pre-War Japan: The Failure of a Concept," in *Journal of Asian Studies* 39, no. 1 (November 1979), 39–76.

Even at the height of Japanese imperialism, even as they diligently mouthed empty theories about the superiority of the Yamato race, the Japanese people were unable to suppress their interest in foreigners [*ihōjin*] and their desire to approach them as human beings.

As we can see, therefore, we Japanese are exceptionally human by nature, and it is surely a cause for celebration that our first reaction to the loss of humanity represented by the phenomenon of antisemitism in Nazi Germany has been to find it incomprehensibly alien. To have caused a senseless war and in the end to have met with ignominious defeat is the common fate of Germany and Japan, but we are fortunate in not having had our good name sullied by the crime of genocide.

Unlike the Nazis, it is hard to imagine that because of bigotry we Japanese would put modern science and technology in the service of an inhuman goal like the eradication of a particular people. At the same time, however, past experience has shown that the Japanese way of thinking has a tendency to become fixated on particular ideas. It is at such moments that crimes against humanity are liable to occur. Therefore, it is impossible to say with certainty that in the distant future, in a particular situation, the Japanese might not come to harbor feelings of resentment and hatred against another people that would lead them to perpetrate barbaric acts.[79]

If the Japanese did not perpetrate Nazi-like crimes during the war, it follows in this reading of events that they must have been victims of the war. One of the earliest examples of this reformulation appeared in Dazai Osamu's enduring 1947 novel, *The Setting Sun* (*Shayō*). In the novel, the character Naoji muses,

> I wonder if we are to blame, after all. Is it our fault that we were born aristocrats? Merely because we were born in such a family, we are condemned to spend our whole lives in humiliation, apologies, and abasement, like so many Jews.[80,1]

---

[1] Dazai was angered during the war when a rumor was circulated by Haga Mayumi, a member of the Japan Romantic School, with which Dazai was also affiliated, that Dazai was writing a novel titled *Sanetomo the Jew* (*Yudayajin Sanetomo*), sacrilegiously likening the great thirteenth-century poet to the miserly Jews. Dazai had a reputation

The identification with the Jews-as-victims in this passage, combined with the equivocation of wartime responsibility, foreshadowed the way the image of the Jews would most frequently be used in postwar Japanese culture. Naoji's suggestion that perhaps the Japanese were not really responsible for the war, that they were actually its victims, the casualties of birth and circumstance, debased and degraded like so many Jews, is typical of this revisionist view, which came to be enshrined in Japanese school texts and other official renditions of the war.

The epitome of the innocent victim for the Japanese was Anne Frank, and in the postwar period, she joined Shylock as a defining stereotype of the Jews.[m] As in Shylock's case, however, Anne's image reflected the Japanese imagination at this time far more than it reflected the Jewish experience.

The story of Anne Frank is extremely well known in Japan, where her famous *Diary* was originally published in December 1952.[n] It topped the Japanese best-seller list in 1953, and it has since sold more than four million copies, a total exceeded only by sales in the

---

as a nonconformist and was justifiably fearful that, if believed, this rumor could seriously impair his ability to publish. Dazai was actually writing a novel titled *Sanetomo, Minister of the Right* (*Udaijin Sanetomo*), which was published in September 1943. Haga eventually apologized for his mistake. See Tsurumi Shunsuke, *Sengo o ikiru imi* [The Meaning of Living in the Postwar Period] (Chikuma shobō, 1981), pp. 85–86.

[m] In 1962, 64.4 percent of high school and college students questioned could identify this young victim of the Nazis, and in a survey of 88 high school students in 1972, 96.5 percent could identify her correctly. By contrast, the 86.8 percent of respondents who had correctly identified Adolf Eichmann in 1962 had dwindled to 10.2 percent ten years later. See Miyazawa Masanori, *Yudayajin ronkō*, rev. ed. (Shinsensha, 1982), p. 207.

[n] Born in Frankfurt in 1929 of parents whose families had lived there since the seventeenth century, Anne Frank fled to Holland with her family in 1934 to avoid Nazi persecution. When the war broke out and the Germans invaded the Netherlands, the Franks were forced into hiding in an attic over the family business in Amsterdam. Their life in hiding lasted twenty-five months, until they were discovered in August 1944 and sent to Auschwitz. Scholars surmise that Anne died of typhus in Bergen-Belsen during February–March 1945. Only Anne's father, Otto Frank, survived the war, and it was through his efforts that her diary was published in Holland in 1947.

See Ernst Schnabel, *Anne Frank: A Portrait in Courage*, tr. Richard and Clara Winston (New York: Harcourt, Brace, 1958); and David Barnouw and Gerrold van der Stroom, *The Diary of Anne Frank: The Critical Edition*, tr. Arnold J. Pomerans and B. M. Mooyaart-Doubleday (New York: Doubleday, 1989).

●

United States.° By contrast, the German edition of the *Diary* sold fewer than 2.5 million copies in the same period.[81]

Anne Frank and her *Diary* have become an integral, indeed a representative part of postwar Japanese culture. Reading the *Diary* is part of an adolescent Japanese girl's rite of passage into adulthood. So closely has Anne Frank been identified with puberty in Japan that in 1961, a manufacturer calling itself Anne Co., Ltd. introduced the first sanitary napkin proportioned for Japanese women and called it "Anne's Day" (*Anne no hi*), from a reference Anne makes in her *Diary* to her first three menstrual periods.ᴾ Although it has fallen into disuse, "Anne's Day" was for many years a common euphemism for menstruation in Japan.[82]

The popularity of Anne Frank's *Diary* in Japan has not necessarily translated into an understanding of the Jewish experience, however. It has, rather, helped the Japanese reconceive themselves as victims of the war. It has contributed to the tendency to generalize the war experience and avoid coming to terms with the specific problems of wartime responsibility and guilt.

The numerous compositions written about the *Diary* by Japanese teenagers for popular essay contests exemplify this trend. Since its inception in 1955, for example, the essay contest for young readers sponsored by the Japanese Library Council has perennially counted among its winning entries essays on the *Diary*. Similarly, the essay contest sponsored in 1964 by Anne's Japanese publisher to commemorate the hundredth printing of the *Diary* was inundated with more than seven thousand entries, despite the fact that eligibility was limited to teenage girls.[83]

The most striking characteristic of these essays is their lack of

---

° Anne Frank's *Diary of a Young Girl* was originally translated by Kaitō Kōzō and published by Bungei shunjū in 1952 as *Hikari honoka ni: Anne no nikki* [A Light Ever so Fragile: Anne's Diary]. A new translation by Fukamachi Mariko titled simply *Anne no nikki* [Anne's Diary] was reissued by the same publisher in 1986. Kaitō's 1952 translation sold a total of three million copies; Fukamachi's translation (which was published on November 20, 1986) had sold 255,000 copies during the first year. (Inoue Hisashi, "Besuto-seraa sengoshi: Anne Furanku, *Hikari honoka ni*" [A History of Postwar [Japan] Through Its Best-Selling Books], *Bungei shunjū*, February 1988, p. 372.

ᴾ Anne's reference to menstruation appears in her entry for January 5, 1944.

•

originality. Length limitations and other contest requirements help to explain some of the uniformity, but most of the essays, ostensibly written about Anne Frank's experience, are actually faithful reproductions of Japan's postwar ideology, which holds that "war" is evil but the causes of "war" are imponderable. The essays thus dutifully decry the evils of war and Nazi cruelty, express sympathy and admiration for Anne's courage, and, on occasion, refer to contemporary problems of prejudice and discrimination in other contexts—blacks in America or the traditional pariah caste (*hisabetsu burakumin*) in Japan. But conspicuous by their absence are any discussions of Anne's Jewishness or the reasons why she was killed.[84]

Obviously, Anne Frank's death was not unrelated to war. Echoing Eleanor Roosevelt, who in her introduction to the American edition of the *Diary* called it "one of the wisest and most moving commentaries on war and its impact on human beings that I have ever read,"[85] Kaitō Kōzō, the *Diary*'s first Japanese translator, expressed the hope that it would teach the Japanese to hate war. It was not unreasonable, therefore, for readers to conclude that war in a generic sense was to blame for Anne's death. It was precisely this therapeutic ideology of generic war, devoid of political or historical content, that the *Diary* has therefore been understood to convey.

Writing in the *Asahi Journal* in 1966, Inui Tomiko did introduce a rare example of a young essayist who took an interest in Jewish issues as a result of her encounter with the *Diary*. "It seems to me," the high school sophomore from Nagano prefecture wrote, "that war is not sufficient to explain the persecution and annihilation of more than six million Jews for no reason other than that they were Jews; there must have been something more." And Inui goes on to wonder if it is really enough for the Japanese, who were allied with the Nazis, to simply hope fervently that such tragedies not be repeated. She asks whether there might not be something more substantial required to come to terms with Japan's war responsibility, for in generic war, no one is responsible. Inui points out that Anne Frank's popularity in Japan is due to the function she serves to help the Japanese decry the evils of war without delving too deeply into the political or historical specifics.[86]

●

Inui's probing candor is rare, however; so rare, in fact, that when Barbara Rogasky's illustrated history of the Holocaust, *Smoke and Ashes*, appeared in Japanese in 1992, the translator titled it *Why Was Anne Frank Killed?* as a corrective to the obfuscation of history that Anne Frank had come to represent.[q]

This use of Anne Frank to obscure the historical realities of war is far from unique to Japan. The Dutch, for example, use her to bolster their reputation for tolerance and to draw attention away from the fact that only 25 percent of Dutch Jews survived the Holocaust, the

---

[q] In her afterword, the translator, Fujimoto Kazuko, wrote,

Why . . . have I changed the Japanese title from the original *Smoke and Ashes* to *Why Was Anne Frank Killed?* I have to explain.

The diary that the young Jewish girl Anne Frank wrote in her Amsterdam hideaway has been widely read in Japan. But why, exactly, did she have to go into hiding? I have long felt that young readers did not really understand the historical circumstances of Anne's story. . . . Until now, the emphasis has almost always been placed on certain aspects of the story: how a sensitive and insightful adolescent girl fought valiantly against despair in the extreme situation of her hiding place and ended her brief life without losing hope or her faith in humanity. That interpretation is correct as far as it goes, and those are certainly important aspects [of Anne's story]. But what about the reason why Anne was forced to lead this kind of life, the historical background of the story? Most explanations have contented themselves with explaining Anne's tragedy with vague references to "the evils of war." . . .

Before Germany's formal declaration of war, the Jews were already being deprived of their human and civil rights, and the flight of the Frank family had already begun. Even without the war, the Nazis would probably have murdered Anne. The German invasion and occupation of the other European countries made it easier for them to kill the Jews in those countries, but the plan to exterminate the Jews was by no means a by-product of the war. Even when the signs of Germany's defeat were unmistakable and the Germans were facing serious shortages of labor and supplies, the Nazis, far from scaling back their efforts to implement their plan to eradicate the Jews, actually increased their efforts to do so.

The reason I have changed the title of this book from the original *Smoke and Ashes* to *Why Was Anne Frank Killed?*, therefore, is to place Anne's life and death back in its historical context.

[Translator's Afterword to Barbara Rogasky, *Anne Furanku wa naze korosareta ka: Yudayajin gyakusatsu no kiroku*, tr. Fujimoto Kazuko (Iwanami shoten, 1992), pp. 262–63. This is a translation of Barbara Rogasky, *Smoke and Ashes: The Story of the Holocaust* (New York: Holiday House, 1988).]

•

highest "kill rate" in Western Europe, exceeded only by Poland in the East.[87]

The Germans also read Anne Frank as the Japanese do. In Germany, young readers identify with Anne as "the prototype of all youth—helpless, imprisoned, at the mercy of elders, defiant of the outside world and terrified within," but they overlook the historical circumstances and political background that caused her death.[88] Japanese and Germans share the tendency to affirm the tragedy of war while denying historical responsibility for it. Both stress the famous entry of July 15, 1944, where Anne declares that "in spite of everything I still believe that people are really good at heart,"[89] and they transform her into a symbol of universal forgiveness and forgetfulness. In both Germany and Japan, Anne facilitates historical amnesia and self-expiation.[90]

The fact that Anne Frank has lost her Jewish identity and become the generic victim of generic war is not simply the result of the obtuseness of readers from the former Axis countries, however. From the outset, Otto Frank was anxious that the universality of his daughter's story not be compromised by her Jewishness, and he actively opposed emphasizing her Jewish identity. "Do not make a Jewish play of it," he wrote Meyer Levin, who was originally slated to write the dramatic adaptation of the *Diary*[91]; and when it was subsequently adapted for the stage by the husband-and-wife team of Albert Hackett and Frances Goodrich, Anne's Jewish identity was successfully obscured: " 'The Diary of Anne Frank' is not in any important sense a Jewish play," wrote the reviewer for the New York *Daily News*. "Anne Frank is a Little Orphan Annie brought into vibrant life."[92] In effect, the Hacketts' play, which was performed nationwide in Japan by the Mingei troupe from September 1956 to May 1957,[93] all but deprived Anne of her Jewish identity and depicted her "as a general symbol of martyred innocence, who stood for but also transcended the lot of suffering humanity."[94] It glossed over the fact that Anne had been killed, along with one million other children, for no other reason than that she was Jewish.[95]

This universalist construction of the *Diary*, which is especially noticeable in the stage and film adaptations, was also the product of the social and political milieu that prevailed in the United States in the 1950s, when the "melting pot" was in vogue and expressions of ethnic particularism were discouraged. During these years, insisting on one's ethnicity (not just Jewish ethnicity) was frowned upon, and being "different" was a deviation from the approved social and political norms.[96]

In sum, then, Anne Frank's *Diary* became a canonical text in Japan in large measure because it enabled the Japanese to relate to the Holocaust and World War II without having to consider hard historical realities. It enabled them to feel good about the war, to identify with a nonthreatening, forgiving victim of a conflict they had reformulated as a sort of natural disaster, and to get on with the task of reconstruction. This universalization and de-Judaization of Anne Frank is not unique to Japan but is observable elsewhere, particularly in Germany, and was legitimated by Anne's father and by the special ethos of American culture reflected in the stage and film adaptations of the *Diary*.

This is not to say that Japanese affection for Anne Frank and her *Diary* is insincere or meaningless. On the contrary, because it is so widely read in Japan, Anne Frank's *Diary of a Young Girl* remains an important source of knowledge and insight into the Jewish experience for the Japanese. Anne had a strong and remarkably mature sense of herself as a Jew and as a participant in Jewish history.[r] Through her,

---

[r]Anne articulated this sense of herself as a Jew in her diary entry of April 11, 1944, for example:

We have been pointedly reminded that we are in hiding, that we are Jews in chains, chained to one spot, without any rights, but with a thousand duties. We Jews mustn't show our feelings, must be brave and strong, must accept all inconveniences and not grumble. . . .

What has inflicted this upon us? Who has made us Jews different from all other people? Who has allowed us to suffer so terribly up till now? It is God that has made us as we are, but it will be God, too, who will raise us up again. If we bear all this suffering and if there are still Jews left, when it is over, then Jews, instead of being doomed, will be held up as an example. Who knows, it might even be our religion from which the world and all peoples learn good, and for that reason and that reason only do we have to suffer now. We can never become just Netherlanders, or just English, or representatives of any country for that matter, we will always remain Jews, but we want to, too.

•

Japanese readers come into contact, at least potentially, with an authentic Jewish life.

The identification of the atomic bombing of Hiroshima and Nagasaki with the Holocaust is another example of Japanese attempts to link their wartime experience to the victimization of the Jews.

The idea that a significant relationship exists between Hiroshima and the Holocaust has become a fixture of international intellectual life. It has been accepted and elaborated by both Jewish and Japanese intellectuals. Nelly Sachs, the Holocaust survivor and Nobel laureate, linked the two experiences in a poem entitled "Landscape of Screams."[s] Sachs's linkage of Hiroshima and the Maidanek death camp is particularly significant because she was a poet profoundly concerned with *Jewish* suffering.[97] With her poem, she conferred on Hiroshima a moral stature she reserves elsewhere for the Jewish people alone, and her credentials as a great and self-conscious Jewish poet give her recognition of a relationship between the Holocaust and Hiroshima a special authority.

The Italian-Jewish chemist, author, and Auschwitz survivor Primo Levi also linked Hiroshima and the Holocaust. In his 1978 poem "The Girl-Child of Pompei," Levi treats a victim of Pompeii, Anne Frank, and "the Hiroshima schoolgirl/A shadow printed on a wall by the light of a thousand suns,/Victim sacrificed on the altar of fear" as

---

[Anne Frank, *The Diary of a Young Girl*, pp. 186–87. See also, Rosenfeld, "Popularization and Memory," p. 257.]

[s] Sachs' poem reads in part,
    Above Moria, the falling off cliffs to God,
        there hovers the flag of the sacrificial knife
        Abraham's scream for the son of his heart,
        at the great ear of the Bible it lies preserved. . . .
    Job's scream to the four winds
        and the scream concealed in Mount Olive
        like a crystal-bound insect overwhelmed by impotence.
    O knife of evening red, flung into the throats
        where trees of a sleep rear blood-licking from the ground,
        where time is shed
        from the skeletons of Hiroshima and Maidanek. . . .

    [Nelly Sachs, *O the Chimneys*, trans. Michael Hamburg et al. (New York: Farrar, Straus and Giroux, 1967), pp. 127, 129.]

casualties of a single lethal continuum; and in the final lines he implores the "Powerful of the earth, masters of new poisons,/Sad secret guardians of final thunder" to refrain from resorting to nuclear war.[98]

Another Nobel laureate, Elie Wiesel, has also linked the threat of nuclear war to the Holocaust, suggesting that with the proliferation of nuclear weapons all humanity has become Jewish. Like Jews during the Nazi terror, in Wiesel's vision, every man, woman, and child on earth has become subject to the imminent threat of utterly arbitrary, meaningless death.[99]

The Japanese poet Kurihara Sadako (1913–), a survivor of Hiroshima, has also written poems and essays linking the atomic bomb experience to the Holocaust. In a recent verse, "Hiroshima, Auschwitz: We Must Not Forget," Kurihara writes,

What is left from Auschwitz—
mounds of striped inmate uniforms,
    of children's small shoes,
a mound of girls' red ribbons,
eating bowls that served also as chamber pots,
soap made from human blubber,
cloth woven from human hair.

What is left from Auschwitz—
turn all the world's blue skies and seas into ink
and it still wouldn't be enough to express
    the sadness, the anger,
the moans of those burned to death in the ovens.

What is left from Hiroshima and Nagasaki—
a person's form burned onto stone,
black rain streaking a wall,
radioactivity inside bodies,
microcephalic babies irradiated in the womb,
voices of the dead ringing from the Heavens,
voices of the dead ringing
    from the bowels of the earth.

•

Hiroshima, Auschwitz: we must not forget.
Nagasaki, Auschwitz: we must not forget.
Even if the first time was a mistake,
the second time will be malice aforethought.
The vow we made to the dead: we must not forget.[100]

Jewish efforts to memorialize the Holocaust and the relationship Jews have striven to maintain with this and other catastrophic experiences in their history have served some Japanese survivor writers as a model of their desired relationship to their experience. In her 1963 story "The Ritual" (*Gishiki*), the *hibakusha* (survivor) writer Takenishi Hiroko (1929–) identifies her efforts to immortalize her Hiroshima experience with Jewish memorial practices:

Like the People of Israel, longing for freedom on the festival of Passover, awake to their history and reading its dark record year after year—"Our fathers were slaves in Egypt!"—I want to live without ever laying that day [of the bombing] to rest. As they perform that ritual, they are doubtless thinking: Anyone who can casually bury his own history will not be qualified to become the hero of the history to come.[101]

In identifying her enterprise with the Jews' memorialization of their bondage in Egypt, Takenishi was groping toward a Japanese equivalent of the rich tradition of Jewish literary responses to catastrophe known as *h̩urban* literature. She wanted to use Jewish memory and Jewish practices, she wrote, as a paradigm for her own desired relationship to her atomic bomb experience.[t]

In the graphic arts, Maruki Iri and Toshi have also connected the Holocaust to Hiroshima. The Marukis, husband and wife, devoted the entire postwar period to painting monumental murals of the aftermath of the Hiroshima and Nagasaki bombings.[102] They were

---

[t] Alan Mintz has explained how the Hebrew literature of the Holocaust has come to reflect and been integrated into the tradition of the Jewish literature of memorialization from the Book of Lamentations forward in his *H̩urban: Response to Catastrophe in Hebrew Literature* (New York: Columbia University Press, 1984).

not in Hiroshima when the bomb was dropped but arrived just days afterward and spent a month working with the survivors. Iri's father, uncle, and two nieces were killed in the blast.

The Marukis did not limit their work to Hiroshima and Nagasaki but eventually moved beyond these events to contemplate other incidences of human cruelty. In 1975 they completed a large (4 × 8 meter), monochromatic mural of *The Rape of Nanking*; and in 1977, they completed their largest work, a gargantuan black-and-white painting measuring 3.4 × 16 meters titled *Auschwitz*.

Auschwitz is a sincere attempt to visualize the Holocaust. But while it is a strong protest against man's inhumanity to man, it does not have the power of the Marukis' other paintings. Lacking the cultural understanding that animates their Japanese work, the *Auschwitz* mural merely reproduces on a grand scale anonymous mass death without cultural identity. Thus, while the mural constitutes a significant attempt to visualize Auschwitz, it does not escape the problem of exculturation and de-Judaization that has plagued other Japanese conceptions of the Holocaust.[u]

In the early 1980s, Inoue Fumikatsu (1945–), a Japanese architect who had spent many years living and working in Israel, also began planning to build a memorial to the victims of Hiroshima and Auschwitz. The memorial was to be built in Kurose, a town of fifteen thousand that lies twelve miles east of Hiroshima and is the sister-city of Oświęcim, Poland, the site of Auschwitz. It was conceived by Inoue, an architect who had also helped design buildings

---

[u] John Dower assesses the mural somewhat differently as follows:

Executed in somber tones of grey, brown, and green, "Auschwitz" virtually abandoned scale and perspective. The contrast to "The Rape of Nanking" was startling, for that prior portrayal of atrocity had been almost photographic in its blunt realism. Here, by contrast, large and minuscule figures were tumbled together, and although the eye was inexorably drawn from right to left, where unseen death chambers waited, innumerable details compelled scrutiny along the way.... "Auschwitz" ... introduced a freedom of scale and form which carried over to many of their subsequent collaborative works.

[John W. Dower, "War, Peace, and Beauty: The Art of Iri Maruki and Toshi Maruki" in Dower and Junkerman, eds., *The Hiroshima Murals*, p. 22. A reproduction of the Auschwitz mural may be found on pp. 96–101.]

for the Hebrew University and other Israeli institutions, as a testament to the common humanity of the victims of the two catastrophes. The project was never completed, owing to a lack of funds, questions about the need for a Holocaust memorial in Japan, and the opposition of pro-Palestinian groups, but it did receive substantial support from both government and private groups before it was abandoned.[103][v]

Some Japanese have objected to the linkage of Hiroshima and Auschwitz on the grounds that the extensive attention paid to Auschwitz has detracted from the Hiroshima experience and led to an undervaluation of the misery caused by the atomic bomb. Writers in this vein choose to ignore the vastly different scale of the two tragedies (approximately one hundred forty thousand died within five months as a result of the bombing of Hiroshima compared to 3 million slaughtered at Auschwitz), to overlook the continuing trauma of the murder of two-thirds of the Jewish population of Europe, and to emphasize instead the ongoing, insidious nature of exposure to nuclear radiation. Kanai Toshihiro, an editorial writer for a Hiroshima newspaper, raised this objection in 1962, saying, "While the realities of the Auschwitz holocaust perpetrated by Nazi Germany against the Jews [are] well known around the world, the Hiroshima experience is not so well known, even though the scope of the misery caused in Hiroshima far exceeds that of Auschwitz."[104] And Kurihara Sadako iterates a similar sense that the misery of Hiroshima and Nagasaki had been greater than the Holocaust but that the

---

[v] One hundred forty-five artifacts from Auschwitz were obtained for display in the Kurose memorial. (See "Chinkon no shimboru heiwakan" [The Peace Memorial: Symbol of the Pacification of Souls], *Yomiuri shimbun*, August 13, 1983.) These were eventually returned, along with ¥8.9 million (about $85,000) in contributions that had been collected when it became clear that the memorial in Japan would not be built. (See "Kifu 890-man en tsūkon no henkan" [¥8.9 Million Returned With Great Sorrow], *Asahi shimbun*, December 18, 1993.)

About twenty artifacts from Maidanek are on permanent display in the Kyoto Museum for World Peace at Ritsumeikan University in Kyoto. Another recent attempt to establish a Japanese museum of the Holocaust is being undertaken in Fukuyama, another city in Hiroshima prefecture, by Pastor Ōtsuka Makoto. Among the objects he has collected for display are six items Anne Frank's father, Otto Frank, used while in Auschwitz. See "Anne no chichi no ihin todoku" [Mementos left by Anne's father arrive], *Asahi shimbun*, August 12, 1993.

●

atomic tragedies had been overshadowed by the Jewish experience.[105]

The linkage of Hiroshima and Nagasaki with the Holocaust is thus widely accepted and has been the basis of compelling works of art by both Japanese and Jews seeking to plumb the depths of human cruelty. These, however, are exceptional cases. In general, the Japanese have shown surprisingly little interest in the historical particulars of the Hiroshima and Nagasaki catastrophes, let alone the Holocaust. Literature by survivor writers has attracted little popular attention and has been dismissed as propaganda by the literary establishment. Political movements have been quick to exploit the emotional impact of the tragedies, but, as the novelist Ōe Kenzaburō has complained, they have almost completely ignored the victims.[106]

Much more common than the probing works of artists, therefore, is the popular use of Hiroshima as a convenient means to trump the Holocaust and obscure Japanese history and wartime responsibility. Reacting to criticism of an article in which he questioned the legitimacy of the U.S. Holocaust Museum, for example, Sadamori Daiji, the deputy foreign editor of the *Asahi shimbun*, replied to his critic in 1993, "Let me tell you that, as a Japanese who lost several relatives in the atomic bombing of Hiroshima, I am as sensitive to 'man's inhumanity to man' as any Jew in the world." This facile invocation of Hiroshima to trump the Holocaust and to establish Japanese parity as victims of the war is far more common in Japan than the insightful candor of creative artists.[107]

Like their identification with Anne Frank, the Japanese identification of Hiroshima and Nagasaki with the Holocaust has led only seldom to an understanding of the Jewish (or, for that matter, the Japanese) experience. It strives instead to bestow on the entire Japanese wartime experience a moral stature that is simply not appropriate. It seeks to blur the elementary distinction between victim and aggressor and to obscure the fact that the Japanese were far more analogous to the Germans during the war than to the Jews. Japanese like Sadamori Daiji who equate Hiroshima with the Holocaust in this way doubly pervert history by simultaneously implying that the Jews did something to deserve what befell them while the Japanese did not.

The atomic bombing of Hiroshima may have been disproportionate, unjustifiable, and even criminal, but it was nevertheless the logical consequence of Japanese aggression. Understood as the equivalent of the Holocaust, Hiroshima loses its unique historical meaning. It becomes a gimmick to avoid confronting unpleasant reality. And that is unconscionable from both the Japanese and the Jewish point of view.

The best-selling book in Japan in 1971 was Isaiah Ben-Dasan's *The Japanese and the Jews* (*Nihonjin to Yudayajin*). The book won the second Ōya Prize for Nonfiction and, by the time an English translation appeared in 1972, it had sold more than a million copies.[108] In many ways, the book was a culmination of trends in Japanese thinking about the Jews in the postwar period.

The Japanese and the Jews is a work of popular theology by a Japanese Christian that uses Jews and Judaism to establish Japanese uniqueness. While it is much more accessible and fashionably rationalistic than the postwar theologies of Matsumoto Fumi, Okusho Kazuo, Fujita Himiko, and Teshima Ikurō, it nonetheless fulfills the same basic function in the same way: it establishes Japanese uniqueness through the authority of the Jews. The book is at once an extension of the thousand-year-old Japanese tradition of manipulating images of foreigners to define "Japaneseness," one of the innumerable expositions on Japanese uniqueness that abounded in the postwar period called *Nihonjinron* (literally, "theories of Japaneseness"),[109] and a recent contribution to the continuing stream of Japanese Christian theorizing about the Jews that began with Saeki Yoshirō in 1908.

The Japanese and the Jews was written by Yamamoto Shichihei (1921–91), who was also the book's publisher. Yamamoto adopted the pseudonym Isaiah Ben-Dasan and insisted for years that Ben-Dasan was a reclusive Jew born in Kobe and raised in Japan who had fought in the Israeli war of independence and settled in (of all places) Terre Haute, Indiana. Despite forays into the wilds of Middle America, Japanese journalists were unable to locate Ben-Dasan, however, and

Yamamoto eventually conceded that he had written the book him-self.[110]

Yamamoto's book was written from a traditional Christian per-spective. His description of Jews and Judaism consists almost exclu-sively of pre-Talmudic examples. He follows Christian convention in presenting the Jews as legalistic Pharisees and Judaism as a loveless religion of laws.[111] In typical Japanese fashion, he confuses Judaism and Christianity, however, and he nonsensically has his alter ego, Ben-Dasan, give lengthy disquisitions on the Gospels as a means to explain Jewish beliefs.[112]

The Japanese and the Jews makes no reference to *The Protocols of the Elders of Zion* or to an international Jewish conspiracy, but it repeats many other hoary Jewish stereotypes. The Jews are, for example, "skillful, cautious handlers of money"[113] and "nomads," who, Ya-mamoto suggests, originated the idea of selection that found its ulti-mate expression in Auschwitz.[114]

Like Nakada Jūji, Oyabe Zen'ichirō, Sakai Shōgun, and others, Yamamoto was motivated by the need to reconcile his Christian identity with his sense of frustrated Japanese nationalism. He had a great deal in common with these thinkers. Like Nakada, he studied at the Methodist Aoyama Gakuin, from which he graduated with a degree in business in 1942. Like Oyabe and Sakai, who were pro-foundly affected by their experience of defeat in the Siberian inter-vention, Yamamoto was shaped by his experience of defeat in the Philippines, where he served as a soldier during World War II, was captured, and remained as a POW until 1947. Besides *The Japanese and the Jews*, Yamamoto wrote a number of other books dealing with religious subjects and his war experience.[115]

While Yamamoto did not acknowledge authorship of *The Japanese and the Jews* until years after it was published, he hinted at his true identity in his pseudonym. Dasan (or Dathan) is a character who appears as a coconspirator in Korah's rebellion against Moses, an episode known in Jewish tradition as "The Great Mutiny" (Numbers 16ff). Isaiah is the prophet most revered in Christianity because he is believed to have foretold the coming of Christ. Thus, while the name Isaiah Ben-Dasan ("Isaiah, Son-of-the-Mutineer") would be inconceivable for a Jew, it accurately described Yamamoto Shichihei, a self-styled mutinous Christian prophet.[116]

The theological character of *The Japanese and the Jews* is clear from Yamamoto's stated purpose in writing it, which is to define "Nihonism" (Japanism), which he claims is "as much a religion as Judaism, Christianity, or Islam."[117] The tenets of Nihonism are the myths of Japanese exceptionalism that the Japanese adopted about themselves after the war to transform Japan's modern history and depict the Japanese as innocent, apolitical creatures who live outside of history and are untouched by it. These myths include the transparent fictions that the Japanese are an inherently liberal and tolerant people who have never produced a despot and who have "made a splendid success of the separation of secular and religious powers."[118] They encompass the idea that the Japanese are exceptionally pragmatic and harmonious,[119] and that they live according to unspoken principles that no foreigner (not even Ben-Dasan) can understand.[120] Yamamoto's purpose is to affirm and reinforce these myths even as he subjects them to gentle and affectionate criticism.

The Japanese and the Jews is perhaps most remarkable, however, for the way it pushes the postwar tendency to identify with the Jews to its logical extreme. For more than sixty years, Japan's syncretic Christian theologians had been using the Jews indirectly to legitimize Japan's "sacred mission," to sanctify Japanese uniqueness, to establish Japan's "chosenness." In the postwar period, from Dazai Osamu's *The Setting Sun* to Anne Frank and the linkage of Hiroshima and Auschwitz, many Japanese had identified with the Jews to establish themselves as innocent victims and exempt themselves from the burdens and responsibilities of their history. With *The Japanese and the Jews*, this tendency achieved its highest expression. A Japanese author literally usurped Jewish identity to affirm Japanese uniqueness. Yamamoto Shichihei *became* the Jew Ben-Dasan and in the guise of a Jew gave the Jews' blessing to Japan's ineffable uniqueness. Never had the monological nature of Japanese debates about the Jews been more obvious. Never had the irrelevance of Jews to the Japanese enterprise of auto-expiation in their name been more manifestly clear.

The postwar period was thus characterized by contradictory

•

trends. On the one hand, it was the first time the Japanese truly encountered the Jews as historical beings. As they grappled with revelations about the Holocaust and events like the Eichmann trial, educated Japanese achieved an unprecedented level of understanding and a degree of sympathy with the Jews that compares well with European countries.

On the other hand, the postwar period was a time of obfuscation and denial. Instead of acknowledging and repudiating them, most Japanese repressed their wartime images of the Jews along with the rest of wartime ideology. They "forgot" the ubiquitous antisemitic rhetoric of the war years and rehabilitated former antisemitic ideologues into "friends of the Jews." When they thought about it at all, they fancied that their wartime antisemitism had actually been an expression of philosemitic affection; and they devised ingenious religious systems that succeeded in combining Japanese ethnic nationalism, Zionism, and the conspiracy theory of *The Protocols of the Elders of Zion* into a dizzying melange. Most important, they identified with the Jews and the Jewish experience as a means to obscure their wartime role and exculpate themselves as the innocent victims, not the perpetrators, of the war.

The result was a bifurcated situation, where an objective appreciation of the Jewish experience could exist side-by-side with traditional and sometimes antisemitic stereotypes. In 1972, *The Protocols of the Elders of Zion* was reissued under the title *The Jews and World Revolution*, and in 1977, the intellectual journal *L'Esprit d'Aujourd'hui* (*Gendai no esupuri*) published a compendium of ostensibly serious articles on the Jews that included learned disquisitions on the international Jewish conspiracy.[121]

In short, the accurate information about Jews and Judaism that proliferated in the postwar period augmented but did not displace traditional Japanese stereotypes of the Jews, which survived the defeat and provided the foundation for future antisemitic writing.

•

VII

THE SOCIALISM OF FOOLS

LEFT-WING ANTI-ZIONISM AND ANTISEMITISM

ON MAY 30, 1972, three Japanese terrorists attacked disembarking passengers in the baggage area of Tel Aviv's Lod Airport with machine guns and hand grenades. The raid was planned jointly by the Japanese Red Army Faction (*Nihon sekigun-ha*) and the Popular Front for the Liberation of Palestine (PFLP), one of the most radical factions in the Palestine Liberation Organization (PLO). The attack left twenty-four people dead and seventy-six wounded. Seventeen of those killed were Puerto Rican tourists. Of the three Japanese perpetrators, only one, Okamoto Kōzō, survived. He served thirteen years of a life sentence in an Israeli jail before being released in 1985 as part of an exchange that traded 1,150 Palestinian prisoners for 3 Israeli soldiers captured during the 1982 invasion of Lebanon.[1]

The incident evoked diverse reactions in Japan. Left-wing students praised the raid as an act of heroism, and signs like those at Kyoto University reading, "Hurray for the Arab Fighters! Israeli Officials, Release Political Prisoners!" appeared on campuses throughout the country. A collection of militant essays titled "International Assembly to Remember Two Japanese Warriors" was published by the Committee to Support the Tel Aviv Struggle, which, under the name "Rescue Committee for the Tel Aviv Struggle," also collected contributions to aid Okamoto.

The Japanese Communist Party, on the other hand, was less enthusiastic. Ordinarily anti-Zionist but anxious to distinguish itself from the Red Army Faction, the JCP denounced Okamoto Kōzō and his slain companions as terrorists and declared that they had "exposed their true, destructive nature as enemies of the people."[2]

The pro-Israel Japan-Israel Friendship Association, headed by the conservative politician Sakomizu Hisatsune (1902–77), publicly deplored the raid and tried to contain the damage to the friendly relations Japan and Israel had established. Two days after the attack, it sent out a mailing to its members, soliciting donations "to express our condolences to the numerous victims."

Japan's Christian Zionists were deeply shocked. Teshima Ikurō, founder of the Makuya sect, rushed to Israel and contributed an ambulance to Lod Airport as a token of Japanese remorse. Ōtsuki Masaru, the second-generation pastor of the Holy Ecclesia of Jesus, organized a "Prayer Meeting to Repent Before God and the Citizens of Israel in Mourning for the Victims" and proclaimed, "As Japanese, we love Israel as much as life itself!"[3]

The Japanese government condemned the attack and sent former Chief Cabinet Secretary Fukunaga Kenji to Israel to apologize and offer the government's condolences to the victims' families. At the same time, however, it refused to seek international police assistance in apprehending the Japanese terrorists still at large, and when Arab governments protested, it sent a second emissary to apologize to them for Japan's overture to Israel.[a]

---

[a] An article in the *Daily Yomiuri* of January 21, 1989, explained Japan's refusal to seek international police help:

The Lod Airport massacre revealed the way the left took control of Japanese perceptions of the Jews and Israel during the 1970s and early 1980s. Inspired by the Palestinians and led by their sympathizers in Japan, the left set the agenda and defined the terms in which the Jews and Israel would be discussed. A broad-based consensus emerged, ratified by government policy, that the Jews' existence as a people and the legitimacy of the state of Israel were dubious at best. By the mid-1980s, the interconnected notions that the Jews did not constitute a people, that Zionism was a retrograde ideology, and that the state of Israel was an unnatural creation of Western imperialism without intrinsic value and the major obstacle to peace in the Middle East had become widely accepted in Japan. Taken together, these notions, in the form of anti-Zionism, reinforced earlier negative images of the Jews and degenerated, finally, into antisemitism.

Japanese authorities Thursday requested member nations of the International Criminal Police Organization to arrest 13 suspected Japanese Red Army terrorists, the first time Japan has made such a request since it joined the organization in 1952.

"Blue" requests had been issued in the past to the 147 ICPO member countries asking for surveillance reports on suspected Japanese left-wing terrorists.

However, since the Japanese Red Army is reported to be gearing up and calling for destruction of the Imperial system, police changed the status of their request to the stronger "red" request, which calls for the arrest of suspects.

Police fear that the suspects may try to take action on the day of the funeral ceremony of Emperor Showa on Feb. 24, according to police.

The 13 Red Army commandos mentioned in the request include Fusako Shigenobu, 43, Japanese Red Army leader, and Kozo Okamoto, 41, who was arrested for the 1972 assault on Lod airport in Tel Aviv, Israel, police said.

In the past, Japan has avoided making similar requests because it does not want to be obliged to honor similar requests made by other member nations. Japanese police have feared that such cooperation would make Japan a target for international terrorists, according to officials.

One of the terrorists still at large is Shigenobu Fusako (1945–). On her activities and the Japanese Red Army, see *New York Times*, September 30, 1977; and Shigenobu Fusako, *Waga ai, waga kakumei* [My Love, My Revolution] (Kōdansha, 1974).

Regarding Japan's decision to send a second delegate to the Middle East, see Shillony, *The Jews and the Japanese*, p. 204.

●

Before the left began to sympathize actively with the Palestinians in 1967, the Japanese took only a passing interest in the Middle East. Following World War I, Japan had endorsed the Balfour Declaration and backed the establishment of a Jewish homeland in Palestine.[b] This endorsement was part of Japan's general support for British policy and not an independent expression of interest in the Middle East or commitment to the Jewish cause, however.[4] The decision taken at the Five Ministers Conference in December 1938 determined Japanese policy toward the Jews during World War II and precluded an active Japanese involvement with Jewish nationalism. Marginal groups like the Holiness Churches supported Zionism (at considerable cost to themselves), and chauvinists like Inuzuka Koreshige dreamed of harnessing Jewish power to serve the Japanese empire, but both of these impulses were discouraged because they ran counter to government policy.

After the war, the Japanese were preoccupied with their own project of national reconstruction and took little notice of the United Nations partition of Palestine in November 1947 or the establishment of the state of Israel in May 1948. In April 1952, when the Occupation ended, Japan immediately established full diplomatic relations with Israel as part of the process of normalizing diplomatic ties with many nations, and those relations have continued uninterrupted since. But Japanese foreign policy in the postwar period has been dictated largely by the need to maintain cordial relations with the United States, and this overriding consideration has governed Japan's relations with Israel as it has with most of the rest of the world. In essence, because

---

[b] "The Japanese Government gladly take note of the Zionist aspirations to establish in Palestine a national home for the Jewish people," Japanese Ambassador to Great Britain Chinda Sutemi wrote to Chaim Weizmann on January 6, 1919, "and they look forward with sympathetic interest to the realization of such desire upon the basis proposed." Quoted in Naoki Maruyama, "Japan's Response to the Zionist Movement in the 1920s," *Bulletin of the Graduate School of International Relations*, International University of Japan 2 (December 1984), 29.

the United States was Israel's staunchest ally, Japan had little real option but to maintain friendly relations with the Jewish state, even during periods of extreme tension.[5]

Egypt was the real focus of Japanese interest in the Middle East during the 1950s. Egypt was one of Japan's major trading partners, and Japanese intellectuals recognized the importance of Nasser's 1952 revolution in Egypt and understood that it represented the emergence of a new Arab nationalism that would henceforth shape the Middle East. Japanese intellectuals identified with Egypt and with Nasser's resistance against Western imperialism, so when the Afro-Asian People's Solidarity Movement was initiated at Bandung, Indonesia, in April 1955 and when Cairo was designated the headquarters of the movement in 1958, the same year Egypt and Syria were federated as the United Arab Republic, these events confirmed Egypt's importance in their mind.

Japanese newspapers gave full coverage to the Sinai conflict of 1956—Nasser's nationalization of the Suez Canal, Israel's campaign against Egypt, and the dispatch of British and French troops to the Suez. A consensus began to emerge that Israel was an imperialist power indistinguishable from England and France, but Israel was not yet cast as the villain in the Middle East drama. That role was reserved for Anthony Eden's England; Nasser's Egypt, which had "bravely resisted the onslaught of the imperialists," was the undisputed hero.

As Japanese interest in the Eichmann trial shows, however, in the early sixties the Japanese, while sometimes critical, were not inveterately hostile toward Israel, and some things about the new Jewish state actually fired their imagination.

The institution of the kibbutz was particularly inspiring. In 1962, Tezuka Nobuyoshi, a retired industrialist who had spent thirty years working on hydroelectrification in rural Hokkaido, visited Israel for sixteen days and became fascinated with Israel's unique cooperative settlements. He returned to Japan to found the Japan Kibbutz Association (*Nihon kibutsu kyōkai*) in October 1963 and its organ, *Kibbutz Monthly* (*Gekkan kibutsu*), which began publishing the following De-

cember.[c] The association sponsored the first group of Japanese kibbutz volunteers who traveled to Israel in September 1964, and five
more groups followed by October 1968, totaling 148 people. A semi-
official group in Israel calling itself the Japanese Kibbutz Study
Groups Committee (*Ha'vaada l'inyanei kvutzot Yapaniot bekibbutzim*)
was established to coordinate Japanese volunteers coming to Israeli
kibbutzim.[6] In 1989, one veteran of the Japanese kibbutz movement
estimated that all told more than two thousand Japanese had spent
time on Israeli kibbutzim.[7]

Tezuka regarded the kibbutz as an institution that would realize
the basic human right to happiness. "To the great majority of people
who lack economic security," he wrote, "freedom and equality are
really no more than a picture of a piece of cake. Ironically, the free
economies of the democracies victimize the vast majority of their
citizens. Below the surface of cultural efflorescence there is neither
freedom nor equality." In Tezuka's view, "all history is the history of
the rise and fall of exploitative civilizations." The kibbutz was the
way he saw to end this history of exploitation.[8]

The Japanese kibbutz movement was one of several utopian experiments attempted in Japan in the modern period.[9] It was essentially a reaction to Japan's rapid economic growth, urbanization, and
the loss of traditional communal values.[10] Although it was sincere and
die-hard remnants still exist, it failed to attract a significant following
and has gone virtually unnoticed in the larger society since its heyday
in the 1960s.

The Japanese who worked as volunteers on Israeli kibbutzim during that period communicated their exhilarating experience of kibbutz
life vividly back to Japan. The Yokohama University professor Nuita
Seiji (1922–), whose descriptions of kibbutz life were published by the
Japanese Foreign Ministry,[11] and Ishihama Mikaru (1941–), who lived
on a kibbutz while she was a student at Kōbe Jogakuin Women's College, were particularly effective. The positive image of the gregarious,
energetic Israeli that has remained a permanent part of the Japanese

---

[c] After 116 issues, *Kibbutz Monthly* changed its name in April 1974 to *Gekkan kyōdōtai*
[Cooperative Life], and it was subsequently renamed *Rokken bunka* [Verdant Culture],
a term coined by the prewar ultranationalist ideologue Ishiwara Kanji.

conception of Israel derived in significant measure from Ishihama's popular *Shalom, Israel*, which was published in 1965.[12]

But things had already begun to change by this time. The year 1960 was a watershed in Japanese politics, and the forces set in motion affected all aspects of Japanese life, including Japanese perceptions of the Jews.

On June 15, 1960, the United States–Japan Mutual Security Treaty was renewed over the vehement protests of many Japanese, especially those on the left. For months, mass demonstrations convulsed the country, leading, among other things, to the cancellation of a visit to Japan by U.S. President Dwight D. Eisenhower. Hundreds of thousands of demonstrators filled the streets, but the government of the born-again liberal democrat Kishi Nobusuke used highly questionable parliamentary tactics to force renewal of the Treaty.[13]

Renewal of the Mutual Security Treaty had two major consequences: it paved the way for the untrammeled pursuit of high-growth economic policies by the Liberal Democratic government by ensuring continued U.S. military protection for Japan; and it permanently weakened the Japanese opposition, especially the Communist Party, which had served as the major organizer of the protests.

The renewal of the Mutual Security Treaty strengthened the Liberal Democratic government's ability to implement the Yoshida Doctrine and devote its primary attention to economic growth. It had this effect because, by allowing the United States to station troops on Japanese soil and placing Japan under the U.S. nuclear umbrella, it freed Japan of the need to provide for its own defense. Thus, one of the first things Ikeda Hayato did after succeeding Kishi Nobusuke as prime minister on July 19, 1960, was to announce a plan to double Japan's national income within ten years, and this income-doubling scheme set Japan on the road to high economic growth that eventually led to its ascension to the position of the world's second-largest economy.

The second major consequence of the renewal of the Mutual Security Treaty was to definitively weaken the left-wing opposition. The credibility of the Japanese Communist Party, already damaged by Khrushchev's 1956 revelations of Stalin's crimes, was further hurt by the security treaty debacle. Many dissidents who had come of age

•

in the postwar period had set aside their differences with the JCP to forge a common front against treaty renewal. With the failure of the struggle, the need for a common front disappeared, and many radical New Left sects emerged. Three of the most important were the Core Faction (*Chūkaku-ha*) and Revolutionary Marxist Faction (*Kakumaru-ha*), which were founded in 1963, and the Red Army Faction (*Sekigun-ha*), which emerged in 1969 out of student struggles in the Osaka-Kyoto area. Composed of members disaffected with the JCP and frustrated by the sense that meaningful political action through the parliamentary process or even traditional leftist protest was impossible, these sects made headlines in the 1960s and 1970s with their resistance to the construction of the new international airport at Narita (the Core and Revolutionary Marxist Factions); and with spectacular bank robberies, airplane hijackings, and, in 1972, the deadly raid on Israel's Lod Airport (the Red Army Faction).

LDP high-growth policies exacerbated the predicament of the left by creating a national consensus that gave economic growth priority over all other national goals and depriving the left of its major issues and constituencies.[d]

In the short term, rapid economic expansion had a salutary effect on Japanese culture, stimulating creative activity. The labor shortage and the easy availability of short-term and part-time employment (*arubaito*, from the German *arbeit*, work) made it easier than ever before for artists to support themselves while pursuing their creative endeavors.[14] The 1960s were thus a period of prodigious cultural and artistic activity in Japan.[15]

There was also considerable sympathy for Jews and Judaism at this time. As early as 1954, Yoshimoto Takaaki (1924–), a leading leftist intellectual, had written an essay on the Gospel according to Matthew, in which he criticized the style of movement epitomized by Christianity and implicitly held up Judaism as an alternative model.[16] This

---

[d] For a fuller summary of the way the left was gradually coopted following the failure of the security treaty demonstrations, see John W. Dower, "Peace and Democracy in Two Systems: External Policy and Internal Conflict," in Andrew Gordon, ed., *Postwar Japan as History* (Berkeley: University of California Press, 1993), pp. 3–33. See especially pp. 22–28.

•

essay by Yoshimoto, as well as his other writings, exercised a profound influence on the generation of protesters looking for an alternative style of movement in the 1960s, and by the late 1960s, there was considerable interest in Jews, Judaism, and Jewish intellectual style.[17] In 1971, the novelist and playwright Abe Kōbō wrote an important essay discussing his sense of affinity with Jewish writers,[18] and the anthropologist Yamaguchi Masao published an essay inspired by George Steiner's *Language and Silence*, affirming a distinct Jewish contribution to Western civilization.[19] In 1969, the fifteen-volume complete works of the German-Jewish critic Walter Benjamin began to appear in Japanese[20]; a three-volume collection of essays by the preeminent scholar of Jewish mysticism Gershom Scholem was also published between 1972 and 1975[21]; and works of fiction by Philip Roth, Chaim Potok, Isaac Bashevis Singer, Elie Wiesel, and other Jewish writers were translated and published in rapid succession.[e]

In the long term, however, the LDP's high-growth policies had a deleterious impact on Japanese culture, intellectual life, and perceptions of the Jews. The tendency toward the commercialization of culture that government policies encouraged was exacerbated by the inflation and recession that followed the Arab oil embargo of 1973. As oil prices rose, so did the cost of paper, distribution, and the like, precipitating a major shakeout in the publishing industry. *Tenbō* [Perspective], a magazine that was virtually synonymous with postwar intellectual life, ceased publication in 1978. Important publishers of intellectual books like Kawade and Chikuma either declared bankruptcy or narrowly escaped it.

The quality of Japanese cultural production also declined. The independent Japanese filmmakers (*dokuritsu puro*) who had made strikingly original films in the 1960s gave way to the soft porn of the Nikkatsu Company in the 1970s. Japanese literature became increasingly trivial and petulant. The theater became obsessed with images of childhood and the attendant themes of escapism and irresponsibility.[22]

---

[e] The books by Roth, Potok, and Singer published in 1971 were, respectively, *Portnoy's Complaint*, *The Chosen*, and *Gimpel the Fool*. Wiesel's *Tales of Our Time* was published in Japan in 1972.

•

Deprived of any realistic hope of assuming power, the left became increasingly preoccupied with symbolic issues and symbolic action. The most extreme manifestation of this was the self-destructive sectarian violence that characterized the New Left in the 1970s. The epitome of this tendency came in 1972, when twelve members of the United Red Army (*Rengō sekigun*), an offshoot of the Red Army Faction, were murdered by their compatriots for "ideological deviation." The nine-day siege of their stronghold at Mt. Asama, north of Tokyo, in February 1972, which resulted in the death of two police officers and a local villager, was broadcast live on national TV, attracting a record 98.2 percent of the Tokyo viewing audience. By 1980, some twenty members of the Revolutionary Marxist Faction had been killed by their Core Faction rivals. These incidents, which involved murder over incomprehensible abstractions, were widely publicized, shocked the nation, and further diminished popular support for the left.[23]

Stymied at home, the Japanese left increasingly sought vicarious gratification through identification with and symbolic participation in "people's struggles" abroad. Of these, the Palestinian struggle against Israel was second in importance only to the struggle of the Viet Cong against the United States.[24]

Japanese Marxists were predisposed to be hostile toward Israel and Zionism. Lenin had explicitly damned Jewish nationalism, saying, "Anyone directly or indirectly putting forward the slogan of Jewish 'national culture' is (whatever his good intention) an enemy of the proletariat"[25]; and Stalin had disqualified the Jews as a people entitled to national aspirations or a nationalist movement by defining a nation as a "historically evolved stable community of language, territory, economic life and psychological make-up manifested in a community of culture."[26]

The Soviet Union had backed the establishment of the state of Israel in 1948, but beginning with the 1952 trial of Rudolf Slánsky, the Jewish-born general secretary of the Czechoslovak Communist Party, on charges of heading a "Trotskyite-Titoist-Zionist" plot to overthrow the socialist order in Czechoslovakia, the theory of a worldwide Jewish conspiracy became a staple of Communist propaganda. The Soviet Union and its satellites became the principal source of antisemitic screed in the world, casting the Israelis and their Jewish-American supporters as latter-day Elders of Zion in innumerable publications and policies.[27]

Japanese Marxists inherited this legacy. "The concept of a Jewish people," they insisted, "is unscientific and, in terms of its political significance, reactionary."[28] Their thinking on the Middle East was predicated on the supposition that Zionism was "an abnormal form of bourgeois nationalism [befitting] a people that has no objective existence but possesses the distinct reactionary capacity to distract the working class from its great mission in the world."[29]

This Marxist disenfranchisement of the Jewish people was reinforced by prestigious non-Soviet and even Jewish left-wing thinkers. Jean-Paul Sartre's 1946 treatise *Anti-Semite and Jew*, translated into Japanese in 1956, was particularly influential.[30] Sartre offered interesting insights into how pariah groups are created in the minds of those who hate them, but focusing on the Jews as an example, he had denied the historical existence of the Jewish people to prove his point. Jews, he asserted magisterially, "cannot take pride in any collective work that is specifically Jewish, or in any civilization properly Jewish, or in a common mysticism."[31] "Twenty centuries of dispersion and political impotence," he went on, "forbid [the Jewish community] having a *historic past*"[32]; and he therefore reasoned that, because there was no such thing as a Jew, "it is not the Jewish character that provokes anti-Semitism but, rather, it is the anti-Semite who creates the Jew."[33f]

Scrupulously honest but ambivalent works by leftist Jewish intellectuals like *The Non-Jewish Jew* by Isaac Deutscher, the eminent biographer of Stalin and Trotsky, were also read in Japan (incorrectly) as denials of Jewish peoplehood and tended to reinforce the

---

[f] During an interview in 1977, Gershom Scholem related to me that Sartre had told him during a visit to Israel in 1967 that he no longer advocated these views, but Sartre had never made his change of heart public, Scholem noted. See David Goodman, "Yudayashi no benshōhō o ikite: Gershom Scholem to no kaiwa" [Living the Dialectic of Jewish History: A Conversation with Gershom Scholem], *Tenbō* 225 (September 1977), 116–29. The exchange regarding Sartre appears on p. 117.

An abbreviated version of this interview with Scholem also appears in my *Isuraeru: koe to kao* [Israel: Voices and Faces], (Asahi shimbunsha, 1979).

•

view that what makes a person Jewish is not history and culture but solidarity with the oppressed.[g]

Before 1967, the denial of Jewish peoplehood was the proprietary perspective of Marxist ideologues. After the Six Day War of June 1967, however, the idea that the Jews did not constitute a people began to enter the mainstream of Japanese political discourse. High-profile intellectuals and academics promoted the idea as part of their support for the Palestinian cause; and after 1973 it was ratified by the Japanese government's new, pro-Arab Middle East policy. From 1973 on, the notion that the Jews were not a people, that "Jewish nationalism" was somehow an oxymoron, and that everything Israel did was thus inherently suspect became widely accepted in Japan.

The founding of the Palestine Liberation Organization in 1964 attracted relatively little attention in Japan, but as their domestic predicament worsened, Japanese leftists increasingly identified with the Palestinian cause and came to advocate the political principles laid out in the PLO's founding covenant, the Palestinian National Charter.

The Palestinian National Charter, as it was revised in 1968, took four basic positions with respect to the Jews and Israel. First, it denied that the Jews were a people who could have a competing claim to the

---

[g] The Japanese interpretation derives from Deutscher's own ambivalence toward his Jewish identity. "To speak personally once again," he writes, "to me the Jewish community is still only negative. I have nothing in common with the [ultraorthodox] Jews of, say *Mea Shaarim* or with any kind of Israeli nationalists.... Religion? I am an atheist. Jewish nationalism? I am an internationalist. In neither sense am I, therefore, a Jew. I am, however, a Jew by force of my unconditional solidarity with the persecuted and exterminated. I am a Jew because I feel the Jewish tragedy as my own tragedy; because I feel the pulse of Jewish history; because I should like to do all I can to assure the real, not spurious, security and self-respect of the Jews." Isaac Deutscher, *The Non-Jewish Jew* (New York: Hill and Wang, 1968), p. 51; published in Japan as *Hi-Yudayateki Yudayajin*, tr. Suzuki Ichirō (Iwanami shoten, 1970).

land. "Judaism, being a religion, is not an independent nationality," it said. "Nor do Jews constitute a single nation with an identity of its own; they are citizens of the states to which they belong."

Second, it asserted that, because the Jews did not constitute a nation, Zionism was not the national liberation movement of the Jews, as the Jews claimed, but "a political movement organically associated with international imperialism and antagonistic to all action for liberation and to progressive movements in the world. It is racist and fanatic in its nature, aggressive, expansionist and colonial in its aims, and fascist in its methods." "The partition of Palestine in 1947 and the establishment of the state of Israel," the charter proclaimed thirdly, are therefore "entirely illegal, regardless of the passage of time"; and it declared finally that "Armed struggle is the only way to liberate Palestine."[34]

Especially after the Six Day War of 1967, when Israel occupied the West Bank and Gaza, bringing large numbers of Palestinians under Israeli control, the Palestinian issue took on extreme symbolic, almost amuletic importance for the Japanese left. Like their counterparts in other countries, Japanese leftists increasingly empathized with the Palestinians, whose struggle against Israel gave them a sense of vicarious participation in a meaningful political movement, and they came to faithfully espouse the principles of the Palestinian National Charter.[35] Three men in particular epitomized this pro-Palestinian, anti-Zionist mentality in Japan: Hirokawa Ryūichi, Itagaki Yūzō, and Oda Makoto.

The photojournalist Hirokawa Ryūichi's personal identification with the Palestinian cause was paradigmatic of the way leftists in Japan, like their counterparts in other countries, shifted their loyalties away from Israel and to the Palestinians following the Six Day War. Hirokawa was born in Tientsin, China, in 1943, the child, as it were, of Japanese imperialism in Asia. After graduating from the Education Department of Waseda University in March 1967, he left immediately for Israel, where he arrived on May 22. He had read Martin Buber on the kibbutz movement and identified with Israel as a bold socialist experiment. The Arab-Israeli conflict, which he understood only vaguely as a tribal rivalry with roots in the immemorial past, did not concern him.[36]

The Six Day War broke out on June 5, two weeks after his arrival in Israel. It changed Hirokawa's perceptions radically. "I began to feel," he wrote, "that out of ignorance I was committing an irrevocable sin [by aiding Israel]." He read Cecil Roth's *A History of the Jews* and other books to try to understand what had happened, but they depicted the Jews as eternal victims and did not elucidate the reality of Jewish power. In the wake of the Six Day War, Hirokawa became convinced that the Jews had forfeited their role as the eternal victims of history and had assumed the identity of oppressors instead.

Disillusioned, Hirokawa moved to a kibbutz affiliated with the Israeli Communist Party and became involved with Mazpen, an ultra–left-wing Israeli organization. After attending Mazpen's weekly meetings, he began to understand the Arab-Israeli conflict "as a complex of Zionism—the ideology of Israeli statehood—imperialism, Arab feudalism, and the chauvinism of the Jewish and Arab peoples." The original inhabitants of Palestine, Hirokawa concluded, were the tragic victims of this complex of interrelated forces, and he resolved to champion their cause. His identification with Israel, in other words, was transferred to the Palestinians, and after his return to Japan in 1970, he worked indefatigably as an outspoken critic of Israel and the Jews and as a prolific advocate of the Palestinian cause. His personal experience in Israel, his marriage to a French-Jewish-Israeli woman,[h] and his deep personal involvement with the Palestinians gave him a unique authority in Japanese debates on the Middle East.

Upon his return to Japan, Hirokawa met Itagaki Yūzō (1931–), a prominent professor of modern Arab history and a pro-PLO activist.

---

[h]Hirokawa married Routie Joskowicz, the daughter of Holocaust survivors, whose book *Watakushi no naka no "Yudayajin"* [The "Jew" Within Me] (Shūeisha, 1982; San'ichi Shobō, 1989) received the Playboy Prize for Nonfiction (*Dokyumento fuairu taishō*) awarded by the Japanese edition of America's *Playboy* magazine. The couple were subsequently divorced, but for many years Joskowicz, who was highly critical of Jews, Judaism, and Israel, gave Hirokawa and his anti-Zionist views a unique credibility and prestige. For a critique of Joskowicz's book, which argues convincingly that it is the typical product of a second-generation Holocaust survivor, see Fujimoto Kazuko, "Shisha o se ni ou onna-tachi" [Women Who Carry the Dead on Their Back] in *Shisō no kagaku* 31 (April 1983), 14–21.

•

Itagaki was teaching at the Tokyo University of Foreign Languages. He moved shortly afterward to Tokyo University, where he remained a professor until his retirement in 1992.[i]

Itagaki claims to be "a student of historical science,"[37] but his views actually derive slavishly from Arab and Soviet propaganda.[j] He founded the Palestine Liaison Committee (*Paresuchina renraku kaigi*), a group that coordinated the efforts of Japanese groups and the PLO; he helped edit *Palestine Quarterly*, one of several pro-Palestinian publications in Japan[k]; and he was instrumental in efforts to establish a PLO office in Tokyo in 1977. In 1991, Baker Abdel Munem, the PLO representative in Japan since 1983, publicly acknowledged Itagaki's aid in establishing a PLO presence in the country.[l]

It is perfectly acceptable for academics to have political opinions, but Itagaki Yūzō has consistently ignored the essential distinction between scholarship and political advocacy. In particular, he has pro-

---

[i] Since his retirement, Itagaki has been professor at Tokyo Keizai [Economics] University.

[j] As early as October 1967, the Aoyama Gakuin University professor Kondō Shin'ichi compared Itagaki's pronouncements with published statements by the Arab League, Soviet Premier Aleksei Kosygin, and the Japanese Communist Party newspaper *Akahata* and showed how Itagaki cleaved faithfully to the Party line. See Kondō Shin'ichi, "Marukusu-Reninshugi, Soren tai Yudayajin, Shionizumu, Isuraeru (1): aru chūtō funsō zushiki no seiritsu katei" [Marxist-Leninism and the Soviet Union Against the Jews, Zionism, and Israel, 1: The Development of a Schematic Approach to the Middle East Conflict], in *Takushoku daigaku ronshū*, 58 (1967), 21–23. Even a cursory review of Soviet and Arab propaganda during this time reveals the consistently derivative nature of Itagaki's thought. Compare, for example, Itagaki's ideas with the summary of Soviet and Arab ideology in Wistrich, *Hitler's Apocalypse*, pp. 194–255.

[k] *Kikan Paresuchina*, published by the Palestine Liaison Committee. Other pro-Arab publications have included the monthly *Arab Review* and *Arab Topics*, published by the office of the Arab League in Tokyo; and *Filastin Biladi*, published by the Tokyo office of the PLO. Pro-Arab publications issued by Japanese include *Chūtō tsūhō* (*Middle East Report*) published by the Middle East Institute of Japan (Chūtō chōsa kai), and *Chūtō jaanaru* (*Middle East Journal*) published by the Middle East Center for Economic Research (Chūtō keizai kenkyūjo). By contrast, only one publication, *Israel Monthly* (*Gekkan Isuraeru*), published by the Israeli Embassy, has consistently presented the Israeli point of view in Japanese.

[l] "Tokyo University professor and Middle East specialist Itagaki Yūzō and photojournalist Hirokawa Ryūichi, who had been active prior to my arrival, were particularly helpful," Munem wrote. "Every month I would meet with them and a group of prominent Japanese friends of Palestine for advice." Baker Abdel Munem, *Waga kokoro no Paresuchina* [My Heart's Home Palestine] (Shakai hihyōsha, 1991), pp. 232–33.

•

moted as objective fact the political position of the PLO, enunciated in the Palestinian National Charter, that the Jews are not a historical people. In his scholarly work, for example, he routinely puts "the Jews" in quotation marks to indicate his disapproval of "the notion (false consciousness) of 'the Jews' as 'a nation,' and the pretense to a 'nationalism' based on it."[38] This denial of Jewish peoplehood appears in no less authoritative a source than the prestigious *Iwanami History of the World*, where the dubious existence of "the Jews" is indicated by quotation marks throughout, even in the statistical tables.

In less scholarly forums, Itagaki has been even more strident. In the second of eleven interviews given just after the Yom Kippur War in November 1973, he told the *Mainichi* newspaper that Judaism was a "religion of intolerance"; that "the existence of Israel is based largely on ideology"; and that the racist Nazi "Nuremberg decrees . . . were carried on in the laws of Israel to define the status of citizenship and repatriation."[39] Echoing Sartre, whose influence he acknowledges,[40] Itagaki asserted that the Jews do not exist, that "in the modern sense, the Jews are those people who are referred to as Jews by society in general; that is, the designation serves as a symbol of social discrimination."[41] None of these ideas is original; they all derive from foreign sources.[42]

Itagaki has been extremely prolific, but two articles in particular give a clear picture of his thought: "Nasser's Failure and the Egotism of the Great Powers," published in June 1967, immediately after the Six Day War[43]; and "Nazism and Zionism," published in 1978.[44] These articles did not appear in marginal left-wing publications but in the *Asahi Journal*, a widely read newsweekly published by the *Asahi* newspaper,[m] and *World (Sekai)*, one of the most prestigious intellectual monthlies in Japan.

In "Nasser's Failure and the Egotism of the Great Powers," Ita-

---

[m] Reporting on the announcement that the *Asahi Journal* would cease publication in June 1992, *Newsweek* magazine characterized it hyperbolically as "Japan's *Mother Jones*, the bible of the counterculture that took root in the early '60s." While the *Asahi Journal* was never a "counterculture bible," it was at the peak of its popularity and influence in 1967, when Itagaki's article appeared. ("Japan's Vanishing Counterculture," *Newsweek*, June 1, 1992. See also "Era of Radical Journalism Ends with Asahi Journal Closure" in *Japan Times Weekly International Edition*, June 1–7, 1992.)

•

gaki sought to demolish the view that the Arab-Israeli conflict was the recrudescence of a centuries-old ethnic rivalry and was therefore somehow inevitable (*shukumeiteki*). He asserted instead that the whole notion of an "Arab-Jewish conflict" was a myth concocted by the Western imperialist powers. "This 'common sense' approach is truly one of the great myths of our time," he wrote. "It is a long-standing fiction created for popular consumption in the twentieth century by the Western powers for reasons of political expediency."[45]

According to Itagaki, it was wrong "to understand the Arab-Israeli conflict on the same level as the [legitimate national] conflicts between India and Pakistan or Indonesia and Malaysia" or "to discuss the conflict in isolation from other issues."[46] The threat to peace in Palestine derived, in his view, neither from the "backwardness" of Arab society nor from some innate incompatibility of Arabs and Jews but solely from "the existence of a Zionist Israel and its military reinforcement by the great powers."[47] Following the Palestinian National Charter, Itagaki asserted that Israel was not simply a threat to peace but a wedge driven into the Arab world, that it represented all the counterrevolutionary military force and political reaction that obstructed social revolution in the Arab states.[48] "Only when Zionism disappears will it be possible to formulate and solve the problem of how 'Jews' can exist in this vast region, participating and cooperating in a broad Arab community," he asserted.[49]

In subsequent pronouncements, Itagaki made it clear that he regarded this analysis as definitive, and because the "myths" of the Arab-Israeli conflict had been exposed, there could be no neutrality in the Middle East situation. Anyone who did not accept his theory that Zionism was the sole obstacle to peace in the Middle East was "helping to prolong a distorted view of the Palestinian and Jewish questions."[50]

According to Itagaki's "correct" view, Zionism was a form of "antisemitism." Originally this argument was based on the premise that instead of solving the problem of antisemitism within their own societies, the West had promoted the myth that "the Jewish problem" could be solved only through the creation of a Jewish state. Zionism Itagaki described as "a kind of 'metamorphosis' of antisemitism," and he reasoned that to recognize the legitimacy of the state of Israel was tantamount to legitimizing the unresolved antisemitism of the West.[51]

In his 1978 *World* article, Itagaki augmented this formulation to equate Zionism with Nazism. A symbiotic relationship had existed between Nazism and Zionism, he claimed,[n] and he concluded, "There is no way to avoid the problem of the Zionistic nature of Nazism and the antisemitic nature of Zionism."[52] "Taking their cue from Nazi terminology, the Zionists contended that a new time of *awakening* had arrived for 'the Jewish people,' for 'the Jewish race,' and they therefore welcomed the pogroms, boycotts, and purges from public office that the Nazis were using against 'the Jews.' . . . One has to recognize in the activities of the Zionists that they actually hoped for an increase in the social discrimination against 'Jews' in order to further their movement."[53]

Contacts between Zionists and the Nazis did take place, but in Itagaki's view they were not antagonists but partners. According to Itagaki, because Nazi antisemitism had "benefited" the Zionists in some sense, the Nazis must have been Zionists. He points out that the Nazi ideologue Alfred Rosenberg had at one point urged the National Socialists to support Zionism to rid Germany of its Jews; that Adolf Eichmann had been inspired by Theodore Herzl's *Der Judenstaat* and had worked with the Haganah, the military arm of the Zionist movement, to expel Jews from Vienna; that at one point Hitler himself had supported a policy of expelling Jews to Palestine over the objections of the German Foreign Ministry; and that "Zionist secret agents sent into Germany [had] cooperated with the SS and participated in the process of selecting 'Jews,' particularly young men, to emigrate."[54]

According to Itagaki, the shift of emphasis from this joint Nazi-Zionist expulsion plan to murder and extermination was simply the result of logistical complications. The state of war brought such a large number of Jews under Nazi control that expulsion became

---

[n] Itagaki bases his argument in part on Hannah Arendt's depiction of Zionist-Nazi "cooperation" in the 1930s. For example, she characterizes the Nazis as "pro-Zionist" at this time. See Hannah Arendt, *Eichmann in Jerusalem: A Report on the Banality of Evil*, rev. ed. (New York: Penguin, 1964), pp. 58–60. The reference to Arendt in Itagaki's piece can be found on p. 27.

•

impossible, and mass murder somehow became the only feasible alternative. The imposition of Jews on Palestine was thus a Nazi crime, and, Itagaki argued, "an approach to 'Nazi crimes' that does not criticize the Zionistic character of Nazism is a political ploy." For Itagaki, the state of Israel represented the survival of Nazism in the postwar period, and anyone who failed to acknowledge this was ignoring the facts for "political" motives.[55]

Itagaki was quick to exculpate the Palestinians of any responsibility for their situation. Even the notorious pro-Nazi Grand Mufti of Jerusalem, Amin el-Husseini, was defended by Itagaki as a hapless prisoner of the mythical "Arab-Jewish conflict" trumped up by the West to deceive the passive and innocent Arabs.[°]

If the Zionists were Nazis, then from Itagaki's perspective the oppressed Palestinians were Jews, and the state of Israel was an antisemitic state. "On the basis of the position in which they have been placed," Itagaki concluded, "the Palestinians today are the best qualified people in the world to understand the 'Jewish' question."[56]

Itagaki's views were highly influential in the 1970s and 1980s. Instead of being condemned as the politically motivated distortion of the facts they were,[P] they were accepted and promoted by Japan's

---

[°]Itagaki writes,

> The malicious slander is being spread abroad that the Palestinians want to drive "the Jews" into the sea. In order to avoid confronting the fact that the Zionists were in contact with the Nazi regime, the tale is being endlessly repeated of the "Arab" leader Amin el-Husseini, who fell into the preset trap of the "Arab-Jewish conflict" and wound up cooperating with the Nazis. The debts of Western society are continually being obscured by moralistic sermons about how Arabs should welcome "the Jews" into the Middle East and live with them in peace and by international political intervention in the guise of "peace" initiatives. (Itagaki, "Nachizumu to Isuraeru," p. 29.)

Itagaki uses quotation marks in this paragraph to indicate that the Mufti was not a *real* Arab, to portray his enthusiastic alliance with the Nazis as a "tale," and to exclude him from the realm of "facts."

[P] Itagaki's equation of Nazism and Zionism went virtually unchallenged. *Sekai*, the influential journal that featured his article identifying Zionism with Nazism, dutifully published a rebuttal by the Hebrew University professor R. J. Zvi Werblowsky, but the editors made a point of specifying that Werblowsky's article was an unsolicited contribution (*tōkō*). (R. J. Zvi Werblowsky, "Isuraeru e no kyokkai—Itagaki Yūzō shi ni hanron suru" [A Perverse Interpretation of Israel: A Response to Itagaki Yūzō], *Sekai*,

mass media as objective and authoritative. On December 1 and 2, 1980, the *Mainichi* newspaper even sponsored an international conference in Tokyo on the status of Jerusalem organized and chaired by Itagaki to which no Israeli or Jewish delegate was invited.[57]

Oda Makoto (1932–), a charismatic organizer and prolific writer, contributed a patina of philosophical legitimacy to the anti-Zionist dogma of Itagaki Yūzō.

Oda has been a presence in Japanese intellectual and political life for more than thirty years.[q] After receiving a degree in ancient Greek literature from Tokyo University, he traveled to the United States in 1958 and spent a year as a Fulbright exchange student at Harvard. After his return to Japan in 1961, he made a name for himself as a freethinking world traveler with a book titled *Take on the World* (*Nan de mo mite yarō*), which became a best seller. Free from the trauma of failure that preoccupied those who had been involved in the security treaty debacle, Oda took a leading role in founding the League for Peace in Vietnam (*Beheiren*), a grassroots movement to oppose the Vietnam War, and he remained its magnetic leader for ten years. With the end of the war in 1975, the league disbanded and Oda

---

November 1978, pp. 348–351.) The long-time Tokyo resident Harold Solomon sarcastically labeled the Tokyo University professor's ideas "Itagakism." (Harold Solomon, "Nachizumu to Itagakizumu" [Nazism and Itagakism], *Chūtō tsūhō*, September 1979.) The only direct Japanese response was by the writer and translator Fujimoto Kazuko, who condemned Itagaki's "astonishingly slipshod" article as a grotesque perversion of the facts. (Fujimoto Kazuko, *Sabaku no kyōshitsu* [Classroom in the Desert] [Kawade shobō shinsha, 1978], p. 230.) Outside of Japan, Solomon's "Japan—Pro-Arab?" was a courageous attempt to criticize Itagaki's ideas.

[q] "Everyone knows Oda," the well-known critic Katō Shūichi has said. "He is very productive and is recognized as an established professional writer. Even his literary foes take him seriously, unlike certain obscure writers affiliated with the JCP who are more active in politics than in literature." Havens, *Fire Across the Sea*, p. 58. Havens offers a brief biography of Oda on p. 57–63 and recounts his leadership of the anti-Vietnam War movement throughout his book.

For another description of Oda's contribution to Japanese political and intellectual life, see J. Victor Koschmann, "Intellectuals and Politics," in Gordon, ed., *Postwar Japan as History*, pp. 414–15.

For examples of Oda's writing, see Oda Makoto, "Making Democracy Our Own, *Japan Interpreter* 6, no. 3 (Autumn 1970), 235–53; and "A Writer in the Present World: A Japanese Case History," in Schlant and Rimer, eds., *Legacies and Ambiguities*, pp. 263–77.

•

turned his prodigious energies to other causes, in particular, the cause of the Palestinians.

In his own way, Oda is a man of intellectual courage. "If it were not for writers like Oda," one sympathetic Western critic has written, "revisionists and patriots claiming that the rape of Nanking was a figment of Chinese propaganda, that the Greater East Asia War was justified, and that all Japanese should bow their heads at the Yasukuni shrine [the symbol of wartime State Shinto], would be but feebly resisted." Oda's intellectual courage is counterbalanced by political irresponsibility and recklessness, however. There are few radical causes he has not espoused, and during the course of his career he has defended the likes of Pol Pot, Ayatollah Khomeini, and others because they were opponents of American imperialism.[58]

Oda's thought is similarly bifurcated into opposing dimensions. In his writings, he is a skeptical Sophist who delights in debunking all claims to a knowledge of Truth. In his politics, however, Oda is a Manichean who views the world in starkly dualistic terms as a war of the forces of light against the forces of darkness.

These characteristics are evident in Oda's writings on the Middle East. Two works are particularly revealing. The first is an essay titled " 'Deir Yassin' and 'Auschwitz,' " which appeared in the September 1977 issue of *Tenbō*.[59][r] The other is a book titled *In a Time of Historical Transition: Toward the 21st Century*, which was published in 1980.[60]

In " 'Deir Yassin' and 'Auschwitz,' " Oda argues that the massacre of Palestinian civilians by Jewish extremists at the village of Deir Yassin in 1948 "canceled out" Auschwitz (the Holocaust) and deprived Israel of the moral basis for its existence.[s]

---

[r] Oda's article was published back-to-back with my interview with Gershom Scholem, and his perspective contrasts sharply with Scholem's central assertion of the continuity and integrity of Jewish history and culture. See David Goodman, "Yudaya-shi no benshōhō o ikite" in the same issue of *Tenbō*, pp. 116–29.

[s] Oda bases his argument on an account of Deir Yassin written by Hirokawa Ryūichi, who asserted, following the Arab version of events, that Palestinian civilians had been intentionally massacred by Jews to stampede their brethren and drive them from the land:

This was an application of the relativizing sophistry that characterizes Oda's work. In his 1981 novel, *Hiroshima*, translated into
English as *The Bomb*, for example, Oda elaborates his theory that all
victims are necessarily also victimizers and that therefore all claims to
moral superiority based on victimhood are insupportable.[61] In " 'Deir
Yassin' and 'Auschwitz,' " Oda uses "Deir Yassin" in the same way to

---

On April 9, the Irgun and Lehi, two right-wing Jewish military groups, surrounded the village of Deir Yassin near Jerusalem, and 250 unresisting people,
including old people, women, and children, were massacred. Those who survived were paraded through central Jerusalem in a "victory procession" in their
blood-soaked clothes. The point of this act was to encourage the Arabs to flee
from Palestine.

[Hirokawa, *Yudaya kokka to Arabu gerira*, pp. 74–76.]

Non-Arab sources dispute this version of events, arguing that, while the Jewish
extremists may have intended to drive out the inhabitants of Deir Yassin, the massacre
was not premeditated. Oda had access to at least two such sources, Muramatsu Takeshi,
"Erusaremu e no michi" [The Road to Jerusalem], *Shūkan Asahi*, special issue, June 25,
1967; and Michel Riquet, "Imi aimai na Paresuchina mondai, 2" [The Ambiguous
Palestinian Problem, 2], *Gekkan Isuraeru*, October-November, 1973. Oda, who knows
English well, also could have consulted English-language source material.

The Israeli historian Benny Morris has written what is probably the most accurate
and dispassionate account of what took place at Deir Yassin:

Ironically, it was not a Haganah but a joint IZL-LHI [Irgun-Lehi] operation,
undertaken with the reluctant, qualified consent of the Haganah commander
in Jerusalem, which probably had the most lasting effect of any single event of
the war in precipitating the flight of Arab villagers from Palestine. On 9 April,
IZL and LHI units, for part of the battle supported by Haganah mortars,
attacked and took Deir Yassin, a generally nonbelligerent village on the western outskirts of Jerusalem. The attack loosely meshed with the objective of
Operation Nahshon, which was to secure the western approaches to Jerusalem.
After a prolonged firefight, in which Arab family after family were slaughtered, the dissidents rounded up many of the remaining villagers, who included
militiamen and unarmed civilians of both sexes, and children, and murdered
dozens of them. Altogether some 250 Arabs, mostly non-combatants, were
murdered; there were also cases of mutilation and rape. The surviving inhabitants were expelled to Arab-held East Jerusalem. The weight of the evidence
suggests that the dissident troops did not go in with the intention of committing
a massacre but lost their heads during the battle, which they found unexpect-
edly tough-going. It is probable, however, that the IZL and LHI commanders
from the first had intended to expel the village's inhabitants. The massacre was
roundly condemned by the mainstream Jewish authorities, including the
Haganah, the Jewish Agency and the Chief Rabbinate, and Ben-Gurion sent a
message to King Abdullah condemning it.

●

trump "Auschwitz," arguing that any special claims to moral superiority the Jews might make based on their victimization at Auschwitz
were voided by the equivalent massacre they committed at Deir
Yassin.

Oda is a profoundly ahistorical thinker. For him, all atrocities,
regardless of time, place, circumstance, or scale are equal. Implying
that Auschwitz was the German response to some unidentified Jewish
provocation, Oda writes of the Holocaust that "terror called forth
terror and revenge invited revenge."[62] Germans had murdered Jews,
and Jews had murdered Palestinians. Therefore, after Deir Yassin,
" 'Auschwitz' [became] just one of the numberless mass murders that
have taken place throughout history."[63]

By murdering Arab civilians at Deir Yassin, the Jews showed
themselves to be mass murderers just like the Germans and thus
"redeemed" the Germans from their terrible historical distinctive-
ness.† "In essence, by virtue of the universality [of Auschwitz], history
seemed to have reached a dead end," Oda wrote in a typically con-
voluted sentence, "but in fact, its very universality opened a hole in
the dead end of history, and *pre*-Auschwitz and *post*-Auschwitz time
connected. . . . Israel became indistinguishable from the Germans [*hitotsu no ana no mujina*] . . . and ironically the Germans were *redeemed*."[64] In other words, precisely because it was "universal"—that
is, repeatable by anyone, including the Jews—the Holocaust lost its
value as a definitive historical event. The atrocities of the Jews an-
nulled the crimes of the Germans, and Deir Yassin canceled out the
Holocaust.

Characteristically for a left-wing thinker, Oda discounts Jewish
peoplehood and assumes that "Auschwitz" is the sole justification for
Israel's existence. He accuses the Jews of manipulating "Auschwitz"
for their own political self-aggrandizement, reducing it "to a symbolic

---

[Benny Morris, *The Birth of the Palestinian Refugee Problem, 1947–1949* (New
York: Cambridge University Press, 1987), pp. 113–14.]
† Oda's argument was prefigured in the debate between Arnold Toynbee and Yaacov
Herzog at McGill University in Montreal on January 31, 1961. Toynbee presented
Oda's argument equating the Jews and the Germans, and Herzog revealed its essential
speciousness. See Yaacov Herzog, *A People That Dwells Alone* (London: Weidenfeld
and Nicolson, 1975), pp. 25–30.

•

and endlessly mutable value whose meaning is apparent only to themselves." Because this is fundamentally illegitimate, it will only prolong the endless cycle of violence and revenge, and Oda predicts that "one 'Deir Yassin' [will] necessarily lead to the next."[65]

Oda satisfies himself that he is being fair by applying across the board this principle that every victim is necessarily, in some way, shape, or form, also a victimizer. Put most simply, he is arguing nothing more arcane than that two wrongs do not make a right, and he takes the United States, the Soviet Union, Japan, and Germany to task for justifying the wrongs they have committed on the basis of past injustices done to them. He even criticizes the Palestinians, "who should have been able to create a new 'Third World' [but who] have been distracted by 'Deir Yassin' and are unable to do so."[66]

The problem is, of course, that this kind of extreme ahistoricism, simplicity, and moral relativism are no basis for a practical politics, so underlying Oda's surface Sophism is a practical, Manichean politics that bifurcates the world into opposing "positive" and "negative" factors (seikō and fukō). Israel is a "negative factor" in the world,[67] and Egypt, which was a "positive factor," became "a negative existence" (fukō no sonzai) in 1979 when it made peace with Israel.[68]

If Israel and Egypt represent the forces of darkness for Oda, then the Palestinians embody the forces of light, and solidarity with the Palestinians is the litmus test of political morality. "Only those who throw themselves headlong against [these 'negative existences'] can constitute the positive, central existence [seikō no chūshin sonzai],"[69] he argues; and he asserts that the Palestinians superseded Egypt and the other Arab states as "the avatar of [the] positive value (seikō to shite no gugentai)" of nationalism, because, possessing no state of their own, "they could argue the case of 'Arab nationalism' in a much more idealistic way." Thus, according to Oda, "support for and proximity to the Palestinian liberation movement is the proof of the justice and progressive character" of the existing states.[70]

In 1982, Oda put this Manichean perspective into practice by organizing an "International People's Tribunal" to put Israel on trial for its invasion of Lebanon. He was joined by Itagaki Yūzō, Hirokawa Ryūichi, and others, who appointed themselves judges to publicize Israel's "criminality" and pronounce sentence on the Jewish state.[71] The tribunal was the culmination of the processes of intense personal identification with the Palestinians, the willful distortion of knowledge on their behalf, and the radical oversimplification of the world that Hirokawa, Itagaki, and Oda had indulged in for more than a decade.

The anti-Zionist dogma developed by Hirokawa Ryūichi, Itagaki Yūzō, Oda Makoto, and other leftist intellectuals[u] was popularized by innumerable other writers. By the 1980s, it had became so prevalent that it assumed the unassailable character of common sense.

One writer who helped popularize anti-Zionism was Ishigaki Ayako, who must be counted among twentieth-century Japan's most fascinating women. Born in 1903, Ishigaki was influenced by the Christian socialist Kagawa Toyohiko and in 1926 emigrated to the United States, where she became involved with Agnes Smedley and other left-wing American journalists. In 1940, she published *Restless Wave*, an English-language autobiography that is a sort of gentle, cherry-blossom version of Smedley's hard-scrabble *Daughter of Earth* (1929).[72] Ishigaki participated in the Spanish Civil War and during World War II produced anti-Japanese propaganda for the American government. Accused of being a Communist sympathizer during the McCarthy era, she returned to Japan in 1951 to become a leading

---

[u] In the early 1970s, left-wing intellectuals concerned with the Middle East were aligned in three factions. The main, "moderate" faction, to which Itagaki also belonged, consisted primarily of intellectuals affiliated with the Japanese Communist Party (JCP) and included Okakura Koshirō, Ōta Iwao, and Yamamoto Tadashi. A second faction to their left consisted of members of the Mao Tse-tung Study Group (*Mō-Takutō shisō kenkyū kai*), including Kai Shizuma, Ikegami Mikinori, Nakamura Seiichi, and Nagashima Matao. Even as they accused them of the evils of Soviet revisionism, this Maoist faction concurred with the JCP group on the issue of Israel. The third faction comprised members of the New Left like Hayashi Takeshi and Hirokawa Ryūichi, Abe Masao, and Azuma Shōhei. Oda Makoto can be seen as an older mentor of this group, which was characterized by its close, personal identification with the Palestinian nationalist cause.

•

liberal and feminist writer of the postwar era. Her numerous books on liberalism and feminism helped to shape Japanese thinking throughout the postwar period.

Ishigaki traveled to the Middle East immediately after the Yom Kippur War. She was seventy at the time. Her dispatches typified the romantic vision of the Middle East conflict that was to dominate mainstream journalism for many years. In the following passage, for example, she describes her experiences after having been made to wait at the Jordan River before entering Israel. Her explicit identification of Jews as Nazis and her implied identification of the Palestinians as oppressed "Jews" show how this role reversal entered the Japanese popular consciousness through journalism.

> We crossed into Israel, where we were forced off our bus, treated like cattle, and had our luggage subjected to a minute inspection. Even our toothpaste and medicine bottles were taken out and inspected. After that, we were herded into cubicles and strip searched. The Israelis were nervous about weapons and bombs to the point of paranoia. As I was not an Arab, I was treated somewhat better than the others. The Israeli officials who dealt with us were as arrogant as Nazis, ordering us about with their chins. The exception to this rule was a busload of American tourists. They were treated politely and sent on their way after only a cursory inspection. They were not pitiful refugees. The refugees had been chased off their land and had been living in the Arab countries. When they go to visit the land of their birth, they are treated as subhumans. It is hard to imagine how they must feel as they are herded about by Israeli officials. Each one of them will go on to become a potential spark to trigger the Palestinian struggle to regain their home-land.[73]

The intolerance of Judaism and the unnatural character of Zionism are stressed in another passage, where Ishigaki contrasts orthodox Jews with barefoot Palestinian women:

> With a fanatical look in their eyes, [the Orthodox Jews] look down with contempt on the Arabs they pass, exuding a thick air of intolerance. I

•

had the feeling I was in the Middle Ages. Despite the fact that they were persecuted themselves as a homeless people and were subjected to massacre after massacre during the Nazi era, they have stolen the Palestinians' land and, having come into possession of a state of their own, are behaving like an arrogant Elect. In the cities, modern high-rise buildings are going up in rapid succession. They are built on the backs of Palestinian laborers, but they are occupied by Israelis. Passing the gate of a kibbutz, a barefoot Palestinian woman is conscripted into hard labor. "Zionism," which until now had been only a word to me, took on tangible form. . . . Was it inevitable that [the Jews] should become so cruel, trampling on those weaker than themselves, as soon as they acquired power courtesy of a foreign regime? I felt as if I had had my nose rubbed in human egotism.[74]

It is not hard to imagine the hurtful situations Ishigaki describes, and her indignation may have been justified. But what is most salient in these passages is the way she tries to deal with these situations by reproducing in popular journalism the increasingly familiar tropes and suppositions of ideological anti-Zionism.

Ishigaki indulges in an extreme romanticization of the Palestinian "revolution." For her, it is not a concrete political struggle but a cathartic, metaphysical experience. The women in the refugee camps, she writes, "seem so much more alive than Japanese women, despite the fact that they are forced to live the worst possible kind of life. It is probably because their passion for the revolution has been distilled and all worldly concerns have been washed away."[75] Accepting without question the legitimacy of commando raids on Israel, Ishigaki praises the Palestinian women because they are "not simply brave, they are full-fledged Palestinian guerrillas."[76]

Ishigaki's romantic idealization of the beleaguered Palestinians was carried on by others, like the journalist Shiba Mitsuyo, who visited Lebanon during the summer of 1978. Shiba does not attempt to understand the real conditions of Palestinian life or the political conditions that keep them in it, but simply identifies with them and by so doing "redeems" herself. "Lost in conversation in the dark, cramped houses of the camp with people who had been expelled [from Israel]," she writes, "I would suddenly have the sense that I had simply stepped into the apartment next to mine back home. The people were open, kind, and full of humor. Experiencing the true love and limitless kindness that is characteristic of those who have been oppressed and abused, I felt my ailing, strained nerves soothed and my everyday life redeemed."[77]

Shiba's emotional identification is explicitly romantic and nonrational: "Even though we did not speak each other's language," she writes, "we understood each other's feelings perfectly."[78] This emotional identification combined with the other tenets of anti-Zionist dogma to produce a powerful ideological formulation that casts the Jews as racist-imperialists and the Palestinians as innocent harbingers of the human future:

> In the midst of their fierce struggle toward liberation, the Palestinian people, who for thirty-one years have been deprived of their right to survival and their right to exist as a people by the atrocities of the racist-imperialist Zionists, have produced a philosophy to liberate even the Jews who stole their homeland and a sensibility to free mankind from all discrimination. The voices of Palestinian children who fight joyfully, single-mindedly will be the first to reach the human future.[79]

These rhapsodic paeans did not appear in marginal left-wing journals but in the *Asahi* and *Mainichi* newspapers. Their purpose was not to explain the situation in the Middle East but to provide the Japanese with a sense that they were connected to a meaningful political movement. Similarly, in 1972, the playwright Kara Jūrō led his troupe, the Situation Theatre (*Jōkyō gekijō*), to perform in Palestinian refugee camps in Lebanon and Syria. Kara had no understanding of the Middle East conflict, but upon his return to Japan, he published an account of his experiences titled *Our Theater in the Wind, Pistols in Our Breast* in which he romanticized the Palestinians and derided the Jews' misguided attempt to embrace "the rotten flesh of the nation-state."[80v] In a like vein, the artist Washimi Tetsuhiko visited Lebanon

---

[v] Apparently sobered by the real political consequences his extravagant rhetoric implied

and Syria at the invitation of the PLO in 1979 and was embraced by PLO chairman Yasir Arafat. "I felt," he wrote in the *Kyoto shimbun*, "the strength of his resolve to liberate his homeland in Mr. Arafat's supple smile and the firm muscles of his shoulders and arms."[81] This was the level to which Japanese left-wing political discourse, which had formulated a trenchant critique of the state in the 1950s and organized massive demonstrations to drive the point home in the 1960s, had descended by the late 1970s.

In sum, during the 1970s, the anti-Zionist ideology of the Palestinian National Charter entered Japan and was domesticated and legitimized by prominent Japanese academics and intellectuals. Popularized by the mass media, it entered the popular consciousness, and a romantic identification with the Palestinians became one of several acceptable substitutes for the practical politics that had become impossible for the left-wing in Japan.[w] Perceptions of Israel as a "racist-imperialist" state, Judaism as an inherently intolerant religion, the Jews as "Nazis," and the Palestinians as "the new Jews," which originated in Soviet and Arab propaganda, thus came to be integrated into the reservoir of Japanese images of the Jews.

On the thirty-seventh anniversary of *Kristallnacht*, November 10, 1975, the United Nations General Assembly adopted a resolution denouncing Zionism as a form of racism. The infamous resolution was intended to foster an international consensus for the highly critical definition of Zionism contained in the Palestinian National Charter, and it was part of an international drive by the Palestine Liberation

---

in the Middle East, Kara subsequently withdrew from overt political activity, and his work took a more poetic turn. See Goodman, *Japanese Drama and Culture in the 1960s*, pp. 233–34.

[w] Other approved alternatives to practical politics were environmentalism and opposition to nuclear weapons. These are unquestionably legitimate issues, but a sentimental espousal of these causes has frequently substituted for practical political activity. Regarding enivronmentalism and antinuclearism as symbolic issues in Japan in the 1970s, see Dower, "Peace and Democracy in Two Systems," pp. 25–28.

Organization and its allies to delegitimize the state of Israel and gather support for the Palestinian cause.[x] Backed by Arab, Third World, and Soviet bloc states, the resolution passed easily by a vote of 72 to 35 with 32 abstentions. All the industrialized democracies opposed the resolution with the exception of Japan, which abstained.

Japan's refusal to join the United States and the European countries was the result of a new independence in Japanese foreign policy that developed in the early 1970s. It was the product of the air of cynicism that surrounded the Vietnam War, the sense of betrayal that followed President Richard Nixon's secret rapprochement with the People's Republic of China in 1971, and, most significantly, the threat to the Japanese economy posed by the Arab oil embargo of 1973. It was also the result of a growing confluence of interests between the conservative government and the left-wing opposition.

Japanese government policy toward the Middle East changed precipitously in 1973. On October 6, the Yom Kippur War began. Ten days later, the Organization of Petroleum Exporting Countries (OPEC) raised the posted price of crude oil 70 percent, and the following day, the Organization of Arab Petroleum Exporting Countries (OAPEC) announced it would cut oil production 5 percent from its September level and would refuse to sell oil to states that did not support Arab political goals. Because Japan imported virtually all its petroleum and was dependent upon the Arab states and Iran for 78.4 percent of its supply in 1973, this sudden increase in oil prices and the threat of an embargo had very serious implications. The threat to Japan was perceived to be so serious that it caused the Japanese government to depart from its unswerving support for United States foreign policy and adopt a pro-Arab Middle East stance.[82]

The decision to side with the Arabs in the Middle East conflict was a rational and pragmatic one. It was not taken out of an animus for (or even a knowledge of) the Jews and Israel; nor, for that matter, was it the result of any particular sympathy for or knowledge of the

---

[x] Among other supporters of this drive was the Ugandan tyrant Idi Amin, who received a standing ovation in the General Assembly this same year following a speech in which he denounced the "Zionist-American conspiracy" and called for the extermination of the Jewish state.

Palestinians. The government of Japan adopted a pro-Arab policy to protect its oil supply. As a by-product, however, it ratified, reinforced, and promoted the left's hostile image of the Jews and Israel.

Japan's pro-Arab tilt was signaled by Chief Cabinet Secretary Nikaidō Susumu in a statement on November 22, 1973, which "deplored Israel's continued occupation of Arab territories"; stressed that Japan had always "been prompt in supporting the United Nations General Assembly Resolution concerning the rights of the Palestinian people for self-determination"; urged that "the legitimate rights" of the Palestinians be recognized; and "depending on future developments" threatened "to reconsider its policy toward Israel."[y]

---

[y] Here is Nikaidō's statement:

1. The Japanese government has consistently hoped that a just and lasting peace in the Middle East will be achieved through the prompt and complete implementation of Security Council Resolution 242 and has continued to request the efforts of the parties and countries concerned. It has been prompt in supporting the United Nations General Assembly Resolution concerning the rights of the Palestinian people for self-determination.

2. The Government of Japan is of the view that the following principles should be adhered to in achieving a peace settlement.
(1) The inadmissability of acquisition and occupation of territories by use of force;
(2) The withdrawal of Israeli forces from all the territories occupied in the 1967 war.
(3) The respect for the integrity and security of the territories of all the countires in the area and the need of guarantees to that end; and
(4) The recognition of and for the legitimate rights of the Palestinian people in accordance with the Charter of the United Nations in bringing about a just and lasting peace in the Middle East.

3. The Government of Japan urges that every possible effort be made to achieve a just and lasting peace in the Middle East in compliance with the above-mentioned principles. Needless to say, it is the intention of the Government of Japan to make as much contribution as possible towards that end. The Government of Japan, deploring Israel's continued occupation of Arab territories, urges Israel to comply with those principles. The Government of Japan will continue to observe the situation in the Middle East with grave concern and, depending on future developments, may have to reconsider its policy toward Israel.

[Maruyama, "Japan's Middle Eastern Policy in a Dilemma," pp. 273–74. The Japanese text appears in Hōri Shōichi, *Nihon no chūtō gaikō "sekiyu gaikō" kara no dakkyaku* (Kyōikusha, 1980), pp. 26–28.]

•

Unconstrained by the need to placate the United States, Japanese opposition parties were even more caustic in their condemnation of Israel. The Japanese Communist Party demanded that the government break diplomatic relations with the Jewish state, and other opposition parties expressed their displeasure with the government's "half-hearted" response. Kawasaki Kanji of the Japan Socialist Party warned, "Unless the government reassesses its total devotion to the United States and fundamentally supports the Arab states, its attitude will be backward-looking at best." Masaki Yoshiaki of the Clean Government Party (Kōmeitō) said, "Even as it makes the Japanese people pay the price of its pro-American mismanagement of the country's affairs, the government has failed to develop a clear policy position of its own." And Kawamura Masaru of the Social Democratic Party said, "Out of its concern for America, the government has distorted the basic line of peace diplomacy. Its responsibility for this is grave indeed."[83] In sum, the consensus among Japanese opposition politicians was that Japan should break with America and develop its own independent foreign policy. They concurred in the government's pro-Arab policy but were critical of the government for being insufficiently zealous in implementing it.

In the ensuing months and years, Japan did everything possible to ingratiate itself with the Arab states. On December 10, the government sent Deputy Prime Minister Miki Takeo as a special envoy to the Middle East. Subsequently, Nakasone Yasuhiro, then minister of international trade and industry (MITI), Special Ambassador Kosaka Zentarō, and MITI Minister Kōmoto Toshio all visited the Arab countries. In February 1977, the government granted the Palestine Liberation Organization permission to establish an office in Tokyo. In July 1979, MITI Minister Ezaki Masumi visited the Middle East, followed by former Foreign Minister Sonoda Sunao as special emissary from the Prime Minister in February 1980. In April 1980, Prime Minister Ōhira Masayoshi announced his support for the establishment of a Palestinian state. And in 1981, Yasir Arafat, ostensibly on a private visit, was welcomed to Japan by the country's top leadership, including the prime minister and foreign minister.

During this period of intense pro-Arab diplomacy, no cabinet-level

•

Japanese official visited Israel. Indeed, the first visit by a Japanese government minister to the Jewish state took place on June 26, 1988, when Foreign Minister Uno Sōsuke visited the country.

The Japanese government also condoned the Arab boycott of Israel, and it refused to censure the many companies that complied with it. Nissan was one such company. In a letter dated July 9, 1969, the Japanese carmaker explicitly refused to export to Israel because of the Arab boycott. It later denied that it was boycotting Israel, but the Anti-Defamation League of B'nai B'rith characterized these denials as "totally false and part of Nissan's continuing pattern of double talk."[84] In 1980, Zennoh, the Japanese Agricultural Cooperative Association, notified the Dead Sea Works in Israel that after twenty-six years of doing business it would no longer import potash from Israel, a move attributed to the Arab boycott. In 1986, Toshiba refused to sell mail-sorting machines to the Israeli Ministry of Communications because of the boycott. Toyota refused to export cars to Israel for decades, and in 1987 an American reporter was told by a Toyota executive that "Toyota has a special policy not to export to Israel."[85] In fact, until 1991, when Toyota began exporting to Israel, Subaru was the only Japanese car sold in the country. Toshiba, Nippon Steel, Hitachi, and Cannon were among Japanese companies still refusing to trade with Israel in 1991.[86] There has been virtually no Japanese investment in Israel. Japan Air Lines does not land there, nor has any Japanese-flag ship entered an Israeli port. Japanese banks, among the largest in the world, have refused to finance exports of investment goods to Israel; and there has been no Japan External Trade Organization (JETRO) office in the country to promote trade.[87]

As the Anti-Defamation League of B'nai B'rith observed in 1986, "The government of Japan not only persists in refraining from condemning the boycott, but is unwilling to do anything to prevent its application in Japan or to discourage Japanese business from cooperating with it."[88] And the *Economist* wrote in 1988, "Talk about trading with Israel is taboo in Japan. South Africa is considered far more respectable."[89]

The liberal media not only supported but idealized the tilt toward the Arab side in the Middle East conflict. In its popular "Vox Populi,

Vox Dei" (*Tensei jingo*) column the *Asahi shimbun* of December 27, 1973, lauded the Arab oil embargo as a latter-day version of the storming of the Bastille. Even if "there are certain inconsistencies," the paper wrote, "we should not lose sight of the fact that with this the Third World has succeeded in using the weapon of natural resources as a means to inaugurate its own liberation movement." And it concluded, "The Japanese have so far been unconcerned with the fate of these countries. . . . Now we know the error of our ways. That is the nature of history." The paper argued that Arab actions were representative of a major historical shift whose importance transcended any minor ethical problems with the embargo itself.

On January 1, 1974, the well-known novelist Ōoka Shōhei published an article in the *Asahi*, arguing that the willingness of the Japanese government to make pro-Arab statements was a necessary first step in developing an independent Japanese foreign policy:

> The present crisis arose from the fact that Japan has gone out of its way
> to accommodate the State of Israel, which the United States created. It
> has been embarrassing to watch Japanese spokesmen tripping over
> themselves to make pro-Arab statements, but that is the necessary first
> step in the de-Americanization of Japanese foreign policy. If I feel that
> the postwar period may have ended, it is because of this [willingness to
> act independently of the United States].[90]

"The Japanese people should reflect long and hard," an *Asahi* editorial of January 5 urged, "on the fact that, while they have aided and abetted the United States, they have had no clear understanding of the fact that they were accomplices in its crimes."

In short, Japan's decision not to oppose the General Assembly resolution equating Zionism with racism was the result of disaffection with American foreign policy and reflected an effective political alliance between left- and right-wing forces in Japan. Because it wished to repudiate American imperialism during the Vietnam War, the left justified government policy with the self-deluding argument that capitulation to Arab pressure constituted an independent foreign policy for Japan. The government, on the other hand, accepted the left's

•

position that an uncritical acceptance of the political platform of the Palestinian National Charter constituted a true understanding of the Middle East situation because it needed a rationale for its unprincipled, economics-driven foreign policy.

The consensus to support the Palestinians thus served the political interests of each side, but it also revealed a paucity of principled political thinking, and it concealed two widely divergent images of Japan and its future. Where the left supported the Palestinians as a means to repudiate capitalist imperialism, the government supported the Palestinians to ensure that Japan would continue unhindered to develop as a capitalist power. The left's vision of Japan as a nonaligned nation akin to the Third World made strange bedfellows with the government's vision of Japan as a leader of the capitalist economies, and the arrangement had a corrosive effect on both sides. It coopted the left-wing opposition into supporting government policy, and it retarded the government's development of a well-informed Middle East stance. The underlying conflict between these two competing images of Japan remained unresolved through the 1980s and continued to affect Japanese Middle East policy through the Gulf War.

The compatibility of left-wing anti-Zionist ideology with antisemitism became clear in 1985–86, when Hirokawa Ryūichi and a group calling itself "The Committee for Palestinian and Jewish Studies" published a two-volume work titled simply *The Jews*. The first volume was a collection of essays subtitled *What Is a Jew?* in which the authors repeated the by now familiar assertions of their creed: that the Jews are nothing more than a religious denomination, that Zionism employs a Nazi-based racist definition of the Jews, and that Israel is a Nazi-racist state in Palestine created by Western imperialism. Jews, the authors argued, should reject racist Zionism, dismantle the state of Israel, and accept the status of a tolerated minority in the Islamic world.[91]

The second volume, titled *The Jews: Merchants of Diamonds and*

Death, took a different tack. In his introduction, Hirose Takashi went out of his way to distinguish it from the conspiracy theories of the right,[z] but he claimed that the volume revealed the *real* Jewish conspiracy—among Israel, South Africa, and Taiwan.

> These three countries have entered into a tacit alliance of murder. Devoting their energies to the most illicit of industries, they are in fact shaping world events. Most people looking superficially at these countries as "states" will probably dismiss them as third-rate nations not worth discussing. But the fact is that early on they secretly cooperated in developing the atomic bomb. Not only have they given birth to the most dangerous alliance in terms of global strategy, but they have been directly involved in every conflict and war and are sending an endless stream of arms, munitions, and military advice into the fields of battle. As their reward, they clench in their fists filthy lucre drenched in blood. The diamonds referred to in the title of this book are the symbol of these ill-gotten gains.[92]

Hirose, who subsequently attributed the 60 percent drop in the Nikkei stock average in 1989 to the machinations of the Jews, here propounds a left-wing conspiracy theory derived from Soviet propaganda that portrays the Jews (in the guise of the Israelis) as manipulators of world events large and small with vast fortunes and nuclear blackmail. This is the Japanese version of what has fittingly been called "the socialism of fools." It is the kind of chimerical hostility toward Jews that can only be called antisemitic.[aa]

---

[z] He writes, "There are many people who have been poisoned by disreputable conspiracy theories of history running rampant in society that hold that the world is about to be overthrown by the 'Jewish secret society of Freemasons.' I hope readers will distinguish carefully between this sort of dubious theorizing and the present work. The Israel Lobby that exists in Europe and America is not an abstraction like the Freemasons but a specific group of real bankers and speculators." Hirokawa Ryūichi and the Committee for Palestinian and Jewish Studies, ed., *Daiyamondo to shi no shōnin: Isuraeru no sekai senryaku* [Merchants of Diamonds and Death: Israel's Global Strategy], *Yudayajin* [The Jews], vol. 2 (Sanyūsha, 1986), p. 5.

[aa] Hirose deduced his conclusion from the fact that a share in the Wall Street firm of Goldman Sachs had been bought by the Sumitomo Bank, which also had an interest in Bank of America, whose president was the brother of Michael Armacost, then U.S.

•

Hirose Takashi is an exceptional case. Not all or even most Japanese on the left would accept his extreme views. But the Japanese left's consistent villainization of Israel and its persistent, categorical denigration of Jewish peoplehood, history, and culture have left an enduring legacy. In the late 1980s and early 1990s, this legacy had two significant consequences. It helped to account for Japan's ambivalence in the Gulf War and for the almost universal refusal of Japan's intellectuals to publicly condemn resurgent antisemitism.

---

ambassador to Japan, who is Jewish. See "Kinkyū keikoku: 'kabuka ichiman-en' de 'Yudaya shihon' ni nerawareru Nihon kigyō" [Urgent Alert: Japanese Industry Threatened by "Jewish Capital" When Stock Prices Hit ¥10,000], *Shūkan Post*, July 10, 1992, pp. 31–35.

On the relationship between left-wing conspiracy theories and Soviet propaganda, see Wistrich, *Hitler's Apocalypse*, pp. 212–13.

The phrase "socialism of fools" was originally coined by August Bebel. See Seymour Martin Lipset, *The Socialism of Fools: The Left, the Jews and Israel* (New York: Anti-Defamation League of B'nai B'rith, 1969); and Michael Lerner, *The Socialism of Fools: Antisemitism on the Left* (Oakland, Calif: Tikkun Books, 1992).

•

VIII

A SIGNAL FAILURE

RECRUDESCENT ANTISEMITISM AND JAPAN'S "SPIRITUAL CONDITION"

BY THE LATE 1980s, Japan had emerged as an economic superpower. Japanese exports grew fourteenfold between 1970 and 1989, from $19.318 billion to $269.57 billion. By 1989, Japan was producing one out of every four automobiles in the world and dominated high-tech industries like cameras, video recorders, silicon memory chips, and robotics. Japanese overseas development assistance exceeded U.S. foreign aid in 1989 by $2 billion. And by 1991, Japanese per capita income was estimated to be $23,570, nearly $2,000 more than per capita income in the United States.[1]

The country's economic success led to a transformation in the way people both at home and abroad thought about Japan. Japanese writers have often stressed Japan's cultural uniqueness, but in the immediate postwar period that uniqueness was usually viewed as a negative characteristic. The Japanese were different from others—more feudalistic, more militaristic—and that had led to the rise of fascism and the debacle of the war. By the 1970s, however, the uniqueness of Japanese culture was more and more being perceived as the source of Japan's economic success. The group-oriented, consensus-building society that had once been regarded as a feudalistic throwback was now increasingly touted as a model of social organization particularly well suited to the postindustrial age.[2] The Harvard sociologist Ezra Vogel captured the spirit of this new perception in the title of his book, *Japan As Number One*.[3]

Renewed pride and self-confidence engendered a new nationalism, and the chauvinist thinkers and politicians who had been on the defensive for most of the postwar period took advantage of the change of mood to assert themselves. In 1982, Nakasone Yasuhiro, an ardent nationalist who as early as 1950 had petitioned Gen. Douglas MacArthur to allow Japan to rearm, became prime minister. Paralleling his contemporaries, Ronald Reagan in the United States and Margaret Thatcher in the United Kingdom, Nakasone injected a strident new nationalism into politics in Japan.

His primary goal as prime minister was to reverse the policies of Yoshida Shigeru, who had made the choice early in the postwar period to sacrifice a degree of Japan's political autonomy for economic advantage. In attempting to reverse the Yoshida Doctrine, Nakasone sought during his five-year tenure as prime minister to reclaim the political autonomy Japan had given up. His "Grand Design" was to restore Japan's pride in itself and create a "healthy nationalism," without which he believed Japan would not be able to take its proper place in international affairs. Nakasone conceived of Japan's national interests as inextricably intertwined with and dependent upon the international system, but he was convinced his country could not play an active leadership role in that system without an active sense of nationalistic pride.[4]

There are varying interpretations of Nakasone's neonationalism. Some have regarded it as a farsighted attempt to internationalize Japan[5]; others have seen it as a menacing resurgence of the wartime mentality.[6] Both views are correct. Nakasone sincerely wanted to establish the basis for greater Japanese participation in international institutions and affairs. To do so, however, he reopened the Pandora's box of Japanese nationalist sentiment, releasing a panoply of forces that he was hard-pressed to control.

Nakasone's attempts to renew Japanese self-esteem culminated in his visit to Yasukuni Shrine on August 15, 1985, the fortieth anniversary of Japan's World War II surrender. Nakasone made this ostentatious visit to the main shrine of wartime State Shinto in the company of 15 cabinet ministers and 172 Liberal Democratic Party (LDP) Diet members, becoming the first sitting prime minister ever to visit the shrine on the day of the surrender. Nakasone compounded the reactionary implications of his visit by making a contribution to the shrine from state funds, thus intentionally contravening the constitutional separation of church and state.[7]

The reactionary mentality behind Nakasone's politics led him to legitimize the racist thinking and rhetoric of Japanese ethnic nationalism. Typical of the kind of thinking Nakasone encouraged was the statement by a Japanese official in 1982 who asserted, "The Japanese are a people that can manufacture a product of uniformity and superior quality because the Japanese are a race of completely pure blood, not a mongrelized race as in the United States."[8] Nakasone's own comments at an LDP seminar in September 1986, extolling the virtues of Japan's "monoracial society" (*tan'itsu minzoku shakai*) and contending that blacks and Hispanics lower the level of intelligence in the United States, epitomized the mindset and reproduced patterns of Japanese xenophobia going back to Aizawa Seishisai.[9a]

Nakasone's actions and rhetoric encouraged those nationalists whose postwar transformation into "liberal democrats" had been more

---

[a] In a remarkable precursor to the rhetoric of the 1980s, Aizawa wrote in 1825, for example, "As for the land amidst the seas which the Western barbarians call America, it occupies the hindmost region of the earth; thus, its people are stupid and simple, and are incapable of doing things." Ryusaku Tsunoda et al., eds., *Sources of Japanese Tradition*, vol. 2 (New York: Columbia University Press, 1964), p. 89.

On the prevalence of racist rhetoric among top LDP politicians at this time, including Nakasone, see Buruma, "A New Japanese Nationalism," *The New York Times Magazine*, April 12, 1987, pp. 23–26, 29, 38; "Prejudice and Black Sambo," *Time*, August 15, 1988; and "Japan Apologizes for a Racial Slur," *New York Times*, August 16, 1988.

•

apparent than real. Unreconstructed chauvinists like Minister of Education Fujio Masayuki had to be sacked in 1986 for suggesting that the rape of Nanking had not violated international law and that Japan had colonized Korea at the Koreans' behest. Two years later, in May 1988, Okuno Seisuke had to be fired as director of the National Land Agency for equivocating Japan's responsibility for invading China in the 1930s. Even after he left office, Nakasone's legacy continued. In 1989, Prime Minister Takeshita Noboru expressed doubts about Japanese wartime responsibility and even about whether Hitler's policies could be classified as aggression.[10]

Outside of government, too, right-wing thinkers were emboldened to express views that had hitherto been regarded as disreputable if not exactly taboo. Etō Jun, a respected academic and prominent literary critic who had long argued that the postwar constitution had emasculated Japan and that Occupation censorship had stunted the growth of Japanese literature, published *The Japanese-American War Is Not Over* (*Nichibei sensō wa owatte inai*) in 1987. In the book, Etō argued that Japan should use its technological superiority as leverage to regain its political independence from the United States. The controversial potboiler *The Japan That Can Say No* (*"No" to ieru Nihon*) by Diet member Ishihara Shintarō and Sony chairman Akita Morio made a similar point in 1989.[11]

Despite increased wealth and a government intent on translating economic power into international influence, however, there was a growing sense of impotence and frustration among Japan's broad middle class. Japanese workers toiled incessantly, earning the label "economic animals," but they received few tangible or even spiritual rewards for their efforts. By the mid-1980s, half the Japanese were dissatisfied with the quality of their life, and one in three office workers were reportedly being treated for a stress-related illness.[12]

Many Japanese also felt they were being victimized by the United States. A New York Times/CBS/Tokyo Broadcasting System poll conducted in May-June 1990 found that more than two-thirds (68 percent) of respondents said the United States was blaming Japan for its economic problems.[13] The same poll repeated in December 1992 revealed that the number of people who believed the United States was using Japan as a scapegoat had increased to 78 percent. More than three-quarters (77 percent) said that Americans were contemptuous of Japanese, and nearly half (46 percent) characterized relations between Japan and the United States as "unfriendly."[14]

Heightened expectations combined with the absence of tangible rewards produced intense feelings of frustration and even rage among some Japanese, and these feelings had an impact on Japanese culture, particularly the publishing industry. The inflation caused by the rise in oil prices following the Arab oil embargo of 1973 had seriously weakened the proud, medium-sized publishers whose imprints had meant intellectual quality and responsibility during the first quarter-century of the postwar period. Publishers like Misuzu, Iwanami, Heibonsha, Kawade, and Chikuma were increasingly displaced in the market by small, sensationalist presses that specialized in the work of dubious "experts" (kenkyūka) and "commentators" (hyōronka), who, although they had few recognizable credentials, often responded more acutely to the interests of the affluent, relatively well-educated, but frustrated middle class than the "high-brow" intellectuals published by the quality houses.[15]

A wave of easy explanations about Japan's present and future situation inundated the market. In 1990, books concerning the prophecies of Nostradamus sold so well that the phenomenon was reported in the Japanese press.[16] Even more popular were books that explained Japan's predicament as the work of a powerful Jewish conspiracy bent on destroying the country, and Japanese book stores set up special "Jewish corners" to better serve their voracious clientele.[b]

The antisemitic books that began filling Japanese bookstores in the mid-1980s were not necessarily written by obvious crackpots. Some, like the two volumes of Yamakage Motohisa's *The Jewish Plot to Control the World*, were by overt Shinto nationalists[17]; but others, like *The Expert Way of Reading the Jewish Protocols* by Yajima Kinji (1919–   ), which went through fifty-five printings in its first year of publication, were by internationally recognized scholars with strong

---

[b] Popular publishers that achieved particular prominence by publishing antisemitic books during this period included Tokuma shoten (founded in 1954), Nihon bungeisha (founded in 1948), and Dai'ichi kikaku (founded in 1981).

•

academic credentials.[18c] Still others, like *The Secret of Jewish Power That Moves the World* by Saitō Eisaburō (1913–), were by prominent politicians.[d]

The most successful antisemitic author to emerge in the mid-1980s, however, was Uno Masami (1941–). Uno is important for three reasons. First, he reactivated and exploited traditional Japanese images of the Jews more thoroughly than any other author. Second, he forged international alliances with antisemites and Holocaust deniers in other countries, introducing their work and ideas to Japan. And third, he revealed the acceptability of antisemitic thinking in Japan today by the high degree of credibility his contentions received in mainstream journalism and politics.

Uno's main achievement is to have breathed new life into old Japanese ideas about the Jews. His central thesis, that Japan faced a mortal threat from the adherents of an alien occult religion, refurbished xenophobic nationalist arguments going back to Aizawa Seishisai, Ukai Tetsujō, and Ōhashi Totsuan. In Uno's version, the United States was secretly controlled by an all-powerful Jewish "shadow government," Japanese-U.S. relations were actually Japanese-*Jewish*

---

[c] Yajima, a professor of international relations at Aoyama Gakuin University, was cited twice by *Time* magazine in 1987 as a reliable expert on economic affairs, despite his public assertions that the world economy was controlled by a global Jewish conspiracy. See *Time*, April 6 and November 9, 1987.

[d] Saitō Eisaburō, *Sekai o ugokasu yudaya pawaa no himitsu* [The Secret of Jewish Power that Moves the World] (Nihon keizai tsūshinsha, 1984). Saitō was elected to the Diet in 1974 and has held the cabinet-level post of director of the Agency of Science and Technology as well as serving as vice minister of labor. He claims to hold doctorates in law, literature, and business from three separate universities and to have authored 180 books. His name appears frequently, along with that of Linus Pauling, in two-page advertisements in the *New York Times Book Review* for "Prof. Dr. Hisatoki Komaki's Four Steps to Absolute Peace," a uniquely Japanese attempt to create a dialogue between Buddhism and Christianity. See, for example, the *New York Times Book Review*, March 14, 1993, pp. 16–17.

Saitō charges in his book that Franklin Roosevelt was thirty percent Jewish and became president of the United States as a Jewish spy (pp. 134–35); that the Jews had declared World War I the beginning of Armageddon, which they believed would bring the Messiah (pp. 171–72); and that the postwar Japanese constitution was imposed on Japan by the Freemasons, who were indistinguishable from the Jews (p. 129). Saitō also informs his readers that the state of Israel was established by Harry Truman, who sent 100,000 American Jews to Palestine aboard U.S. Navy ships, which shelled the land and drove out the native inhabitants (p. 186).

●

relations, and therefore the threat posed to Japan by the United States was actually a Jewish threat.[19] All of Japan's democratic institutions, which had been mandated by the American-inspired postwar constitution, were, according to Uno, a Jewish plot to destroy Japan.[20] He announced that democracy and internationalism amounted to "the Judaization of Japan," and he urged his compatriots to emulate Hitler and devise policies that would protect the interests of the Japanese ethnic nation (*minzoku no rieki*).[21]

Christian theology also played an essential role in Uno's thought. A fundamentalist minister in the Osaka Bible Christian Church (*Ōsaka seisho kirisuto kyōkai*), he followed in the footsteps of nationalistic Christian theorists of the Jews like Oyabe Zen'ichirō, Sakai Shōgun, and Nakada Jūji. Uno has published explicit works of Christian prophecy, including *Great Prophecies of the Old Testament: The Jews and Armageddon* and *Great Prophecies of the Old Testament, Continued: Armageddon and the Qualifications of the Leader*, both of which appeared in 1982.[22e] He preaches that the Jews' ultimate aim is to precipitate World War III to bring about the Messianic Age,[23] which will follow the Soviet invasion of Israel,[24] which Uno says the prophet Ezekiel foretold and the Jews believe fanatically.[25] After the war, which the Jews will win, a Jewish autocrat will benevolently rule the world from the rebuilt Temple in Jerusalem, but the Jewish dictatorship will last only three-and-a-half years, after which time the real Messiah, the returned Jesus, will appear on the Mount of Olives to usher in the true Millennium.[26,27f]

---

[e] *Great Prophecies of the Old Testament: The Jews and Armageddon* was published in March 1982, after which Uno left immediately for his sixth visit to Israel. The day before he was to return to Japan, Israel invaded Lebanon, confirming Uno's apocalyptic theories. Upon his arrival back in Japan, he issued the sequel to his earlier book, *Great Prophecies of the Old Testament, Continued: Armageddon and the Qualifications of the Leader*.

Uno met Prime Minister Menachem Begin in May 1981, and a photograph of Uno with Begin's arm around his shoulder appears in *Kyūyaku seisho no dai-yogen*, p. 85.

[f] Uno's argument is based on the Book of Revelation (13:5–8) and closely resembles the apocalyptic theology of the American premillennialist preacher Hal Lindsey, whose immensely popular *The Late Great Planet Earth* was first published in 1970 and had reportedly sold eighteen million copies in the United States by the mid-1980s. The cataclysm Uno predicts is identical to the one Lindsey describes, and he uses the same

•

In the two works that brought him international notoriety in 1987,[28] Uno combined this xenophobic ethnic nationalism and Christian fundamentalism with the conspiracy theory of *The Protocols of the Elders of Zion* to explain current events.[g] The two books—*If You Understand the Jews, You Will Understand the World* and *If You Understand the Jews, You Will Understand Japan*—so appealed to Japanese

---

exegetical evidence. See Hal Lindsey, *The Late Great Planet Earth* (New York: Bantam, 1973), especially pp. 135–68.

[g] Over the course of a few months in the fall of 1985, the value of the yen appreciated rapidly relative to the U.S. dollar. Where the dollar had been worth ¥240 in September 1985, it was trading in a range between ¥140 and ¥150 by the beginning of 1986. This rapid appreciation made it more difficult for the Japanese to export goods to the United States and made U.S. imports more affordable in Japan, thus putting the export-oriented Japanese economy under severe pressure.

The restructuring of the yen-dollar relationship was the result of a coordinated policy worked out by the finance ministers of the five leading industrial nations (G5), who met at the Plaza Hotel in New York on September 22, 1985. The Plaza Hotel Accord was an attempt to rectify the U.S.-Japan trade imbalance by adjusting the rate of exchange to make U.S. goods more attractive in the Japanese market.

Uno Masami interpreted these events according to *The Protocols of the Elders of Zion*. The precipitous rise in the value of the yen, he wrote, was part of a premeditated Jewish plot to destroy Japan (Uno, *Yudaya ga wakaru to sekai ga miete kuru* [*Sekai*], pp. 21, 24, and passim). Because the revaluation of the yen would not achieve this purpose, Uno claimed that the Jews, who had engineered the stock market crash of 1929, were plotting a similar "economic apocalypse" for 1990. Having lured all of Japanese liquid assets into U.S. financial markets, which they controlled, the Jews would orchestrate a global panic in that year, causing a return to the gold standard. Japanese investments, denominated in dollars, would be lost; Japan would be destitute; and the Jews would proceed to buy up Japan on the cheap (Uno, *Sekai,* pp. 254–59). Having taken control of Japan, the Jews would transport masses of black and Hispanic workers into the country, robbing the Japanese of their jobs and raping their women, thus simultaneously polluting Japanese culture and the Japanese gene pool (Uno, *Yudaya ga wakaru to Nihon ga miete kuru* [*Nihon*], pp. 130–31).

According to Uno, "International Jewish Capital" already functioned as a global "shadow government" that determined everything that happened in the world (Uno, *Sekai,* pp. 31–33). International Jewish Capital had, he charged, already taken complete control of the United States (Uno, *Sekai,* p. 108), and Ronald Reagan was nothing but a "robot president" controlled by "Jewish" advisers like George Shultz (Uno, *Sekai,* p. 41; *Sekai,* p. 121–23). Even Reagan's cancer surgery in 1985 was alleged by Uno to have been Jewish retaliation for Reagan's advocacy of school prayer and his visit to the Bitburg cemetery in West Germany, where Nazi SS troops are interred (Uno, *Sekai,* pp. 124–32).

According to Uno, the real rulers of America are the Jews, who manipulate the country through four great "Jewish" families—the Rockefellers, the Morgans, the Duponts, and the Mellons—and a fifth financial empire built around Citicorp. The fact that none of these families is in fact Jewish did not concern Uno. By his lights, Commodore Matthew Perry, Christopher Columbus, V. I. Lenin, Franklin Roosevelt,

readers that they sold a combined total of over a million copies in fewer than six months.[29]

Far from being criticized as dangerously atavistic, Uno's theories were treated as a plausible explanation for Japan's economic woes in mainstream journalistic and political circles. He was quoted approvingly in the mass media, including the *Yomiuri shimbun*, Japan's most widely read daily newspaper,[h] and he appeared as a featured speaker at a Constitution Day rally sponsored by the Liberal Democratic Party.[i]

---

and even former Saudi Oil Minister Sheikh Ahmad Zaki Yamani were all Jews. (For references to the "Jewish" origins of these historical figures, see the following: Four great "Jewish" families: Uno, *Nihon*, pp. 108–11; Perry: Uno, *Sekai*, p. 174; Columbus: Uno, *Nihon*, p. 111; Lenin: Uno, *Nihon*, pp. 166–67; Roosevelt: Uno, *Nihon*, p. 114; Yamani: Uno, *Nihon*, p. 129.)

Uno calculated that the "Jewish" Rockefellers alone possessed 10 percent of the world's wealth (Uno, *Sekai*, p. 113). According to his reckoning, they controlled six of America's ten biggest banks, six of its ten biggest insurance firms, and more than a hundred multinational corporations, including Exxon, Texaco, and Standard Oil; General Motors, Ford, and Chrysler; IBM, GE, and USX; First National City Bank and Chase Manhattan Bank (Uno, *Sekai*, p. 113).

Not only do the Jews have a stranglehold on the United States—the world's greatest military, economic, and political power—but, according to Uno, they also have a monopoly on the world's supplies of energy, food, information, and capital (Uno, *Sekai*, pp. 6–7, 218–19).

In Uno's view, in 1985–86, only Japan and the Soviet Union stood between the Jews and their goal of total world domination, and the Jews had already devised the downfall of these two remaining adversaries (Uno, *Sekai*, p. 7). By revaluing the dollar, strengthening Korea as an economic rival to Japan, and reestablishing diplomatic relations between the United States and China, the Jews were seeking to contain and eventually destroy Japan (Uno, *Sekai*, p. 7 and passim). Drawing heavily on *The Protocols*, Uno argued that the Jews were in the final stages of their plot to destroy Japan, despoiling the Japanese spirit through television and mindless popular culture (Uno, *Sekai*, pp. 62–64), bleeding the nation of its financial resources by encouraging stock market speculation, and luring Japanese companies away from Japan to establish factories overseas (Uno, *Nihon*, p. 6).

If Japan was to survive, Uno argued, it would have to awake to the fact that the principal opposition in global politics was not East versus West or North versus South but the Jews against the world (Uno, *Sekai*, pp. 7, 25).

[h] In a major article in the business section, the *Yomiuri* cited Uno's theory that the Jews had plotted the revaluation of the yen to punish Japan as a credible explanation of the country's economic woes. "En: haisui no kōbō" [The Yen: Last Ditch Defense], January 17, 1987.

[i] The 1987 rally was sponsored by a conservative faction of the LDP headed by Kishi Nobusuke, the wartime ultranationalist and born-again Liberal Democratic premier who had forced through the renewal of the U.S.-Japan Mutual Security Treaty in 1960. See "Backers, Protesters Mark Constitution's 40th Year," *Japan Times*, May 4, 1987.

•

What accounted for the popularity and acceptability of Uno's work was the way it reactivated *familiar* images of the Jews. The xenophobic notion that Japan was being threatened by an alien religious force, Christian prophecies regarding the Jews, and the conspiracy theory of *The Protocols* were by no means alien to Japan.[30] Uno's ideas were thus neither original nor aberrant but a continuation of longstanding trends in Japanese intellectual history, and this accounts for their popularity and the alacrity with which Japanese readers accepted them.

Two things did distinguish Uno from his predecessors, however. First, he was a professional antisemite, a creature of the commercialization of Japanese culture in the 1970s and 1980s. Unlike Oyabe Zen'ichirō, Sakai Shōgun, or even Inuzuka Koreshige, who were motivated by an idealistic albeit extreme and often bizarre nationalism, Uno was self-aggrandizing and clearly motivated by the quest for profit. He thrived on the fame international criticism brought him, and in 1993 he capitalized on his reputation as a Jew-baiter in a new book titled *I Fought the Jews and Understood the World*.[31]

Uno was also distinguished by the extent of his overseas alliances. Despite their xenophobia, Japanese antisemites have always had strong ties to ethnic nationalists in other countries. Shiōden Nobutaka visited Hitler's Germany, and his ideas were strongly influenced by the Nazis. More recently, Yajima Kinji lifted his theories almost verbatim from an American contemporary named Gary Allen, a John Birch Society ideologue and speechwriter for the late Alabama Governor George Wallace.[j] Uno, similarly, is part of the

---

[j] Allen was a contributing editor to both the *Conservative Digest* and the John Birch Society's *American Opinion* magazine. His most popular books in Japan are *Rokkuferaa teikoku no inbō* [The Rockefeller File], tr. Takahashi Yoshinori (Jiyū kokuminsha, 1987); and *Insaidaa* [None Dare Call It Conspiracy], tr. Yuasa Shin'ichi (Taiyō shuppan, 1986).

Yajima explicitly identifies the Jews as Allen's "Insiders," "power elite," and "Eastern Establishment" (Yajima, pp. 37ff). He contends that the United States and Soviet Union are both controlled by an "invisible empire" or shadow government (Yajima, pp. 80ff). This invisible empire is composed of three "secret societies," all of which grew out of the eighteenth-century secret order known as the Illuminati, and it aims to unite the world under its control. Following Allen, Yajima considers liberal policy groups like the Round Table Groups, the Council on Foreign Relations, and the Royal Insti-

international network of right-wing antisemites and Holocaust deniers who have been increasingly active in recent years.[32k] Like them, he denies that he is hostile to Jews, but he idealizes Hitler and Stalin.[33] Like them, he claims that the Holocaust is a Jewish fabrication.[34] Like French Holocaust-denier Robert Faurisson, whose work he cites, Uno claims Anne Frank's *Diary* is a forgery.[35] And like German revisionist historians, he argues that while they may have killed hundreds of thousands of Jews, Stalin and Hitler did so only in self-defense.[36]

Uno's international connections go beyond these intellectual affinities, however. He heads the Japanese branch of the Washington-based Liberty Lobby,[37] which the Anti-Defamation League of B'nai B'rith described in 1988 as "the most active anti-Semitic organization in the [United States]."[38] In addition to his own monthly publication, *Enoch*, Uno publishes *New American View: International Edition*, a version of the newsletter published by the Liberty Lobby that first appeared in September 1987. The editor of *New American View*, Victor Marchetti, appears on the cover of Uno's 1990 book, *Confessions*

---

tute for International Affairs to be "secret societies." All this is taken directly from Gary Allen. (Compare Yajima on the Illuminati, pp. 83–84, with Gary Allen and Larry Abraham, *None Dare Call It Conspiracy* [Seattle: Double A Publications, 1971, 1983], pp. 30n, 91. Compare also the chart on "Financing Bolshevik Revolution" [Allen, p. 80] with Yajima's chart on p. 75. Compare further, Allen, *None Dare Call It Conspiracy*, pp. 92–94, on the Round Table Groups, the Royal Institute for International Affairs, and the Council on Foreign Relations with Yajima, pp. 82–86.)

For a description of Yajima's intellectual lineage, see George Johnson, *Architects of Fear: Conspiracy Theories and Paranoia in American Politics* (Boston: Tarcher, 1983).

Uno also cites Gary Allen's conspiracy theories. See *Sekai*, pp. 187–89.

[k] In 1989, an American journalist expressed the suspicion that Uno was on the Arab payroll. "Western intelligence agents in the Far East," he wrote, "have for some time been investigating possible ties between author Uno and the well-funded Arab propaganda effort in Japan." (Willy May Stern, "David and Godzilla," *New Republic*, February 27, 1989, p. 18.) The basic alliance between Arab interests and the left wing in Japan makes Arab support for right-wing extremists like Uno extremely unlikely, however, and indeed Itagaki Yūzō and Arab representatives in Japan have openly criticized his ideas. (See, for example, Abdelwahab Chalbi, "A Windfall for Israeli Apologists" in the *Asahi shimbun*, September 3, 1987; Itagaki Yūzō's comments in the *Asahi shimbun*, March 28, 1987; and Itagaki's comment quoted in " 'Jewish Conspiracy' a Figment of an Author's Imagination," *The East* 23, no. 2 (June 1987), 43.)

•

of the Jews: Behind the Scenes of the Japanese Economy and in ads for
New American View: International Edition.[39,40]

Another Liberty Lobbyist with whom Uno works is Dale P. Crowley Jr., a fundamentalist Baptist minister who describes himself as "fanatically insane, raving right-wing."[41] Crowley speaks Japanese, which
he presumably learned as a missionary, and visits Japan frequently. The
Liberty Lobby's weekly tabloid, *The Spotlight*, reported on one of his
visits in the following terms: "A staunch America firster, Crowley
spent two weeks in Japan as the guest of Pastor Masami Uno, an economist and clergyman who is concerned about the growing Zionist influence in his country. Crowley, who is fluent in Japanese, addressed
groups of business executives, many of whom were CEOs of their companies."[42] A videotape of one of Crowley's joint lecture appearances
with Uno is available and can be rented at Japanese video stores.[43] In
1991, Uno published *The International Jewish Conspiracy: An American Account*, which he cobbled together from Crowley's antisemitic
work.[44]

Uno is also linked to American political extremist and antisemite
Lyndon LaRouche.[45] Uno published *Confessions of the Jews*, which
was purportedly authored by two American Jews, Paul Goldstein and
Jeffrey Steinberg, and translated by Uno. Goldstein and Steinberg are
listed on the masthead of LaRouche's magazine *EIR* (*Executive Intelligence Review*) as "Directors of Counterintelligence." In 1987, both
men were indicted for obstruction of justice in connection with
LaRouche's trial for fraud in his 1984 presidential campaign. Among
other things, *Confessions of the Jews* accuses the Anti-Defamation
League of being an international criminal conspiracy that runs drugs
and maintains rings of prostitutes to raise funds for its manipulation
of U.S. corporations, a charge that Steinberg developed in articles like
his 1990 "Tax-Exempt Treachery: A Profile of the Anti-Defamation
League."[46] Steinberg has also accused Amnesty International of being
a "support organization for Soviet-sponsored international terrorism."[47]

Uno has translated the work of legitimate foreign authors, in-
sinuating that they share his antisemitic views. He has translated
Arthur Koestler's *The Thirteenth Tribe: The Khazar Empire and Its*

Heritage,[48] which casts doubt on the historical continuity of the Jewish people,[1] and two books that were critical of Israel and Zionism—Robert I. Friedman, *The False Prophet: Rabbi Meir Kahane—From FBI Informant to Knesset Member*[49] and Alfred M. Lilienthal, *The Zionist Connection II: What Price Peace?*[50,m]

In sum, therefore, the recrudescence of Japanese antisemitism that began in the mid-1980s, epitomized by the work of Uno Masami, was not a novel or aberrant phenomenon but a logical product of Japanese history and the reiteration of longstanding Japanese images of Jews. It was an extreme expression of the neonationalism of the Nakasone regime, which had been made possible by Japan's economic success. It was driven by the sense of frustration and rage many Japanese felt as their economic achievements failed to translate into international respect and a better, freer, more meaningful life. And it was popularized by pseudo-intellectuals, unscrupulous "commentators," and sensationalist publishers who had gained prominence in the 1970s because of the commercialization of Japanese culture.

---

[1] Of this theory, the Princeton historian Bernard Lewis has written, "Some [Arab writers] limit this denial [of the continuity of Jewish peoplehood] to European Jews, and make use of the theory that the Jews of Europe are not of Israelite descent at all but are the offspring of a tribe of Central Asian Turks converted to Judaism, called the Khazars. This theory, first put forward by an Austrian anthropologist in the early years of this century, is supported by no evidence whatsoever. It has long since been abandoned by all serious scholars in the field, including those in Arab countries, where Khazar theory is little used except in occasional political polemics." Bernard Lewis, *Semites and Anti-Semites* (New York: Norton, 1987), p. 48.

The theory nevertheless continues to be treated as credible in Japan, promoted by both the left and the right. See "Yudaya teikoku Hazaaru maboroshi no shuto?" [Was This the Lost Capital of the Jewish Khazar Empire?], *Asahi shimbun*, August 20, 1992, which reports on the leftist writer Hirokawa Ryūichi's recent investigations.

[m] It is doubtful that Uno personally wrote and translated all these works. Willy Stern reports that Uno's *If You Understand the Jews* books were ghostwritten by his editor, Takahashi Teruo. See Willy May Stern, "David and Godzilla," *New Republic*, February 27, 1989, p. 17.

•

The basic reaction to the recrudescence of antisemitism in Japan was denial. "Anti-Semitism has no roots in Japan's cultural history," asserted one government official in a typical statement.[51] Implying that the problem was not antisemitism in Japan but Jewish paranoia abroad, the Japanese Foreign Ministry issued a memorandum to the Japanese Association of Publishers in 1989 that read in part, "Although it is true that Japan has no history of anti-Semitism, the Jewish community fears that the spread of such derogatory literature in Japan will do irrevocable damage to Japanese perceptions of and attitudes toward the Jewish people."[52]

To reinforce this highly selective, self-serving reading of history, the Japanese government also resurrected Sugihara Chiune as the exemplar of Japanese wartime policy toward the Jews. Sugihara, who issued transit visas to as many as six thousand Lithuanian Jews in 1940, had been consigned to oblivion for more than fifty years. His wife Yukiko had refused all contact with Foreign Ministry officials after the war, blaming them for punishing her husband for his humanitarianism. In October 1991, however, Vice-Minister for Political Affairs Suzuki Muneo found it expedient to express the ministry's regrets to Mrs. Sugihara. "On behalf of the Foreign Ministry," he said, "I would like to take the occasion of the establishment of diplomatic relations with Lithuania to assure you that we honor your husband and his extraordinary deeds and hold his memory in the highest esteem."[53] A story reporting that a street in the newly independent Lithuanian capital had been named Sugihara Street appeared in the Japanese press.[54] In March 1992, Prime Minister Miyazawa Kiichi, in response to a question from a member of parliament, answered, "Vice-Consul Sugihara's judgment and actions were humanitarian and courageous in an extreme situation, the Nazi persecution of the Jews. I would like to commend both his judgment and his deeds."[55] A memorial park honoring Sugihara was also dedicated in August 1992 near the diplomat's birthplace in Yaozu, close to Nagoya,[56] and books also appeared celebrating his life. Shino Teruhisa's *Long Journey to the Promised Land*[57] and Sugihara Yukiko's *The Visa of Life for Six Thousand*[58] told his story, and in 1991 a one-hour documentary entitled "Sugihara Chiune" was aired on the Yomiuri television network.[59]

While Sugihara presents a model of individual moral courage and common-sense compassion of which the Japanese can justifiably be proud, he was no more representative of Japanese wartime policies and attitudes than Oskar Schindler was of the policies of the Germans. In the context of the war, Sugihara was a renegade who was disciplined for his insubordination, and the Japanese government's efforts to identify itself with him were a transparent attempt to deflect attention away from Japan's history of antisemitism.

Notwithstanding these denials and obfuscations, the Japanese government did alter some of its policies toward Israel in the late 1980s, but these changes in foreign policy had virtually no impact on domestic thought.

There were three reasons for the shift in Japanese policy toward Israel. First, the Arabs were weaker and the Japanese were stronger in 1987 than they had been in 1973. Slackening oil prices had weakened Arab economies.[n] At the same time, the Japanese had taken defensive measures and were less vulnerable to Arab pressure than they had been fifteen years earlier. An underground reserve amounting to a five-month supply of oil had been created and conservation measures had been instituted. By the late 1980s, although the Japanese economy was approximately 60 percent the size of the U.S. economy, it used only about 20 percent of the energy.[60] In addition, Japan was less dependent on Arab markets than it had been. Where the Arab states had once purchased 10 percent of Japan's total exports, in 1988 they bought less than 4 percent.[61] And the steady decline in the ability of the Soviet Union to sponsor the Arab states made them far more dependent on Japan politically than Japan was on them.

Second, the Japanese government gradually became aware that, contrary to the representations of left-wing ideologues, Israel did not

---

[n] Between 1984 and 1987, the Office of Anti-Boycott Compliance of the United States Commerce Department reported a 50 percent decline in the number of complaints it received, about 20,000 a year, down from between 35,000 and 40,000 in previous years. ("Arabs' Boycott of Israel Is Alive, But Hardly Flourishing," *New York Times*, August 23, 1987.)

•

constitute the major obstacle to peace and stability in the Middle East. It became obvious that issues that had nothing to do with Israel, like the Iran-Iraq war, were far more significant destabilizing factors than the bogeyman of Zionism.[62]

Finally, negative publicity generated by revelations about Japanese adherence to the Arab boycott and reports of the widespread stereotyping of Jews in Japan affected government policy. During a visit to Tokyo in November 1985, New York Mayor Ed Koch told the powerful Japanese Economic Business Council (*Keidanren*) that Japan could not insist on free trade with the United States while complying with the Arab boycott of Israel. Koch was told in private talks with Prime Minister Nakasone that Japan had no intention of changing its support for the Arab boycott, but it is clear in retrospect that Koch made an impression.[63] The embarrassment caused by the *New York Times* revelation on March 12, 1987, of the popularity of antisemitic books in Japan, diplomatic protests from the Israeli government, letters from U.S. congress members, and threats of a Jewish boycott of Japanese products in the United States further embarrassed the Japanese government, which tried to neutralize criticism by improving relations with Israel and the American Jewish community.[°]

The Japanese government began making gestures of friendship toward Israel in late 1987, just months after the *New York Times* story appeared. In November of that year, the Japanese philanthropist and power broker Sasakawa Ryōichi contributed $1.5 million to the Tikotin Museum of Japanese Art in Haifa.[64] In December, the exchange of trade missions between Japan and Israel that had been suspended ten years earlier was resumed.[65] On June 26, 1988, Foreign Minister Uno Sōsuke became the first cabinet-level Japanese dignitary

---

[°] Senator Arlen Specter (R-PA) and Representative Charles Schumer (D-NY) cosigned an angry letter to Prime Minister Nakasone immediately after the *New York Times* story appeared. Charles Chi Halevi called for a boycott of Japanese goods in the *Chicago Tribune*, April 28, 1987. See also the letter from Morton Marcus in *Moment*, January–February 1988. Another letter urging free trade with Israel signed by 101 members of Congress was sent to Prime Minister Kaifu Toshiki and Korean premier Kang Young Hoon in August 1989; and nine senators wrote with a similar message to Prime Minister Kaifu in March 1991. See Jennifer Golub, *Japanese Attitudes Toward Jews* (New York: Pacific Rim Institute of the American Jewish Committee, 1992), p. 13.

•

to visit Israel. And in December 1988, he was followed by Itoyama Eitarō, chairman of the Diet's foreign affairs committee and one of the world's ten wealthiest men.[66]

These contacts were not unequivocal expressions of friendship. During Foreign Minister Uno's visit, the Japanese diplomat met with Prime Minister Yitzhak Shamir and made the obligatory pilgrimage to Yad Vashem, the Holocaust memorial, then proceeded immediately to the Deheishe refugee camp south of Bethlehem, where he pledged a quarter of a million dollars for the construction of a community center and ostentatiously reaffirmed Japan's support for the creation of a Palestinian state.[P]

Despite the equivocal character of Japan's new policy toward Israel, the improvement in Japanese-Israeli relations between 1987 and the Gulf War of 1991 was real. Total trade between Japan and Israel, which had been $385 million in 1985, grew to $827 million by 1987 and reached $1.38 billion in 1991. Also in 1991, Toyota, Nissan, and Mazda announced that they would begin direct auto sales to Israel, ending years of strict observance of the Arab boycott.[67]

After the interruption of the Gulf War, relations between Japan and Israel continued to improve. The Japanese became increasingly impatient with the Palestine Liberation Organization after it sided with Iraq during the war. In May 1991, Tada Toshio, the former ambassador to Damascus and Riyadh and head of the Middle East Institute in Tokyo, labeled PLO leaders "professional protesters" only interested in perpetuating the Middle East conflict to keep themselves employed.[68] On December 16, Japan voted with the United States and 109 other nations to repeal the UN General Assembly's 1975 resolution equating Zionism with racism. On December 3, 1992, Foreign Minister Watanabe Michio set a precedent by meeting with a delegation of American Jewish leaders from the American Jewish Committee, using the opportunity to announce that Japan had taken a series of steps to end Japanese compliance with the Arab boycott.[69] In

---

[P] See "Chutzpah in Japanese," *Washington Jewish Week*, July 7, 1988. The Deheishe community center was personally dedicated on June 1, 1991, by Foreign Minister Nakayama Tarō, who called on Israel "to be more flexible for the sake of peace." See "Nakayama Dedicates Center at Deheishe," *Jerusalem Post*, June 2, 1991.

January 1993, a tax treaty was signed between Japan and Israel, eliminating the problem of double taxation in the two countries. Although minor by most standards, it was nevertheless the first treaty ever signed between Israel and Japan and the result of thirty years of negotiations.[70]

Japan also took an active role as a cosponsor of the multilateral peace talks between Israel and its Arab neighbors that began in May 1992. Japan hosted working groups on the environment and participated in others on water and the economy. During a December 1992 visit to Japan, Israeli Foreign Minister Shimon Peres praised the Japanese and urged them to play an even more active role in the peace process.[71]

Japanese antisemitism has always been an issue of *domestic* ideology, however, and Japanese foreign policy toward Israel and the Jews had little impact on domestic life and thought. When on September 4, 1987, Foreign Minister Kuranari Tadashi condemned Japanese antisemitism in a statement before the Foreign Affairs Committee of the Diet, therefore, his statement was clearly made for foreign consumption and was duly ignored by the Japanese press. It had no impact whatsoever on the acceptability of antisemitic thought in Japan.

The most egregious recent example of the discontinuity between the Japanese government's foreign and domestic policy was the World Conference of Historical Cities held in Kyoto in November 1987. The conference was organized by the Kyoto city government with the support of the Foreign Ministry. Thirty-five cities from around the world were invited to attend, each with a history of at least 1,200 years and a population exceeding 500,000. Tunis and Katmandu were invited to attend, but Jerusalem, certainly one of the world's most venerable cities, was not. Kyoto city officials repeatedly denied any political motivation behind their refusal to invite Jerusalem, but in a letter to Jerusalem Mayor Teddy Kollek, Mayor Imagawa Masahiko acknowledged the political nature of the decision.[72] The Kyoto city government's decision to exclude Jerusalem, condoned by the Foreign Ministry and virtually ignored by the Japanese press, amounted to a government-sponsored cultural boycott of Israel.

•

Reacting to the exclusion of Jerusalem and the blatant rebuff to Israel, Mayor Ray Flynn of Boston withdrew his city from the conference. A relatively young city, Boston did not meet the conference's criteria for participation, but it had been Kyoto's sister city since 1959, and without it no U.S. city would have been included. The *Boston Herald* ran a blistering editorial, supporting Mayor Flynn's decision to withdraw from the parley and condemning Kyoto's snub as a manifestation of Japanese antisemitism.[73]

Japanese scholars have generally refused to make an issue of antisemitism. While they have produced a substantial body of research on Jewish subjects, they have for the most part elected not to respond to the resurgence of antisemitism in Japan.

Recent Japanese scholarship on Jews and Judaism includes works on virtually every aspect of Jewish culture. *Jewish Thought*, two volumes in a sixteen-volume series on Eastern thought, were issued by the Iwanami Publishing Company in 1988–89. Kogishi Akira's *The Jews Expelled from Spain*, published in 1992, explores the expulsion of Jews from Spain in 1492. More than twenty accounts and memoirs of the Holocaust were translated and published in the period between 1989 and 1992, including Mochida Yukio's *The Nazi Hunt: Postwar Germany*, Ōsawa Takeo's *Jews and Germans*, and Shinoda Kōichirō's *Closed Space, Closed Time: The Literature of the Nazi Concentration Camps*.[74] Books on subjects ranging from Jewish interpretations of the Bible to the history of the state of Israel have also been published by Miltos Publishing, which specializes in Judaica.[75]

A few authors previously identified with the pro-Arab left have begun to express more balanced views. Doi Toshikuni's *American Jews* remains critical of Israel, but the author spent time in the United States acquainting himself with the American Jewish community, and he points out that the Jews are a complex and dynamic people. Similarly, in his *The American Jewish Community: The Reality of Jewish Power and Antisemitism*, Maruyama Naoki discusses the American Jewish community and its relationship to Japan-U.S. relations. Maruyama criticizes Japan for allowing antisemitic books to flourish and Japanese politicians for making racist remarks that jeopardize a basically cordial relationship.[76]

•

Virtually every important foreign work has also been translated into Japanese, and many good introductions to Judaism and Jewish history written from a variety of perspectives are readily available in Japanese bookstores. Examples include Isidore Epstein's *Judaism: A Historical Presentation*, Cecil Roth's *History of the Jews*, the six-volume *History of the Jewish People* edited by H. H. Ben-Sasson, and Max Dimont's popular *Jews, God and History*.[77] A few of the individual Jewish authors whose works are available in Japanese include Martin Buber, Gershom Scholem, Walter Benjamin, George Steiner, Elie Wiesel, Isaac Bashevis Singer, Philip Roth, and Saul Bellow. Lucy Dawidowicz's *The War Against the Jews*, Joan Peters's *From Time Immemorial*, and Charles Silberman's *A Certain People* are all available in Japanese. Books as diverse as *The Memoirs of Gluckel of Hameln* and Lenny Bruce's *How to Talk Dirty and Influence People* can be read in Japanese translation.[78]

Despite the wealth of good, representative writing about the Jews and Jewish culture in Japanese, Japanese readers show little interest in them, and they sell far fewer copies and have a much smaller impact than the more sensational books and articles. Published in 1973, the translation of Nobel Laureate Elie Wiesel's *Tales of Our Time*, for example, had sold fewer than 4,500 copies by April 1992. First published in Japanese in 1971, *Gimpel the Fool* by Nobel prize-winner I. B. Singer had sold a similar number of copies in the same period. Despite continuing tensions in the Middle East and the 1991 Gulf War, books about Israel have not sold particularly well. *In the Land of Israel*, Amos Oz's self-critical portrait, first published in 1985, had sold fewer than 2,800 copies by April 1992. And in contrast to Anne Frank's phenomenally popular *Diary of a Young Girl*, the more mature and provocative diary of another Holocaust victim, Etty Hillesum's *An Interrupted Life*, sold fewer than 3,000 copies between 1989 and 1992.[79]

The value of the continuing efforts by Japan's community of conscientious scholars and publishers cannot be overestimated. With patience and perseverance they have produced a body of work that provides a solid basis for an accurate understanding of Jews, Jewish culture, and Jewish history in Japan. But reticent to be distracted from their academic pursuits, Japanese scholars have generally refused to engage in the undignified task of promoting their work or refuting antisemitic demagogues, and they have thus not entirely fulfilled the promise contained in the founding "Prospectus" of the Japan Association for Jewish Studies to give their scholarly findings a "social expression."

To their credit, a number of individuals have stepped forward to denounce Japanese antisemitism and have candidly identified it as a throwback to Japan's ultanationalist past. Miyazaki Masahiro's sardonically titled *If You Spend Too Much Time Thinking About the Jews, You Won't Understand Anything* point by point debunked Uno Masami's analysis of world events.[80] The highly respected scholars Katō Shūichi, Yamaguchi Yasushi, and Muramatsu Takeshi all wrote op-ed pieces linking Uno to Nazism and reminded Japanese readers of their country's wartime alliance with Germany.[81] Nakagawa Ken'-ichi, a Protestant minister and television evangelist, also published a book trying to set the record straight.[82] These remained individual expressions of opinion, however. They were not echoed by other Japanese intellectuals and were not embraced by the media. Consistent with their refusal to acknowledge the existence and continuity of antisemitic thought in Japan, no major Japanese newspaper has ever editorialized against it.[83]

As was true of the government, the basic reaction of Japanese intellectuals to reports of antisemitism in Japan was categorical denial.[84] Typical of this trend was Chikushi Tetsuya, a prominent liberal journalist, former editor of the *Asahi Journal*, and an anchorman for TV Asahi. He accurately condemned "the uncritical acceptance of a racist myth" as evidence of "an abysmal ignorance of history and international politics [and] a sad commentary on our spiritual condition, too." But his condemnation was vitiated by his refusal to acknowledge antisemitism as a Japanese problem: "Japan is one of the few countries," he declared, "with no history of anti-Semitism."[85]

Chikushi was unusually outspoken in his denial. Most Japanese intellectuals simply rejected out of hand the notion that they bore any responsibility for confronting the antisemitism in their midst. The decision to award Kometani Foumiko's novella *Passover* two of Japan's most prestigious literary prizes exemplified this insensitivity and spoke volumes about the mentality of Japanese intellectuals today.

Passover concerns Michi, Kometani's thinly disguised alter ego, who came to the United States looking for the freedom she missed in Japan. In the U.S., Michi married a Jewish man and gave birth to a mentally retarded son. Instead of freedom, she found herself enslaved to an unreasoning offspring and a childish, self-indulgent mate. When her son is finally institutionalized after many years, Michi, finally free, uses the occasion of a Passover seder to declare her own liberation from bondage and walks out on her husband and family.

This plot is full of possibilities, but Kometani develops it without humor, insight, or irony. The wife of Hollywood screenwriter Josh (*Harry and Tonto*) Greenfeld, Kometani is the mother of Noah, the autistic son about whom Greenfeld has written several widely praised books,[86] and her purpose in writing *Passover* was to vent the frustration and rage she had accumulated over the years of caring for her handicapped son. "It began to hit me when I translate [Josh's books about Noah]," Kometani confessed to an American interviewer in 1988. "Nothing left for me. What I can do for my life now when I'm taking care of kids all the time? Always cleaning up the filth of Noah, always him pulling my hair, hurting me. And I had emotions left, a lot of complaints, and I had to put them somewhere. His Noah books, always he is the hero, my problems are not there. I want to write my side of the story."[87]

In writing her side of the story, Kometani grossly overcompensates, stooping to racial stereotypes of Jewish noses and worn-out calumnies about Jewish cliquishness.[88] The Passover seder becomes, in her portrayal, a display of Jewish hypocrisy and ugliness that she argues through her alter ego is typical not only of Jews but of Western civilization in general. The west is a uniquely intolerant civilization, according to Kometani; Judaism is the source of that intolerance; and Jews are the embodiment of intolerance.[q] In the final

---

[q] The outlandish charge that Jews and Judaism are the source of all religious intolerance is hardly new. Gavin Langmuir recounts the conclusions of Austrian Count Coudenhove-Kalergi, who, writing in 1901, found the origins of religious bigotry in the promulgation of the Torah under Ezra in the mid-fifth century B.C.E. In terms almost

pages of her book, Kometani accuses Judaism of being responsible for all the evils of Western civilization, including "colonialism, missionizing, and Nazism."[89r]

Some of the critics who read Kometani's book in Japanese found its description of Jews so extreme as to deserve the label "antisemitic." Kometani relates that she was first asked if she intended to write an anti-Jewish book at the party celebrating her receipt of the Shinchō Prize in August 1985.[90] *Passover* was described as antisemitic in a letter to the *New York Times* in March 1987.[91] Mistakenly identified as the chairman of the jury that awarded Kometani the Akutagawa Prize (which has no chair),[92] the respected Roman Catholic novelist Endō Shūsaku defended his earlier failure to criticize the book by publicly deploring "the anti-Semitism in this novel."[93] And the former Princeton University professor, novelist, and scholar of early Japanese poetry Ian Hideo Levy characterized Kometani's descriptions as "grotesque" and "bordering on racism."[94]

Several reviewers who read *Passover* in Kometani's 1989 English translation defended her against the charge of antisemitism.[95] Part of the difference in perception had to do with Kometani's rendering of

---

identical to those employed by Kometani, Coudenhove-Kalergi attributed all subsequent religious fanaticism and bigotry to the Jews. According to his thesis, Christianity and Islam had taken over the intolerant fanaticism of Judaism and turned it back on the Jews as antisemitism. Like Kometani, he condemned religious intolerance as a violation of what he considered genuine religious principles and attributed its origin to the Jews. See Gavin I. Langmuir, *History, Religion, and Antisemitism* (Berkeley: University of California Press, 1990), pp. 22–23.

[r] The charge that religious intolerance is a uniquely Western phenomenon is a common Japanese conceit. While Japan has been largely free of phenomena like the Crusades, there are many examples of religious intolerance in Japan, including the persecution of Christians and the suppression of Buddhism during the Tokugawa period. A particularly egregious twentieth-century example is Japanese colonial policy in Korea during the period from 1936 to 1945, when Koreans in their own country were not only made to speak Japanese and take Japanese names but were also required to worship Japanese gods. See Eugene C. Kim, "Education in Korea Under the Japanese Colonial Rule," in Andrew C. Nahm, ed., *Korea Under Japanese Colonial Rule* (Kalamazoo, Mich.: Center for Korean Studies, Western Michigan University, 1973), especially pp. 142–44. See also the title story in Richard E. Kim, *Lost Names: Scenes from a Korean Boyhood* (New York: Praeger, 1970), pp. 87–115.

•

her work, which altered key passages.⁵ Koemtani's self-serving English translation notwithstanding, however, the success of her Japanese original depends entirely on the ostentatious way it exploits Japanese stereotypes of Jews. As Fumiko Ikeda Feingold wrote in a letter to the *New York Times*, "Whatever the author's intentions, particularly in a climate of growing Japanese anti-Semitism, the effect of her story is bound to confirm the worst prejudices and falsest stereotypes."⁹⁶

Passover exploits Japanese stereotypes of Jews and of the West to prosecute the personal vendetta of its author. Writing in *World Literature Today*, New York critic Waka Tsunoda described the work as

---

⁵ One key passage will serve to illustrate how Kometani sanitized her translation. Toward the end of *Passover,* Michi complains,

> The people sitting here [around the seder table] are wondering why I don't convert to Judaism like Marilyn Monroe or Elizabeth Taylor. Other religions don't exist for them. Christianity and Islam inherited this intolerance from Judaism, and they ended up killing each other. That's the meddling West that won't leave people and their beliefs alone! That's colonialism, [Christian] missionizing, and Nazism.

[Kometani, *Sugikoshi no matsuri*, pp. 155–56.]

The key language is, "*Kō iu haitasei ga Yudaya-kyō kara Kirisuto-kyō ya Kaikyō ni uketsugare, sono sue wa otagai ni koroshiau yō ni natta no da. Hito no shugi o damatte hotte okenai osekkai na seiyō. Sore ga shokuminchi-shugi de ari, senkyō de ari, Nachizumu de aru.*" The clear implication is that Judaism is a particularly intolerant religion and the source of all the intolerance in the West, including Nazism.

Criticized for the antisemitic implications of this passage (David G. Goodman, Letter to the Editor, *Los Angeles Times Magazine*, August 21, 1988, p. 6), Kometani altered it in her translation:

> The people at the Seder table were probably wondering why I had not converted to Judaism, like Marilyn Monroe and Elizabeth Taylor. For them, no other religion could have any possible validity. *This exclusively, this clannish conviction that they alone were the sole repositories of ultimate truth, is something found not only in Judaism but also in Christianity and in Islam, and in the end they often killed each other because of it.* In the West, ideologies and theologies traditionally proselytized, unable to leave foreign cultures alone; resulting inevitably in imperialism, evangelism, and even in Nazism.

[Kometani, *Passover*, p. 78; emphasis added.]

Where in the Japanese original Kometani clearly implies that Judaism is the source of the West's "unique" intolerance, she has altered the passage for English readers, denying the special responsibility of Judaism and blaming all the monotheistic religions instead.

●

"not much more than a schoolchild's uninspired composition."[97] *Publisher's Weekly* wrote, "Kometani's narrative, dominated by the protagonist's whining self-pity and spiteful vituperation, is a nasty diatribe."[98] And *Hadassah Magazine* suggested, "More than the contempt and alarm it has evoked, the main thing [*Passover*] deserves is neglect."[99]

Japanese critics saw it differently. They praised *Passover* as the best that contemporary Japanese literature had to offer. In 1985, perhaps because it seemed to resonate with the rage many Japanese were feeling toward the United States at the time, they honored it with two of Japan's most prestigious literary awards, the Akutagawa Prize and the Shinchō Prize for New Writers.[100] Incredibly, in 1991, Kometani was even featured in a series on the world's "Great Jewish Writers" by a regional literary magazine.[101]

Kometani responded to American criticism of *Passover* with an autobiographical sequel entitled *Professor Dear* in 1991.[102] True to form, she chose to answer her critics by depicting them as illiterate homosexuals. Far from being condemned as a juvenile harangue, the book was praised in the *Asahi shimbun* by the well-known novelist Ōe Kenzaburō because, he said, it revealed what it was *really* like for a Japanese to live abroad.[103]

By ignoring flagrant expressions of antisemitism and rewarding overt hostility toward Jews and Judaism with literary prizes, the Japanese intellectual establishment has allowed antisemitism to persist in Japan and has contributed to its spread.

The willingness of Japanese newspapers to advertise flagrantly antisemitic books without fear of sanction is further evidence of this fact. All of Japan's mass-circulation dailies carry ads for antisemitic books.[104†] On July 27, 1993, the *Nihon keizai* (*Nikkei*) *shimbun*, widely

---

† Japanese daily newspapers like the *Yomiuri* and *Asahi* are papers with very large circulations. The national morning edition of the *Yomiuri* has a circulation of almost ten million; the morning edition of the *Asahi* has a circulation of more than eight million. Circulation figures for the Tokyo morning edition of the *Yomiuri*, *Asahi*, and *Nihon keizai* alone are as follows: *Yomiuri* = 5,820,000; *Asahi* = 4,290,000; *Nihon keizai* = 1,630,000. (These are 1989 figures from the 1990 edition of *Zasshi shimbun sō-katarogu*.) Consequently, advertisements carried in these papers have an impact of their own independent of book sales.

regarded as the Japanese counterpart of the *Wall Street Journal*, carried a one-third-page ad for the three volumes of the pseudonymous Jacob Morgan's *Get Japan, The Last Enemy: The Jewish Protocols for World Domination*. The *Asahi* had carried a similar ad four months earlier.[105] Emblazoned with Jewish stars and an image of Satan, the ad claimed that "Jewish cartels surrounding the Rothschilds control Europe, America, and Russia and have now set out to conquer Japan!" It outlined the Jewish scenario to destroy the Japanese economy, blaming the Jews for everything from the cut in Japanese interest rates in 1987 to the Gulf War and predicting the "re-occupation" of Japan by the Jews by the end of the decade. It asserted that the potential development of a two-party system in Japan was a Jewish plot to destroy the country and that Japanese currency contained hidden "Jewish" symbols that ridiculed Japan's imperial family.

At least as shocking as the ad itself, however, was the reaction of *Nikkei* officials when challenged about the ethics of carrying it. When questioned, a *Nikkei* official replied that the newspaper had a policy against running slanderous ads but that the advertisement for Morgan's books could not be considered slanderous. In a written response to a reporter's question, Umeda Shigeaki, head of the *Nikkei*, asserted, "We don't make any judgments on ideology, opinion, thought and beliefs in advertisements." Similarly, when challenged about its decision to publish the books in the first place, the publisher, Dai'ichi kikaku, replied simply, "We are satisfied that the author checked his facts."[106]

As in the case of Kometani's *Passover*, the question about the *Nikkei* ad for Jacob Morgan's books ultimately has less to do with the ad itself than with what it reveals about the judgment and standards of those who have published and defended it. Like the decision by the Japanese literary establishment to applaud Kometani's *Passover* as the best of contemporary Japanese literature, the decision of the *Nikkei* to defend a blatantly antisemitic advertisement reveals a provincialism, moral obtuseness, and historical myopia that was all too typical of the time.[u]

---

[u] Many knowledgeable observers have commented on the debilitated state of Japanese intellectual life in the late 1980s. The Cornell University historian J. Victor Koschmann

•

The signal failure to deal meaningfully with the recrudescence of antisemitism in Japan had political consequences during the Gulf crisis of 1990–91.

The Iraqi invasion of Kuwait in August 1990 precipitated a dilemma for the Japanese. Never before had events in the Middle East impinged so personally on their lives. For the first time, Japanese businessmen and their families were held hostage as "guests" in Iraq. Delegations of Diet members shuttled between Tokyo and Baghdad to negotiate their release, and the nation became emotionally engrossed in their fate.

Pressure from the United States exacerbated the sense of crisis. Japan was under intense pressure to contribute to the war effort, because, it was argued, the campaign was being mounted in significant part to protect Japan's oil supply. Eventually, the Japanese government did contribute $13 billion to defray the cost of the war, but only belatedly, after a grueling debate.

In general, the Japanese opposed the use of military force against Iraq. Their reasons were diverse but logical. Following the Yoshida

---

has written, for example, "If 1960 marked the apex of effective intellectual criticism in postwar [Japanese] history . . . then the end of the Shōwa period in 1989 might very well emerge as its nadir" (J. Victor Koschmann, "Intellectuals and Politics," in Andrew Gordon, ed., *Postwar Japan as History* [Berkeley: University of California Press, 1993], p. 423.) The University of Chicago scholar Norma Field presents a similarly devastating appraisal in her study entitled *In the Realm of a Dying Emperor: A Portrait of Japan at Century's End* (New York: Pantheon Books, 1991), as does the journalist Ian Burumain his chapter on Japan in *God's Dust* (New York: Farrar Strauss and Giroux, 1989), pp. 227–62.

Japanese intellectuals may counter that they in fact opposed antisemitism in Japan in an appropriate fashion by refusing to dignify it with attention (*mokusatsu*). They may also argue that Japan is a highly compartmentalized society (*takotsubo shakai*), where unsavory phenomena like racism and antisemitism are best treated by isolating them to certain unenlightened segments of the population. These approaches are not completely implausible, but they have been manifestly unsuccessful in discouraging or containing antisemitic thought and rhetoric in Japan. They are in fact themselves manifestations of the characteristic moral paralysis of the time.

•

Doctrine, which dictated that Japanese avoid participating in any kind of collective security arrangement, conservative politicians and businessmen took the position that Japan should contribute to the war effort only to the extent necessary to protect Japan's oil supply and preserve its relationship with the United States.[107] The Japanese people at large opposed the use of force because of their abhorrence of war as a generic evil. Left and liberal elements distrusted American foreign policy vis-à-vis the Third World and saw the assault on Iraq as yet another expression of American imperialism. Across the board, people invoked Article Nine of the Japanese constitution, which forbids Japan to use military force as an instrument of national policy, construing it broadly to prohibit not only the deployment of Self-Defense Force personnel but the contribution of humanitarian support as well.

Japanese opposition to the war against Iraq was justified on these economic, moral, and legal grounds, but beyond these reasoned arguments there was a degree of incoherence in the Japanese debate that astonished many observers.[108] Ignorance lay at the root of this incoherence. The Japanese simply knew very little about the Middle East and what was transpiring there. Without an academic tradition of area studies, few trained professionals and little reliable information on the Middle East were available.[v] Moreover, the weight of accumulated misinformation distorted, diluted, and compromised the resources that did exist. Lacking the capacity to inform themselves

---

[v] This problem was not limited to the Middle East. Japan had considerable difficulty administering its foreign aid program in the early 1990s because it lacked foreign expertise. Although Japan donated more in foreign aid than any other country, including the United States ($11.51 billion versus $10.72 billion), and although only 20% of that aid was tied to contracts with Japanese companies (as opposed to the 53% of French aid and the 54% of German aid that were tied in 1991), Japan was forced to entrust the administration of part of its aid to Britain's Crown Agents and was considering seeking the help of American aid workers as well because there were few Japanese area studies experts and people with experience in nongovernmental organizations (NGOs) to staff its program. See "Into Africa," *Economist*, October 9, 1993. For a Japanese argument for the need for more nongovernmental organizations to assist in foreign aid, see Matsui Yayori, *Shimin to enjo* [Citizens and Aid], Iwanami shinsho no. 133 (Iwanami shoten, 1990). See also David G. Goodman, ed., *Japan and the Developing World, Swords and Ploughshares: The Bulletin of the Program in Arms Control, Disarmament, and International Security*, 7, no. 4, University of Illinois (Summer 1993).

•

about unfolding events, the Japanese public had to depend on American news broadcasts beamed in by satellite as the sole consistent source of reliable information on the war.

The confused nature of the situation can be gathered from the publishing activity that took place surrounding the crisis. Between 1989 and 1991 there was a threefold increase in publishing related to Israel and the Middle East, with the total number of books published each year rising from 56 in 1989 to 151 in 1991.^w Special corners were set up in bookstores to display the many books that appeared. Junkudō, a major bookstore in Kyoto, set up a special Middle East section in the fall of 1990, for example. During the first week of February 1991, six of the thirty titles on the store's best-seller list were on the Middle East, and Junkudō was having difficulty keeping titles in stock.[109] In this and other bookstores around the country, however, no distinction was made among serious, objective analyses, antisemitic conspiracy theories, and anti-Zionist ideological tracts. All were dis-

---

^w The number and type of books published between 1989 and 1991 is set out in the following table.

	Original Works in Japanese	Translations	Total
1989	26	30	56
Antisemitic	3	0	
General	5	5	
1990	41	35	76
Antisemitic	3	3	
General	17	3	
1991	90	61	151
Antisemitic	5	4	
General	42	15	

In this table, the upper row for each year gives the total number of books published on Jews and Israel. Books that make no direct reference to Israel are not included. The second row tallies the books that were unequivocally antisemitic. The third row gives the number of books on general Middle East topics, including the Gulf crisis. Translations from foreign languages include books on the Holocaust, books on the Middle East, books on Judaism and Jewish thought, books on Jewish history, spy novels, and popular fiction.

Regarding the disproportionate sales of antisemitic titles, see "Wangan sensō ga hi o tsuketa 'Yudayabon' ninki no kiken" [The Danger of the Popularity of "Jewish Books" Inflamed by the Gulf War], *Asahi Journal*, May 3–10, 1991, pp. 100–101.

played together, without differentiation, as equally valid perspectives on the Middle East situation.[x]

In this environment, the distorting influence of ideologues was profound. Those readers who followed conspiracy theorists like Uno Masami could only conclude that the Gulf War was a stratagem of "the Jewish shadow government" that controls America, that the conflict was one of the endless wars of attrition predicted in *The Protocols of the Elders of Zion*, and that demands for Japanese monetary contributions to the war effort were part of the ongoing Jewish conspiracy to weaken and impoverish Japan.

The distorting impact of left-wing writers was even more pronounced. The scholars and journalists surrounding Itagaki Yūzō were particularly prolific during the crisis, promoting the view that Saddam Hussein's invasion of Kuwait was a response to the Israeli occupation of the West Bank and Gaza Strip and an attempt to liberate the Palestinians. In October 1990, eleven of these writers contributed to *Making Sense of "The Kuwait Crisis": Trends in Iraq and the Japanese Perspective*; in December, twelve authors contributed to *Middle East Perspective: Twelve Chapters Forecasting Changes in the Middle East*; and in February 1991, just before the outbreak of the Gulf War, thirty-six writers contributed to *The Middle East Gulf War and Japan: Proposals from Middle East Specialists*. In June 1991, the group published a postmortem titled *Middle East Analysis: Conditions in the Middle Eastern Countries in the Aftermath of the Gulf War*. During the crisis, the contributors to these volumes were in demand as lecturers, and many of their remarks were subsequently published in pamphlets and other formats.[110]

Protestant ministers from the United Church of Christ in Japan

---

[x] This inability to discriminate between serious and fallacious, reputable and disreputable arguments is also observable in individual works. An example of this phenomenon is *Yudaya bukku* [Jewish Books: Books and Reviews on Jews and Judaism], a volume prepared by "Sources of the 21st Century," an ad hoc group of ten or fifteen people with no discernible academic credentials formed in 1985 to study the occult. *Jewish Books* is a well-intentioned attempt to make sense out of the many theories of the Jews circulating in Japan today, including Jewish conspiracy theories, Japanese-Jewish common ancestry theories, and the like, but the result is to validate all of them. See Gurūpu 21 seiki gensho no kai, *Yudaya bukku* (Tokuma shoten, 1988).

•

(*Nihon Kirisutokyōdan*) also criticized Israel relentlessly and blamed it for the war. Led by Reverend Murayama Moritada, they sought to express their "solidarity with the Palestinian people as [their] means of solving the Palestinian problem, by extension, the Jewish problem, and achieving the liberation of Japanese workers."[111] Invoking the by now familiar transposition of Palestinians and Jews, Reverend Murayama asserted, "The intellectual and political structure that was formerly employed to eradicate the Jews has now been shifted to the Palestinians. 'The Palestinian issue' stands today as 'the new Jewish question.' "[112] Having previously supported the Iranian revolution as a progressive cultural struggle, Murayama defended Saddam Hussein during the Gulf crisis as the anti-Zionist champion of the Palestinian cause.[113]

Munakata Motoi, another minister in the United Church of Christ, demonstrated the essential identity of some left-wing and right-wing thinking. America had embarked on the Gulf War, he claimed, because of inordinate Jewish power in the United States. "It is obvious that any attempt to deal with the Palestinian problem would lead to the collapse of [Bush's] presidency," he wrote; and he lamented what he regarded as the end of democracy in America. Japan, he argued, was right not to participate in the Gulf War because it "must not contribute to the decline of America and of democracy, nor cooperate with bigotry and destruction, nor trample on fairness [*kōhei*] in the name of some short-sighted justice [*seigi*]."[114]

These left-wing denials of Jewish peoplehood and criticisms of Israel were especially significant because they shaped Japanese news coverage and therefore popular perceptions of the Gulf War. One particularly influential journalist was Hirayama Kentarō, a senior commentator (*kaisetsu iin*) with NHK, Japan's government-sponsored radio and television network. Hirayama, who made his reputation with sympathetic coverage of Third World struggles against the United States, was NHK's chief expert on Middle Eastern affairs during the Gulf War. The views he expressed throughout the crisis were summarized in his 1992 book, *To Whom Does Jerusalem Belong?*, in which he characterizes Israel as a fanatical right-wing state, declares Hebrew "an ersatz language" (*jinkōteki na gengo*), and flatly denies that the Jews exist as a historical people.[115]

•

Left-wing anti-Zionism shaped news broadcasts on commercial networks as well. Nishimori Mari (1961–), a polyglot graduate of the Tokyo University of Foreign Languages who studied at Cairo University and speaks fluent Arabic in addition to English, French, and Russian, appeared regularly on TV Asahi, the CNN affiliate in Japan. During the Gulf War she was featured on the weekend shows "Super Saturday" and "The American Way," regularly editorializing on the conflict. Similarly, Koike Yuriko (1952–), a 1976 graduate of Cairo University, appeared as a newscaster on TV Tokyo. Koike originally made a name for herself by interviewing Mu'ammar Gadhafi and Yasir Arafat, and she was also the founder of Inter-Communication Forum, a PR firm specializing in promoting Third World interests.[116]

Certainly, the Iraqi and Third World perspective needed to be heard on Japanese news broadcasts, and the Japanese had every right to oppose the Gulf War on principled grounds. But by assigning a disproportionately large role in the Gulf crisis to an illegitimate Israel and conniving Jews, newscasters like Hirayama, Nishimori, and Koike hampered the development of an accurate understanding of the Gulf conflict in Japan.

In short, the Japanese intellectual community has done little to stop or even retard the spread of antisemitic thinking in Japan, which is the continuation of a tradition of ethnic nationalist xenophobia and religious bigotry stretching back two hundred years. Their provincialism, moral obtuseness, and historical myopia have left their compatriots vulnerable to the distortions of dedicated ideologues and have impaired Japanese ability to deal effectively with the world around them in crisis situations like the Gulf War.

IX

JAPAN'S JEWISH PROBLEM

IMPLICATIONS IN A MULTICULTURAL WORLD

THE FUNDAMENTAL POLITICAL context of Japanese debates on the Jews and Israel changed after the Gulf War. The end of Communist support for the hard-line Arab states that accompanied the collapse of the Soviet Union and the coincidence of U.S. and Russian interests in the Middle East led to Iraq's defeat in 1991 and eventually resulted in the peace accord between Israel and the PLO in September 1993. In his September 9 letter to Israeli Prime Minister Yitzhak Rabin, PLO Chairman Yasir Arafat explicitly renounced "terrorism and other acts of violence" and affirmed "that those articles of the Palestinian Covenant which deny Israel's right to exist ... are now inoperative and no longer valid."[1] As its original proponents and major foreign sponsors abandoned it, the leftist position that Israel was the creation of Western imperialism with no intrinsic legitimacy became untenable.

Domestic politics also weakened the left. In nationwide Diet elections on July 18, 1993, the Socialist Party, recently renamed the Social Democratic Party, lost almost half of its 134 seats, reducing its total representation in the 511-seat body to just 70 members; and the Communist Party lost 1 seat, leaving it just 15 representatives. Public rejection of the Socialists and Communists reflected their disillusionment with policies and positions that seemed out of step with post–Cold War realities.

The conservatives, too, suffered an historic setback in the elections. Defectors had created two new parties with former Liberal Democratic politicians, and the loss of four seats in the national balloting cost the LDP its thirty-eight-year-old political hegemony.

The implications of this defeat for Japan's political culture were immediately obvious. A new coalition government headed by the reform-minded Hosokawa Morihiro took power, and one of the new prime minister's first acts was to reverse former LDP policy and publicly acknowledge Japan's responsibility for World War II. "I would . . . like to take this opportunity," he said in an address to the Diet on August 23, 1993, "to express anew our profound remorse and apologies for the fact that past Japanese actions, including aggression and colonial rule, caused unbearable suffering and sorrow for so many people."[2] Because the antisemitic boom of the 1980s was based in part on the denial of war responsibility and the revival of wartime nationalist and xenophobic thinking by the Nakasone regime, Prime Minister Hosokawa's forthright acknowledgment of Japan's wartime role was a step toward delegitimizing the foundations of contemporary antisemitic thought.

The decline of the ideological left and the rise of liberal forces within Japan's conservative political establishment suggested that relations with Israel would improve and antisemitic theorizing would diminish in Japan in the coming years. At the same time that these hopeful political developments were taking place, however, Japan was struggling with an economic recession, and old stereotypes of

•

the Jews, rather than disappearing, began a new transformation.

Economic conditions began to worsen in 1990, and Japan entered the worst recession of the postwar period. In the year ended June 1993, Japan's real gross domestic product shrank by 0.5 percent. More than a thousand Japanese businesses went bankrupt each month during the first half of 1993, and a Labor Ministry survey conducted in September revealed that three-fifths of the companies polled had recently cut wages. Breaking with the hallowed tradition of lifetime employment, Japanese companies laid off workers and imposed new standards of performance based on achievement on those who remained. In February 1993, Nissan announced it would close its Zama factory outside Tokyo, reducing its work force by five thousand employees.[3]

Economic insecurity led to a new round of antisemitic publishing activity. Writing in 1992, for example, Ōta Ryū (1930–) offered his readers an introduction to the Jewish Peril that traced the Jewish plot to destroy Japan back 1,200 years to the Nara period.[4] In 1993, Jacob Morgan, the pseudonymous author whose work was advertised in the *Nikkei* newspaper and who is probably identical to his "translator," Oshino Shōtarō, asserted that the Japanese Ministry of Finance and the Bank of Japan were controlled by Jews and that the well-known business consultant Ohmae Ken'ichi was a Jewish agent dedicated to selling out Japan to the Jews. Morgan charged that "Jewish" insignia could be found on Japanese paper money and identified Fukuzawa Yukichi, Nitobe Inazō, and Natsume Sōseki, the modern historical figures whose likenesses appear on Japanese currency, as (Jewish) Freemasons.[5] Seeking to exploit the lucrative antisemitic market, Japanese publishers and authors thus competed to produce books of escalating vulgarity and absurdity.

The increasing number of foreign workers in Japan during this recessionary period also reignited Japanese xenophobia. In 1990, the number of illegal immigrants in Japan was officially put at 100,000, but 300,000 was suggested as a more accurate figure. The visible presence of a relatively large number of dark-skinned Pakistanis and Iranians caused particular concern. The concentrated presence of the estimated 4,000 Iranian men who assembled in Yoyogi Park in central

Tokyo each Sunday caused alarm; and in December 1989, the National Police Agency circulated a memo asserting that Pakistanis had
"a unique body odor," carried infectious diseases, and routinely lied in
the name of Allah.[6]

Most Japanese took a liberal stance toward immigrant workers.
According to a 1989 survey, 56 percent of Japanese favored continuing
to admit foreign workers while 33 percent opposed the policy. Forty-
five percent favored giving legal status to those illegal aliens already
working in Japan, and an additional 16 percent favored applying
immigration laws leniently. Only 34 percent of respondents to the
survey wanted to strictly enforce existing laws and expel illegal aliens.[7]

Some Japanese were less compassionate, however. Starting in 1991,
bright red handbills emblazoned with swastikas began to appear on
lampposts in Tokyo and surrounding areas. The posters were distributed by the League of National Socialists (*Kokka shakaishugisha
dōmei*), a group of small businesspeople dismayed by the increasing
number of foreign workers in Japan and anxious over Japan's economic future. The group reportedly had only fifteen or sixteen core
members, but they managed to distribute 3,500 handbills in Tokyo
and adjoining Saitama prefecture each Sunday.[8] The handbills, which
measured eight by eleven inches, blamed Jewish multinational corporations for rising consumer prices, and they demanded that Japan
be protected from a plot by the Freemasons to admit alien races to the
country. One handbill posted near the Israeli embassy in Tokyo on
May 25, 1993, read, "Remember Kristallnacht! Get the illegal aliens in
Japan who threaten Japan's security! Fight the Zionist occupation
government! Smash international Jewish power and free the world
from diabolical Judaism!"

This new, economically driven xenophobia achieved an important
symbolic victory in July 1992, when the first antisemitic political party
in Japanese history appeared on the ballot for the Upper House Diet
election.[a] The Global Restoration Party (*Chikyū ishin tō*) fielded can-

---

[a] Shiōden Nobutaka had run on an antisemitic platform in the 1942 Diet election and
had polled more votes nationwide than any other candidate, but there had been no
political parties in this fascist election, all existing parties having been folded into the
Taisei yokusankai (Imperial Rule Assistance Association).

•

didates in Tokyo, the Osaka-Kobe area, and Gumma prefecture, and, as a recognized party, received national television time and newspaper space to promote its message.[b]

That message was unequivocal. According to the campaign literature for one of its candidates, Fujinami Norio, the party's purpose was to "smite the traitors who are selling out Holy Japan to the diabolical Jewish cult." "The Global Restoration Party," a campaign notice read, "denounces the ambitions of the Jews (Pharisees) to conquer the world and turn it into a global pasture for the human race and promotes the establishment of a world order under the rule of the Emperor and the Imperial Principle of Universal Brotherhood [*hakkō ichiu*]." Echoing wartime antisemites who regarded the Jews as Japan's true enemy, the handbill asserted that Japan had been defeated and occupied not by America but by the Jews, and that it was the urgent task of the Japanese to throw off this Jewish yoke. Another candidate, Suzuki Hisashi, called for the defeat of proposals to allow Japanese soldiers to participate in United Nations peacekeeping operations and for the creation of a Japanese foreign legion to fulfill Japan's international duties instead. Self-contradictorily, he also demanded revival of the Japanese martial spirit (*Yamatogokoro to bushidō seishin*), which the Jews had allegedly suppressed, revision of the constitution to allow for the establishment of an imperial army, navy, and air force, and an end to Jewish control over Japanese society.

While the Global Restoration Party polled only 11,883 votes, or a tiny 0.03 percent of the electorate, and was one of several unconventional parties to participate in the election, its presence on the ballot was important because it signaled that even on a minute scale, antisemitic thought was being translated into political action in 1990s Japan.[c]

---

[b] All that is required to become a candidate in an election of this kind is posting a bond of between ¥2 million and ¥4 million ($20,000 to $40,000) called *kyōtakukin* that is forfeited if the candidate fails to receive a minimum number of votes. No petition or other evidence of popular support is required.

[c] Election results from the *Asahi shimbun*, July 27, 1992. The UFO Party (*UFO-tō*), which has fielded candidates in previous elections, received 37,552 votes (0.08 percent); the World Renewal Party. (*Yonaoshi tō*) received 46,713 votes (0.10 percent). Two

Japanese experts have differing opinions on the significance of this organized antisemitic and antiforeign activity. Komai Hiroshi, a professor of international relations at Tsukuba University, has suggested that groups like the League of National Socialists are the Japanese counterpart of neo-Nazi groups in Germany, and he has urged that they be taken seriously. On the other hand, Nishio Kanji, a prominent specialist in German literature at Denki Tsūshin University, is more sanguine. He doubts that the xenophobia expressed by groups like the League of National Socialists is shared by most Japanese, but he himself has advocated blood tests, intelligence tests, and criminal investigations before permitting immigrants to enter Japan.[9]

While it is unlikely that neo-Nazi-style movements like the League of National Socialists and the Global Restoration Party will develop into a significant political force in Japan in the foreseeable future, the xenophobia, religious fanaticism, and political reaction they represent are also present in mainstream politics. The May 1994 book by Ogai Yoshio (45), an official of the Tokyo branch of the Liberal Democratic Party, advocating the electoral strategies of Adolf Hitler, is a case in point. The book was quickly removed from circulation after its publication was reported in the *New York Times*, but it was preapproved by party officials and its perspective was entirely consistent with the ethnic nationalist tradition in Japanese conservative politics. Further examples of this trend were the May statement by Justice Minister Nagano Shigeto that the rape of Nanking never happened and the shot fired the same month by a right-wing militant in a Tokyo hotel near former Prime Minister Hosokawa Morihiro to punish him for his acknowledgment of Japan's wartime responsibility.[d] The newest manifestations of Japanese antisemitism are thus significant because they show that, despite liberalization efforts by politicians like

---

parties received fewer votes than the Global Restoration Party: the Spirit Purification Society (*Jōreikai*) received 9,779 votes (0.02 percent), and the Stream of Sincerity Party (*Seiryūsha*) received 7,294 votes (0.02 percent).

[d] On the other hand, the historian Ienaga Saburō's twenty-nine-year court battle to have government efforts to censor his unvarnished account of the Nanking [Nanjing] massacre found illegal ended in qualified victory on May 10, 1994, when the government failed to meet the deadline for filing an appeal. See "Scholar Wins Ruling on Nanjing Atrocity," *New York Times*, May 13, 1994.

•

Hosokawa Morihiro, xenophobic ethnic nationalism continues to exercise an influence over Japanese politics.[10]

What then is to be done? Jews have taken a number of steps to combat Japanese antisemitism. The Anti-Defamation League of B'nai B'rith has documented and criticized Japanese antisemitism and has tried with mixed success to correct Japanese misunderstandings of Jews.[e] The Simon Wiesenthal Center has publicized Japanese antisemitism in its fundraising campaigns.[f] The American Jewish Committee has worked with government and business leaders to help effect meaningful changes in Japanese policy and government behavior.[g] And in 1994, with the support of foreign donors and long-time

[e] The ADL (along with the American Jewish Committee and the Greenberg Center for Judaic Studies at the University of Hartford) was a primary sponsor of the symposium "Japan and the Jews: Past, Present, and Future" held at the Japan Society in New York on April 10 and 11, 1989. Among its publications are "Japan and Anti-Semitism: The Proliferation of Anti-Jewish Literature," an *ADL International Report*, April 1987; and Burton S. Levinson and Abraham H. Foxman, "Yugamerareta Yudayajin-zō" [The Distorted Image of the Jewish People], *Chūō kōron*, September 1987, pp. 180–189. Levinson and Foxman are respectively National Chairman and National Director of the ADL.

[f] In a March 1994 solicitation, the Wiesenthal Center cited "hundreds of Japanese antisemitic books and tracts" as an example of "a virulent new strain of antisemitism around the world." While it is true that individual antisemites like Uno Masami have established far-flung contacts with like-minded ideologues in other countries, contemporary Japanese antisemitism as a whole is highly ethnocentric and has little interest in participating in any kind of international network.

[g] Shortly after the intensity of antisemitic activity in Japan became known, the AJC convened a colloquy of scholars to define the problem and develop a strategy for dealing with it. Neil Sandberg, who had recently retired from the AJC's Los Angeles office, was asked to head the Pacific Rim Institute, a new branch of the AJC formed to improve relations between Jews and the peoples of Asia, including the Japanese. Over the next six years, Sandberg, the AJC's executive director David Harris, and other AJC members visited Japan, Korea, and China, initiating exchange programs and establishing rapport with government officials and private businesspeople. They argued forcefully that compliance with the Arab boycott of Israel and the lack of a strong government response to antisemitic publications were not in Japan's best interests.

AJC efforts to establish an ongoing dialogue paid off. The Japanese government issued statements to the Japanese Publishers Association, informing them that antise-

Jewish residents of Japan, a Jewish Cultural Center is scheduled to open in the Jewish Community Center in Tokyo to better inform the Japanese about Jews and Judaism.

But there is no shortage of accurate information about Jews and Judaism in Japan today, and a dearth of accurate information is not the reason antisemitism exists there. Antisemitism exists in Japan for the same reason bigotry exists in any other society: because a vocal minority actively espouses it and a much larger number of often well-educated and sometimes influential citizens accept and condone it.

Japanese antisemitism is an eruption of the darkness in modern Japanese history. It is a malign version of the basic patterns of Japanese culture. It derives from the virulent political obscurantism of Japanese xenophobes, who pandered paranoid fantasies throughout the modern period to assuage their feelings of insecurity and anomie. It is an integral component of the ideology that, in the 1930s, assumed control of Japan and precipitated World War II. It is the hidden, grotesque face of the wartime chauvinism that survived, transformed, after the war. To deny the historical roots of Japanese antisemitism is

---

mitic books were damaging Japan's international reputation; it pledged to discourage Japanese companies from complying with the Arab boycott; and it took other steps to improve Japan's relations with the state of Israel. Some of these actions might have been taken without the AJC, and some of them were largely cosmetic. The Arab boycott was weakening and Japanese compliance was proving counterproductive in any case. Government warnings to publishers were pro forma, couched in equivocal language, and backed by no threat of sanctions for noncompliance. In the post–Cold War era, it was obvious to the Japanese that improved relations with Israel were to Japan's advantage. Nevertheless, the AJC's efforts clearly accelerated the process and made the government's response more meaningful. The AJC's dignified, low-key, equable approach should serve as a model for future activism.

See David A. Harris, " 'The Elders of Zion' in Tokyo: What Should We Do About Japanese Anti-Semitism?" *Moment*, October 1987, pp. 32–37; and David Harris, "Fostering Japanese-Jewish Understanding: A Need to Address the Ignorance About Jews in Asia," *AJC Journal*, Summer 1989, pp. 11–12. On the impact of AJC diplomacy, see J. J. Goldberg, "Bagels and Sushi," *The Jerusalem Report*, June 17, 1993, p. 34. See also Jennifer Golub, *Japanese Attitudes Toward Jews* (New York: The Pacific Rim Institute of the American Jewish Committee, 1992).

AJC efforts did not escape Uno Masami, whose international edition of *New American View* commented on them, implying that the Jews were manipulating the Japanese government. See "Nihon ni harareta Yudaya lobii" [The Jewish Lobby Comes to Japan], *New American View* (Japanese edition), January 15, 1994, pp. 4–5.

•

to ignore the historical legacy of Japanese ethnic nationalism and to deny the historical continuity of Japan.

Japanese antisemitism and the refusal to acknowledge the history it represents hobble Japan's efforts to play a constructive role in the world community. The spectacle of Japanese incoherence during the Gulf War demonstrates this. In the post–Cold War era, when the successful management of international relations will increasingly depend upon the ability to deal with the volatile forces of race, ethnicity, and religion, Japanese antisemitism and the cultural contradictions it reifies will continue to impede Japan's ability to contribute effectively to international society.

The implications of antisemitism's persistence in Japan are thus serious and far-reaching. Ultimately, only the Japanese themselves can solve this problem by acknowledging that Japanese antisemitism is a product of Japanese history. Japanese antisemitism will cease to be a problem when and to the extent that the Japanese people, and particularly Japanese intellectuals, renew their commitment to face up to and resist their own history. Then and only then will antisemitism cease to be the canker it is in Japan today.

NOTES

Unless otherwise indicated, Japanese sources were published in Tokyo.

CHAPTER 1. WHAT THE JAPANESE THINK OF JEWS AND WHY ANYONE SHOULD CARE

1. "Japanese Writers are Critical of Jews," *New York Times*, March 12, 1987.

2. Regarding Uno's appearance: "Backers, Protesters Mark Constitution's 40th Year," *Japan Times*, May 4, 1987. The *Yomiuri* article is "En: haisui no kōbō" [The Yen: Last-Ditch Defense], *Yomiuri shimbun*, January 17, 1987.

3. The number of books with "Jew" in the title is from Tokyo Shuppan Hanbai, one of Japan's major book distributors, cited in *New York Times*, March 12, 1987. The books referred to are Yamakage Motohisa, *Yudaya no sekai shihai senryaku: miezaru sekai seifu no kyōi* [The Jewish Plot to Control the World: The Threat of the Invisible World Government] (Management-sha, 1985); Yajima Kinji, *Yudaya purotokōru chō-urayomi-jutsu* [The Expert Way of Reading the Jewish Protocols] (Seishun shuppansha, 1986); and Saitō Eisaburō, *Sekai o ugokasu yudaya pawaa no himitsu* [The Secret of Jewish Power That Moves the World] (Nihon keizai tsūshinsha, 1984).

4. "Anti-Semitic Book Ad Assailed," *Japan Times*, July 31, 1993.

5. "Kinkyū keikoku: 'kabuka ichiman-en' de 'Yudaya shihon' ni nerawareru Nihon kigyō" [literally: Urgent Alert: Japanese Industry Threatened by "Jewish Capital" When Stock Prices Hit ¥10,000], *Shūkan Post*, July 10, 1992, pp. 31–35; and "Senritsu! Kurinton o ayatsuru Yudaya shihon no tainichi senryaku" [The Ominous Strategy of the Jewish Capital That Controls Clinton], *Shūkan gendai*, December 5, 1992, pp. 24–28. Circulation figures are from *Shuppan nenkan* [Publishing Annual] (Shuppan nyūsusha, 1992). The comment about Jewish manipulation of poll results is attributed to Fujii Noboru of the Cambridge Forecast Group. See also "Kurinton shikkyaku no hi" [The Day of Clinton's Downfall] in *Sapio,* April 14, 1994, pp. 6–9, in which Fujii, who claims to have attended graduate school at Harvard, argues that the Jewish media responsible for Bill Clinton's election were now trumping up scandals like Whitewater to bring about his downfall and punish him for supporting the peace agreement between Israel and the PLO.

6. *Asahi shimbun*, international satellite edition, April 7 and 30, 1993.

7. William Watts, "Anti-Semitism in Japan: A Survey Research Study—A

Report to the Anti-Defamation League of B'nai B'rith," December 19, 1988, pp. 3–4, 18.

8. Isaiah Ben-Dasan, *Nihonjin to Yudayajin* (Yamamoto shoten, 1970); Isaiah Ben-Dasan, *The Japanese and the Jews*, tr. Richard L. Gage (Tokyo: Weatherhill, 1972). Sales figures from the English edition, front cover overleaf, and from *New York Times*, March 12, 1987.

9. Jacob Raz, *Aspects of Otherness in Japanese Culture, Performance in Culture 6* (Tokyo: Institute for the Study of Languages and Cultures of Asia and Africa, Tokyo University of Foreign Studies, 1992), p. vii. See also Yamaguchi Masao, "Yudayajin no chiteki jōnetsu" [The Intellectual Passion of the Jews], in *Hon no shinwagaku* [The Mythology of the Book] (Chūō kōronsha, 1971), pp. 37–72. Shimada Masahiko, "A Callow Fellow of Jewish Descent," tr. Hiroaki Sato, in Helen Mitsios, ed., *New Japanese Voices: The Best Contemporary Fiction from Japan* (New York: Atlantic Monthly Press, 1991), pp. 1–22.

10. These theories have been treated in some detail by Sugita Rokuichi, in *Higashi Ajia e kita Yudayajin* [Jews Who Came to East Asia] (Otowa shobō, 1967); *Nichiyu dōsoron o otte* [In Pursuit of Japanese-Jewish Common Ancestry Theories] (Otowa shobō, 1972); and "Nichiyu dōso-ron, sono-go" [Japanese-Jewish Common Ancestry Theories Reprised] in *Yudaya Isuraeru kenkyū*, nos. 5–6, 1970. See also Satō Aiko, *Akahana no Kirisuto—Tsugaru fūryū tan* [Jesus with a Red Nose: Tall Tales of Tsugaru] (Kōbun-sha, 1972).

11. *Sekai nazo no Yudaya* [The Jews: Enigma of the World], special issue of *Rekishi tokuhon* [History Reader] 32, no. 6 (March 1987), 9–17, 166–255.

   Circulation figures for 1990 according to *Zasshi-shimbun sō-katarogu* [Comprehensive Catalog of Magazines and Newspapers] (Media Research Center, 1990).

12. Herman Dicker, *Wanderers and Settlers in the Far East: A Century of Jewish Life in China and Japan* (New York: Twayne, 1962), pp. 164–65.

13. Tokayer's books include *Yudaya hassō no kyōi* [The Wonder of Jewish Thought], tr. Kase Hideaki (Jitsugyō no Nihonsha, 1972); *Yudaya jōkushū* [Jewish Humor], tr. Sukegawa Akira (Jitsugyō no Nihonsha, 1973); *Yudaya kakugenshū* [Jewish Proverbs], tr. Sukegawa Akira (Jitsugyō no Nihonsha, 1975); *Yudaya to Nihon: nazo no kodaishi* [The Jews and Japan: The Riddle of Ancient History], tr. Hakozaki Sōichirō (Sangyō nōritsu daigaku shuppanbu, 1975); and *Yudayajin no hassō* [The Way Jews Think], tr. Kase Hideaki (Tokuma shoten, 1978).

14. See Jack Halpern, *Yudaya kankaku o nusume! sekai no naka de dō ikinokoru ka* [Steal the Jewish Sensibility (For Yourselves)! How to Survive in the World] (Tokuma shoten, 1987); and Jack Halpern, ed., *New Japanese-English Character Dictionary* (Kenkyūsha, 1990).

•

15. See David Biale, *Power and Powerlessness in Jewish History* (New York: Schocken, 1986).

16. Bernard Glassman, *Anti-Semitic Stereotypes Without Jews: Images of the Jews in England, 1290–1700* (Detroit: Wayne State University Press, 1975).

17. Paul Lendvai, *Anti-Semitism Without Jews: Communist Eastern Europe* (New York: Doubleday, 1971).

18. Muramatsu Takeshi, "Mata arawareta 'Nachi no bōrei' " ["The Nazi Ghost" Appears Again], *Sankei shimbun*, April 10, 1987. Katō Shūichi, "Nihon ni okeru han-Yudayashugi" [Antisemitism in Japan], *Asahi shimbun*, evening edition, June 15, 1987. Yamaguchi Yasushi, "Naze ureru 'han-Yudaya-bon': shin-nashonarizumu ka" [Why "Antisemitic Books" Sell: A New Nationalism?] *Asahi shimbun*, April 8, 1987, evening edition. Ian Buruma, "A New Japanese Nationalism," *New York Times Magazine,* April 12, 1987, pp. 22–29, 38.

19. Yoshi Tsurumi, "Anti-Semitism in Japan: The Ghost That has Returned to Haunt," *Pacific Basin Quarterly* (Winter-Spring 1990), 21–22. David G. Goodman, "Han-Yudayashugisha to shite no Momotarō" [Momotarō as Antisemite], *Sekai*, January 1988, pp. 329–39. Fujiwara Hajime, "Tōsakuteki sakoku seishin o haisu" [(We Should) Reject the Perverted Spirit of a Closed Country], *Sekai shūhō*, April 14, 1987, pp. 4–5.

20. David G. Goodman, "Japanese Anti-Semitism," *The World and I*, November 1987, pp. 401–9. David G. Goodman, "Current Japanese Attitudes Toward the Jews and Their Implications for US-Japan Relations," *Occasional Paper*, September 1989, Program in Arms Control, Disarmament, and International Security, University of Illinois at Urbana-Champaign. Robert J. J. Wargo, "The Jewish Conspiracy Scare: An Exercise in Paranoia," *PHP Intersect* (January 1988), 30–34.

21. A number of books have been written about the Jewish experience in the Far East, including Dicker, *Wanderers and Settlers in the Far East*; David Kranzler, *Japanese, Nazis and Jews: The Jewish Refugee Community of Shanghai, 1938–1945* (New York: Yeshiva University Press, 1976); Ben-Ami Shillony, *The Jews and the Japanese: The Successful Outsiders* (Rutland, Vt.: Tuttle, 1991); Marvin Tokayer and Mary Swartz, *The Fugu Plan* (New York: Paddington Press, 1979); and Cheryl A. Silverman, "Jewish Emigres and Popular Images of Jews in Japan," (Ph.D. diss., Columbia University, 1989).

CHAPTER 2. MOMOTARŌ AS ANTISEMITE

1. For general, anthropological insight into the role outsiders play in Japanese culture and religion, see Teigo Yoshida, "The Stranger as God: The Place of the Outsider in Japanese Folk Religion," *Ethnology* 20, no. 2 (1981), 87–89;

Masao Yamaguchi, "Kingship, Theatricality, and Marginal Reality in Japan," in Ravindra K. Jain, ed., *Text and Context: The Social Anthropology of Tradition* (Philadelphia: Institute for the Study of Human Issues, 1977), pp. 151–79; Hori Ichirō, "Mysterious Visitors from the Harvest to the New Year," *Studies in Japanese Folklore*, ed. Richard M. Dorson (New York: Arno Press, 1980), pp. 76–106; and Hori's *Folk Religion in Japan* (Chicago: University of Chicago Press, 1968).

For more specific insight into *marebito* in traditional Japanese theater, see Jacob Raz, *Audience and Actors: A Study of Their Interaction in the Japanese Traditional Theatre* (Leiden: E. J. Brill, 1983), esp. pp. 25–33. Regarding contemporary theatre, see David G. Goodman, *Japanese Drama and Culture in the 1960s: The Return of the Gods* (Armonk, N.Y.: M. E. Sharpe, 1988). In Japanese, see, for example, Orikuchi Shinobu, *Nihon geinōshi rokkō* [*Six lectures on the history of the Japanese performing arts*], *Origuchi Shinobu zenshū*, vol. 18 (Chūō kōronsha, 1976), pp. 356–367.

2. David Pollack, *The Fracture of Meaning: Japan's Synthesis of China from the Eighth through the Eighteenth Centuries* (Princeton: Princeton University Press, 1986), p. 185 and passim.

3. Ronald P. Toby, *State and Diplomacy in Early Modern Japan: Asia in the Development of the Tokugawa Bakufu* (Princeton: Princeton University Press, 1984), pp. 211–30.

4. Toby, *State and Diplomacy in Early Modern Japan,* passim; and Ronald P. Toby, "Carnival of the Aliens: Korean Embassies in Edo Period Art and Popular Culture," *Monumenta Nipponica,* 41, no. 4 (Winter 1986), 415–56. See also Toby's "Kinsei shomin bunka ni arawareru Chōsen tsūshinshi-zō: sezoku-shūkyō-jō no hyōgen" [Korean Missions in Early Modern Japanese Culture: Expressions in Secular and Religious Life], *Kan* 110 (July 1988), 106–58.

5. On the application of the Momotarō archetype in the context of World War II, see John W. Dower, *War Without Mercy: Race and Power in the Pacific War* (New York: Pantheon, 1986), pp. 251–61; and Tsuno Kaitarō, *Monogatari: Nihonjin no senryō* [The Japanese as Occupiers: A Narrative], Asahi sensho 269 (Asahi shimbunsha, 1985).

On the relationship between Japanese mythology and Japanese attitudes towards Jews, see David G. Goodman, "Hanyudayashugisha to shite no Momotarō" [Momotarō as Antisemite], *Sekai,* January 1988, pp. 329–39. See also Ben-Ami Shillony, "Imaginary Devils," in *Politics and Culture in Wartime Japan* (New York: Oxford University Press, 1981), pp. 156–71.

For one of the innumerable examples of the life-or-death struggle as it is described in recent antisemitic literature, see Yamakage Motohisa, *Yudaya no sekai shihai senryaku: miezaru sekai seifu no kyōi* [The Jewish Plot to Control the

●

World: The Threat of the Invisible World Government] (Management-sha, 1985), p. 381.

6. On the evolution of Japanese nationalism and xenophobia out of the constructive response to this internal crisis, see H. D. Harootunian, *Things Seen and Unseen: Discourse and Ideology in Tokugawa Nativism* (Chicago: University of Chicago Press, 1988). See also Peter Nosco, *Remembering Paradise: Nativism and Nostalgia in Eighteenth Century Japan*, Harvard-Yenching Institute monograph series, 31 (Cambridge, Mass.: Council on East Asian Studies, Harvard University, 1990).

7. The extent and profundity of Buddhist influence is described in William R. LaFleur, *The Karma of Words: Buddhism and the Literary Arts in Medieval Japan* (Berkeley: University of California Press, 1983); and James H. Sanford, William R. LaFleur, and Masatoshi Nagatomi, eds., *Flowing Traces: Buddhism in the Literary and Visual Arts of Japan* (Princeton: Princeton University Press, 1992).

8. Fukuda Gyōkai (1806–88), quoted in Kishimoto Hideo, *Japanese Religion in the Meiji Period*, tr. John F. Howes (Tokyo: Ōbunsha, 1956), p. 111. Cited in Martin Collcutt, "Buddhism: The Threat of Eradication," in Marius B. Jansen and Gilbert Rozman, eds., *Japan in Transition: From Tokugawa to Meiji* (Princeton: Princeton University Press, 1986), p. 143.

9. Joseph M. Kitagawa, *Religion in Japanese History* (New York: Columbia University Press, 1966), pp. 175; 219–20.

10. George Wilson, "Pursuing the Millennium in the Meiji Restoration," in Tetsuo Najita and J. Victor Koschmann, eds., *Conflict in Modern Japanese History: The Neglected Tradition* (Princeton: Princeton University Press, 1982), pp. 186–87. For a fuller treatment of these themes, see Wilson's *Patriots and Redeemers in Japan: Motives for the Meiji Restoration* (Chicago: University of Chicago Press, 1992).

11. Translations of contemporary descriptions of the antinomian mass hysteria that swept Japan in the final years of the Tokugawa period may be found in John W. Dower, ed., *Origins of the Modern Japanese State: Selected Writings of E. H. Norman* (New York: Pantheon, 1975), pp. 343–55.

12. For a complete translation and commentary on the Aizawa's *New Theses*, see Bob Tadashi Wakabayashi, *Anti-Foreignism and Western Learning in Early-Modern Japan: The New Theses of 1825* (Cambridge, Mass.: Council on East Asian Studies, Harvard University, 1986). Excerpts may also be found in Ryusaku Tsunoda et al., eds., *Sources of Japanese Tradition*, vol. 2 (New York: Columbia University Press, 1964), pp. 88–96.

References to Japan's "spiritual void" appear in Wakabayashi, pp. 122, 124.

●

13. Wakabayashi, *Anti-Foreignism and Western Learning in Early-Modern Japan*, pp. 133, 140–41.

14. This summary is based on ibid., pp. x–xi.

15. Helen Hardacre, *Shinto and the State, 1868–1988* (Princeton: Princeton University Press, 1989), pp. 27ff.

16. Wakabayashi, *Anti-Foreignism and Western Learning in Early-Modern Japan*, pp. xi–xii.

17. See George Elison, *Deus Destroyed: The Image of Christianity in Early Modern Japan* (Cambridge, Mass.: Council on East Asian Studies, Harvard University, 1973).

18. Wakabayashi, *Anti-Foreignism and Western Learning in Early-Modern Japan*, p. 142.

19. Aizawa Seishisai, *Shinron*, in *Meiji bunka zenshū*, vol. 15 (Nihon hyōronsha, 1929), p. 12; Wakabayashi, *Anti-Foreignism and Western Learning in Early-Modern Japan*, p. 168.

20. Aizawa, *Shinron*, p. 28; Wakabayashi, *Anti-Foreignism and Western Learning in Early-Modern Japan*, p. 209.

21. Aizawa, *Shinron*, pp. 24–25; Wakabayashi, *Anti-Foreignism and Western Learning in Early-Modern Japan*, pp. 200–201.

22. Aizawa, *Shinron*, p. 55; Wakabayashi, *Anti-Foreignism and Western Learning in Early-Modern Japan*, p. 273.

23. Wakabayashi, *Anti-Foreignism and Western Learning in Early-Modern Japan*, p. 72.

24. Ibid., pp. 56–57.

25. "Ideology of hatred" is Wakabayashi's phrase. See ibid., p. 51.

26. Kiyū Dōjin, *Hekija kanken-roku* [On Understanding and Rejecting Heresy] (Enzan, 1861), pp. 2–3.

27. Ibid., p. 4.

28. For a general introduction to Ōhashi's thought, see Carmen Blacker, "Ōhashi Totsuan: A Study in Anti-Western Thought," in *Transactions of the Asiatic Society of Japan* 3, no. 7 (November 1959), 147–68.

29. Ōhashi Totsuan, *Hekija shōgen* [Comments on Heresy], in *Meiji bunka zenshū*, vol. 15, p. 80.

30. Ibid., p. 62.

31. Ibid., p. 121.

32. Ibid., p. 130.

33. H. W. Fowler and F. G. Fowler, eds., *The Concise Oxford Dictionary of Current English*, 4th ed. (Oxford: Clarendon Press, 1914).

34. Kawatake Toshio, *Zoku hikaku engeki-gaku* [Comparative Drama, Continued], (Nansōsha, 1974), pp. 482; 530. If Chikamatsu had knowledge of Shakespeare's work, it would presumably have come from European missionaries.

35. Ibid., p. 432.

36. Ibid., p. 492.

37. Ibid., p. 492.

38. Ibid., p. 499.

39. For a thorough analysis of the play, see Kawatake Toshio, "Kabukika-sareta 'Benisu no shōnin,' " [Kabuki Versions of *The Merchant of Venice*], in *Hikaku engeki-gaku* [Comparative Drama] (Nansōsha, 1967), pp. 513–526.

40. See, for example, the figure of Kuheiji in *The Love Suicides at Sonezaki* and Tahei in *The Love Suicides at Amijima*. Both plays are by Chikamatsu Monzaemon (1653–1725) and are available in English in Donald Keene, tr., *Major Plays of Chikamatsu* (New York: Columbia University Press, 1961).

41. Kawatake, *Zoku hikaku engeki-gaku*, p. 530.

42. Yoko Chiba, "Sada Yacco and Kawakami: Performers of *Japonisme*," in *Modern Drama* 35 (1992), 41–42.

43. Kawatake, *Zoku hikaku engeki-gaku*, p. 469.

44. William Archer, *World*, July 24, 1901, p. 28, quoted in Chiba, "Sada Yacco and Kawakami," p. 42.

45. Kawatake, *Zoku hikaku engeki-gaku*, p. 470.

46. Shimizu Jirō, " 'Benisu no shōnin' no enshutsu ni chūmoku" [With Special Attention to the Direction of "The Merchant of Venice"], *Teatoro* 34, no. 10 (September 1967), 78–81.

47. Odashima Yūshi, "Benisu no Yudayajin" [The Jew of Venice], *Shingeki*, 15, no. 3 (March 1968), 53.

48. For reviews of the production, see, for example, Amino Kiku, "Watashi no gekihyō—'Benisu no shōnin' hoka" [My Theatre Review: "The Merchant of Venice" and Other Plays], *Higeki kigeki* 21, no. 3 (March 1968), 47–50; Endō Tameharu, " 'Benisu no shōnin' ima mukashi" ["The Merchant of Venice," Then and Now], *Higeki kigeki* 21, no. 4 (April 1968), 8–11; Odashima Yūshi, "Benisu no Yudayajin," *Shingeki* 15, no. 3 (March 1968), 50–53; and Ozu Jirō,

"Gunshū no naka ni Shakespeare ga hoshii" [I Want a Shakespeare Among the Masses], *Teatoro* 296 (March 1968), 31–34.

49. Ōba Kenji, "Seitō no fukkatsu o mezashite" [Toward a Revival of Orthodoxy], *Teatoro* 367 (September 1973), 65–67.

50. Watanabe Minojirō, *Yudaya minzoku no sekai-teki katsudō* [The Global Activities of the Jews] (Ōsaka Mainichi shimbun and Tokyo Nichinichi shimbun, 1923), p. 1.

51. Cheryl A. Silverman, "Jewish Emigres and Popular Images of Jews in Japan," (Ph.D. diss., Columbia University, 1989), pp. 200–201.

52. Iwai Katsuhito, *Benisu no shōnin no shihonron* [The Theory of Capitalism in *The Merchant of Venice*] (Iwanami shoten, 1985). The book had gone through six printings in its first six months. Iwai, who received his Ph.D. from MIT and taught at Yale from 1973 to 1979, is also the author of *Disequilibrium Dynamics* (New Haven: Yale University Press, 1981).

53. Kawatake, *Zoku hikaku engeki-gaku*, p. 486.

54. James Edward Ketelaar, *Of Heretics and Martyrs in Meiji Japan: Buddhism and Its Persecution* (Princeton: Princeton University Press, 1990), p. 12.

55. Kawatake, *Zoku hikaku engeki-gaku*, pp. 486, 533.

56. An excerpt from Mori's novel is included in Donald Keene, ed., *Modern Japanese Literature* (New York: Grove Press, 1960), pp. 232–41.

57. James Shapiro, *Shakespeare and the Jews*, The Parkes Lecture (University of Southampton, 1992).

58. John K. Fairbank, Edwin O. Reischauer, and Albert M. Craig, *East Asia: The Modern Transformation* (Boston: Houghton Mifflin, 1965), pp. 521–27.

59. John W. Dower, *War Without Mercy: Race and Power in the Pacific War* (New York: Pantheon, 1986), p. 204.

60. Ibid., pp. 164–65.

61. See Toshihiko Sato, "Henrik Ibsen in Japan" (Ph.D. diss., University of Washington, 1966); and Brian Powell, "Matsui Sumako: Actress and Woman," in W. G. Beasley, ed., *Modern Japan; Aspects of History, Literature and Society* (Berkeley: University of California Press, 1975).

CHAPTER 3. GOD'S CHOSEN PEOPLE

1. Carol Gluck, *Japan's Modern Myths: Ideology in the Late Meiji Period* (Princeton: Princeton University Press, 1985), pp. 134–35.

2. F. G. Notehelfer, *American Samurai: Captain L. L. Janes and Japan* (Princeton: Princeton University Press, 1985).

3. For a description of the most significant of these strategies, see Shūichi Katō, *A History of Japanese Literature: Volume 3, The Modern Years*, tr. Don Sanderson (New York: Kodansha International, 1990), pp. 107–87.

4. Uchimura Kanzō, "Two J's," in Tsunoda et al., eds., *Sources of Japanese Tradition*, vol. 2, p. 349.

5. Tatsuo Arima, *The Failure of Freedom* (Cambridge, Mass.: Harvard University Press, 1969), p. 27.

6. Uchimura Kanzō, "The Non-Church Movement," in Tsunoda et al., eds., *Sources of Japanese Tradition*, vol. 2, pp. 347–48.

For a fuller explanation of *Mukyōkai* Christianity, see Carlo Caldarola, *Christianity: The Japanese Way*, Monographs and Theoretical Studies in Sociology and Anthropology in Honour of Nels Anderson, publication 15 (Leiden, The Netherlands: E. J. Brill, 1979), especially pp. 50–191.

7. Uchimura Kanzō, "Japanese Christianity," in Tsunoda et al., eds., *Sources of Japanese Tradition*, vol. 2, pp. 348–49.

8. See *The Complete Works of Kanzo Uchimura*, vol. 1 (Kyobunkwan, 1971), pp. 26–28, for the text of the "Covenant" in English.

9. "Kirisuto sairin o shinzuru yori kitarishi yo no shisōjō no henka" [The Changes in My Thought That Have Come from My Belief in the Second Coming of Christ], in *Seisho no kenkyū*, February 1918. *Uchimura Kanzō zenshū* [The Complete Works of Uchimura Kanzō], vol. 24 (Iwanami shoten, 1982) p. 384.

10. "Seisho kenkyūsha no tachiba yori mitaru Kirisuto no sairai" [The Second Coming of Christ from the Point of View of a Biblical Scholar] in *Seisho no kenkyū*, February 1918. *Uchimura Kanzō zenshū*, vol. 24, p. 59.

11. Ibid., p. 60.

12. "Kirisuto sairin o shinzuru yori kitarishi yo no shisōjō no henka," *Uchimura Kanzō zenshū*, vol. 24, p. 60.

13. Ibid., p. 60

14. "Seisho kenkyūsha no tachiba yori mitaru Kirisuto no sairai," *Uchimura Kanzō zenshū*, vol. 24, p. 60.

15. For a critical account of Uchimura's doctrine of the Second Coming, see Arima, *The Failure of Freedom*, pp. 29–32.

16. "Seisho no yogen to Paresuchina no kaifuku" [Biblical Prophecies and the Restoration of Palestine] in *Seisho no kenkyū*, July 1918. *Uchimura Kanzō zenshū*, vol. 24, p. 248.

17. "Erusaremu daigaku no setchi" [The Establishment of the Hebrew Uni-

versity in Jerusalem] in *Seisho no kenkyū*, September 1918. *Uchimura Kanzō zenshū*, vol. 24, pp. 315–316.

18. Ibid., p. 315.

19. "Kirisuto sairin no shōmeisha to shite no Yudayajin" [The Jews as Witnesses to the Second Coming] in *Seisho no kenkyū*, June 1918. *Uchimura Kanzō zenshū*, vol. 24, p. 221.

20. "Erusaremu daigaku no setchi," *Uchimura Kanzō zenshū*, vol. 24, p. 316.

21. Ibid., p. 317.

22. Ibid., p. 317.

23. George M. Marsden, *Fundamentalism and American Culture: The Shaping of Twentieth-Century Evangelicalism, 1870–1925* (New York: Oxford University Press, 1980), p. 151.

24. "Erusaremu daigaku no setchi," *Uchimura Kanzō zenshū*, vol. 24, p. 317.

25. See "Sairin saishō no hitsuyō" [The Need to Reiterate the Second Coming], written May 1929, published in *Seisho no kenkyū*, April 1930. *Uchimura Kanzō zenshū*, vol. 24, p. 48.

26. See "Yo ga Kirisuto no sairin ni tsuite shinzezaru koto domo" [Things I Do Not Believe Regarding the Second Coming of Christ], in *Seisho no kenkyū*, February 1918.

27. Yoneda Isamu, *Nakada Jūji den* [Biography of Nakada Jūji], (Fukuin senkyōkai, 1979), pp. 255–56.

28. "Sairin shinkō no shikibetsu" [Distinguishing Between Various Beliefs in the Second Coming] in *Nakada Jūji zenshū* [Complete Works of Nakada Jūji], vol. 7 (Inochi no kotobasha, 1973), p. 91.

29. "Ten no shigyō" [The Work of Heaven], in *Nakada Jūji zenshū*, vol. 6 (Nakada Jūji zenshū kankō kai, Inochi no kotobasha, 1975), p. 133.

30. Marsden, *Fundamentalism and American Culture*, p. 7.

31. Gene A. Getz, *MBI: The Story of the Moody Bible Institute* (Chicago: Moody Press, 1969), p. 176.

32. Marsden, *Fundamentalism and American Culture*, p. 33.

33. Ibid., p. 32–33.

34. "Nihon seito no shimei" [The Mission of Japanese Christians], in *Nakada Jūji zenshū*, vol. 6, p. 374.

35. Bishop Juji Nakada, *Japan in the Bible*, tr. David T. Tsutada (Oriental Missionary Society, Japan Holiness Church Publishing Department, 1933). Unless otherwise noted, translations are from this text.

36. "Preface," in *Nakada Jūji zenshū*, vol. 2, pp. 31–32. Translation by DGG.

37. Nakada, *Japan in the Bible*, pp. 10ff.

38. Ibid., pp. iii–iv.

39. Ibid., pp. 51–61.

40. Ibid., p. 61; *Nakada Jūji zenshū*, vol. 2, pp. 91–92.

41. Nakada, *Japan in the Bible*, pp. 85–86; *Nakada Jūji zenshū*, vol. 2, p. 123.

42. Nakada, *Japan in the Bible*, p. 80; *Nakada Jūji zenshū*, vol. 2, p. 112.

43. Nakada, *Japan in the Bible*, p. 106; *Nakada Jūji zenshū*, vol. 2, pp. 137–38.

44. Nakada, *Japan in the Bible*, p. 107; *Nakada Jūji zenshū*, vol. 2, p. 139.

45. Nakada, *Japan in the Bible*, pp. 107–08; *Nakada Jūji zenshū*, vol. 2, p. 139.

46. Nakada, *Japan in the Bible*, pp. 110–111; *Nakada Jūji zenshū*, vol. 2, pp. 140–41.

47. Nakada, *Japan in the Bible*, pp. 82–83; *Nakada Jūji zenshū*, vol. 2, p. 115.

48. Nakada, *Japan in the Bible*, pp. 80–81; *Nakada Jūji zenshū*, vol. 2, pp. 112–13.

49. Nakada, *Japan in the Bible*, p. 82; *Nakada Jūji zenshū*, vol. 2, p. 114.

50. Nakada, *Japan in the Bible*, pp. 82–83; *Nakada Jūji zenshū*, vol. 2, p. 115.

51. "Minzoku no sukui" [The Salvation of the (Japanese) Nation], in Yoneda, *Nakada Jūji den*, pp. 462–63.

52. Yoneda, *Nakada Jūji den*, p. 461.

53. Ibid., p. 520.

54. Nakada, *Japan in the Bible*, p. 34.

55. Nakada, *Japan in the Bible*, pp. 36–43.

56. Norman McLeod, *Epitome of the Ancient History of Japan* (Nagasaki: Rising Sun Office, 1875; "Appended Edition," 1879).

57. Harold S. Williams, *Foreigners in Mikadoland* (Rutland, Vt.: Tuttle, 1963), p. 168.

58. Ibid., p. 275.

59. The first complete Japanese translation of McLeod's work was N. McLeod, *Nihon to Yudaya: nazo no sanzennenshi* [Japan and the Jews: The Three Thousand Year History of an Enigma] (Jiyū kokuminsha, 1987). "Nihon kodaishi no shukuzu," in *Rekishi tokuhon*, March 1987, pp. 218–27, claims to be the first time the work was introduced to a Japanese readership.

McLeod's theories were given credence earlier by Marvin Tokayer in his *Yudaya to Nihon: nazo no kodaishi* [The Jews and Japan: The Riddle of Ancient History] (Sangyō nōritsu daigaku shuppanbu, 1975). See Silverman, "Jewish Emigres and Popular Images of Jews in Japan," pp. 226–27; and Tarakida Ryūzen, "Nichiyu dōsoron wa koko made risshō dekiru" [Japanese-Jewish Common Ancestry Theories Can Be Proven to This Extent], in *Rekishi tokuhon*, March 1987, p. 173.

60. See Joseph Jacobs, "Anglo-Israelism" in *The Jewish Encyclopedia* (1964), 1:600–601; and Albert M. Hyamson, "Anglo-Israelism," in James Hastings, ed., *Encyclopedia of Religion and Ethics* (New York: Scribner's, 1913), 1:483–84.

61. Howard Brotz, *The Black Jews of Harlem: Negro Nationalism and the Dilemmas of Negro Leadership* (New York: Schocken, 1970), p. 4.

62. Hyamson, "Anglo-Israelism," pp. 483–84.

63. Brotz, *The Black Jews of Harlem*, p. 10.

64. Ibid., pp. 1–2, 7.

65. Ibid., p. vi and passim.

66. Jacqueline Carol Berry, "Black Jews: A Study of Status Malintegration and (Multi) Marginality" (Ph.D. diss., Syracuse University, 1977), p. 85.

67. Quoted in ibid., p. 28.

68. Saeki Yoshirō's "Uzumasa o ronzu" was first published in *Chiri rekishi,* January 1908. It was subsequently appended to *Keikyō hibun kenkyū* [Research on Nestorian Inscriptions] (Tairō shoin, 1911), pp. 46–50.

69. Saeki, *Keikyō hibun kenkyū*, p. 46.

70. For a detailed study of one important example of this syncretic or "combinative" phenomenon, see Allan G. Grapard, *The Protocol of the Gods: A Study of the Kasuga Cult in Japanese History* (Berkeley: University of California Press, 1992).

71. Saeki Yoshirō, "Kyokutō ni okeru saisho no Kirisutokyō ōkoku, Yuzuki, oyobi, sono minzoku ni kansuru shomondai" [Various Problems Regarding Yuzuki, The First Kingdom of Christians in the Far East, and Its People], ed. Ide Katsumi, in *Shikan* [Historical Views], *Waseda daigaku shigakkai*, vol. 74, October 1966, pp. 14–28.

72. See the nine pages of color photographs of these sites in *Rekishi tokuhon* [History Reader], March 1987.

73. Oyabe Zen'ichirō, *Nippon oyobi Nippon kokumin no kigen* [The Origin of Japan and the Japanese People] (Kōseikaku, 1929), pp. 21–22.

•

74. Oyabe's life history is described in detail in Sugita Rokuichi, *Isuraeru-shi zakkō*, pp. 380–85, and Mimura Saburō, *Yudaya mondai to uragaeshite mita Nihon rekishi* [Japanese History Seen as an Inversion of the Jewish Problem] (Nichiyu kankei kenkyū kai, 1953), pp. 228–38.

75. The book was reissued in both Japanese and English in 1991. See Jenichiro [sic] Oyabe, *A Japanese Robinson Crusoe* (Issunsha, 1991).

76. *Jingisukan wa Minamoto no Yoshitsune nari* [Genghis Khan was Minamoto no Yoshitsune] (Fuzanbō, 1924).

77. "Oyabe Zen'ichirō," in Ebisawa Arimichi et al., eds., *Nihon kirisutokyō rekishi daijiten* [Historical Dictionary of Christianity in Japan] (Kyōbunkan, 1988).

78. Oyabe Zen'ichirō, *Nippon oyobi Nippon kokumin no kigen*, preface.

79. Ibid., p. 392.

80. Ibid., pp. 390–92.

81. Kawamorita Eiji, *Nihon Heburu shiika no kenkyū*, 2 vols. (Kyōbunkan, 1956–1957). A condensed version of this work was published in 1990 under the title *Nihon no naka no Yudayajin* [The Jews in Japan].

82. Kawamorita Eiji, *Nihon Heburu shiika no kenkyū*, vol. 1, p. 1.

83. Ibid., pp. 4–8; *Nihon no naka no Yudaya*, pp. 4–5.

84. Kawamorita, *Nihon Heburu shiika no kenkyū*, Preface, p. 3.

85. Sakai Katsuisa (a.k.a. Shōgun), *Sekai no shōtai to Yudayajin* [The True Nature of the World and the Jews] (Naigai shobō, 1924), pp. 218–19.

CHAPTER 4. THE PROTOCOLS OF ULTRANATIONALISM

1. J. A. White, *The Siberian Intervention* (Princeton: Princeton University Press, 1950); and James W. Morely, *The Japanese Thrust into Siberia, 1918* (New York: Columbia University Press, 1957).

2. Norman Cohn, *Warrant for Genocide*, Brown Judaic Studies 23 (Chico, Calif.: Scholars Press, 1981), p. 119.

3. *The Protocols* served the same purpose in Germany. See ibid., p. 133.

4. This account of *The Protocols* is based on Cohn, *Warrant for Genocide*.

5. Kitagami Baiseki, *Yudayaka* [The Jewish Peril] (Naigai shobō, 1923).

6. Ibid., p. 242.

7. "Sakai Shōgun," in Ebisawa Arimichi et al. eds., *Nihon kirisutokyō rekishi daijiten* [Historical Dictionary of Christianity in Japan] (Kyōbunkan, 1988).

•

8. The Japanese titles are, respectively, *Yudaya no sekai seiryaku undō* (hereafter *Seiryaku*), *Yudaya minzoku no daiinbō* (hereafter *Daiinbō*), and *Sekai no shōtai to Yudayajin* (hereafter *Shōtai*). All three were published by Naigai shobō.

9. Sakai, *Daiinbō*, p. 221.

10. Ibid., p. 3.

11. Sakai, *Seiryaku*, p. 445.

12. Sakai, *Shōtai*, p. 221.

13. Sakai, *Seiryaku*, p. 464; *Daiinbō*, p. 211; *Shōtai*, p. 213; and passim.

14. Sakai, *Shōtai*, pp. 213–14.

15. Ibid., pp. 213–14.

16. Sakai, *Seiryaku*, p. 470.

17. Sakai, *Daiinbō*, p. 77.

18. Ibid., p. 296. A similar argument may be found in the preface to *Seiryaku*.

19. Sakai, *Shōtai*, p. 218.

20. Ibid., p. 289.

21. Ibid., p. 218. In his entry for Sakai in *Nihon kirisutokyō rekishi daijiten*, Aizawa Genshichi gives "Japanese-Israelism" as the English for *Nichiyu-shugi*.

22. Yoshino Sakuzō, "Iwayuru sekaiteki himitsu kessha no shōtai" [The Truth About the So-Called Global Secret Societies], *Chūō kōron*, June 1921. See also Yoshino Sakuzō, "Yudayajin no sekaiteki tenpuku no inbō ni tsuite" [Concerning the Theory of a Jewish Conspiracy to Overthrow the World], *Chūō kōron*, May 1921.

23. Mitsukawa Kametarō, *Yudayaka no meimō* [The Illusion of the Jewish Peril] (Heibonsha, 1929).

24. Nishi Yoshiyuki, *Hitoraa ga soko e yatte kita* [There Came Hitler] (Bungei shunjū, 1971), p. 267.

25. Matsuuchi Norizō, *Orinpikku kara juneevu e* [From the Olympics to Geneva] *Chūō kōron*, March 1933.

26. Editorial, *Asahi shimbun*, May 8, 1933.

27. Katsumoto Seiichirō, "Yudayajin junan kenbunki" [Observations on the Sufferings of the Jewish People] *Chūō kōron*, July 1933, pp. 349–362. Baba Tsunego, "Hitoraa-ron" [On Hitler], *Chūō kōron*, May 1933, pp. 247–55; Kagawa Toyohiko, "Hōrōteki Yudaya minzoku no unmei" [The Fate of the Wandering Jews], *Kaizō*, January 1934, pp. 16–26; Minobe Ryōkichi, " 'Daisan teikoku' ni taizai shite" [On Visiting "The Third Reich"], *Kaizō*, November

1934, pp. 1–16; Kuwaki Gen'yoku, "Doitsu ni okeru Yudayajin mondai" [The Jewish Problem in Germany], *Teiyū rinriḵai rinri ḵōenshū*, July 1933, pp. 31–38; Hoashi Riichirō, "Nachisu no kyōbō to jimetsu o isogu minzokushugi" [Nazi Fury and the Self-Destructiveness of Ethnic Nationalism], *Teiyū rinriḵai rinri ḵōenshū*, July 1933, pp. 51–52.

28. Minobe, " 'Daisan teikoku' ni taizai shite," p. 8.

29. Katsumoto, "Yudayajin junan kenbunki," p. 362.

30. Murase Okio, *Doitsu gendai shi* [A History of Contemporary Germany] (Tokyo University, 1954), p. 312.

31. Minobe, " 'Daisan teikoku' ni taizai shite," p. 16.

32. Baba, "Hitoraa-ron," pp. 248–55.

33. Kuwaki, "Doitsu ni okeru Yudayajin mondai." However, three years later, in the December 1936 issue of the same periodical, Kuwaki expressed a slightly different view in an article entitled "Yudayakyōto ken'o no ichi riyū" [One Reason for Hating Jews], pp. 61–68.

34. Hoashi, "Nachisu no kyōbō to jimetsu o isogu minzokushugi," p. 53.

35. Yanaihara Tadao, *Yanaihara Tadao zenshū* [The Complete Works of Yanaihara Tadao], vol. 1 (Iwanami shoten, 1963), p. 532. This article was originally published as "Shion undō (Yudaya minzoku kyōdo kensetsu undō) ni tsuite" [On the Zionist Movement (The Movement to Build a Homeland for the Jewish People)], in *Keizaigaku ronshū* (Published by the Economics Department of Tokyo Imperial University) (October 1923), II(2). A revised version was included in *Shoḵumin seisaḵu no shinkichō* [A New Basis for Colonial Policy] (Kōbundō, 1927).

36. Yanaihara Tadao, "Nachisu kyōtei to jiyū" [The Nazi Pact and Freedom], *Fujin no tomo*, January 1937. In another article titled "Kokka to risō" [The State and Ideals] in *Chūō ḵōron* (September 1937), Yanaihara criticized the expulsion of the Jews and scrutinized Hitler. This essay was one of the causes for Yanaihara's own expulsion from Tokyo University. He subsequently published the essay at his own expense, but the authorities forbade it to be distributed in 1938.

37. Kiyosawa's diary of the war years, *Ankoḵu nikki* [Diary of Darkness] (1954), is a remarkable document from this period.

38. Kiyosawa Kiyoshi, "Hitoraa wa naze ni ninki ga aru ka—Doitsu ni kite Nachisu undō o miru" [Why Is Hitler Popular? Thoughts on Coming to Germany and Seeing the Nazi Movement], *Chūō ḵōron*, February 1938, pp. 214–27.

39. Adolf Hitler, *Waga tōsō* [Mein Kampf], tr. Ōkubo Yasuo (Mikasa shobō,

1937). Alfred Rosenberg, *Nijusseiki no shinwa*, tr. Suita Junsuke and Kamimura Kiyonobu (Chūō kōronsha, 1938). Alfred Stosz, *Yudaya to Nihon no tatakai* [Der Kampf zwischen Juda und Japan] (Seikyōsha, 1938).

40. Walther Brewitz, *Yudaya yonsen-nen-shi* [Four Thousand Years of Jewish History], tr. Yonemoto Sanji (Daidō shoin, 1943), pp. 19–21.

41. Ibid., pp. 19–21.

42. Hazumi Ichirō, *Yudayaka no sekai* [The World of the Jewish Peril] (Kasumigaseki shobō, 1941), pp. 24–25.

43. Thomas R. H. Havens, *Valley of Darkness: The Japanese People and World War Two* (New York: Norton, 1978), pp. 21–23.

44. Hasegawa Taizō, "Nunokawa Magoichi sensei o itamu" [In Memory of Professor Nunokawa Magoichi], *Yudaya kenkyū*, May–June 1944, p. 57.

45. Yamagata Tōkon [Nunokawa Magoichi], "Yudaya minzoku no seikaku ni tsuite" [Regarding the Characteristics of the Jewish People], *Teiyū rinrikai rinri kōen shū*, February 1926, p. 87.

46. Ibid., pp. 101–2.

47. Ibid., p. 102.

48. Nunokawa Seien [Nunokawa Magoichi], "Yudaya himitsuryoku no ura-kōsaku" [The Secret Machinations of Covert Jewish Power], *Teiyū rinrikai rinri kōenshū*, July 1938, p. 108.

49. Nunokawa Seien [Nunokawa Magoichi], "Shisōsen no ABC" [The ABC's of the Ideological War], *Teiyū rinrikai rinri kōenshū*, April 1938, p. 110.

50. Nunokawa Seien, "Shisōsen to Yudaya minzoku no kankei" [The Relationship Between the Ideological War and the Jewish People], part one, *Teiyū rinrikai rinri kōenshū*, September 1938, pp. 113–14.

51. Nunokawa, "Shisōsen no ABC," p. 110.

52. Hasegawa, "Nunokawa Magoichi sensei o itamu," p. 57.

53. The history of the *Shinjinkai* is detailed in Henry D. Smith III, *Japan's First Student Radicals* (Cambridge, Mass.: Harvard University Press, 1972).

54. Shunsuke Tsurumi, *An Intellectual History of Wartime Japan 1931–1945* (London: KPI Limited, 1986), p. 9.

55. Shisō no kagaku kenkyūkai [Association for the Scientific Study of Thought], ed., *Tenkō*, vol. 1 (Heibonsha, 1955), p. 99.

56. Smith, *Japan's First Student Radicals*, p. 42.

57. Tsurumi, *An Intellectual History of Wartime Japan*, pp. 10–11.

58. For detailed analysis and description of the *tenkō* phenomenon, see Patricia Golden Steinhoff, "*Tenkō*: Ideology and Societal Integration in Prewar Japan" (Ph.D. diss., Harvard University, 1969); and Kazuko Tsurumi, *Social Change and the Individual: Japan Before and After Defeat in World War Two* (Princeton: Princeton University Press, 1970).

59. Robert Jay Lifton, Shūichi Katō, and Michael R. Reich, *Six Lives, Six Deaths: Portraits from Modern Japan* (New Haven: Yale University Press, 1979), p. 177.

60. The initial collation of thoughts on the subject appeared as Shisō no kagaku kenkyūkai, ed., *Tenkō*, 3 vols. (Heibonsha, 1955).

61. "Panama unga dai-gigoku monogatari: Yudaya-teki yarikuchi no kōtekirei" [The Scandal of the Panama Canal: A Prime Example of Jewish Perfidy], *Kokusai himitsuryoku no kenkyū*, no. 2, March 1937, p. 257.

62. The interview he published in the *Asahi shimbun* on January 1, 1932, was the first installment in a special series of articles titled "Relaxed Conversations with the World's 'Number Ones'" (*Sekai no numbaa wan to hogaraka ni kataru*).

63. Nishi, *Hitoraa ga soko e yatte kita*, p. 268.

64. Kuroda Reiji, *Doreifyusu jiken kenkyū* [Study of the Dreyfus Affair] (Hanza shoten, 1936).

65. "Dorefyusu jiken" [The Dreyfus Affair], *Kaizō*, May and July-October 1930.

66. Kuroda Reiji, "Panama unga dai-gigoku monogatari: Yudaya-teki yarikuchi no kōtekirei," *Kokusai himitsuryoku no kenkyū*, no. 5, December 1938, p. 258.

67. Ibid., p. 258.

68. Ibid., p. 388.

69. "Shimpuson fujin, Nihon eiga ni kunrin suru Yudaya kinken, Nichidoku bōkyō kyōtei zadankai" [Panel Discussion on Mrs. Simpson, The Jewish Money that Rules Over the Japanese Film Industry, and The Anti-Comintern Pact], *Kokusai himitsuryoku no kenkyū*, no. 2, pp. 147–48.

CHAPTER 5. JEWS AS THE ENEMY

1. Tokutomi Iichirō, *Hisshō kokumin tokuhon* [A Citizen's Reader for Certain Victory] (Mainichi shimbunsha, 1944), pp. 69–71; 139–40. Quoted in Ben-Ami Shillony, *Politics and Culture in Wartime Japan* (New York: Oxford University Press, 1981), p. 161. Tokutomi is referred to as "the dean of Japan's nationalist

writers" in Ryusaku Tsunoda et al., eds., *Sources of Japanese Tradition*, vol. 2 (New York: Columbia University Press, 1964), p. 291.

2. Cited in John W. Dower, *War Without Mercy: Race and Power in the Pacific War* (New York: Pantheon, 1986), pp. 224–25.

3. Ibid., p. 258.

4. Itō Ken, "Dainiji Ōshū taisen to Yudaya mondai" [The Second Great European War and the Jewish Problem], *Kokusai chishiki oyobi hyōron*, January 1940, pp. 74–75.

5. Atago's real name was Okutsu Hikoshige. See Kobayashi Masayuki, *Yudayajin: sono rekishizō o motomete* (Seikō shobō, 1976), p. 269.

6. Atago Hokuzan, *Yudaya no sekai shihai kōryō* [The Jewish Plan to Control the World] (Seikei shobō, 1941), pp. 7–8, 373; and *Yudaya to sekai sensō* [The Jews and the World War] (Daiyamondosha, 1943), p. 271.

7. Kumamoto Arihisa, "Yudaya kenkyūsha no taisenkan o hihan su" [A Critique of Jewish Scholars' Views of the War], *Teiyū rinrikai rinri kōenshū*, September 1941, pp. 62–63.

8. Takeda Seigo, *Shimbun to Yudayajin* [Newspapers and the Jews], (Ōa Tsūshinsha, 1944), p. 256.

9. Ibid., pp. 257–59.

10. *Yomiuri shimbun*, January 22, 1944.

11. "Yudaya kyūketsuki-domo no gokuaku-hidō" [The Inhuman Machinations of the Jewish Vampires], *Yomiuri shimbun*, August 8, 1948.

12. *Asahi shimbun*, April 21, 1944.

13. *Ōsaka Mainichi shimbun*, evening edition, October 19, 1938.

14. *Ōsaka Mainichi shimbun*, November 12, 1938.

15. Irokawa Daikichi, *Aru Shōwa-shi: jibunshi no kokoromi* [One Man's History of the Shōwa Era: An Attempt at a Self-History], (Chūō kōronsha, 1975), pp. 91–92; 115.

For an example of Irokawa's historical work in English, see Irokawa Daikichi, *The Culture of the Meiji Period*, ed. Marius B. Jansen (Princeton: Princeton University Press, 1985).

16. For another translation and interpretation, see David Kranzler, *Japanese, Nazis and Jews: The Jewish Refugee Community of Shanghai, 1938–1945* (New York: Yeshiva University Press, 1976), pp. 232–33, 265n. Kranzler views these principles as somehow "pro-Jewish."

17. Kranzler, *Japanese, Nazis and Jews,* p. 19.

18. For a full account of Japanese press coverage of the Jewish refugees, see Miyazawa Masanori, "Nihon e hinan Yudayajin to shimbun" [The Jewish Refugees and Newspapers in Japan], *Yudaya-Isuraeru kenkyū* (October 1988), 10:43–49.

19. Cheryl A. Silverman, "Jewish Emigres and Popular Images of Jews in Japan" (Ph.D. diss., Columbia University, 1989), pp. 51–64.

20. Sugita Rokuichi, *Higashi Ajia ni kita Yudayajin* [Jews Who Came to East Asia] (Otowa shobō, 1967), p. 155.

21. Higuchi Kiichirō, *Attsu-Kisuka gun-shireikan no kaisōroku* [Memoirs of the Military Commander of Attu and Kiska] (Fuyō shobō, 1971), p. 354. Attu and Kiska are islands in the Aleutian chain and today part of the state of Alaska. They were occupied by Japanese forces in 1942. On May 11, 1943, an amphibious assault by U.S. forces began, and the Japanese were driven out after nineteen days of heavy fighting and mass suicides (*gyokusai*) by the defenders. Three months later, on August 15, U.S. and Canadian forces landed on Kiska, but the Japanese had already evacuated the island.

22. Inuzuka Koreshige, "Nippon no 'Aushubittsu' wa rakuen datta" [The Japanese "Auschwitz" was a Paradise], *Sekai to Nippon*, May 1961. This article was reprinted in *Jiyū*, February 1973, pp. 228–35.

23. Ben-Ami Shillony, *The Jews and the Japanese: The Successful Outsiders* (Rutland, Vt.: Tuttle, 1991), p. 188; and David Kranzler, "How Japan Saved Jews from Hitler," *Washington Post*, November 14, 1982.

24. Hilda Rabau, "Shanghai Revisited," *Bulletin of Igud Yotzei Sin in Israel* (*Association of Former Residents in China*) (May 1991), 317:22.

25. Kase Hideaki, "Nihon no naka no Yudayajin" [Jews in Japan], *Chūō kōron*, May 1971, pp. 238–40.

26. Wada Yōichi et al., eds., *Tokkō shiryō ni yoru senji-ka no Kirisuto-kyō undō* [The Christian Movement in Wartime Japan As Seen in the Records of the Special Higher Police], vol. 2 (Shinkyō shuppansha, 1972), pp. 141–42.

27. Ibid., p. 143.

28. Wada Yōichi et al. eds., *Tokkō shiryō ni yoru senji-ka no Kirisuto-kyō undō*, vol. 3, p. 144.

29. Ibid., p. 144.

30. Ibid., pp. 58–59.

31. See Kasahara Yoshimitsu and Morioka Iwao, *Kirisutokyō no sensō sekinin* [Christianity's Responsibility for the War] (Kyōbunkan, 1974), p. 29.

32. Masuda Masao, "Kakudai shikitareru ōbei no haiyu undō ni tsuite (ge)"

[The Expansion of the Antisemitic Movement in the West, Part II], In *Yudaya kenkyū*, May-June 1944.

33. Masuda Masao, "Kanmatsu dokugo " [Afterword] in *Yudaya kenkyū*, January-February 1944.

34. Masuda Masao, "Kono sensō wa Nihon o chūshin to suru sekai fukko no taisen de aru" [This War Is the Great War of Restoration of the World with Japan at the Center], in *Yudaya kenkyū*, December 1943.

35. Kubota Michiatsu, "Nichiyu dōso-ron o haigeki su!" [I Denounce Common Ancestry Theories], in *Yudaya kenkyū*, March 1942.

36. The following testimony is recorded in Masuda Masao, "Kanmatsu dokugo" [Afterword], *Yudaya kenkyū*, January-February 1944, pp. 64–65; and "Teikoku gikai ni okeru Yudaya mondai" [The Jewish Problem (Discussed) in the Imperial Diet], *Yudaya kenkyū*, March 1944, pp. 45–49.
   For a discussion of the role played by the notion of "proper place" in Japan's wartime ideology, see Dower, *War Without Mercy*, pp. 278–84.

37. Koyama Takeo, *Tōa to Yudaya mondai* [East Asia and the Jewish Problem], ed. Mantetsu kōhōka [Public Relations Department of the South Manchurian Railroad], Tōa shinsho (Chūō kōronsha, 1941), p. 115.

38. Ibid., p. 117.

39. Ibid., p. 117.

40. Ibid., p. 118.

41. Ibid., p. 127.

42. Ibid., pp. 87–88.

43. For a discussion of these tropes, see Dower, *War Without Mercy*, pp. 203ff.

44. Fujiwara Nobutaka [Shiōden Nobutaka], *Yudaya minzoku no kenkyū* [Studies on the Jewish People] (Naigai shobō, 1925), p. 245.

45. Ibid., p. 265.

46. Quoted in Norman Cohn, *Warrant for Genocide*, Brown Judaic Studies 23 (Chico, Calif.: Scholars Press, 1981), pp. 242–43.

47. Shiōden Nobutaka, "Yudaya minzoku riyō-ron no kikensei" [The Dangers in the Notion of Using the Jews], in *Nihon oyobi Nihonjin* (published by Seikyōsha), October 1939, p. 12.

48. Ibid., p. 103.

49. Ibid., p. 103.

50. Shiōden Nobutaka, "Hinan Yudayajin to Beikoku shihai no keikaku"

[The Jewish Refugees and the Plan to Take Over America], *Yudaya kenkyū*, May 1941, p. 18.

51. In *Shisō kenkyū shiryō* [Ideological Studies Material], issues number 87–88.

52. Examples of Inuzuka's antisemitic writings from this period are quoted in Kranzler, *Japanese, Nazis, and Jews*, pp. 172–73.

53. From the Cabinet Information Bureau (*Naikaku jōhōbu*), *Shisōsen kōshūkai kōgi sokki* [Shorthand Transcripts of Lectures Delivered Before Seminars on Ideological Warfare], nos. 1–4, 1938, pp. 23–112.

54. Utsunomiya Kiyo [Inuzuka Koreshige], *Yudaya mondai to Nippon—fu kokusai himitsuryoku no kenkyū* [The Jewish Problem and Japan—A Supplement to Studies in the World's Secret Powers] (Naigai shobō, 1939), pp. 478–79.

55. Ibid., p. 488.

56. Ibid., p. 423.

57. Ibid., pp. 423–24.

58. Ibid., pp. 481–84.

59. See Inuzuka Kiyoko, *Kaigun Inuzuka kikan no kiroku: Yudaya mondai to Nippon no kōsaku* [Records of the Navy's Inuzuka Operation: The Jewish Problem and Japan's Maneuvers] (Nihon kōgyō shimbunsha, 1982), pp. 85–86.

60. Inuzuka Kiyoko, "Yudayajin o hogo shita teikoku kaigun" [The Imperial Navy Protected the Jews], *Jiyū*, February 1973, pp. 236–37.

61. Kranzler, *Japanese, Nazis, and Jews*, p. 237.

62. Oyabe Zen'ichirō, *Nippon oyobi Nippon kokumin no kigen* (Kōseikaku, 1929), pp. 390–92.

63. See Kase, "Nihon no naka no Yudayajin," pp. 241–43.

64. Sugihara Yukiko, *Rokusennin no inochi no biza* [The Visas That Saved Six Thousand Lives] (Asahi sonorama, 1990; 2d ed., Taishō shuppan, 1993).

CHAPTER 6. IDENTIFICATION AND DENIAL

1. The statistics in these paragraphs, unless otherwise noted, are taken from John W. Dower, *War Without Mercy: Race and Power in the Pacific War* (New York: Pantheon, 1986), pp. 295–99.

2. Van C. Gessel, "Postoccupation Literary Movements and Developments in Japan," in Ernestine Schlant and J. Thomas Rimer, eds., *Legacies and Ambi-*

guities: *Postwar Fiction and Culture in West Germany and Japan* (Washington, D.C.: Woodrow Wilson Center Press, 1991), p. 207.

3. Maruyama Masao, "Kindai Nihon no chishikijin: [Modern Japanese Intellectuals], in Maruyama Masao, *Kōei no ichi kara* (Miraisha, 1982), pp. 113–30.

4. Carol Gluck, "The Idea of Showa," *Daedalus* 119, no. 3 (Summer 1990), 12.

5. From the translator's introduction to Leo Baeck, *Yudayakyō no honshitsu* [The Essence of Judaism], tr. Ariga Tetsutarō (Zenkoku shobō, 1946).

6. Maruyama Masao, *Thought and Behavior in Modern Japanese Politics*, ed. Ivan Morris (New York: Oxford University Press, 1963).

7. Publisher's introduction to Viktor E. Frankl, *Yoru to kiri: Doitsu kyōsei shūyōjo no taiken kiroku*, tr. Shimoyama Tokuji (Misuzu shobō, 1956). The Japanese translation appeared three years before the book was published in the United States by Beacon Press in 1959.

8. Okakura Koshirō, *Paresuchina monogatari* [Tales of Palestine] (Nihon hyōronsha, 1950). Also included in *Okakura Koshirō kokusai seiji ronshū*, vol. 5 (Keisō shobō, 1969). Takebayashi Fumiko, *Geshutapo—seiki no yajū to tatakatta Yudayajin hiwa* [Gestapo—The Untold Story of How the Jews Fought the Beast of the Century] (Kantōsha, 1950). *Isuraeru* [Israel], Iwanami shashin bunko (Iwanami shoten, 1954). Kai Shizuma, *Chūkintō* [The Middle East], Iwanami shinsho (Iwanami shoten, 1957). Sugita Rokuichi, *Kokusai funsō no shōten Isuraeru: sono jitsujō to rekishi* [Israel: Focus of International Struggle] (Kyōbunkan, 1957). Takeyama Michio, "Ningen seishin no hōkai: Nachizumu no Yudayajin tairyō satsuriku jiken ni tsuite" [The Collapse of the Human Spirit: On the Nazi Mass Murder of the Jews], *Bungei shunjū*, November 1957 through April 1958. This essay is also included in Takeyama, *Zoku Yōroppa no tabi* [Travels in Europe, Continued], (Shinchōsha, 1959).

9. Anne Frank, *Hikari honoka ni: Anne no nikki* [A Light Ever So Fragile: Anne's Diary], tr. Kaitō Kōzō (Bungei shunjū, 1952). Jean-Paul Sartre, *Yudayajin*, tr. Andō Shinya, Iwanami shinsho (Iwanami shoten, 1956). Elie Cohen, *Kyōsei shūyōjo ni okeru ningen kōdō*, tr. Shimizu et al. (Iwanami shoten, 1957). Lord Russell of Liverpool, *Jinkō jigoku: Nachisu sensō hanzai shōshi*, tr. Ōsawa Motoi (Misuzu shobō, 1957).

10. Ben-Ami Shillony, *The Jews and the Japanese: The Successful Outsiders* (Rutland, Vt.: Tuttle, 1991), p. 152.

11. "Nihon-Isuraeru bunka kenkyūkai setsuritsu no shui" [Prospectus], in *Nihon-Isuraeru kenkyū* [Studies on Jewish Life and Culture], October 1961. The translation of *Nihon Isuraeru-bunka kenkyūkai* as "The Japan Association for Jewish Studies" is the association's.

12. Rolf Hochhuth, *The Deputy* [Der Stellvertreter], tr. Richard and Clara Winston (New York: Grove Press, 1964), p. 102.

•

13. Ibid., p. 156.

14. Eric Bentley, *The Storm Over The Deputy* (New York: Grove Press, 1964). Bentley's book does not attempt to be exhaustive, but it includes a seventeen-page bibliography of critical commentary by David Beams. See pp. 237–54.

15. Guenter Lewy, *The Catholic Church and Nazi Germany* (New York: McGraw-Hill, 1964); and John H. Morley, *Vatican Diplomacy and the Jews During the Holocaust, 1939–1943* (New York: KTAV, 1980).

16. See, for example, Takeyama Michio's article in *Tokyo shimbun*, April 21, 1963; and Tokyo University German literature professor Nishi Yoshiyuki's "Doitsu chishikijin to Rōma hōō" [German Intellectuals and the Pope], *Jiyū*, June 1963.

17. Among his other works are Tatsuki Shin, *Kirisuto to Marukusu: Tōō shisō kikō* [Christ and Marx: An Intellectual Journey Through Eastern Europe] (Simul, 1972).

18. Michio Takeyama, *The Harp of Burma*, tr. Howard Hibbett (Rutland, Vt.: Tuttle, 1966). The film, directed by Ichikawa Kon, was released in 1956.

19. Richard L. Rubenstein proposes a similar thesis in *The Cunning of History: The Holocaust and the American Future* (New York: Harper and Row, 1975), esp. pp. 78–97.

20. See Takeyama Michio, "Seisho to gasu-shitsu" [The Bible and the Gas Chambers], *Jiyū*, July-October 1963. These articles are also collected in Takeyama Michio, *Ningen ni tsuite* [On Man] (Shinchōsha, 1966).

21. Tatsuki Shin, "Rōma hōō ni sekinin wa nakatta: *Dairisha* to Vachican" [The Pope Was Not Responsible: *The Deputy* and the Vatican], *Jiyū*, May 1964. This essay is also included in Tatsuki, *Kirisuto to Marukusu*.

22. "Zaiseki: Rōma hōō to tennō no baai" [Responsibility: The Pope and the Emperor Compared], *Kokoro*, November 1964, p. 22.

23. Tatsuki Shin, "Yudayajin no shukumei—Takeyama Michio-shi no oshie o kou" [The Fate of the Jews: A Question for Takeyama Michio], *Jiyū*, February 1965, p. 121.

24. Takeyama Michio, "Yōroppa to watakushi" [Europe and I], *Jiyū*, May 1973.

25. Hannah Arendt, *Eichmann in Jerusalem: A Report on the Banality of Evil*, rev. ed. (New York: Penguin, 1965, 1977).

26. This point of view was explained, although not necessarily advocated, in all the major newspapers. See, for example, the analysis in the *Yomiuri shimbun*, December 16, 1961. Some "Letters to the Editor" did advocate this view.

See, for example, the letters from Tanii Shōji and Furuzuka Takeo in the *Asahi shimbun*, June 6, 1962.

27. Kaikō Takeshi, *Koe no kariudo* (Iwanami shoten, 1962), p. 41.

28. Muramatsu Takeshi, *Tairyō satsujin no shisō* (Bungei shunjū, 1961), pp. 91–92.

29. Inukai Michiko, "Kokuren ga sabaku beki datta," *Shūkan Asahi*, December 29, 1961; and *Asahi shimbun*, December 16, 1961.

30. Inukai Michiko, "Aihiman shikei hanketsu ni omou" [Thoughts on the Eichmann Death Sentence], *Asahi shimbun*, December 16, 1961.
    Buber's views are cited in Arendt, *Eichmann in Jerusalem*, pp. 251–52.

31. See, for example, the editorial, "Aihiman saiban ni omou" [Thoughts on the Eichmann Trial], *Asahi shimbun*, April 12, 1961.

32. "Tensei jingo" [Vox Populi, Vox Dei], *Asahi shimbun*, December 17, 1961.

33. "Kyō no mondai" [Today's Issue], *Asahi shimbun*, December 16, 1961.

34. "Kyō no mondai," *Asahi shimbun*, December 16, 1961.

35. Inoue Makoto, "Aihiman no shokei" [Eichmann's Execution], *Ronsō*, September 1962.

36. Ibid.

37. Kaikō Takeshi, *Koe no kariudo*, pp. 67–70.

38. Muramatsu, *Tairyō satsujin no shisō*, p. 99.

39. Ibid., p. 240.

40. Aoki Shigeru, "Shinkō-koku Isuraeru" [The New Country, Israel], January 1961. Shirai Kensaku, "Isuraeru, motto shitte yoi kuni" [Israel: A Country We Should Get to Know], July 1964. Yoshizawa Kōji, " 'Erabareta tami' no kokoku Isuraeru" [Israel: Homeland of 'The Chosen People'], January 1965. Kuroda Kiyoshi, "Chichūkai kara Nihon e" [From the Mediterranean to Japan], July 1965.

41. Nishitani Misao, "Yudaya seisaku o shire," *Tenshō* 2, no. 2 (March 1954), 15–16.

42. Inuzuka Kiyoko, *Kaigun Inuzuka kikan no kiroku: Yudaya mondai to Nippon no kōsaku* [Records of the Navy's Inuzuka Operation: The Jewish Problem and Japan's Maneuvers] (Nihon kōgyō shimbunsha, 1982), pp. 436–48; 488–90.

43. David Kranzler, *Japanese, Nazis and Jews: The Jewish Refugee Community of Shanghai, 1938–1945* (New York: Yeshiva University Press, 1976), p. 174. See also Ernie Meyer, "A Present for Purim," *Jerusalem Post*, March 12, 1982.

44. Marvin Tokayer and Mary Swartz, *The Fugu Plan: The Untold Story of the*

Japanese and the Jews during World War II (New York: Paddington Press, 1979), pp. 11, 272–73.

45. Herman Dicker, *Wanderers and Settlers in the Far East: A Century of Jewish Life in China and Japan* (New York: Twayne, 1962), p. 179. See also the illuminating three-part colloquy among Sugita Rokuichi, Kobayashi Masayuki, and Miyazawa Masanori, "Nihon ni okeru Yudaya mondai rongi," subtitled in English, "Japanese Anti-semites and Philo-semites," in *Yudaya-Isuraeru kenkyū* [Studies in Jewish Life and Culture] (1970, 1975, 1980), numbers 5–6, 7, 8–9; pp. 57–71, 32–49, 58–71, respectively.

46. Shillony, *The Jews and the Japanese*, p. 216. Inuzuka Kiyoko, *Kaigun Inuzuka kikan no kiroku: Yudaya mondai to Nippon no kōsaku*, p. 44.

47. Mimura Saburō, *Sekai no nazo Nihon to Isuraeru* [Japan and Israel: Enigmas of the World], Nichiyu kankei kenkyū sōsho 1 (Nichiyu kankei kenkyūkai, 1950); and Mimura Saburō, *Yudaya mondai to uragaeshite mita Nihon rekishi* [Japanese History Seen as an Inversion of the Jewish Problem] (Nichiyu kankei kenkyūkai, 1953). These works were republished in a combined edition in 1984 as Mimura Saburō, *Yudaya mondai to uragaeshite mita Nihon rekishi; furoku—Sekai no nazo Nihon to Isuraeru* [Japanese History Seen as an Inversion of the Jewish Problem, With an Appendix—Japan and Israel: Enigmas of the World] (Hachiman shoten, 1984).

48. Mimura, *Yudaya mondai to uragaeshite mita Nihon rekishi*, pp. 227 and 272.

49. Ibid.

50. Sugita, *Nichiyu dōsoron o otte*, p. 44.

51. Mimura, *Yudaya mondai to uragaeshite mita Nihon rekishi*, pp. 188, 226.

52. Hori Ichirō, *Folk Religion in Japan: Continuity and Change*, ed. Joseph M. Kitagawa and Alan L. Miller (Chicago: University of Chicago Press, 1968), pp. 217–18.

53. Shillony, *The Jews and the Japanese*, pp. 212–13.

54. Yossi Klein Halevi, "Samurai Chassidim: Japan's Lovers of Zion," *Moment* (March 1986), p. 48.

55. Teshima Ikurō, *Uzumasa no kami—Hachiman shinkō to Kirisuto Keikyō ni tsuite* (Tokyo Kirisuto seisho-juku, 1971). Teshima also develops his views in the magazine of the Makuya Bible Seminary, *Seimei no hikari* [Light of Life].

56. Carlo Caldarola, *Christianity: The Japanese Way*, Monographs and Theoretical Studies in Sociology and Anthropology in Honour of Nels Anderson, publication 15 (Leiden, The Netherlands: E. J. Brill, 1979), pp. 193, 204.

57. Halevi, "Samurai Chassidim," p. 52; Caldarola, *Christianity: The Japanese Way*, p. 198.

58. "Isuraeru no Nipponjin 'giyūhei' " [A Japanese Army Volunteer in Israel], *Asahi Journal*, July 23, 1967.

59. *Sekai tenpuku no daiinbō Yudaya protokōru* [The Jewish Protocols: The Great Conspiracy to Overthrow the World] (Haja kenshōsha, 1938).

60. Matsumoto Fumi, *Fuji Kaidan'in konryū* (Fujisan Myōkōin, 1958), p. 3.

61. Ibid., p. 107.

62. Ibid., pp. 107–8.

63. Ibid., pp. 113–14.

64. See note on page 157 above.

65. Okusho's sources include Takenouchi Yoshimiya's *Jindai no bankokushi* [A History of the World in the Age of the Gods] (1970) and *Jindai no jidai no hanashi* [Stories of the Gods from the Age of the Gods] (1969), both published by Kōso kōtai jingū amatsukyō sōchō [Headquarters of the Universal Religion of the Shrine of the Imperial Ancestors]; and Yano Yūtarō, *Shinrei seiten* [Scriptures of the Holy Spirit] (1932).

66. Okusho Kazuo, *Kyūseishu no shutsugen to chijō tengoku* [The Appearance of the Messiah and the Earthly Paradise] (Kasumigaseki shobō, 1972), pp. 358–59.

67. Ibid., pp. 24, 66.

68. Ibid., pp. 127–28.

69. Ibid., pp. 250–51.

70. Ibid., pp. 252–53.

71. Ibid., pp. 254–55.

72. Ibid., p. 278.

73. Ibid., p. 59.

74. The myth of the Heavenly Cave is recounted in Donald L. Philippi, tr., *Kojiki* (Princeton: Princeton University Press, 1969), pp. 81–86; and W. G. Aston, *Nihongi: Chronicle of Japan from Earliest Times to A.D. 697* (Rutland, Vt.: Tuttle, 1972), pp. 41–45.

75. Okusho, *Kyūseishu no shutsugen to chijō tengoku*, pp. 25, 59, 235.

76. Masuda Masao, "Kono sensō wa Nippon o chūshin to suru sekai fukko no taisen de aru" [This War Is a Great War of Global Renaissance Centering on Japan], *Yudaya kenkyū*, December 1943, p. 1.

77. The following account is based on Ben-Ami Shillony, "The Princess of the Dragon Palace: A New Shinto Sect is Born," *Monumenta Nipponica* 39, no. 2 (1984), 177–82.

•

78. Wolfgang Scheffler, *Nachisu to Yudayajin: 600-man-nin gyakusatsu no kiroku* [Judenverfolgung in Dritten Reich, 1933–1945] (Kōdansha, 1961).

79. Translator's afterword to Scheffler, *Nachisu to Yudayajin*.

80. Dazai Osamu, *The Setting Sun*, tr. Donald Keene (New York: New Directions, 1956), p. 158.

81. Alvin H. Rosenfeld, "Popularization and Memory: The Case of Anne Frank," in Peter Hayes, ed., *Lessons and Legacies: The Meaning of the Holocaust in a Changing World* (Evanston: Northwestern University Press, 1991), p. 262.

82. Kittredge Cherry, *Womansword: What Japanese Words Say About Women* (New York: Kodansha International, 1987), pp. 17–18. See also Inoue, "Besutoseraa sengoshi: Anne Furanku, *Hikari honoka ni*," pp. 373–74.

83. Inui Tomiko, "Anne no nikki: teikō to shi to ai to" [The Diary of Anne Frank: Resistance, Death, and Love], "Sengo no besuto seraa 21," *Asahi Journal*, March 6, 1966, pp. 38–39.

84. See the essays included in *Seishōnen dokusho kansōbun-shū* published annually by the *Mainichi shimbun*.

85. Anne Frank, *The Diary of a Young Girl* (New York: Simon and Schuster, 1953), p. ix.

86. Inui "Anne no nikki: teikō to shi to ai to." The young essayist's name was Arai Kinue.

87. Judith Miller, *One By One By One: Facing the Holocaust* (New York: Simon and Schuster, 1990), p. 97.

88. Norbert Muhlen, "The Return of Anne Frank," *ADL Bulletin* 2 (June 1957), cited in Rosenfeld, "Popularization and Memory," p. 266.

89. Anne Frank, *The Diary of a Young Girl*, p. 237.

90. Rosenfeld, "Popularization and Memory," pp. 262–71.

91. Letter from Otto Frank to Meyer Levin, June 28, 1952, cited in Doneson, "The American History of Anne Frank's Diary," p. 152.

92. *Daily News*, October 6, 1955, quoted in Rosenfeld, "Popularization and Memory," p. 254.

93. The play was translated and directed by Sugawara Taku. See *Gikyoku Anne no nikki*, tr. Sugawara Taku (Bungei shunjū, 1957).

94. Rosenfeld, "Popularization and Memory," pp. 257–60.

95. Lawrence Langer, "The Americanization of the Holocaust on Stage and Screen," in Sarah Blacher Cohen, ed., *From Hester Street to Hollywood: The Jewish-American Stage and Screen* (Bloomington: Indiana University Press, 1983), pp. 214–15.

96. Judith E. Doneson, "The American History of Anne Frank's Diary," *Holocaust and Genocide Studies* 2, no. 1 (1987), 149–50, 158.

97. Sidra DeKoven Ezrahi, *By Words Alone: The Holocaust in Literature* (Chicago: University of Chicago Press, 1980), p. 140.

98. Primo Levi, *Primo Levi: Collected Poems*, tr. Ruth Feldman and Brian Swann (London: Faber and Faber, 1988), p. 34. I am grateful to Richard Minear for bringing this poem to my attention.

99. Robert Jay Lifton and Eric Markusen, *The Genocidal Mentality: Nazi Holocaust and Nuclear Threat* (New York: Basic Books, 1990), p. 1.

Lifton's work itself is eloquent testimony to the linkage postwar (Jewish) intellectuals have made between Hiroshima and the Holocaust. See especially his *Death in Life: Survivors of Hiroshima* (New York: Basic Books, 1967) and *The Nazi Doctors: Medical Killing and the Psychology of Genocide* (New York: Basic Books, 1986).

100. Translated by Richard H. Minear. This translation appears in Minear's introduction to his translation of Kurihara's "The Literature of Auschwitz and Hiroshima: Thoughts on Reading Lawrence Langer's *The Holocaust and the Literary Imagination*," *Holocaust and Genocide Studies* 7, no. 1 (Spring 1993), 82. See also Richard H. Minear, tr., "Five Poems (1974–91) by the Hiroshima poet Kurihara Sadako," *Bulletin of Concerned Asian Scholars* 23, no. 1 (January-March 1991), 26–30.

For a representative collection of Kurihara's work in English, see Kurihara Sadako, *Black Eggs*, tr. Richard Minear, Michigan Monograph Series in Japanese Studies, 21 (Ann Arbor: University of Michigan Center for Japanese Studies, 1994).

101. Ōe Kenzaburō, ed., *Nan to mo shirenai mirai ni* (Shūeisha, 1983), p. 254. For a complete translation of the story, see "The Rite," tr. Eileen Katō, in Ōe Kenzaburō, ed., *The Crazy Iris and Other Stories of the Atomic Aftermath* (New York: Grove Press, 1985), pp. 169–200. The translation here is by DGG.

102. For reproductions and a discussion of the Marukis' work, see John W. Dower and John Junkerman, eds., *The Hiroshima Murals: The Art of Iri Maruki and Toshi Maruki* (New York: Kodansha International, 1985).

The Marukis are also the subject of a film directed by John Junkerman, *Hellfire: A Journey from Hiroshima* (New York: First Run Features, 1986).

103. Interview with Inoue Fumikatsu, *Asahi shimbun*, December 16, 1982; "Auschwitz Memorial Planned in Kurose," *Japan Times*, January 12, 1983; "Hiroshima and the Holocaust, *Japan Times*, February 20, 1983.

104. Ōe Kenzaburō, *Hiroshima Notes*, trans. Toshi Yonezawa, ed. David L. Swain (Tokyo: YMCA Press, 1981), p. 150.

•

105. Kurihara, "The Literature of Auschwitz and Hiroshima," pp. 23–24.

106. Richard H. Minear, ed. and trans., *Hiroshima: Three Witnesses* (Princeton: Princeton University Press, 1990), p. 6. Ōe Kenzaburō, *Hiroshima nōto* [Hiroshima Notes] (Iwanami shoten, 1965). The combination of self-righteousness and ignorance that characterizes popular Japanese attitudes toward Hiroshima has been noted by many observers. See, for example, Ian Buruma, *God's Dust* (New York: Farrar Straus and Giroux, 1989), pp. 259–62; and Dave Barry, *Dave Barry Does Japan* (New York: Random House, 1992), pp. 173–80.

107. Sadamori Daiji, "Tokuhain memo" [Foreign Correspondent's Memo], *Asahi shimbun*, April 24, 1993. Letter from Neil Sandberg to Sadamori Daiji, August 2, 1993. Response by Sadamori dated August 11, 1993.

108. Isaiah Ben-Dasan, *Nihonjin to Yudayajin* (Yamamoto shoten, 1970); Isaiah Ben-Dasan, *The Japanese and the Jews*, tr. Richard L. Gage (Tokyo: Weatherhill, 1972). Sales figures from the English edition, front cover overleaf.

109. See Asami Sadao, *Nise Yudayajin to Nihonjin* [The Counterfeit Jew and the Japanese] (Asahi shimbunsha, 1983). For a discussion of *Nihonjinron* in English, see Peter N. Dale, *The Myth of Japanese Uniqueness* (New York: St. Martin's Press, 1986). See also Aoki Tamotsu, *"Nihonron" no henyō* [The Evolution of "Theories of Japan"], (Chūō kōronsha, 1990).

110. Shillony, *The Jews and the Japanese*, p. 214.

111. Ben-Dasan, *The Japanese and the Jews*, pp. 96, 133–51.

112. Ibid., pp. 142–48, for example.

113. Ibid., p. 133.

114. Ibid., pp. 36–37.

115. For example, Yamamoto Shichihei, *Watakushi no naka no Nihongun* [The Japanese Army Within Me] (Bungei shunjū, 1975); and *Kyūyaku seisho monogatari* [Tales from the Old Testament] (Sanseidō, 1984).

116. We are grateful to Marvin Tokayer for this exegesis.

117. Ben-Dasan, *The Japanese and the Jews*, p. 102.

118. Ibid., pp. 52, 73.

119. Ibid., p. 75.

120. Ibid., pp. 113, 100.

121. Nara Hiroshi, ed., *Yudayajin*, a special issue of *Gendai no esupuri*, no. 121 (August 1977).

A much superior special issue on the Jews was published by *Gendai no shisō* this same year. See *Yudayateki chisei to gendai* [The Jewish Mind and the

Present], a special issue of *Gendai no shisō* [Revue de la pensée d'aujourd'hui], no. 12 (November 1977).

Nagafuchi Ichirō, *Yudayajin to sekai kakumei* [Jews and World Revolution] (Shinjinbutsu ōraisha, 1971).

CHAPTER 7. THE SOCIALISM OF FOOLS

1. Patricia G. Steinhoff, "Portrait of a Terrorist: An Interview with Kozo Okamoto," *Asian Survey* 16, no. 9 (September 1976), 830–45; Ben-Ami Shillony, *The Jews and the Japanese: The Successful Outsiders* (Rutland, Vt.: Tuttle, 1990), pp. 203–4.

2. *Akahata*, June 25, 1967.

3. Ōtsuki Masaru "Onaji Nihonjin to shite magokoro kara no tsugunai o!!" [Let Us Make Wholehearted Atonement as Members of the Same Japanese People (Who Committed This Crime)], *Gekkan Isuraeru*, July 1972, p. 12.

4. Shillony, *The Jews and the Japanese*, pp. 151–57.

5. See Robert M. Immerman, "Japanese Diplomacy: An Overview," in David G. Goodman, ed., *Japan and the Developing World*, Swords and Ploughshares: The Bulletin of the Program in Arms Control, Disarmament, and International Security, 7, no. 4, University of Illinois (Summer 1993), pp. 3–5.

6. Avraham Altman, "The Japan Kibbutz Association," *Asian and African Studies* 6 (1970), 176, 180–81.

7. Kusakari Zenzō, "Kibutsu kenshūgaku joron" [An Introduction to Kibutz Study], in Ueno Masahito, *Kibutsu gaido* [Kibbutz Guide] (Tochigi Prefecture: Nihon kyōdōtai kyōkai, 1989), p. 5.

8. Tezuka Nobuyoshi, *Isuraeru ni tanjō shita atarashii nōgyō kibutsu* [The New Agricultural Kibbutz Born in Israel], in *Sekai jaanaru* (1963), pp. 24–27, quoted in Altman, "The Japan Kibbutz Association," p. 177.

9. David W. Plath, "Modernization and Its Discontents: Japan's Little Utopias," *Journal of Asian and African Studies* (1969), 1–17.

10. Zenzo Kusakari, Michael M. Steinbach, and Moshe Matsuba, eds., *The Communes of Japan*, 2d rev. ed. (Kibbutz Akan, Akan-gun, Hokkaido: Japanese Commune Movement, 1979).

11. See, for example, Nuita Seiji, "Kibutsu no seikatsu taiken" [Life on the Kibbutz], *Asahi Journal*, December 10, 1961; *Kibutsu: Isuraeru no yūtopia-teki jikken* [The Kibbutz: Israel's Utopian Experiment] (Middle East-Africa Section, Japanese Foreign Ministry, 1963); "Isuraeru no yūtopia kyōdōtai: kibutsu" [Israel's Utopian Community: The Kibbutz], *Gaimushō chōsa geppō* (1966), vol. 7, nos. 9–10, 11–12.

•

12. Ishihama Mikaru, *Sharōmu Isuraeru* (Orionsha, 1965). In 1966, Ishihama married the writer Takahashi Osamu. She spent fifteen months in Palo Alto, California, beginning in the spring of 1979 while her husband was a resident scholar at the Hoover Institution at Stanford University. She recorded her impressions in *Kariforunia no suteki na gakkō* [A Wonderful School in California] (Shinchōsha, 1982).

13. The classic description of the security treaty crisis is George R. Packard III, *Protest in Tokyo: The Security Treaty Crisis of 1960* (Princeton: Princeton University Press, 1966).

14. Kan Takayuki, *Sengo engeki* [Postwar Theatre], Asahi sensho 178 (Asahi shimbunsha, 1981), p. 194.

15. See David G. Goodman, *Japanese Drama and Culture in the 1960s: The Return of the Gods* (Armonk, N.Y.: M. E. Sharpe, 1988). See also, David Desser, *Eros Plus Massacre: Introduction to the Japanese New Wave Cinema* (Bloomington: Indiana University Press, 1988).

16. Yoshimoto Takaaki, "Machiu-sho shiron" [An Essay on Matthew], in Yoshimoto Takaaki, *Geijutsuteki teikō to zasetsu* [Artistic Resistance and Despair], 2d ed. (Miraisha, 1963), pp. 7–77.

17. See David G. Goodman, *Fuji-san mieta: Satoh Makoto ni okeru kakumei no engeki* [Mt. Fuji Perceived: The Revolutionary Theatre of Satoh Makoto] (Hakusuisha, 1983); and Goodman, *Japanese Drama and Culture in the 1960s*.

18. Abe Kōbō, *Uchinaru henkyō* [Inner Margins] (Chūō Kōronsha, 1971). The essay may also be found in *Abe Kōbō zen-sakuhinshū* [The Complete Works of Abe Kōbō], vol. 15 (Shinchōsha, 1973), pp. 30–57.

19. Yamaguchi Masao, "Yudayajin no chiteki jōnetsu" [The Intellectual Passion of the Jews], in *Hon no shinwagaku* [The Mythology of the Book] (Chūō kōronsha, 1971), pp. 37–72.

20. Published by Shōbunsha. The fifteen-volume set was completed in 1981.

21. Gershom Scholem, *Yudayashugi no honshitsu* [The Essence of Judaism], tr. Takao Toshikazu (Kawade shobō shinsha, 1972); *Yudayashugi to seiō* [Judaism and Western Europe], tr. Takao Toshikazu (Kawade shobō shinsha, 1973); *Yudayakyō shimpishugi* [Jewish Mysticism], tr. Takao Toshikazu (Kawade shobō shinsha, 1975).

22. On film, see Desser, *Eros Plus Massacre: Introduction to the Japanese New Wave Cinema*. On literature, see Irmela Hijiya-Kirschnereit, "Post-World War II Literature: The Intellectual Climate in Japan, 1945–1985," in Ernestine Schlant and J. Thomas Rimer, eds., *Legacies and Ambiguities: Postwar Fiction and Culture in West Germany and Japan* (Washington, DC: Woodrow Wilson

Center Press, 1991), esp. pp. 104–6. On theater, see Robert T. Rolf, "Japanese Theatre from the 1980s: The Ludic Conspiracy," *Modern Drama* 31, no. 1 (March 1992), 127–36.

23. Patricia G. Steinhoff, "Portrait of a Terrorist," p. 837; David E. Apter and Nagayo Sawa, *Against the State: Politics and Social Protest in Japan* (Cambridge, Mass.: Harvard University Press, 1984), pp. 111–28; and Patricia G. Steinhoff, "Death by Defeatism and Other Fables: The Social Dynamics of the Rengō Sekigun Purge," in Takie Sugiyama Lebra, ed., *Japanese Social Organization* (Honolulu: University of Hawaii Press, 1992), pp. 195–224.

24. Regarding the Vietnam War and Japan, see Thomas R. H. Havens, *Fire Across the Sea: The Vietnam War and Japan, 1965–1975* (Princeton: Princeton University Press, 1987).

25. Hyman Lumer, ed., *Lenin on the Jewish Question* (New York: International Publishers, 1974), p. 107. Quoted from Nora Levin, *While Messiah Tarried: Jewish Socialist Movements, 1871–1917* (New York: Schocken, 1977), p. 364.

26. Joseph Stalin, "Marxism and the National and Colonial Question" (1913), quoted in Levin, *While Messiah Tarried*, p. 361.

27. A succint history of Soviet antisemitism and anti-Zionism is given in Robert Wistrich, *Hitler's Apocalypse: Jews and the Nazi Legacy* (New York: St. Martin's Press, 1985), pp. 194–215. See also Paul Johnson, *A History of the Jews* (New York: Harper and Row, 1988), pp. 569–576.

28. Yamamoto Tadashi, "Chūtō funsō no haikei to ikutsu ka no mondai" [The Background of the Middle East Conflict and a Number of Problems], *Zen'ei*, February 1971.

29. Ōta Iwao, "Chūtō sensō to Isuraeru mondai" [The Mideast War and the Problem of Israel], *Zen'ei*, September 1976.

30. Jean-Paul Sartre, *Yudayajin*, tr. Andō Shinya (Iwanami shoten, 1956).

31. Jean-Paul Sartre, *Anti-Semite and Jew*, tr. George J. Becker (New York: Schocken, 1948, 1965), p. 85.

32. Ibid., p. 66. Emphasis in the original.

33. Ibid., p. 143.

34. "The Palestinian National Charter of 1968," *The Arab-Israeli Conflict*, vol. 3, ed. John Norton Moore (Princeton: Princeton University Press, 1974), pp. 705–11.

35. For discussions of this phenomenon, see Robert S. Wistrich, ed., *Anti-Zionism and Antisemitism in the Contemporary World* (New York: New York

University Press, 1990); Jacques Givet, *The Anti-Zionist Complex* (Englewood, N.J.: SBS Publishing, 1979); and Arnold Forster and Benjamin R. Epstein, *The New Anti-Semitism* (New York: McGraw-Hill, 1974).

36. This account is drawn from Hirokawa Ryūichi, *Yudaya kokka to arabu gerira* [The Jewish State and the Arab Guerrillas] (Sōshisha, 1971), pp. 1–3.

37. Itagaki Yūzō, Oda Makoto, and Shiboh Mitsukazu, eds., *The Israeli Invasion of Lebanon, 1982—Inquiry by the International People's Tribunal* (Sanyūsha, 1983), p. xxi.

38. Itagaki Yūzō and Okakura Koshirō, "Dai-ichiji sekai taisen to jūzoku sho-chiiki" [The First World War and the Various Regional Dependencies], *Iwanami kōza sekai rekishi*, vol. 24 (Iwanami shoten, 1971), p. 235.

39. *Mainichi Daily News*, November 27, 1973; "Arabu to Isuraeru" [The Arabs and Israel], *Mainichi shimbun*, November 2, 1973. The interviews were carried in *Mainichi shimbun*, November 1–13, 1973, and in the *Mainichi Daily News* between November 26 and December 8, 1973.

40. Itagaki acknowledges Sartre as the source of his views in "Naseru no zasetsu to taikoku no egoizumu," p. 13.

41. *Mainichi Daily News*, November 27, 1973.

42. Bernard Lewis, *Semites and Anti-Semites* (New York: Norton, 1987), esp. pp. 192–253.

43. Itagaki Yūzō, "Naseru no zasetsu to taikoku no egoizumu," *Asahi Journal*, June 25, 1967.

44. Itagaki Yūzō, "Nachizumu to Isuraeru," *Sekai*, July 1978.

45. Itagaki, "Naseru no zasetsu to taikoku no egoizumu," p. 12.

46. Ibid., p. 19.

47. Ibid., p. 19.

48. Ibid., pp. 17–18.

49. Ibid., p. 19.

50. Itagaki Yūzō, " 'Arabu-Isuraeru no tairitsu' o koeru mono" [Beyond "Arab-Israeli Confrontation"], *Yomiuri shimbun*, May 28, 1973.

51. Itagaki, "Naseru no zasetsu to taikoku no egoizumu," p. 13.

52. Itagaki, "Nachizumu to Isuraeru," p. 27.

53. Ibid., p. 26.

54. Ibid., p. 27.

55. Ibid., p. 28.

56. Ibid., p. 29.

57. "Erusaremu mondai o rikai suru tame ni" [In Order to Understand the Problem of Jerusalem], *Mainichi*, November 28, 1980.

58. Ian Buruma, "The Devils of Hiroshima," *New York Review of Books*, October 25, 1990, p. 16.

59. Oda Makoto, " 'Aushuvittsu' to 'Deiru Yashin'—'kyōsei' e no genri, 3" ["Auschwitz" and "Deir Yassin"—Principles for Coexistence, 3], *Tenbō* 225 (September 1977), 130–46.

60. Oda Makoto, *Rekishi no tenkan no naka de—21 seiki e* [In a Time of Historical Transition: Toward the 21st Century] (Iwanami shoten, 1980).

61. Oda Makoto, *The Bomb*, tr. D. H. Whittaker (New York: Kodansha International, 1990). See also Ian Buruma's favorable review of the book in "The Devils of Hiroshima," pp. 15–19.

62. Oda, " 'Aushuvittsu' to 'Deiru Yashin,' " p. 134.

63. Ibid., p. 136.

64. Ibid., p. 138. Emphasis in the original.

65. Ibid., p. 139.

66. Ibid., pp. 138–39.

67. Ibid., pp. 142–43; 145–46.

68. Oda Makoto, *Rekishi no tenkan no naka de—21 seiki e* [In a Time of Historical Transition: Toward the 21st Century], pp. 27–29.

69. Ibid., p. 29.

70. Ibid., pp. 30–31.

71. Itagaki, Oda, and Shiboh, eds., *The Israeli Invasion of Lebanon, 1982.*

72. Haru Matsui [Ishigaki Ayako], *Restless Wave* (New York: Modern Age Books, 1940).

73. Ishigaki Ayako, "Paresuchina de mita koto" [What I Saw in Palestine], *Mainichi shimbun*, evening edition, August 21, 1974.

74. Ishigaki Ayako, "Nikki kara" [From My Diary], *Asahi shimbun*, evening edition, September 10 and 19, 1974.

75. Ibid.

76. Ishigaki, "Paresuchina de mita koto."

77. Shiba Mitsuyo, " 'Heiwa o!' josei no sakebi mo ōkiku" ["Peace!" Women's Voices Also Cry], *Mainichi shimbun*, evening edition, November 9, 1978.

•

78. Shiba Mitsuyo, "Naisen no Lebanon o yuku" [Traveling Through Lebanon During the Civil War], *Asahi shimbun*, evening edition, November 8, 1978.

79. Shiba Mitsuyo, "Paresuchina no kodomotachi" [The Children of Palestine], in Hirokawa Ryūichi, ed., *Ubawareta kuni no kodomotachi—Paresuchina dokyumentari shashin shū* [Children of a Stolen Land—Documentary Photographs of Palestine] (Daisan shokan, 1979), p. 139.

80. Kara Jūrō, *Kaze ni tento, mune ni wa kenjū: Paresuchina Banguradeshu kikō* [Our Tent (Theatre) in the Wind, Pistols in Our Breast: Record of Journeys to Palestine and Bangladesh] (Kadokawa shoten, 1976), p. 10.

81. Washimi Tetsuhiko, " 'Rekishi' o ikinuku nanmin-tachi" [Refugees Who Survive "History"], *Kyōto shimbun*, October 23, 1979.

82. Maruyama Naoki, "Japan's Middle Eastern Policy in a Dilemma," *Kiyō*, Kokusai Daigaku Chūtō Kenkyūjo [Bulletin of the Middle East Institute of the International University of Japan] 2 (1986), 267–72.

83. *Asahi shimbun*, November 23, 1973.

84. Anti-Defamation League of B'nai B'rith, "Japan and the Arab Boycott," *ADL Bulletin*, November 1986.

85. Willy Stern, "Japan's 'Free Traders' Boycott Israel," *Tokyo Business Today*, November 1987, pp. 26–28.

86. "Is Japan Making Amends?" *Jerusalem Post*, May 24, 1991.

87. Stern, "Japan's 'Free Traders' Boycott Israel," pp. 26–28.

88. Kenneth Jacobson and Jess Hordes, "Japan and the Arab Boycott," *ADL Bulletin*, November 1986, p. 1.

89. "Israel Braces for Uno Who?" *Economist*, May 21, 1988.

90. Ōoka Shōhei, "Daini no sengo ka" [A Second Postwar Period?], *Asahi shimbun*, January 1, 1974.

91. Hirokawa Ryūichi and Paresuchina-Yudayajin mondai kenkyūkai [Society for the Study of the Palestine-Jewish Question], ed., *Yudayajin to wa nani ka*, *Yudayajin*, vol. 1 (Sanyūsha, 1985).

92. Hirokawa Ryūichi and the Committee for Palestinian and Jewish Studies, ed., *Daiyamondo to shi no shōnin: Isuraeru no sekai senryaku* [Merchants of Diamonds and Death: Israel's Global Strategy], *Yudayajin* [The Jews], vol. 2 (Sanyūsha, 1986), pp. 1–2.

CHAPTER 8. A SIGNAL FAILURE

1. Mikiso Hane, *Modern Japan: A Historical Survey*, 2d ed. (Boulder, Colo.: Westview Press, 1992), pp. 379, 387, 394.

2. Aoki Tamotsu, *"Nihonron" no henyō* [The Evolution of "Theories of Japan"] (Chūō kōronsha, 1990).

3. Ezra F. Vogel, *Japan as Number One: Lessons for America* (Cambridge, Mass.: Harvard University Press, 1979).

4. Kenneth B. Pyle, *The Japanese Question: Power and Purpose in a New Era* (Washington, D.C.: AEI Press, 1992), pp. 85–105.

5. Ibid., pp. 85–105; and Kenneth B. Pyle, "In Pursuit of a Grand Design: Nakasone Betwixt the Past and the Future," *Journal of Japanese Studies* 13, no. 2 (Summer 1987), 243–70, especially pp. 261–66.

6. See, for example, Ian Buruma, "A New Japanese Nationalism," *New York Times Magazine*, April 12, 1987, pp. 23–26, 29, 38.

7. Pyle, *The Japanese Question*, p. 99.

8. *Wall Street Journal*, November 19, 1982, quoted in John W. Dower, "Fear and Prejudice in U.S.-Japan Relations," *Ethics and International Affairs* 3 (1989), 161. This essay also appears in John W. Dower, *Japan in War and Peace: Selected Essays* (New York: The New Press, 1993), pp. 301–35.

9. Regarding Nakasone's controversial remarks about the intellectual level (*chiteki suijun*) in America, see "Shushō hatsugen ni kōgi sattō" [Deluge of Protest Over Prime Minister's Remarks], *Yomiuri shimbun*, September 24, 1986; "Jinshu ronsō" [The Race Debate], *Yomiuri shimbun*, November 3, 1986; George Fields, "Racism Is Accepted Practice in Japan," *Wall Street Journal*, November 10, 1986. On a related remark Nakasone made about Japan's Ainu minority, see "Japan's Unmelted Minority Talks Up," *New York Times*, November 5, 1986.

10. Pyle, *The Japanese Question*, p. 17.

11. Etō Jun, *Nichibei sensō wa owatte inai* [The Japanese-American War Is Not Over] (Nesco, 1987). For a critique of Etō's charges regarding Occupation censorship, see Jay Rubin, "From Wholesomeness to Decadence: The Censorship of Literature Under the Allied Occupation," *Journal of Japanese Studies* 11, no. 1 (Winter 1985), 71–103.

Morita Akio and Ishihara Shintarō, *"No" to ieru Nihon* [The Japan that Can Say No] (Tokyo: Kōbunsha, 1989).

12. "Rich Man, Poor Man in Japan: Not an Economic Party for All," *New York Times*, December 26, 1988; "Feeling Poor in Japan," *Economist*, June 11, 1988.

13. "Do It My Way," *Economist*, November 24, 1990.

14. "Gloom Is Lifting in the U.S. and Descending on Japan," *New York Times*, December 29, 1992.

•

15. On changes in Japanese culture and the publishing industry in the 1980s, see Shūichi Katō, "Mechanisms of Ideas: Society, Intellectuals, and Literature in the Postwar Period in Japan," in Ernestine Schlant and J. Thomas Rimer, eds., *Legacies and Ambiguities: Postwar Fiction and Culture in West Germany and Japan* (Washington, D.C.: Woodrow Wilson Center Press, 1991), pp. 249–59.

16. "Nosutoradamusu 'fukkatsu' " [Nostradamus "Rises Again"], *Mainichi shimbun*, February 9, 1991.

17. Yamakage Motohisa, *Yudaya no sekai shihai senryaku: miezaru sekai seifu no kyōi* [The Jewish Plot to Control the World: The Threat of the Invisible World Government] (Management-sha, 1985). See also the sequel, *Yudaya no sekai shihai senryaku part 2: Yudaya no kami wa jinrui o sukuwanai.* [The Jewish Plot to Control the World, Part 2: The God of the Jews Will Not Save Mankind] (Management-sha, 1987).

18. Yajima Kinji, *Yudaya purotokōru chō-urayomi-jutsu* [The Expert Way of Reading the Jewish Protocols] (Seishun shuppansha, 1986).

19. Uno Masami, *Yudaya ga wakaru to sekai ga miete kuru* [If You Understand the Jews, You Will Understand the World] (Tokuma shoten, 1986), p. 147. Hereinafter, *Sekai*.

20. Ibid., pp. 149–50; and Uno Masami, *Yudaya ga wakaru to Nihon ga miete kuru* [If You Understand the Jews, You Will Understand Japan] (Tokuma shoten, 1986), p. 161. Hereinafter, *Nihon*.

21. Ibid., pp. 127, 135, 193–96.

22. Uno Masami, *Kyūyaku seisho no dai-yogen: sekai saishū sensō to Yudayajin* [Great Prophecies of the Old Testament: The Jews and Armageddon] (Tokuma shoten, 1982) and *Zoku kyūyaku seisho no dai-yogen: sekai saishū sensō to shidōsha no jōken* [Great Prophecies of the Old Testament, Continued: Armageddon and the Qualifications of the Leader] (Tokuma shoten, 1982).

23. Uno, *Sekai*, pp. 241–42; *Nihon*, pp. 237–52.

24. Uno, *Nihon*, p. 244.

25. Uno, *Sekai*, pp. 7, 234–36.

26. Uno, *Nihon*, pp. 249–52.

27. Ibid., pp. 225–26.

28. "Japanese Writers are Critical of Jews," *New York Times*, March 12, 1987.

29. According to an advertisement in the *Yomiuri shimbun*, April 6, 1987.

30. Uno openly acknowledges Yasue Norihiro, first translator of *The Protocols*. See *Sekai*, pp. 31–32.

●

31. Uno Masami, *Yudaya to tatakatte sekai ga mieta: hakujin shihai no hōkai to "futatsu no Yudayajin"* [I Fought the Jews and Understood the World: The Collapse of White Domination and "The Two Kinds of Jews"], Kappa Business Books (Kōbunsha, 1993).

32. See Pierre Vidal-Naquet, *Assassins of Memory: Essays on the Denial of the Holocaust*, tr. Jeffrey Mehlman (New York: Columbia University Press, 1992); and Deborah Lipstadt, *Denying the Holocaust: The Growing Assault on Truth and Memory* (New York: Free Press, 1993).

33. "Japanese Writers Critical of Jews," *New York Times*, March 12, 1987; and Uno, *Nihon*, pp. 170–74, 186–99.

34. Uno, *Nihon*, pp. 199–202.

35. Uno Masami, *1992-nen Yudaya keizai senryaku* [The Jewish Economic Strategy for 1992] (Nihon bungeisha, 1989), pp. 3–5.

36. Uno, *Nihon*, pp. 196–199.
    On German historical revisionism, see Ernst Nolte, "Between Myth and Revisionism? The Third Reich in the Perspective of the 1980s," in *Aspects of the Third Reich*, ed. H. W. Koch (New York: Macmillan, 1985), pp. 17–38; and Richard J. Evans, "The New Nationalism and the Old History: Perspective on the West German Historians' Debate," *Journal of Modern History* 59, no. 4 (December 1987), 761–97.

37. Uno Masami, *Hitoraa no gyakushū* [Hitler's Revenge] (Nesco, 1990), p. 287.

38. Anti-Defamation League of B'nai B'rith, *Extremism on the Right* (New York: Anti-Defamation League of B'nai B'rith, 1988), p. 35.

39. Uno Masami, Paul Goldstein, and Jeffrey Steinberg, *Yudaya no kokuhaku: Nihon keizai o rimen kara miru* [Confessions of the Jews: Behind the Scenes of the Japanese Economy] (Enoch shuppan, 1990), cover and p. 286.

40. Anti-Defamation League of B'nai B'rith, *Liberty Lobby: Network of Hate*, ADL Research Report, 1990, pp. 11–12.

41. "Religious Tug of War Delays Burial of Arlington Man," *Washington Post*, January 6, 1988.

42. *Spotlight*, February 27, 1989, p. 13.

43. Uno Masami and Dale Crowley, Jr., *Yudaya ga wakaru to Amerika ga miete kuru* [If You Understand the Jews, You Will Understand America] (Chūtō mondai kenkyū sentaa, 1989). This is a video tape of a joint lecture appearance by Uno and Crowley at the Osaka Nakanoshima Kōkaidō on September 18, 1989. It is one of a series of video and audio tapes produced by Uno's Middle East Problems Research Center.

•

44. *Yudaya no kokusai senryaku: Amerikajin kara no shōgen* [The International Jewish Conspiracy: An American Account].

45. On LaRouche's antisemitism, see Dennis King, *Lyndon LaRouche and the New American Fascism* (New York: Doubleday, 1989), pp. 38–46 and passim.

46. Jeffrey Steinberg, Scott Thompson, et al., "Tax-Exempt Treachery: A Profile of the Anti-Defamation League," *Executive Intelligence Review* (*EIR*), May 18, 1990, pp. 32–49.

47. King, *Lyndon LaRouche and the New American Fascism*, p. 178.

48. *Yudayajin to wa dare ka: dai 13 shizoku kazaaru ōkoku no nazo*. Originally published in the United States in 1976.

49. Japanese title: *Yudaya o hagu: busō tero soshiki JDL no naimaku* [The Jews Unmasked: Inside the Terrorist JDL].

50. Japanese title: *Yudaya konekushon* [The Jewish Connection].

51. Umezu Itaru, "Japanese and Jews," *New York Times*, March 19, 1987. Umezu was the director of the Japan Information Center, a section of the Japanese Consulate in New York.

52. "Japanese Foreign Ministry Memorandum Issued to the Japanese Association of Publishers in September 1989 Regarding the Publication of Anti-Semitic Literature in Japan," unofficial translation prepared by the Japanese Foreign Ministry.

53. *Asahi shimbun*, October 5, 1991.

54. *Asahi shimbun*, September 12, 1991.

55. *Asahi shimbun*, March 14, 1992.

56. "Japanese to Name Park in Memory of Ambassador Who Saved Jews," *Jerusalem Post*, August 5, 1992.

57. *Yakusoku no kuni e no nagai tabi* (Librio shuppan, 1988).

58. *Rokusennin no inochi no biza* (Asahi sonorama, 1990).

59. The program was aired on July 7, 1991.

60. "Japan, Israel Improving Commercial Ties," *Washington Post*, August 7, 1991.

61. *Jerusalem Post*, June 24, 1988.

62. Kurt W. Radtke, "Japan-Israel Relations in the Eighties," *Asian Survey* 28, no. 5 (May 1988), 526–40.

63. Anti-Defamation League of B'nai B'rith, "Japan and the Arab Boycott," *ADL Bulletin*, November 1986.

●

64. *Jerusalem Post*, November 23, 1987.

65. *New York Times*, June 19, 1988.

66. *Jerusalem Post*, December 11, 1988.

67. "Japan Expanding Its Ties with Israel," *New York Times*, June 19, 1988; Golub, *Japanese Attitudes Toward Jews*, p. 13.

68. "Is Japan Making Amends?" *Jerusalem Post*, May 24, 1991.

69. "Japan Will Stop Supporting Arab Economic Boycott," *Jerusalem Post*, December 4, 1991.

70. "Israel, Japan to Sign Tax Treaty," *Jerusalem Post*, January 13, 1993.

71. "Peres Calls for Greater Japanese Role in Region," *Jerusalem Post*, December 15, 1992.

72. " 'Seiji-teki riyū de jogai' to Imagawa shichō" [Mayor Imagawa Admits (Jerusalem) "Excluded for Political Reasons"], *Chūgai nippō*, December 7, 1987.

73. "Lessons in Kyoto," *Boston Herald*, November 18, 1987.

For additional information and opinion about the exclusion of Jerusalem from the World Conference of Historical Cities, see R. J. Zvi Werblowsky, "Rekishi toshi to wa nanika" [What Is a Historical City?], *Chūgai nippō*, October 23 and 26, 1987; "Erusaremu jogai no hamon kakudai" [The Impact of Excluding Jerusalem Increases], *Chūgai nippō*, November 18, 1987; and "Kūkyo na seremonii sekai rekishi toshi" [The World Conference of Historical Cities: An Empty Ceremony], *Chūgai nippō*, December 7, 1987.

74. Nagao et al., eds., *Yudaya shisō, I–II* [Jewish Thought, I–II], in *Iwanami kōza: Tōyōshisō*, vols. 1 and 2 (Iwanami shoten, 1988–89); Shinoda Kōichirō, *Tozasareta jikū: Nachi kyōsei shūyōjo no bungaku* [Closed Space, Closed Time: The Literature of the Nazi Concentration Camps] (Hakusuisha, 1992); Kogishi Akira, *Supein o owareta Yudayajin: Marano no ashiato o tazunete* [The Jews Expelled from Spain: In the Footsteps of the Marranos] (Jinmon shoin, 1992); Mochida Yukio, *Nachisu tsuikyū: Doitsu no sengo* [The Nazi Hunt: Postwar Germany] (Kōdansha, 1990); Ōsawa Takeo, *Yudayajin to Doitsujin* [Jews and Germans] (Kōdansha, 1991). For a summary of these recent publications, see "Nachisu no jidai o shiru" [Learning About the Nazi Period], *Mainichi shimbun*, March 16, 1992.

75. Among the works published by Miltos were translations of Menachem Begin, *The Revolt* (1989); Herman Wouk, *This Is My God: The Jewish Way of Life* (1990); Adin Steinsaltz, *Biblical Images: Men and Women of the Book* (1990). Miltos also published original works, including Itokawa Hideo, *Kōya ni idomu: Tale of Ben-Gurion University of the Negev* (1989); and Ushiyama

Takeshi, *Yudayajin ongakka: sono junan to kōei* [Jewish Musicians: Their Suffering and Their Glory] (1991).

76. Doi Toshikuni, *Amerika no Yudayajin* [American Jews] (Iwanami shoten, 1991); Maruyama Naoki, *Amerika no Yudayajin shakai: Yudaya pawaa no jitsuzō to han-Yudayashugi* [The American Jewish Community: The Reality of Jewish Power and Antisemitism] (Japan Times, 1990).

77. Azumi Eiji and Koizumi Takashi, trans., *Yudaya shisō no hatten to keifu* (Kinokuniya shoten, 1975); Hasegawa Shin and Azumi Eiji, trans., *Yudayajin no rekishi* (Misuzu shobō, 1966); Ishida Tomoo, et al. trans., *Yudaya minzokushi*, six vols. (Rokkō shuppan, 1976–78); Fujimoto Kazuko, trans., *Yudayajin*, 2 vols., Asahi sensho, 265–66 (Asahi shimbunsha, 1984).

78. Uchida Tatsuru, trans., *Shion kenja no giteisho: Yudayajin sekai seifuku inbō no shinwa* [Warrant for Genocide] (Dynamic Sellers, 1986); *Gettō ni ikite: aru Yudaya fujin no shuki* [The Memoirs of Gluckel of Hameln], tr. Hayashi Mizue (Shinjusha, 1974); Fujimoto Kazuko, trans., *Yatsura o shaberitaose!* [How to Talk Dirty and Influence People] (Shōbunsha, 1977).

79. We are grateful to Shōbunsha publishers for making these data available.

80. Miyazaki Masahiro, *Yudaya ni kodawaru to sekai ga mienaku naru* (Futami shobō, 1987).

81. Katō's article appeared in the *Asahi shimbun*, June 15, 1987, evening edition; Yamaguchi's appeared in the *Asahi shimbun*, April 8, 1987, evening edition; and Muramatsu's was published in the *Sankei shimbun*, April 10, 1987.

82. Nakagawa Ken'ichi, *Yudaya nyūmon: sono kyozō to jitsuzō* [An Introduction to the Jews: True and False Images] (Harvest Ministries, 1992).

83. *Sekai nippō*, a small, religiously oriented paper, did criticize the trend in its edition of March 22, 1987.

84. For a French counterpart to this phenomenon, see Edgar Morin, *Rumour in Orléans*, tr. Peter Green (New York: Pantheon, 1971). This is a translation of *La Rumeur d'Orléans* (Paris: Editions du Seuil, 1969). The Japanese edition is *Orulean no uwasa: josei yūkai no uwasa to sono shinwa sayō*, tr. Sugiyama Mitsunobu (Misuzu shobō, 1973).

85. *Asahi shimbun,* June 17, 1987. This passage is quoted from a syndicated translation of Chikushi's article, prepared by the Asia Foundation's Translation Service Center, that appeared in the *Milwaukee Journal,* August 27, 1987.

86. Josh Greenfeld, *A Child Called Noah: A Family Journey* (New York: Holt, Rinehart and Winston, 1972); *A Place for Noah* (New York: Holt, Rinehart and Winston, 1978); *A Client Named Noah: A Family Journey Continued* (New York: H. Holt, 1986).

87. Ellen Hopkins, "Her Story," *Los Angeles Times Magazine,* June 12, 1988, p. 41.

88. Kometani Foumiko, *Sugikoshi no matsuri* [Passover] (Shinchōsha, 1985), pp. 96, 156. The English version is Foumiko Kometani, *Passover,* tr. Foumiko Kometani (New York: Carrol and Graf, 1989).

89. Ibid., pp. 155–56.

90. Ibid., p. 169.

91. David G. Goodman, "Reason for Concern in Japanese Anti-Semitism," Letter to the Editor, *New York Times,* March 25, 1987.

92. Ibid.

93. Shūsaku Endō, Letter to *New York Times,* May 4, 1987.

94. Liibi Hideo [Ian Hideo Levy] and Aoki Tamotsu, "Kokkyō o koeta bungaku: [Literature Without Borders], in *Gendai no shisō: Revue de la pensée d'aujourd'hui* 19, no. 2 (February 1991), 178. Levy's words in Japanese were *dogitsui* and *sabetsu hyōgen girigiri.*

95. For example, Susan Chira, "No One Is Nice Here," Review of *Passover,* in *New York Times Book Review,* October 22, 1989.

96. Fumiko Ikeda Feingold, Letter to the Editor, *New York Times,* May 4, 1987.

97. *World Literature Today,* Autumn 1986.

98. Review of Foumiko Kometani's *Passover, Publishers Weekly,* September 22, 1989, p. 39.

99. Alan M. Tigay, Review of *Passover, Hadassah Magazine,* April 1990, p. 44.

100. The comments of the Akutagawa Prize jury may be found in *Bungei shunjū,* March 1986, pp. 333–37.

101. Hirose Keiji, "Yudaya bungaku no kyoshō-tachi (8): intabyū Kometani Foumiko, *Sugikoshi no matsuri*" [Great Jewish Writers (8): An Interview with Kometani Foumiko—*Passover*], in *Kansai bungaku* 30, no. 6 (June 1992), 44–51.

102. Kometani Foumiko, "Purofessaa deaa" [Professor Dear], *Bungakkai,* January 1991; and *Purofessa deaa* [Professor Dear], (Bungei shunjū, 1992).

103. Ōe Kenzaburō, "Bungei jihyō" [Current Literature], *Asahi shimbun,* April 23, 1992.

104. For examples, see the *Yomiuri,* international edition, May 27, 1987; May 19, 1988. *Asahi,* international edition, November 22, 1991.

105. *Asahi shimbun,* international edition, March 31, 1993.

•

106. "Anti-Semitic Book Ad Assailed," *Japan Times*, July 31, 1993.

107. Pyle, *The Japan Question*, pp. 127–31 and passim.

108. Ibid., p. 127.

109. *Asahi shimbun*, February 7, 1991.

110. *"Kueeto kiki" o yomitoku: Iraku no dōkō to Nihon no shiten* [Making Sense of "The Kuwait Crisis": Trends in Iraq and the Japanese Perspective] (Daisan shokan, 1990); *Chūtō paasupekuchibu: Chūtō no henka o yosoku suru tame no 12 shō*, [Middle East Perspective: Twelve Chapters Forecasting Changes in the Middle East] (Daisan shokan, 1991); *Chūtō wangan sensō to Nihon: Chūtō kenkyūsha no teigen* [The Middle East Gulf War and Japan: Proposals from Middle East Specialists] (Daisan shokan, 1991); *Chūtō anarishisu: wangan sensōgo no Chūtō shokoku jijō* [Middle East Analysis: Conditions in the Middle Eastern Countries in the Aftermath of the Gulf War] (Daisan shokan, 1991).
   " 'Wangan' o meguru shoseki shuppan no ugoki" [Trends in Book Publishing Surrounding "The Gulf"], *Asahi shimbun*, March 24, 1991, summarizes book publishing about the Gulf Crisis, highlighting Itagaki's activities.

111. This statement is from a May 1980 appeal issued by the *Kansai Paresuchina jinmin to rentai suru kai* [Kansai Society for Solidarity with the Palestinian People], a group affiliated with the Abeno Church in Osaka, titled "Paresuchina mondai no tadashii rikai o! Shin no rentai no tame ni" [Understand the Palestinian Problem Correctly! Toward True Solidarity]. The same argument was made in 1990 in Nihon Kirisutokyōdan shakai iinkai, ed., *Paresuchina to Kirisutokyō* [Palestine and Christianity]. Murayama Moritada is the central figure in both organizations.

112. Nihon Kirisutokyōdan shakai iinkai, ed., *Paresuchina to Kirisutokyō* (1991), p. 7.

113. Murayama Moritada, "What Was 'The Gulf War'?" *Seisho to kyōkai* [Bible and Church], May 1991, p. 27.

114. Munakata Motoi, "Seigi to kōsei," *Seisho to kyōkai*, May 1991, pp. 28–29.

115. Hirayama Kentarō, *Erusaremu wa dare no mono ka* [To Whom Does Jerusalem Belong?] (NHK shuppan, 1992), p. 66. See also "Hito," *Asahi shimbun*, February 7, 1991.

116. Koike Yuriko and Itagaki Yūzo, "Sara ni tōnoku kayakuko 'Paresuchina mondai' kaiketsu" [Dimming Prospects for Disarming the Powder Keg of the 'Palestinian Problem'], *President*, April 1991, pp. 190–200.

CHAPTER 9. JAPAN'S JEWISH PROBLEM

1. "The Letters by Arafat and Rabin," *New York Times*, September 10, 1993.

2. "Japan's New Leader Pledges Sweeping Changes in Political System," *New York Times*, August 24, 1993.

3. "Losing Its Way," *Economist*, September 18, 1993; "Breakdown in the Fast Lane," *Economist*, February 27, 1993; "Japanese Start to Link Pay to Performance, Not Tenure," *New York Times*, October 2, 1993.

4. Ōta Ryū, *Yudaya sekai teikoku no Nihon shinkō senryaku* [The Jewish World Empire's Plot to Invade Japan] (Nihon bungeisha, 1992). See also Ōta Ryū, *Ima Nihon ga abunai! Yudayaka nyūmon* [Japan Is in Danger Now! An Introduction to the Jewish Peril] (Nikkei kikaku shuppankyoku, 1992).

5. Jacob Morgan, *Saigo no kyōteki Nihon o ute: zoku Yudaya sekai shihai no giteisho* [Get Japan, The Last Enemy: The Jewish Protocols for World Domination, Continued], tr. Oshino Shōtarō (Daiichi kikaku, 1993).

6. " 'Gaikokujin oidase': tairyō no bira demawaru" ["Out with the Foreigners!": Large Numbers of Handbills Circulated], *Asahi shimbun*, international edition, April 7, 1993; "Toward Fellow Asians, A Lack of Fellowship," *New York Times*, January 3, 1990; "New Indignities for Refugees in Japan," *New York Times*, October 24, 1989; "Issue of Japanese Racism Grows with Immigration," *Los Angeles Times*, January 1, 1990.

7. *Asahi shimbun*, international edition, November 6, 1989.

8. *Asahi shimbun*, international edition, April 7, 1993.

9. " 'Gaikokujin oidase': tairyō no bira demawaru," *Asahi shimbun*, international edition, April 7, 1993; "Toward Fellow Asians, A Lack of Fellowship," *New York Times*, January 3, 1990.

10. Ogai Yoshio, *Hitoraa senkyo senryaku—gendai senkyo hisshō no baiburu* [Hitler Election Strategy: A Bible for Certain Victory in Modern Elections] (Chiyoda Nagata shobō, 1994). See "Japanese Book Praises Hitler for Politics," *New York Times,* June 8, 1994; and "Hitler Book Is Withdrawn by Japanese," *New York Times,* June 15, 1994. Regarding Nagano Shigeto's statement, see "Tokyo Aide Calls 'Rape of Nanking' a Fabrication," *New York Times,* May 5, 1994; and "Minister Fired for Doubting Japan's Guilt," *New York Times,* May 8, 1994. On the intimidation of former Prime Minister Hosokawa, see "Japanese Rightist Fires Shot Near Former Premier: Anger Over Apologies for Tokyo's War Role," *New York Times,* May 31, 1994.

See also an earlier suggestion in the mass-circulation weekly *Shūkan bun-shun* by a major in the Japanese Self-Defense Force, Yanai Shinsaku, that a coup d'état might be the best way to deal with Japan's continuing political scandals: "A Japanese Major Suggests a Cure for Political Scandals," *New York Times,* October 16, 1992.

•

BIBLIOGRAPHY

WORKS IN JAPANESE

Unless otherwise indicated, all books in Japanese were published in Tokyo.

1. Primary Sources

Abe, Kōbō. "Uchinaru henkyō" [Inner Margins]. In *Abe Kōbō zen-sakuhinshū* [The Complete Works of Abe Kōbō], vol. 15. Shinchōsha, 1973, pp. 30–57.

Aizawa, Seishisai. *Shinron* [New Theses]. In *Meiji Bunka zenshū*, vol. 15. Nihon hyōronsha, 1927, pp. 1–57.

Atago, Hokuzan. *Yudaya no sekai shihai kōryō* [The Jewish Plan to Control the World]. Seikei shobō, 1941.

———. *Yudaya to sekai sensō* [The Jews and the World War]. Daiyamondosha, 1943.

Baba, Tsunego. "Hitoraa-ron." [On Hitler]. *Chūō kōron*, May 1933, pp. 247–55.

Ben-Dasan, Isaiah. See Yamamoto, Shichihei.

Doi, Toshikuni. *Amerika no Yudayajin* [American Jews]. Iwanami shoten, 1991.

Etō, Jun. *Nichibei sensō wa owatte inai* [The Japanese-American War Is Not Over]. Nesco, 1987.

Executive Committee of the Common Bible Translation, ed. *Seisho: shin kyōdō yaku* [The Bible: The New Interconfessional Translation]. Japan Bible Society, 1987.

Fujii, Noboru. "Kurinton shikkyaku no hi" [The Day of Clinton's Downfall]. *Sapio*. April 14, 1994, pp. 6–9.

Fujimoto, Kazuko. *Sabaku no kyōshitsu* [Classroom in the Desert]. Kawade shobō shinsha, 1978.

Fujita, Den. *Jissen no yudaya shōhō: chōjōshiki no manee senryaku* [Practical Jewish Business Methods]. KK Bestsellers, 1986.

Gendai no shisō [Revue de la pensée d'aujourd'hui], ed. *Yudayateki chisei to gendai* [The Jewish Mind and the Present], November 1977.

Gurūpu 21 seiki gensho no kai. *Yudaya bukku* [Jewish Books]. Tokuma shoten, 1988.

Hōri, Shōichi. *Nihon no chūtō gaikō: sekiyu gaikō kara no dakkyaku.* [Japan's Middle East Policy: Beyond Oil Politics]. Kyōikusha, 1980.

Hasegawa, Taizō. "Nunokawa Magoichi sensei o itamu" [In Memory of Professor Nunokawa Magoichi]. *Yudaya kenkyū*, May–June 1944, p. 57.

Hayashi, Shigeo. *Sadato to Begin: chūtō heiwa no futari no shuyaku* [Sadat and Begin: Two Leaders in Middle East Peace]. Kyōikusha, 1979.

Hayashi, Takeshi. *Gendai Arabu nyūmon: chūtō mondai no kyozō to jitsuzō* [An Introduction to the Arabs Today: Fact and Fiction about the Middle East Problem]. Nihon keizai shimbun, 1974.

———. "Shohyō *Yudayajin* [Gendai no esupuri] e no hanron" [A rebuttal of the review of *The Jews* in *L'esprit Modern*]. In *Gekkan Isuraeru*, October 1977, pp. 15–16.

———. "Yudayajin, sono kaihō no shinwa: Isuraeru 'kokka' no mujun" [The Myth of Jewish Liberation: Israel's Contradictions as a "Nation"]. *Gendai no esupuri* 121 (1977), 112–28.

Hazumi, Ichirō. *Yudayaka no sekai*. [The World of the Jewish Peril]. Kasumigaseki shobō, 1941.

Hidaka, Yoshiki. *Amerika nairan to hakujin no ronri*. [Civil Strife in America and the White Man's Way of Thinking]. Kōbunsha, 1992.

Higuchi, Kiichirō. *Attsu-Kisuka-gun-shireikan no kaisōroku*. [Memoirs of the Military Commander of Attu and Kiska]. Fuyō shobō, 1971.

Hirayama, Kentarō. *Erusaremu wa dare no mono ka* [To Whom Does Jerusalem Belong?]. NHK shuppan, 1992.

Hirokawa, Routie [Joskowicz, Routie]. *Watakushi no naka no "Yudayajin"* [The "Jew" Within Me]. Shūeisha, 1982.

Hirokawa, Ryūichi. *Yudaya kokka to Arabu gerira* [The Jewish State and the Arab Guerrillas]. Sōshisha, 1971.

———. "Yudaya teikoku Hazaaru maboroshi no shuto. [The Lost Capital of the Jewish Khazar Empire]. *Asahi shimbun*. August 20, 1992.

Hirokawa, Ryūichi and Paresuchina-Yudayajin mondai kenkyū kai [Society for the Study of the Palestine-Jewish Question], eds. *Yudayajin* [The Jews], 2 vols. Sanyūsha, 1985.

Hirose, Keiji. "Yudaya bungaku no kyoshō-tachi (8): intabyū Kometani Foumiko, *Sugikoshi no matsuri*" [Great Jewish Writers (8): An Interview with Kometani Foumiko—*Passover*]. *Kansai bungaku* 30, no. 6 June 1992, 44–51.

Hirose, Takashi. "Isuraeru-PLO no 'rekishiteki wakai' wa 'akai tate' Rosuchairudo-ke no shōchū de okonawareta" [The "Historical Reconciliation" Between Israel and the PLO Was Engineered by the "Red Shield" of the Rothschilds]. *Sapio*, October 28, 1993, pp. 18–22.

Hoashi, Riichirō. "Nachisu no kyōbō to jimetsu o isogu minzokushugi" [Nazi

•

Fury and the Self-Destructiveness of Ethnic Nationalism]. *Teiyū rinrikai rinri kōenshū*, July 1933, pp. 51–53.

Hotta, Yoshie. "Yoru to kiri: hibi no shi no naka de" [Night and Fog: In the Midst of Daily Death]. Sengo besuto seraa monogatari, 40. *Asahi Journal*, July 24, 1966, pp. 35–39.

Inoue, Makoto. "Aihiman no shokei," [Eichmann's Execution]. *Ronsō*, September 1962, pp. 116–122.

Inui, Tomiko. "Anne no nikki: teikō to shi to ai to" [The Diary of Anne Frank: Resistance and Death and Love]. Sengo no besuto seraa, 21. *Asahi Journal*, March 6, 1966, pp. 35–39.

Inukai, Michiko. "Aihiman shikei hanketsu ni omou" [Thoughts on the Eichmann Death Sentence]. *Asahi shimbun*, December 16, 1961.

———. "Kokuren ga sabaku beki datta" [The United Nations Should Have Tried (Eichmann)]. *Shūkan Asahi*, December 29, 1961, pp. 6–7.

Inuzuka, Kiyoko. *Kaigun Inuzuka kikan no kiroku: Yudaya mondai to Nippon no kōsaku* [Records of the Navy's Inuzuka Operation: The Jewish Problem and Japan's Maneuvers]. Nihon kōgyō shimbunsha, 1982.

———. "Yudayajin o hogo shita teikoku kaigun" [The Imperial Navy That Protected the Jews]. *Jiyū*, February 1973, pp. 236–45.

Inuzuka, Koreshige. "Nippon no 'Aushubittsu' wa rakuen datta" [The Japanese "Auschwitz" was a Paradise]. *Sekai to Nippon*, May 1961, reprinted in *Jiyū*, February 1973, pp. 228–35.

——— [Utsunomiya, Kiyo]. *Yudaya mondai to Nippon—fu kokusai himitsuryoku no kenkyū* [The Jewish Problem and Japan—A Supplement to Studies in the World's Secret Powers]. Naigai shobō, 1939.

Ishigaki, Ayako. "Nikki kara" [From My Diary]. *Asahi shimbun*, September 10 and 19, 1974.

———. "Paresuchina de mita koto" [What I Saw in Palestine]. *Mainichi shimbun*, evening edition, August 21, 1974.

Ishihama, Mikaru. *Sharōmu Isuraeru* [Shalom, Israel]. Orionsha, 1965.

Ishinomori, Shōtarō. *Nihon keizai nyūmon* [An Introduction to the Japanese Economy], 4 vols. Nihon keizai shimbunsha, 1986–88.

Isuraeru. Iwanami shashin bunko. Iwanami shoten, 1954.

Itagaki, Yūzō. " 'Arabu-Isuraeru no tairitsu' o koeru mono" [Beyond "Arab-Israeli Confrontation"]. *Yomiuri shimbun*, May 28, 1973.

———. "Arabu to Isuraeru" [The Arabs and the Israelis], *Mainichi shimbun*, November 1–13, 1973.

————, ed. *Chūtō anarishisu: wangan sensō go no Chūtō shokoku jijō* [Middle East Analysis: Conditions in the Middle Eastern Countries in the Aftermath of the Gulf War]. Daisan shokan, 1991.

————, ed. *Chūtō paasupekuchibu: Chūtō no henka o yosoku suru tame no 12 shō* [Middle East Perspective: Twelve Chapters Forecasting Changes in the Middle East]. Daisan shokan, 1990.

————, ed. *Chūtō wangan sensō to Nihon: Chūtō kenkyūsha no teigen* [The Middle East Gulf War and Japan: Proposals from Middle East Specialists]. Daisan shokan, 1991.

————, ed. *"Kueeto kiki" o yomitoku: Iraku no dōkō to Nihon no shiten* [Making Sense of "The Kuwait Crisis": Trends in Iraq and the Japanese Perspective]. Daisan shokan, 1990.

————. "Nachizumu to Isuraeru." *Sekai*, July 1978, pp. 26–29.

————. "Naseru no zasetsu to taikoku no egoizumu" [Nasser's Failure and the Egoism of the Great Powers]. *Asahi Journal*, June 25, 1967, pp. 12–19.

Itagaki, Yūzō and Okakura, Koshirō. "Dai-ichiji sekai taisen to jūzoku shochi-iki" [The First World War and the Various Regional Dependencies]. *Iwanami kōza sekai rekishi*, vol. 24. Iwanami shoten, 1971.

Itō, Ken. "Dainiji Ōshū taisen to Yudaya mondai," [The Second Great European War and the Jewish Problem]. *Kokusai chishiki oyobi hyōron*, January 1940, pp. 71–75.

Iwai, Katsuhito. *Benisu no shōnin no shihonron* [The Theory of Capitalism in *The Merchant of Venice*]. Iwanami shoten, 1985.

Joskowicz, Routie. See Hirokawa, Routie.

Kai, Shizuma. *Chūkintō* [The Middle East]. Iwanami shoten, 1957.

Kaikō, Takeshi. *Koe no kariudo* [Hunter for Voices]. Iwanami shoten, 1962.

Kansai Paresuchina jinmin to rentai suru kai [Kansai Society for Solidarity with the Palestinian People], ed. "Paresuchina mondai no tadashii rikai o! Shin no rentai no tame ni" [Understand the Palestinian Problem Correctly! Toward True Solidarity]. May 1980.

Kara, Jūrō. *Kaze ni tento, mune ni wa kenjū: Paresuchina Banguradeshu kikō* [Our Tent (Theatre) in the Wind, Pistols in Our Breast: Record of Journeys to Palestine and Bangladesh]. Kadokawa shoten, 1976.

————. *Sagawa-kun e no tegami* [Letter to Sagawa]. Kawade shobō shinsha, 1983.

Kasahara, Yoshimitsu and Morioka, Iwao. *Kirisutokyō no sensō sekinin* [Christianity's Responsibility for the War]. Kyōbunkan, 1974.

Katō, Shūichi. "Nihon ni okeru 'han-Yudayashugi' " ["Antisemitism" in Japan]. *Asahi shimbun*, evening edition, June 15, 1987.

Katsumoto, Seiichirō. "Yudaya minzoku junan kenbunki" [Observations on the Suffering of the Jewish People]. *Chūō kōron*, July 1933, pp. 349–62.

Kawamorita, Eiji. *Nihon Heburu shiika no kenkyū* [Japanese Hebrew Songs], 2 vols. Kyōbunkan, 1956.

———. *Nihon no naka no Yudaya* [Jews in Japan]. Tama shuppan, 1990.

Kimura, Hiroshi. "Yudayajin-netsu ni toritsukarete" [Taken Captive by the Jewish Fever]. *Shokun*, January 1971, pp. 212–24.

Kita, Morio. *Dokutoru Manbou konchū-ki* [Dr. Manbou's Entomology]. Chūō kōronsha, 1961.

Kitagami, Baiseki. *Yudayaka* [The Jewish Peril]. Naigai shobō, 1923.

Kitazawa, Masao. "Naserizumu no henyō to Arabu sekai—Arabu minzoku-shugi no shiteki kōzō" [The Transformation of Nasserism and the Arab World—The Historical Structure of Arab Nationalism]. *Sekai*, July 1974, pp. 123–37.

Kiyosawa, Kiyoshi. "Hitoraa wa naze ni ninki ga aru ka—Doitsu ni kite Nachisu undō o miru" [Why Is Hitler Popular? Coming to Germany and Watching the Nazi Movement]. *Chūō kōron*, February 1938, pp. 214–27.

Koike, Yuriko and Itagaki, Yūzō. "Sara ni tōnoku kayakuko 'Pareschina mondai' kaiketsu" [Dimming Prospects for Disarming the Powder Keg of the "Palestinian Problem"]. *President*, April 1991, pp. 190–200.

Kokusai himitsuryoku no kenkyū [Studies in the World's Secret Powers], 6 vols. Kokusai seikei gakkai. [Association for International Political and Economic Studies], November 1936–April 1940.

Kometani, Foumiko. *Purofessaa deaa* [Professor Dear]. Bungei shunjū, 1992.

———. *Sugikoshi no matsuri* [Passover]. Shinchōsha, 1985.

Koyama, Takeo, ed. *Tōa to Yudaya mondai* [East Asia and the Jewish Problem]. Chūō kōronsha, 1941.

Kubota, Michiatsu. "Nichiyu dōsoron o haigeki su!" [I Denounce Japanese-Jewish Common Ancestry Theories]. *Yudaya kenkyū*, March 1942, p. 110.

Kumamoto, Arihisa. "Yudaya kenkyūsha no taisenkan o hihan su" [A Critique of Jewish Scholars' Views of the War]. *Teiyū rinrikai rinri kōenshū*, September 1941, pp. 62–70.

Kuroda, Reiji. See Okanoe, Morimichi.

Kusakari, Zenzō. "Kibutsu kenshūgaku joron" [An Introduction to Kibbutz Study]. In Ueno Masahito, *Kibutsu gaido* [Kibbutz Guide]. Tochigi Prefecture: Nihon kyōdōtai kyōkai, 1989.

•

Kuwaki, Gen'yoku. "Doitsu ni okeru Yudayajin mondai" [The Jewish Problem in Germany]. *Teiyū rinrikai rinri kōenshū*, July 1933, pp. 31–38.

Maruyama, Naoki. *Amerika no Yudayajin shakai: Yudaya pawaa no jitsuzō to han-Yudayashugi* [The American Jewish Community: The Reality of Jewish Power and Antisemitism]. Japan Times, 1990.

Masuda, Masao. "Kakudai shikitareru ōbei no haiyu undō ni tsuite (ge)" [The Expansion of the Antisemitic Movement in the West, Part II]. *Yudaya kenkyū*, May-June 1944, pp. 2–27, 67.

———. "Kanmatsu dokugo" [Afterword]. *Yudaya kenkyū*, January-February 1944, pp. 64–65.

———. "Kono sensō wa Nihon o chūshin to suru sekai fukko no taisen de aru" [This War Is the Great War of Restoration of the World with Japan at the Center]. *Yudaya kenkyū*, December 1943.

———. "Teikoku gikai ni okeru Yudaya mondai" [The Jewish Problem [Discussed] in the Imperial Diet]. *Yudaya kenkyū*, March 1944, pp. 45–49.

Matsumoto, Fumi. *Fuji Kaidan'in konryū* [Building the Altar at Mount Fuji]. Fujisan Myōkōin, 1958.

McLeod, Norman. *Nihon kodaishi no shukuzu* [Epitome of the Ancient History of Japan]. In *Rekishi tokuhon*, March 1987, pp. 218–27.

———. *Nihon to Yudaya: nazo no sanzennenshi* [Epitome of the Ancient History of Japan]. Jiyū kokuminsha, 1987.

Mimura, Saburō. *Sekai no nazo: Nihon to Isuraeru* [Japan and Israel: Enigmas of the World]. Nichiyu kankei kenkyū sōsho 1. Nichiyu kankei kenkyūkai, 1950.

———. *Yudaya mondai to uragaeshite mita Nihon rekishi* [Japanese History Seen as an Inversion of the Jewish Problem]. Nichiyu kankei kenkyūkai, 1953.

Minobe, Ryōkichi. " 'Daisan teikoku' ni taizai shite" [On Visiting 'The Third Reich']. *Kaizō*, November 1934, pp. 1–16.

Mitsukawa, Kametarō. *Yudayaka no meimō* [The Illusion of the Jewish Peril]. Heibonsha, 1929.

Miura, Shumon. "Pio XII wa Nachi no daairinin ka?" [Was Pius XII the Deputy of the Nazis?] *Shokun*, September 1971, pp. 226–33.

Morgan, Jacob. See Oshino, Shōtarō.

Morita, Akio and Ishihara, Shintarō. *"No" to ieru Nihon* [The Japan That Can Say No]. Kōbunsha, 1989.

Munakata, Motoi. "Seigi to kōsei" [Justice and Fairness]. *Seisho to kyōkai*, May 1991, pp. 28–29.

•

Muramatsu, Takeshi. "Erusaremu e no michi" [The Road to Jerusalem]. *Shūkan Asahi,* June 25, 1967, pp. 76–79.

———. "Mata arawareta 'Nachi no bōrei': han-Yudaya-sho būmu ni omou" ["The Nazi Ghost" Reappears: Thoughts on the Antisemitic Book Boom]. *Sankei shimbun,* April 10, 1987.

———. *Tairyō satsujin no shisō* [The Philosophy of Mass Murder]. Bungei shunjū, 1961.

Murayama, Moritada. " 'Wangan sensō' to wa nan na no ka" [What Is 'The Gulf War'?]. *Seisho to kyōkai,* May 1991, pp. 26–27.

Nagafuchi, Ichirō. *Yudayajin to sekai kakumei* [The Jews and World Revolution]. Shinjinbutsu ōraisha, 1971.

Naimu-shō keihōkyoku hoanka [Peace Preservation Section, Police Bureau, Home Ministry], ed. "Purotesutanto-ha kirisuto-sha no yō-chūi gendō" [Remarks and Actions of Protestant Christians Requiring Scrutiny]. *Tokkō Geppō* [The Monthly Newsletter of the Special Higher Police], July 1941.

Nakada, Jūji. *Nakada jūji zenshū* [Complete Works of Nakada Jūji], 7 vols. Inochi no kotobasha, 1973.

Nara, Hiroshi, ed. *Yudayajin.* A special issue of *Gendai no esupuri* [L'esprit Modern], vol. 121, 1977.

Nihon Kirisutokyōdan shakai iinkai, ed. *Paresuchina to Kirisutokyō* [Palestine and Christianity], 1991.

Ninomiya, Nobuchika [Tatsuki, Shin]. *Kirisuto to Marukusu: Tōō shisō kikō* [Christ and Marx: An Intellectual Journey Through Eastern Europe]. Simul, 1972.

———. "Rōma hōō ni sekinin wa nakatta: *Dairisha* to Vachican" [The Pope Was Not Responsible: *The Deputy* and the Vatican]. *Jiyū,* May 1964, pp. 67–70.

———. "Yudayajin no shukumei—Takeyama Michio-shi no oshie o kou" [The Fate of the Jews: A Question for Takeyama Michio]. *Jiyū,* February 1965, pp. 116–121.

Nishi, Yoshiyuki. "Doitsu chishikijin to Rōma hōō" [German Intellectuals and the Pope]. *Jiyū,* June 1963, pp. 60–67.

———. *Hitoraa ga soko e yatte kita* [There Came Hitler]. Bungei shunjū, 1971.

Nishitani, Misao. "Yudaya seisaku o shire," [Beware the Jewish Plot!] *Tenshō* 2, no. 2 (March 1954).

Nuita, Seiji. *Isuraeru no yūtopia kyōdōtai: kibutsu"* [Israel's Utopian Community: The Kibbutz]. Gaimushō chōsa geppō 7 (1966), 9–10, 11–12.

———. *Kibutsu: Isuraeru no yūtopia-teki jikken* [The Kibbutz: Israel's Utopian

Experiment]. Middle East-Africa Section, Japanese Foreign Ministry. 1963.

———. "Kibutsu no seikatsu taiken" [Life on the Kibbutz]. *Asahi Journal*, December 10, 1961, pp. 12–16; December 17, 1961, pp. 67–70.

Nunokawa, Magoichi [Nunokawa, Seien]. "Shisōsen no ABC" [The ABC's of the Ideological War]. *Teiyū rinrikai rinri kōenshū*, April 1938, pp. 105–11.

——— [Nunokawa, Seien]. "Shisōsen to Yudaya minzoku no kankei" [The Relationship Between the Ideological War and the Jewish People]. *Teiyū rinrikai rinri kōenshū*, September 1938, pp. 109–21.

——— [Nunokawa, Seien]. "Yudaya himitsuryoku no urakōsaku" [The Secret Machinations of Covert Jewish Power]. *Teiyū rinrikai rinri kōenshū*, July 1938, pp. 107–17.

——— [Yamagata, Tōkon]. "Yudaya minzoku no seikaku ni tsuite" [Regarding the Character of the Jewish People]. *Teiyū rinrikai rinri kōenshū*, February 1926, pp. 87–103.

Nunokawa, Seien. See Nunokawa, Magoichi.

Oda, Makoto. " 'Aushuvittsu' to 'Deiru Yashin'—'kyōsei' e no genri, 3." ["Auschwitz" and "Deir Yassin"—Principles for Coexistence, 3]. *Tenbō* 225 (September 1977), 130–46.

———. *Rekishi no tenkan no naka de—21 seiki e* [In a Time of Historical Transition: Toward the 21st century]. Iwanami shoten, 1980.

Ōhashi, Totsuan. *Hekija shōgen* [Comments on Heresy], 4 vols. Shiseijuku, 1857. Also in *Meiji bunka zenshū*, vol. 15. Nihon hyōronsha, 1927, pp. 59–140.

Okakura, Koshirō. *Okakura Koshirō kokusai seiji ronshū*, vol. 5. Keisō shobō, 1969.

———. *Paresuchina monogatari* [Tales of Palestine]. Nihon hyōronsha, 1950.

Okanoe, Morimichi [Kuroda, Reiji]. *Doreifyusu jiken kenkyū*. [Study of the Dreyfus Affair]. Hanza shoten, 1936.

———. "Panama unga dai-gigoku monogatari: Yudaya-teki yarikuchi no kōtekirei" [The Scandal of the Panama Canal: A Prime Example of Jewish Perfidy]. *Kokusai himitsuryoku no kenkyū*. 2:257; 3:399–426; 4:286–328; 5:262–388.

Okusho, Kazuo. *Kyūseishu no shutsugen to chijō tengoku* [The Appearance of the Messiah and the Earthly Paradise]. Kasumigaseki shobō, 1972.

Osaragi, Jirō. "Dorefyusu jiken" [The Dreyfus Affair]. *Kaizō*, May and July–October 1930.

Ōsawa, Takeo. *Yudayajin to Doitsujin* [Jews and Germans]. Kōdansha, 1991.

Oshino, Shōtarō [Morgan, Jacob]. *Saigo no kyōteki Nihon o ute: zoku Yudaya sekai shihai no giteisho* [Get Japan, The Last Enemy: The Jewish Protocols for World Domination, Continued]. Daiichi kikaku, 1993.

Ōta, Iwao. "Chūtō sensō to Isuraeru mondai" [The Mideast War and the Problem of Israel]. *Zen'ei,* September 1976, pp. 147–63.

Ōta, Ryū. *Ima Nihon ga abunai! Yudayaka nyūmon* [Japan Is in Danger Now! An Introduction to the Jewish Peril]. Nikkei kikaku shuppankyoku, 1992.

———. *Yudaya sekai teikoku no Nihon shinkō senryaku* [The Jewish World Empire's Plot to Invade Japan]. Nihon bungeisha, 1992.

Ōtsuki, Masaru. "Onaji Nihonjin to shite magokoro kara no tsugunai o!!" [Let Us Make Wholehearted Atonement as Members of the Same Japanese People (Who Committed this Crime)]. *Gekkan Isuraeru,* July 1972, p. 12.

Ōya, Sōichi. *Nihon no jinbutsu kōmyaku* [Mining Japan's People]. Bungei shunjūsha, 1959.

Oyabe, Zen'ichirō [Oyabe, Jenichiro]. *A Japanese Robinson Crusoe.* Issunsha, 1991.

———. *Jingisukan wa Minamoto no Yoshitsune nari* [Genghis Khan Was Minamoto no Yoshitsune]. Fuzanbō, 1924.

——— *Nippon oyobi Nippon kokumin no kigen* [The Origin of Japan and the Japanese People]. Kōseikaku, 1929.

Sadamori, Daiji. "Tokuhain memo" [Correspondent's Memo]. *Asahi shimbun,* April 24, 1993.

Saeki, Yoshirō. "Kyokutō ni okeru saisho no Kirisutokyō ōkoku, Yuzuki, oyobi, sono minzoku ni kansuru shomondai" [Various Problems Regarding Yuzuki, The First Kingdom of Christians in the Far East, and Its People] edited by Ide Katsumi. *Shikan.* In *Waseda daigaku shigakkai* 74 (October 1966), 14–28.

———. "Uzumasa o ronzu." *Chiri rekishi,* January 1908. Reprinted in Saeki, Yoshirō. *Keikyō hibun kenkyū* [Research on Nestorian Inscriptions]. Tairō shoin, 1911, pp. 21–50.

Saitō, Eisaburō. *Sekai o ugokasu yudaya pawaa no himitsu* [The Secret of Jewish Power That Moves the World]. Nihon keizai tsūshinsha, 1984.

Saitō, Takashi. "Rekishi to no deai" [Encounter with History]. *UP,* September 1975.

Sakai, Katsuisa [Sakai, Shōgun]. *Sekai no shōtai to Yudayajin* [The True Nature of the World and the Jews]. Naigai shobō, 1924.

——— [Sakai, Shōgun]. *Yudaya minzoku no daiinbō* [The Great Jewish Conspiracy]. Naigai shobō, 1924.

———— [Sakai, Shōgun]. *Yudaya no sekai seiryaku undō* [The Global Political Machinations of the Jews]. Naigai shobō, 1924.

Satō, Aiko. *Akahana no Kirisuto—Tsugaru fūryū tan* [Jesus with a Red Nose: Tall Tales of Tsugaru]. Kōbunsha, 1972.

Shiba, Mitsuyo. " 'Heiwa o!' josei no sakebi mo ōkiku" ["Peace!" Women's Voices Also Cry]. *Mainichi shimbun*, evening edition, November 9, 1978.

————. "Naisen no Lebanon o yuku" [Traveling Through Lebanon During the Civil War]. *Asahi shimbun*, evening edition, November 8, 1978.

————. "Paresuchina no kodomotachi" [The Children of Palestine]. In *Ubawareta kuni no kodomotachi—Paresuchina dokyumentari shashin shū* [Children of a Stolen Land—Documentary Photographs of Palestine], edited by Hirokawa Ryūichi. Daisan shokan, 1979.

Shigenobu, Fusako. *Waga ai, waga kakumei* [My Love, My Revolution]. Kōdansha, 1974.

Shiōden, Nobutaka. "Hinan Yudayajin to Beikoku shihai no keikaku" [The Jewish Refugees and the Plan to Take Over America]. *Yudaya kenkyū,* May 1941, pp. 18–21.

———— [Fujiwara, Nobutaka]. *Yudaya minzoku no kenkyū* [A Study of the Jewish People]. Naigai shobō, 1925.

————. "Yudaya minzoku riyō-ron no kikensei" [The Dangers in the Notion of Using the Jews]. In *Nihon oyobi Nihonjin,* October 1939, pp. 11–14.

Shirai, Kensaku. "Isuraeru, motto shitte yoi kuni." *Asahi Journal,* July 1964.

Takeda, Seigo. *Shimbun to Yudayajin* [Newspapers and the Jews]. Ōa Tsūshinsha, 1944.

Takenouchi, Yoshimiya. *Jindai no bankokushi* [A History of the World in the Age of the Gods]. Kōso kōtai jingū amatsukyō sōchō, 1970.

————. *Jindai no jidai no hanashi* [Stories of the Gods from the Age of the Gods]. Kōso kōtai jingū amatsukyō sōchō, 1969.

Takeyama, Michio. *Ningen ni tsuite* [On Man]. Shinchōsha, 1966.

————. "Ningen seishin no hōkai: Nachizumu no Yudayajin tairyō satsuriku jiken ni tsuite" [The Collapse of the Human Spirit: On the Nazi Mass Murder of the Jews]. *Bungei shunjū,* November 1957 through April 1958.

————. "Seisho to gasu-shitsu" [The Bible and the Gas Chambers]. *Jiyū,* July–October 1963.

————. "Yōroppa to watakushi" [Europe and I]. *Jiyū* May 1973, pp. 214–224.

————. *Zoku Yōroppa no tabi* [Travels in Europe, Continued]. Shinchōsha, 1959.

●

Tatsuki, Shin. See Ninomiya, Nobuchika.

Teshima, Ikurō. *Uzumasa no kami—Hachiman shinkō to Kirisuto Keikyō ni tsuite* [The God of Uzumasa: Hachiman Worship and Nestorian Christianity]. Tokyo Kirisuto seisho-juku, 1971.

Tezuka, Osamu. *Adorufu ni tsugu* [Aufruf an Adolf], 5 vols. Bungei shunjū, 1988.

Tokayer, Marvin. *Yudaya hassō no kyōi* [The Wonder of Jewish Thought], translated by Kase Hideaki. Jitsugyō no Nihonsha, 1972.

———. *Yudaya kakugenshū* [Jewish Proverbs], translated by Sukegawa Akira. Jitsugyō no Nihonsha, 1975.

———. *Yudaya to Nihon: nazo no kodaishi* [The Jews and Japan: The Riddle of Ancient History], translated by Hakozaki Sōichirō. Sangyō nōritsu daigaku shuppanbu, 1975.

———. *Yudayajin no hassō* [The Way Jews Think], translated by Kase Hideaki. Tokuma shoten, 1978.

Tokutomi, Iichirō. *Hisshō kokumin tokuhon* [A Citizen's Reader for Certain Victory]. Mainichi shimbunsha, 1944.

Uchimura, Kanzō. "Chirigakuteki chūshin to shite no Erusaremu" [Jerusalem as Geographical Center]. *Seisho no kenkyū*, January 1919. *Uchimura Kanzō zenshū*, vol. 24, pp. 437–39.

———. "Erusaremu daigaku no setchi" [The Establishment of the Hebrew University in Jerusalem]. *Seisho no kenkyū*, September 1918. *Uchimura Kanzō zenshū*, vol. 24, pp. 314–17.

———. "Kirisuto sairin no shōmeisha to shite no Yudayajin" [The Jews as Witnesses to the Second Coming]. *Seisho no kenkyū*, June 1918. *Uchimura Kanzō zenshū*, vol. 24, pp. 218–24.

———. "Kirisuto sairin o shinzuru yori kitarishi yo no shisōjō no henka" [The Changes in My Thought That Have Come from My Belief in the Second Coming of Christ]. *Seisho no kenkyū*, December 1918. *Uchimura Kanzō zenshū*, vol. 24, pp. 384–91.

———. "Sairin saishō no hitsuyō." [The Need to Reiterate the Second Coming]. *Seisho no kenkyū*, April 1930. *Uchimura Kanzō zenshū*, vol. 32, pp. 327–29.

———. "Seisho kenkyūsha no tachiba yori mitaru Kirisuto no sairai" [The Second Coming of Christ from the Point of View of a Biblical Scholar]. *Seisho no kenkyū*. February 1918. *Uchimura Kanzō zenshū*, vol. 24, pp. 56–62.

———. "Seisho no yogen to Paresuchina no kaifuku" [Biblical Prophecies and the Restoration of Palestine]. *Seisho no kenkyū*, July 1918. *Uchimura Kanzō zenshū*, vol. 24, pp. 242–48.

————. *Uchimura Kanzō zenshū* [The Complete Works of Uchimura Kanzō], vols. 24, 32. Iwanami shoten, 1982–83.

————. "Yo ga Kirisuto no sairin ni tsuite shinzezaru koto domo" [Things I Do Not Believe Regarding the Second Coming of Christ]. *Seisho no kenkyū*, February 1918. *Uchimura Kanzō zenshū*, vol. 24, pp. 47–49.

Ukai, Tetsujō [Kiyū, Dōjin]. *Hekija kanken-roku* [On Understanding and Rejecting Heresy]. Enzan, 1861.

Uno, Masami. *Hitoraa no gyakushū* [Hitler's Revenge]. Nesco, 1990.

————. *Kyūyaku seisho no dai-yogen: sekai saishū sensō to Yudayajin* [Great Prophecies of the Old Testament: The Jews and Armageddon]. Tokuma shoten, 1982.

————. *1992-nen Yudaya keizai senryaku* [The Jewish Economic Strategy for 1992]. Nihon bungeisha, 1989.

————. *Yudaya ga wakaru to Nihon ga miete kuru* [If You Understand the Jews, You Will Understand Japan]. Tokuma shoten, 1986.

————. *Yudaya ga wakaru to sekai ga miete kuru* [If You Understand the Jews, You Will Understand the World]. Tokuma shoten, 1986.

————. *Yudaya to tatakatte sekai ga mieta: hakujin shihai no hōkai to "futatsu no Yudayajin"* [I Fought the Jews and Understood the World: The Collapse of White Domination and "The Two Kinds of Jews"]. Kōbunsha, 1993.

————. *Zoku Kyūyaku seisho no dai-yogen* [Great Prophecies of the Old Testament, Continued: Armageddon and the Qualifications of the Leader]. Tokuma shoten, 1982.

Uno, Masami and Crowley, Dale Jr. *Yudaya ga wakaru to Amerika ga miete kuru* [If You Understand the Jews, You Will Understand America]. Video. Chūtō mondai kenkyū sentaa, 1989.

Uno, Masami; Goldstein, Paul; and Steinberg, Jeffrey. *Yudaya no kokuhaku: Nihon keizai o rimen kara miru* [Confessions of the Jews: Behind the Scenes of the Japanese Economy]. Enoch shuppan, 1990.

Utsunomiya, Kiyo. See Inuzuka, Koreshige.

Washimi, Tetsuhiko. " 'Rekishi' o ikinuku nanmin-tachi" [Refugees Who Survive "History"]. *Kyōto shimbun*, October 23, 1979.

Watanabe, Minojirō. *Yudaya minzoku no sekai-teki katsudō* [The Global Activities of the Jews]. Ōsaka Mainichi shimbun and Tōkyō Nichinichi shimbun, 1923.

Yajima, Kinji. *Yudaya purotokōru chō-urayomi-jutsu* [The Expert Way to Read the Jewish Protocols]. Seishun shuppansha, 1986.

Yamagata, Tōkon. See Nunokawa, Magoichi.

Yamaguchi, Masao. "Yudayajin no chiteki jōnetsu" [The Intellectual Passion of the Jews]. In *Hon no shinwagaku* [The Mythology of the Book]. Chūō kōronsha, 1971, pp. 37–72.

Yamaguchi, Yasushi. "Naze ureru 'han-Yudaya' bon" [Why Do "Antisemitic" Books Sell?]. *Asahi shimbun*, evening edition, March 28, 1987.

Yamakage, Motohisa. *Yudaya no sekai shihai senryaku: miezaru sekai seifu no kyōi* [The Jewish Plot to Control the World: The Threat of the Invisible World Government]. Management-sha, 1985.

———. *Yudaya no sekai shihai senryaku part 2: Yudaya no kami wa jinrui o sukuwanai* [The Jewish Plot to Control the World, Part 2: The God of the Jews Will Not Save Mankind]. Management-sha, 1987.

Yamamoto, Shichihei. *Hitotsu no kyōkun: Yudaya no kōbō* [One Lesson: The Fall and Rise of the Jews]. Kōdansha, 1987.

———. *Kyūyaku seisho monogatari* [Tales from the Old Testament]. Sanseidō, 1984.

——— [Ben-Dasan, Isaiah]. *Nihonjin to Yudayajin* [The Japanese and the Jews]. Yamamoto shoten, 1970.

———. *Watakushi no naka no Nihongun* [The Japanese Army Within Me]. Bungei shunjū, 1975.

Yamamoto, Tadashi. "Chūtō funsō no haikei to ikutsu ka no mondai" [The Background of the Middle East Conflict and a Number of Problems]. *Zen'ei*, February 1971, pp. 191–224.

Yamane, Kiku. *Kirisuto wa Nippon de shinde iru: ishoku kōshō—uchū kōkogaku no genten* [Christ Died in Japan: Sources of Cosmic Archaeology, An Unorthodox Study]. Tama shuppan, 1958.

Yanaihara, Tadao. "Kokka no risō" [Ideals of the State]. In *Chūō kōron*, September 1937, pp. 4–22.

———. "Nachisu kyōtei to jiyū" [The Nazi Pact and Freedom]. *Fujin no tomo*, January 1937. In *Yanaihara Tadao zenshū*, vol. 18. Iwanami shoten, 1964, pp. 600–10.

———. "Shion undō (Yudaya minzoku kyōdo kensetsu undō) ni tsuite" [On the Zionist Movement (The Movement to Build a Homeland for the Jewish People)]. In *Keizaigaku ronshū*. Published by the Economics Department of Tokyo Imperial University, 2, no. 2 (October 1923), 25–75.

———. *Shokumin seisaku no shinkichō* [A New Basis for Colonial Policy]. Kōbundō, 1927.

———. *Yanaihara Tadao zenshū* [The Complete Works of Yanaihara Tadao], vol. 1. Iwanami shoten, 1963.

●

Yano, Yūtarō. *Shinrei seiten* [Scriptures of the Holy Spirit]. 1932.

Yoshimoto, Takaaki. "Machiu-sho shiron" [An Essay on Mathew]. In Yoshi-moto Takaaki, *Geijutsuteki teikō to zasetsu* [Artistic Resistance and Despair]. Miraisha, 1983, pp. 7–77.

Yoshino, Sakuzō. "Iwayuru sekaiteki himitsu kessha no shōtai." [The Truth About the So-Called Global Secret Societies]. *Chūō kōron*, June 1921, pp. 2–42.

———. "Yudayajin no sekaiteki tenpuku no inbō no setsu ni tsuite" [Concerning the Theory of a Jewish Conspiracy to Overthrow the World]. *Chūō kōron*, May 1921, pp. 65–72.

Yudaya kenkyū [Jewish Studies]. Kokusai seikei gakkai [Association for International Political and Economic Studies], May 1941–December 1944.

2. Secondary Sources

Akita, Kiyoshi. "Nihon no ichi-daigakusei no minzoku kanjō." [The Ethnic Feelings of Students at One Japanese University]. *Jinmongaku* 70. Kyoto: Dōshisha University, (February 1964), 28–47.

———. "SD-hō kara mita Nihon no ichi-daigaku gakusei no minzoku hen-ken" [Racial Prejudice Among the Students of One Japanese University as Determined on the Basis of Semantic Differentials]. *Jinmongaku* 104. Kyoto: Dōshisha University, May 1968, 10–38.

Allen, Gary. *Insaidaa* [None Dare Call It Conspiracy], translated by Yuasa Shin'ichi. Taiyō shuppan. 1986.

———. *Rokkuferaa teikoku no inbō* [The Rockefeller File], translated by Takahashi Yoshinori. Jiyū kokuminsha, 1987.

Amino, Kiku. "Watashi no gekihyō—'Benisu no shōnin' hoka" [My Theatre Review: "The Merchant of Venice" and Other Plays]. *Higeki kigeki* March 1968, pp. 47–50.

Aoki, Tamotsu. *"Nihonron" no henyō* [The Evolution of "Theories of Japan"]. Chūō kōronsha, 1990.

Asami, Sadao. *Nise Yudayajin to Nihonjin* [The Counterfeit Jew and the Japanese]. Asahi shimbunsha, 1983.

Azumi, Eiji and Koizumi, Takashi, eds. *Yudaya shisō no hatten to keifu* [The Growth and Development of Jewish Thought]. Kinokuniya shoten, 1975.

Baeck, Leo. *Yudayakyō no honshitsu* [The Essence of Judaism], translated by Ariga Tetsutarō. Zenkoku shobō, 1946.

Ben-Sasson, H. H., ed. *Yudaya minzokushi* [A History of the Jewish People], translated by Ishida Tomoo et al., 6 vols. Rokkō shuppan, 1976–78.

Brewitz, Walther. *Yudaya yonsennen-shi* [Four Thousand Years of Jewish History], translated by Yonemoto Sanji. Daidō shoin, 1943.

Bruce, Lenny. *Yatsura o shaberitaose!* [How to Talk Dirty and Influence People], translated by Fujimoto Kazuko. Shōbunsha, 1977.

Chikushi, Tetsuya. " 'Han-Yudaya-bon' ryūkō—fuan to muchi no sanbutsu" [The Antisemitic Book Boom: The Product of Insecurity and Ignorance]. Nihon-tataki no shindan, 7. *Asahi shimbun*, morning edition, June 17, 1987.

Cohen, Elie. *Kyōsei shūyōjo ni okeru ningen kōdō* [Human Behavior in the Concentration Camps], translated by Shimizu et al. Iwanami shoten, 1957.

Cohn, Norman. *Shion kenja no giteisho: Yudayajin sekai seifuku inbō no shinwa* [The Protocols of the Elders of Zion: The Myth of a Jewish Plot to Take Over the World], translated by Uchida Tatsuru. Dynamic Sellers, 1986.

Deutscher, Isaac. *Hi-Yudayateki Yudayajin* [The Non-Jewish Jew], translated by Suzuki Ichirō. Iwanami shoten, 1970.

Dimont, Max. *Yudayajin* [Jews, God and History], translated by Fujimoto Kazuko, 2 vols. Asahi sensho 265–66. Asahi shimbunsha, 1984.

Ebisawa, Arimichi et al., eds., *Nihon kirisutokyō rekishi daijiten* [Historical Dictionary of Christianity in Japan]. Kyōbunkan, 1988.

Eidelberg, Joseph. *Yamato minzoku wa Yudayajin datta: shutsu-Ejiputo kara Nihon e no michi* [The Japanese and the Ten Lost Tribes of Israel], translated by Nakagawa Kazuo. Tama shuppan, 1984.

Endō, Tameharu. " 'Benisu no shōnin' ima mukashi" ["The Merchant of Venice," Then and Now]. *Higeki kigeki* 21, no. 4 (April 1968), 8–11.

Ford, Henry. *Kokusai Yudayajin: gendai ni yomigaeru jidōsha-ō Henrii Fōdo no keikoku* [The International Jew: Automobile Magnate Henry Ford's Undying Warning and Its Relevance Today], edited and translated by Shima Kōichi. Tokuma shoten, 1993.

Frank, Anne. *Anne no nikki.* [The Diary of a Young Girl], translated by Fukamachi Mariko. Bungei shunjū, 1986.

———. *Hikari honoka ni: Anne no nikki* [The Diary of a Young Girl], translated by Kaitō Kōzō. Bungei shunjū, 1952.

Frankl, Viktor. *Yoru to kiri: Doitsu kyōsei shūyōjo no taiken kiroku* [Ein Psycholog erlebt das Konzentrationslager], translated by Shimoyama Tokuji. Misuzu shobō, 1956.

Fujimoto, Kazuko. "Shisha o se ni ou onna-tachi" [Women Who Carry the Dead on Their Back]. In *Shisō no kagaku,* 31 (April 1983), pp. 14–21.

Fujita, Shōzō. "Shōwa hachinen o chūshin to suru tenkō no jōkyō" [The *Tenkō* Situation Circa 1933]. In Shisō no kagaku kenkyūkai, ed. *Tenkō*, vol. 1. Heibonsha, 1959, pp. 31–65.

Fujiwara, Hajime. "Tōsakuteki sakoku seishin o haisu" [We Should Reject the Perverted Spirit of a Closed Country]. *Sekai shūhō*, April 14, 1987, pp. 4–5.

Gluckel of Hameln. *Gettō ni ikite: aru Yudaya fujin no shuki* [The Memoirs of Gluckel of Hameln], translated by Hayashi Mizue. Shinjusha, 1974.

Goodman, David G. *Fuji-san mieta: Satoh Makoto ni okeru kakumei no engeki* [Mt. Fuji Perceived: The Revolutionary Theatre of Satoh Makoto]. Hakusuisha, 1983.

———. "Han-Yudayashugisha to shite no Momotarō" [Momotarō as Antisemite]. *Sekai*, January 1988, pp. 329–39.

———. *Hashiru: kokusaika jidai no chichioya-jutsu* [Running: Fatherhood in an International Age]. Iwanami shoten, 1989.

———. "Isuraeru ga miseru 'jisei' no kōzō to wa" [The Structure of Israel's "Self-Restraint"]. *Asahi Journal*, February 15, 1991, pp. 22–26.

———. *Isuraeru: koe to kao* [Israel: Voices and Faces]. Asahi shimbunsha, 1979.

———. "Nihon-hatsu eibun zasshi no susume" [A Call for English-Language Magazines Produced in Japan]. *Asahi shimbun*, evening edition, April 8, 1991.

———. *Tōbōshi: watashi jishin no rekishi dai-saakasu* [My Escapology: My Very Own Great Historical Circus]. Shōbunsha, 1976.

———. "Yudaya-shi no benshōhō o ikite: Gershom Scholem to no kaiwa" [Living the Dialectic of Jewish History: A conversation with Gershom Scholem]. *Tenbō* 225. (September 1977), 116–29.

Hackett, Albert and Goodrich, Frances. *Gikyoku Anne no nikki* [The Diary of Anne Frank], translated by Sugawara Taku. Bungei shunjū, 1957.

Hitler, Adolf. *Waga tōsō* [Mein Kampf], translated by Okubo Yasuo. Mikasa shobō, 1937.

Inoue, Fumikatsu. "Interview." *Asahi shimbun*, December 16, 1982.

Irokawa, Daikichi. *Aru Shōwa shi: jibunshi no kokoromi* [One Man's History of the Shōwa Era: An Attempt at a Self-History]. Chūō kōronsha, 1975.

Itō, Tasaburō. "Bakumatsu ni okeru Yaso-kyō Haigeki" [Anti-Christian Polemics of the Late Tokugawa Period]. *Kinsei-shi no kenkyū* [Studies in Early Modern Japanese History]. Yoshikawa Kōbunkan, 1981.

Itokawa, Hideo. *Kōya ni idomu: Tale of Ben-Gurion University of the Negev*. Miltos Publishing, 1989.

Kan, Takayuki. *Sengo engeki* [Postwar Theatre]. Asahi sensho 178. Asahi shimbunsha, 1981.

Kase, Hideaki. "Nihon no naka no Yudayajin" [Jews in Japan]. *Chūō kōron*, May 1971, pp. 234–47.

Kawatake, Toshio. *Hikaku engeki gaku* [Comparative Drama]. Nansōsha, 1967.

———. *Zoku hikaku engeki-gaku* [Comparative Drama, Continued]. Nansōsha, 1974.

Kobayashi, Masayuki. "Yudaya ryokō memo yori" [From Notes Taken on a Jewish Trip]. *Yudaya-Isuraeru kenkyū* no. 3 (1964), p. 51.

———. *Yudayajin: sono rekishizō o motomete* [The Jews: In Search of Their Historical Identity]. Seikō shobō, 1976.

Kogishi, Akira. *Supein o owareta Yudayajin: Marano no ashiato o tazunete* [The Jews Expelled from Spain]. Jinmon shoin, 1992.

Kondō, Shin'ichi. "Marukusu-Reinin-shugi, Soren tai Yudayajin, shionizumu, Isuraeru (1): aru chūtō funsō zushiki no seiritsu katei" [Marxism-Leninism and the Soviet Union Against the Jews, Zionism, and Israel, 1: The Development of a Paradigm for the Middle East Conflict]. In *Takushoku daigaku ronshū* 58, (1967), 21–39.

Konno, Toshihiko. *Bunmei to kaosu—sabetsu, henken* [Civilization in Chaos: Discrimination, Prejudice]. Yachiyo shuppan, 1980.

Levy, Ian Hideo [Liibi, Hideo]. *Seijōki no kikoenai heya* [The Room Where the Star-Spangled Banner Cannot Be Heard]. Kōdansha, 1992.

Levy, Ian Hideo [Liibi, Hideo] and Aoki, Tamotsu. "Kokkyō o koeta bungaku" [Literature Without Borders]. *Gendai no shisō: Revue de la pensée d'aujourd'hui* 19, no. 2 (February 1991), 162–83.

Lord Russell of Liverpool. *Jinkō jigoku: Nachisu sensō hanzai shōshi* [The Scourge of the Swastika], translated by Ōsawa Motoi. Misuzu shobō, 1957.

Maruyama, Masao. "Kindai Nihon no chishikijin" [Modern Japanese Intellectuals]. In Maruyama Masao. *Kōei no ichi kara*. Miraisha, 1982, pp. 113–30.

———. *Thought and Behavior in Modern Japanese Politics*, edited by Ivan Morris. New York: Oxford University Press, 1963.

Maruyama, Naoki. "Japan's Response to the Zionist Movement in the 1920s." *Bulletin of the Graduate School of International Relations* 2, International University of Japan (December 1984), 27–40.

———. "1930-nendai ni okeru Nihon no han-Yudayashugi" [Japanese Antisemitism in the 1930s]. *Bulletin of the Institute of Middle Eastern Studies* 3, International University of Japan (1987–88), 411–38.

●

Matsui, Yayori. *Shimin to enjo* [Citizens and Aid]. Iwanami shinsho no. 133. Iwanami shoten. 1990.

Matsuuchi, Norizō. "Orinpikku kara juneevu e" [From the Olympics to Geneva]. *Chūō kōron*, March 1933, pp. 305–11.

Miyazaki, Masahiro. *Yudaya ni kodawaru to sekai ga mienaku naru* [If You Spend Too Much Time Thinking About the Jews, You Won't Understand Anything]. Futami shobō, 1987.

Miyazawa, Masanori. "Hai-Yaso to Han-Yudaya—kindai Nihon no haigai shisō." [Anti-Christianity and Antisemitism: Xenophobic Thought in Modern Japan]. *Shakai kagaku kenkyū* 84, Waseda daigaku shakai kagaku kenkyūjo (February 1984), 311–34.

———. *Hokubei Nihonjin Kirisutokyō undō* [A History of Japanese-Christian Movements in North America], PMC shuppan, 1991.

———. "Nihon e hinan Yudayajin to shimbun" [The Jewish Refugees and Newspapers in Japan]. *Yudaya-Isuraeru kenkyū* 10 (October 1988), 43–49.

———. *Nihon ni okeru Yudaya-Isuraeru rongi bunken mokuroku, 1877–1988* [A Bibliography of Debates in Japan on Israel and the Jews, 1877–1988]. Shinsensha, 1990.

———. *Nihonjin no Yudaya-Isuraeru ninshiki* [Japanese Attitudes Toward the Jews and Israel]. Kyoto: Shōwadō, 1980.

———. *Niijima Jō—kindai Nihon no senkakusha* [Niijima Jō: Pioneer of Modern Japan]. Kōyō shobō, 1993.

———. "Saikin no Yudaya-Isuraeru rongi." [Recent Debates in Japan on the Jews and Israel]. *Yudaya-Isuraeru kenkyū* 14, (May 1994), 24–35.

———. *Yudayajinron-kō: Nihon ni okeru rongi no tsuiseki* [Theories Concerning the Jews: An Investigation into Debates in Japan]. Shinsensha, 1973. Rev. ed., 1982.

Munem, Baker Abdel. *Waga kokoro no Paresuchina* [My Heart's Home Palestine]. Shakai hihyōsha, 1991.

Nagao, Masahito et al., eds. *Yudaya shisō, I-II* [Jewish Thought, I-II]. *Iwanami kōza: Tōyō-shisō*, vols. 1 and 2. Iwanami shoten, 1988–89.

Nakagawa, Ken'ichi. *Yudaya nyūmon: sono kyozō to jitsuzō* [An Introduction to the Jews: True and False Images]. Shizuoka: Harvest Ministries, 1992.

Nomura, Michiko. *Terejin no chiisana gaka-tachi* [The Little Artists of Theresienstadt]. Kaiseisha, 1993.

Oba, Kenji. "Seitō no fukkatsu o mezashite" [Toward a Revival of Orthodoxy]. *Teatoro* 367, (September 1973), 65–67.

Odashima, Yūshi. "Benisu no Yudayajin" [The Jew of Venice]. *Shingeki*, March 1968, pp. 50–53.

Ōe, Kenzaburō. *Hiroshima nōto* [Hiroshima Notes]. Iwanami shoten, 1965.

———. Review of Kometani, *Professor Dear*. "Bungei jihyō," *Asahi shimbun*, April 23, 1992.

Ogai, Yoshio. *Hitoraa senkyo senryaku—gendai senkyo hisshō no baiburu* [Hitler Election Strategy: A Bible for Certain Victory in Modern Elections]. Chiyoda Nagata shobō, 1994.

Orikuchi, Shinobu. *Nihon geinōshi rokkō* [Six Lectures on the History of the Japanese Performing Arts]. *Orikuchi Shinobu zenshū*, vol. 18. Chūō kōronsha, 1976, pp. 356–67.

Ozu, Jirō. "Gunshū no naka ni Shakespeare ga hoshii" [I Want a Shakespeare Among the Masses]. *Teatoro* 15, no. 3 (March 1968), 53.

Passin, Herbert. "Jōdan ja nai! Yudaya inbō setsu" [Don't Be Ridiculous! The Theory of a Jewish Conspiracy]. *Bungei shunjū*, April 1987, pp. 262–70.

Riquet, Michel. "Imi aimai no Paresuchina mondai, 2" [The Ambiguous Palestinian Problem, 2]. *Gekkan Isuraeru*, October-November 1973, pp. 3–8.

Rogasky, Barbara. *Anne Furanku wa naze korosareta ka: Yudayajin gyakusatsu no kiroku* [Smoke and Ashes; Literally, Why Was Anne Frank Murdered? A Record of the Mass Murder of the Jews], translated by Fujimoto Kazuko. Iwanami shoten, 1992.

Rosenberg, Alfred. *Nijusseiki no shinwa* [The Myth of the Twentieth Century], translated by Suita Junsuke and Kamimura Kiyonobu. Chūō kōronsha, 1938.

Roth, Cecil. *Yudayajin no rekishi* [A History of the Jews], translated by Hasegawa, Shin and Azumi, Eiji. Misuzu shobō, 1966.

Sartre, Jean-Paul. *Yudayajin* [Anti-Semite and Jew], translated by Andō Shinya. Iwanami shoten, 1956.

Scholem, Gershom. *Yudayakyō shimpishugi* [Jewish Mysticism], translated by Takao Toshikazu. Kawade shobō shinsha, 1975.

———. *Yudayashugi no honshitsu* [The Essence of Judaism], translated by Takao Toshikazu. Kawade shobō shinsha, 1972.

———. *Yudayashugi to seiō* [Judaism and Western Europe], translated by Takao Toshikazu. Kawade shobō shinsha, 1973.

Scheffler, Wolfgang. *Nachisu to Yudayajin: 600-man-nin gyakusatsu no kiroku* [Judenverfolgung in Dritten Reich 1933–1945]. Kōdansha, 1961.

Sekai nazo no Yudaya [The Jews: Enigma of the World]. *Rekishi tokuhon*, March 1987.

Shimizu, Isao, ed. *Taiheiyō sensōki manga* [Cartoons of the Pacific War Period]. Bijutsu dōjinsha, 1971.

Shimizu, Jirō. " 'Benisu no shōnin' no enshutsu ni chūmoku" [With Special Attention to the Direction of "The Merchant of Venice"]. *Teatoro 34*, no. 10 (September 1967), 78–81.

Shino, Teruhisa. *Yakusoku no kuni e no nagai tabi* [Long Journey to the Promised Land]. Librio shuppan, 1988.

Shinoda, Kōichirō. *Tozasareta jikū: Nachi kyōsei shūyōjo no bungaku* [Closed Space, Closed Time: The Literature of the Nazi Concentration Camps]. Hakusuisha, 1992.

Solomon, Harold. "Nachizumu to Itagakizumu" [Nazism and Itagakism]. *Chūtō tsūhō*, September 1979, pp. 48–51, 47.

Stern, Willy. "Makari tōru 'Yudaya inbōsetsu' no uso" [The Bald-Faced Lie of "The Jewish Conspiracy"]. *Asahi Journal*, August 25, 1989, pp. 88–90.

Stosz, Alfred. *Yudaya to Nihon no tatakai* [Der Kampf zwischen Juda und Japan]. Seikyōsha, 1938.

Sugihara, Yukiko. *Rokusennin no inochi no biza* [The Visas That Saved Six Thousand Lives]. Asahi sonorama, 1990. Taishō shuppan, 1993.

Sugita, Rokuichi. *Higashi Ajia e kita Yudayajin* [Jews Who Came to East Asia]. Otowa shobō, 1967.

———. *Isuraeru-shi zakkō* [Miscellaneous Thoughts on the History of Israel]. Kyōbunkan, 1964.

———. *Nichiyu dōsoron o otte* [In Pursuit of Japanese-Jewish Common Ancestry Theories]. Otowa shobō, 1972.

———. "Nichiyu dōsoron, sono-go" [Japanese-Jewish Common Ancestry Theories Reprised]. *Yudaya Isuraeru kenkyū*, nos. 5–6, (1970), pp. 34–39.

———. "Nihon ni okeru Yudaya rongi no tokuisei" [Idiosyncrasies of Discussions of Jews in Japan]. *Isuraeru-shi zakkō*. Kyōbunkan, 1964, pp. 369–96.

———. "Shomotsu kara mita Nihon no Yudaya mondai" [Japan's "Jewish Problem" as Seen in Literature]. *Yudaya-shi kenkyū yodan*. Kyōbunkan, 1962.

———. *Yudaya-shi kenkyū yodan* [Extraneous Thoughts on the Study of Jewish History]. Kyōbunkan, 1962.

Takebayashi, Fumiko. *Geshutapo—seiki no yajū to tatakatta Yudayajin hiwa*

[Gestapo—The Untold Story of How the Jews Fought the Beast of the Century]. Kantōsha, 1950.

Tamamuro, Fumio. "Shinbutsu bunri to haibutsu kishaku no jittai" [The Reality of the Separation of Buddhist and Shinto Deities and the Anti-Buddhist Movement]. *Rekishi kōron*, no. 96 (November 1983).

Tarakida, Ryūzen. "Nichiyu dōsoron wa koko made risshō dekiru" [Japanese-Jewish Common Ancestry Theories Can be Proven to this Extent]. *Rekishi tokuhon*, March 1987, pp. 172–77.

Teshima, Yuroh. " 'Yudaya-bon' wa naze yomareru no ka." *Jitsugyō no Nihon*, May 15, 1987, pp. 86–88.

Toby, Ronald P. "Kinsei shomin bunka ni arawareru Chōsen tsūshinshi-zō: sezoku-shūkyō-jō no hyōgen" [Korean Missions in Early Modern Japanese Culture: Expressions in Secular and Religious Life]. *Kan* 110, (July 1986), 106–58.

Tsuno, Kaitarō. *Monogatari: Nihonjin no senryō* [The Japanese as Occupiers: A Narrative]. Asahi sensho 269. Asahi shimbunsha, 1985.

Tsurumi, Shunsuke. *Sengo o ikiru imi* [The Meaning of Living in the Postwar Period]. Chikuma shobō, 1981.

Ushiyama, Takeshi. *Yudayajin ongakka: sono junan to kōei* [Jewish Musicians: Their Suffering and Their Glory]. Miltos Publishing, 1991.

Wada, Yōichi, et al., eds. *Tokkō shiryō ni yoru senjika no Kirisuto-kyō undō* [The Christian Movement in Wartime Japan as Seen in the Records of the Special Higher Police], 3 vols. Shinkyō shuppansha, 1972.

Werblowsky, R. J. Zvi. "Isuraeru e no kyokkai—Itagaki Yōzō shi ni hanron suru" [A Perverse Interpretation of Israel: A Response to Itagaki Yūzō]. *Sekai*, November 1978, pp. 348–51.

———. "Rekishi toshi to wa nanika" [What Is a Historical City?] *Chūgai nippō*, October 23 and 26, 1987.

Yamashita, Hajime. *Kindai Doitsu-Yudaya seishinshi kenkyū* [Studies in Modern German-Jewish Intellectual History]. Yūshindō, 1980.

Yoneda, Isamu. *Nakada Jūji den* [Biography of Nakada Jūji]. Nakada Jūji den kankō kai, 1959; Fukuin senkyō kai, 1979.

———. *Shōwa no junkyōsha* [Martyrs of Shōwa]. Kirisuto shimbunsha, 1960.

Yoneda, Yutaka and Takayama, Yoshinobu. *Senji Hōrinesu junanki: Shōwa no shūkyō dan'atsu* [The Ordeal of the Holiness Churches During the War: The Oppression of Religion in the Shōwa Period]. Inochi no kotobasha, 1964.

•

WORKS IN ENGLISH

1. Primary Sources

Allen, Gary and Abraham, Larry. *None Dare Call It Conspiracy*. Seattle: Double A Publications, 1971, 1983.

Aston, W. G. *Nihongi: Chronicle of Japan from Earliest Times to A. D. 697*. Rutland, Vt.: Tuttle, 1972.

Avnery, Uri. *Israel Without Zionism: A Plan for Peace in the Middle East*. New York: Collier, 1968, 1971.

Barnouw, David and van der Stroom, Gerrold. *The Diary of Anne Frank: The Critical Edition*, translated by Arnold J. Pomerans and B. M. Mooyaart-Doubleday. New York: Doubleday, 1989.

Ben-Dasan, Isaiah. See Yamamoto, Shichihei.

Ben Yehuda, Shaleak. *Black Hebrew Israelites from America to the Promised Land: The Great International Religious Conspiracy Against the Children of the Prophets*. New York: Vantage Press, 1975.

Bentley, Eric. *The Storm Over the Deputy*. New York: Grove Press, 1964.

Chikamatsu, Monzaemon. *Major Plays of Chikamatsu*, translated by Donald Keene. New York: Columbia University Press, 1961.

Chikushi, Tetsuya. "Japanese Use Anti-Semitism to Explain Economic Woes." *Milwaukee Journal*, August 27, 1987.

Dazai, Osamu. *The Setting Sun*, translated by Donald Keene. New York: New Directions, 1956.

Eidelberg, Joseph. *The Japanese and the Ten Lost Tribes of Israel*. Givatayim, Israel: Sycamore Press. 1980.

Fowler, H. W. and Fowler, F. G., eds. *The Concise Oxford Dictionary of Current English*, 4th ed. Oxford: Clarendon Press, 1914.

Frank, Anne. *The Diary of a Young Girl*. New York: Doubleday, 1952.

Goodman, David G. "Reason for Concern in Japanese Anti-Semitism." Letter to the Editor, *New York Times*, March 25, 1987.

———. Letter to the Editor, *Los Angeles Time Magazine*, August 21, 1988.

Hochhuth, Rolf. *The Deputy* [Der Stellvertreter], translated by Richard and Clara Winston. New York: Grove Press, 1964.

Ishigaki, Ayako [Matsui, Haru]. *Restless Wave: An Autobiography*. New York: Modern Age Books, 1940.

Ishinomori, Shōtarō. *Japan, Inc.: An Introduction to Japanese Economics (The Comic Book)*. Berkeley: University of California Press, 1988.

●

Itagaki, Yūzō. "The Arabs and the Israelis." *The Mainichi Daily News*, November 26 to December 8, 1973.

Itagaki, Yūzō; Oda, Makoto; and Shiboh, Mitsukazu, eds. *The Israeli Invasion of Lebanon, 1982—Inquiry by the International People's Tribunal.* Sanyūsha, 1983.

Kim, Richard E. *Lost Names: Scenes from a Korean Boyhood.* New York: Praeger, 1970.

Kojiki, translated by Donald L. Philippi. Princeton: Princeton University Press, 1969.

Kometani, Foumiko. *Passover,* translated by Foumiko Kometani. New York: Carroll & Graf, 1989.

Kotsuji, Abraham S. *From Tokyo to Jerusalem.* New York: Bernard Geis Associates, 1964.

Kurihara, Sadako. *Black Eggs,* translated by Richard H. Minear. Michigan Monograph Series in Japanese Studies, 21. Ann Arbor: University of Michigan Center for Japanese Studies, 1994.

———. "Five Poems (1974–91) by the Hiroshima Poet Kurihara Sadako," translated by Richard H. Minear. *The Bulletin of Concerned Asian Scholars*, 23, no. 1 (January–March 1991), 26–30.

———. "The Literature of Auschwitz and Hiroshima: Thoughts on Reading Lawrence Langer's *The Holocaust and the Literary Imagination,*" translated by Richard H. Minear. In *Holocaust and Genocide Studies* 7, no. 1 (Spring 1993), 77–106.

Kusakari, Zenzō; Steinbach, Michael M.; and Matsuba, Moshe, eds. *The Communes of Japan,* 2nd rev. ed. Kibbutz Akan, Akan-gun, Hokkaido: Japanese Commune Movement, 1979.

Lindsey, Hal. *The Late Great Planet Earth.* New York: Bantam, 1973.

Matsui, Haru. See Ishigaki, Ayako.

McLeod, Norman. *Epitome of the Ancient History of Japan.* Nagasaki: Rising Sun Office, 1875. Appended edition, 1879.

Minear, Richard H., ed. and trans. *Hiroshima: Three Witnesses*, Princeton: Princeton University Press, 1990.

Moore, John Norton, ed. *The Arab-Israeli Conflict*, vol. 3, Princeton: Princeton University Press, 1974.

Nakada, Bishop Juji. *Japan in the Bible,* translated by David T. Tsutada. Oriental Missionary Society, Japan Holiness Church Publishing Department, 1933.

Oda, Makoto. *The Bomb,* translated by D. H. Whittaker. New York: Kodansha International, 1990.

●

————. "Making Democracy Our Own." *Japan Interpreter* 6, no. 3 (Autumn 1970), 235–53.

————. "A Writer in the Present World: A Japanese Case History." In Schlant and Rimer, eds. *Legacies and Ambiguities*, pp. 263–77.

Ōe, Kenzaburō. *Hiroshima Notes*, edited by David L. Swain, translated by Toshi Yonezawa. Tokyo YMCA Press, 1981.

Rabau, Hilda. "Shanghai Revisited." In *Bulletin of Igud Yotzei Sin in Israel* (*Association of Former Residents in China*) 317, (May 1991), 22.

Sachs, Nelly. *O the Chimneys*, translated by Michael Hamburg et al. New York: Farrar, Straus and Giroux, 1967.

Sartre, Jean-Paul. *Anti-Semite and Jew*, translated by George J. Becker. New York: Schocken, 1948, 1965.

Shimada, Masahiko. "A Callow Fellow of Jewish Descent," translated by Hiroaki Sato. In *New Japanese Voices: The Best Contemporary Fiction from Japan*, edited by Helen Mitsios. New York: Atlantic Monthly Press, 1991, pp. 1–22.

Steinberg, Jeffrey and Thompson, Scott et al. "Tax-Exempt Treachery: A Profile of the Anti-Defamation League." *Executive Intelligence Review* (*EIR*), May 18, 1990.

Takeyama, Michio. *The Harp of Burma*, translated by Howard Hibbett. Rutland, Vt. Tuttle, 1966.

Tanabe, Hajime. *Philosophy as Metanoetics*, translated by Yoshinori Takeuchi. Berkeley: University of California Press, 1986.

Tsunoda, Ryusaku et al., eds. *Sources of Japanese Tradition*, vol. 2. New York: Columbia University Press, 1964.

Uchimura, Kanzō. *The Complete Works of Kanzo Uchimura*, 7 vols. Kyobunkwan, 1971.

Umezu, Itaru. "Japanese and Jews." *New York Times*, March 19, 1987.

Wakabayashi, Bob Tadashi. *Anti-Foreignism and Western Learning in Early-Modern Japan: The New Theses of 1825*. Cambridge, Mass.: Council on East Asian Studies, Harvard University, 1986.

Watts, William. "Antisemitism in Japan: A Survey Research Study—A Report to the Anti-Defamation League of B'nai B'rith." Washington, D.C.: Potomoc Associates, December 19, 1988.

Yamamoto, Shichihei [Ben-Dasan, Isaiah]. *The Japanese and the Jews*, translated by Richard L. Gage, Tokyo: Weatherhill, 1972.

2. Secondary Sources

Ahlberg, Roger [Yoshiwara, R.]. *Sumerian and Japanese: A Comparative Language Study*. Chiba, Japan: Japan English Service, 1991.

Altman, Avraham. "The Japan Kibbutz Association." *Asian and African Studies* 6 (1970), 175–82.

Alvarez, Louis and Kolker, Andrew. *The Japanese Version*, video release. New York: Center for New American Media, 1991.

Amelan, Ralph. Review of *The Japanese and the Ten Lost Tribes*. In *Jerusalem Post*. August 8, 1985.

Anti-Defamation League of B'nai B'rith. *Extremism on the Right*. New York: Anti-Defamation League of B'nai B'rith, 1988.

———. *Japan and Anti-Semitism: The Proliferation of Anti-Jewish Literature*. ADL International Report, April 1987.

———. "Japan and the Arab Boycott." *ADL Bulletin*, November 1986.

Apter, David E. and Sawa, Nagayo. *Against the State: Politics and Social Protest in Japan*. Cambridge, Mass. Harvard University Press, 1984.

Arendt, Hannah. *Eichmann in Jerusalem: A Report on the Banality of Evil*, rev. ed. New York: Penguin, 1977.

———. *The Origins of Totalitarianism*, rev. ed. New York: Harcourt Brace Jovanovich, 1973.

Arima, Tatsuo. *The Failure of Freedom*. Cambridge, Mass. Harvard University Press, 1969.

Barry, Dave. *Dave Barry Does Japan*. New York: Random House, 1992.

Barshay, Andrew E. *State and Intellectual in Imperial Japan: The Public Man in Crisis*. Berkeley: University of California Press, 1988.

Beckmann, George M., and Okubo Genji. *The Japanese Communist Party, 1922–1945*. Stanford: Stanford University Press, 1969.

Berry, Jacqueline Carol. "Black Jews: A Study of Status Malintegration and (Multi) Marginality." Ph.D. diss., Syracuse University, 1977.

Biale, David. *Power and Powerlessness in Jewish History*. New York: Shocken, 1986.

Blacker, Carmen. "Ōhashi Totsuan: A Study in Anti-Western Thought." In *Transactions of the Asiatic Society of Japan* 3, no. 7 (November 1959), 147–68.

Blitzer, Wolf. "Sayonara to the Boycott?" *Hadassah Magazine*, January 1987, pp. 12–13.

Brenner, Lenni. *Zionism in the Age of the Dictators*. Westport, Conn.: Lawrence Hill, 1983.

Bromley, David G., and Shupe, Anson D. Jr. *"Moonies" in America: Cult, Church, and Crusade*. Sage Library of Social Research 92. Beverly Hills: Sage Publications, 1979.

Brotz, Howard. *The Black Jews of Harlem: Negro Nationalism and the Dilemmas of Negro Leadership*. New York: Schocken, 1970.

●

Buckley, William F. Jr. *In Search of Anti-Semitism*. New York: Continuum, 1992.

Buruma, Ian. "A New Japanese Nationalism." *New York Times Magazine*, April 12, 1987, pp. 22–29, 38.

———. "It Can't Happen Here." *New York Review of Books*, April 23, 1992, pp. 3–4.

———. "The Devils of Hiroshima." *New York Review of Books*, October 25, 1990.

Caldarola, Carlo. *Christianity: The Japanese Way*. Leiden, The Netherlands: E. J. Brill, 1979.

Carter, Stephen L. *The Culture of Disbelief: How American Law and Politics Trivialize Religious Devotion*. New York: Basic Books, 1993.

Chiba, Yoko. "Sada Yacco and Kawakami: Performers of *Japonisme*." In *Modern Drama* 35 (1992), 41–42.

Chira, Susan. "No One Is Nice Here." Review of *Passover, New York Times Book Review*, October 22, 1989.

Chryssides, George D. *The Advent of Sun Myung Moon: The Origins, Beliefs and Practices of the Unification Church*. New York: St. Martin's Press, 1991.

Cohn, Norman. *Warrant for Genocide*. Brown Judaic Studies 23. Chico, Calif.: Scholars Press, 1981.

Colcutt, Martin. "Buddhism: The Threat of Eradication." In *Japan in Transition: From Tokugawa to Meiji*, edited by Marius B. Jansen and Gilbert Rozman. Princeton: Princeton University Press, 1986, pp. 143–67.

Cook, Haruko Taya and Cook, Theodore F. *Japan at War: An Oral History*. New York: New Press, 1992.

Cooper, Abraham. "Japanese Anti-Semitism: A Mystery, Absurdity and Threat to Japan's Image." *Japan Times*, June 28, 1988.

Dale, Peter N. *The Myth of Japanese Uniqueness*. New York: St. Martin's Press, 1986.

Desser, David. *Eros Plus Massacre: Introduction to the Japanese New Wave Cinema*. Bloomington: Indiana University Press, 1988.

Deutscher, Isaac. *The Non-Jewish Jew*. New York: Hill and Wang, 1968.

Dicker, Herman. *Wanderers and Settlers in the Far East: A Century of Jewish Life in China and Japan*. New York: Twayne, 1962.

Dikötter, Frank. *The Discourse of Race in Modern China*. Stanford: Stanford University Press, 1992.

•

Dillenberger, John and Welch, Claude. *Protestant Christianity*, 2d ed. New York: Macmillan, 1988.

Doak, Kevin M. *Dreams of Difference: The Japan Romantic School and the Crisis of Modernity*. Berkeley: University of California Press, 1994.

———. "Nationalism as Dialectics: Ethnicity, Moralism, and the State in Early Twentieth Century Japan." Unpublished paper delivered at a symposium on "Zen, the Kyoto School, and the Question of Nationalism." Santa Fe, New Mexico, March 11, 1994.

Doneson, Judith E. "The American History of Anne Frank's Diary." *Holocaust and Genocide Studies* 2, no. 1 (1987), 149–60.

Dower, John W. "E. H. Norman and the Uses of History." In *Origins of the Modern Japanese State: Selected Writings of E. H. Norman*, edited by John W. Dower. New York: Pantheon, 1975.

———. "Fear and Prejudice in U.S.-Japan Relations." *Ethics and International Relations* 3 (1989), 135–62.

———. *Japan in War and Peace: Selected Essays*. New York: New Press, 1993.

———. "Peace and Democracy in Two Systems: External Policy and Internal Conflict." In *Postwar Japan as History*. Edited by Andrew Gordon. Berkeley: University of California Press, 1993, pp. 3–33.

———. "The Useful War." *Daedalus* 90, no. 3 (Summer 1990), 49–70.

———. *War Without Mercy: Race and Power in the Pacific War*. New York: Pantheon, 1986.

Dower, John W. and Junkerman, John, eds. *The Hiroshima Murals: The Art of Iri Maruki and Toshi Maruki*. New York: Kodansha International, 1985.

Duus, Peter and Okimoto, Daniel I. "Fascism and the History of Pre-War Japan: The Failure of a Concept." *Journal of Asian Studies* 39, no. 1 (November 1979), 65–76.

Elison, George. *Deus Destroyed: The Image of Christianity in Early Modern Japan*. Cambridge, Mass.: Council on East Asian Studies, Harvard University, 1973.

Emmott, Bill. *The Sun Also Sets: The Limits to Japan's Economic Power*. New York: Times Books, 1989.

Evans, Richard J. "The New Nationalism and the Old History: Perspective on the West German Historians' Debate." *Journal of Modern History* (December 1987), 761–97.

Ezrahi, Sidra DeKoven. *By Words Alone: The Holocaust in Literature*. Chicago: University of Chicago Press, 1980.

Feingold, Fumiko Ikeda. "Letter to the Editor." *New York Times*, May 4, 1987.

•

Field, Norma. *In the Realm of a Dying Emperor: A Portrait of Japan at Century's End*. New York: Pantheon, 1991.

Fields, George. *Gucci on the Ginza*. New York: Kodansha International, 1989.

———. "Racism Is Accepted Practice in Japan." *The Wall Street Journal*, November 10, 1986.

Fletcher, Miles. "Intellectuals and Fascism in Early Shōwa Japan." *Journal of Asian Studies* 39, no. 1 (November 1979), 39–64.

Forster, Arnold and Epstein, Benjamin R. *The New Anti-Semitism*. New York: McGraw Hill, 1974.

Frost, Ellen. *For Richer or Poorer: The New U.S.-Japan Relations*. New York: Council on Foreign Relations, 1987.

Gates, Henry Louis, Jr. "Black Demagogues and Pseudo-Scholars." *New York Times*, July 20, 1992.

Gessel, Van C. "Postoccupation Literary Movements and Developments in Japan. In Schlant, Ernestine and Rimer, J. Thomas, eds. *Legacies and Ambiguities: Postwar Fiction and Culture in West Germany and Japan*. Washington, D.C.: Woodrow Wilson Center Press, 1991, pp. 207–23.

Getz, Gene A. *MBI: The Story of the Moody Bible Institute*. Chicago: Moody Press, 1969.

Givet, Jacques. *The Anti-Zionist Complex*. Englewood, N.J.: SBS Publishing, 1979.

Glassman, Bernard. *Anti-Semitic Stereotypes Without Jews: Images of the Jews in England, 1290–1700*. Detroit: Wayne State University Press, 1975.

Gluck, Carol. "The Idea of Showa." *Daedalus* 119, no. 3 (Summer, 1990).

———. *Japan's Modern Myths: Ideology in the Late Meiji Period*, Princeton: Princeton University Press, 1985.

Goldberg, J. J. "Bagels and Sushi," *Jerusalem Report*. June 17, 1993, p. 34.

Goldstein, Clifford. "Anti-Semitism in Japan." *Liberty* (March/April 1989), 21–23.

Golub, Jennifer. *Japanese Attitudes Toward Jews*. New York: Pacific Rim Institute of the American Jewish Committee, 1992.

Goodman, David G. *After Apocalypse: Four Japanese Plays of Hiroshima and Nagasaki*. New York: Columbia University Press, 1986. Ithaca, NY: Cornell East Asia Program, 1994.

———. "Creative Language Use and World Order." In *Swords and Ploughshares: The Bulletin of the Program in Arms Control, Disarmament, and International Security* 1, no. 3, University of Illinois at Urbana-Champaign. (May 1987), 3–4.

•

————. "Current Japanese Attitudes Toward the Jews and Their Implications for US-Japan Relations." *Occasional Paper*. Program in Arms Control, Disarmament, and International Security. University of Illinois at Urbana-Champaign. September 1989.

————, ed. *Japan and the Developing World*. A special issue of *Swords and Ploughshares: The Bulletin of the Program in Arms Control, Disarmament, and International Security* 7. no. 4, University of Illinois at Urbana-Champaign, (Summer 1993).

————. "Japanese Anti-Semitism." *The World & I*. November 1987, pp. 401–9.

————. *Japanese Drama and Culture in the 1960s: The Return of the Gods*. Armonk, N.Y.: M. E. Sharpe, 1988.

————, ed. and trans. *Long, Long Autumn Nights: Selected Poems of Oguma Hideo, 1901–1940*. Michigan Monographs Series in Japanese Studies, 3. University of Michigan Center for Japanese Studies, 1989.

————. " 'Reciprovocation' in Recent U.S.-Japan Relations." *JAMA Forum* 9, no. 3. Published by the Japan Automobile Manufacturers Association. March 1991, 3–8.

Gordon, Andrew, ed. *Postwar Japan as History*. Berkeley: University of California Press, 1993.

Grapard, Allan G. *The Protocol of the Gods: A Study of the Kasuga Cult in Japanese History*. Berkeley: University of California Press, 1992.

Halevi, Yossi Klein. "Samurai Chassidim: Japan's Lovers of Zion." *Moment*, March 1986, pp. 47–52.

Hall, Robert King, ed. *Kokutai no Hongi: Cardinal Principles of the National Entity of Japan*. Translated by John Owen Gauntlett. Newton, Mass.: Crofton, 1974.

Halpern, Jack, ed. *New Japanese-English Character Dictionary*. Tokyo: Kenkyūsha, 1990.

Halsell, Grace. *Prophecy and Politics: Militant Evangelists on the Road to Nuclear War*. Westport, Conn.: Lawrence Hill, 1986.

Hane, Mikiso. *Modern Japan: A Historical Survey*, 2d. ed. Boulder, Col.: Westview Press, 1992.

Hardacre, Helen. *Shinto and the State, 1868–1988*, Princeton: Princeton University Press, 1989.

Harootunian, Harry D. *Things Seen and Unseen: Discourse and Ideology in Tokugawa Nativism*. Chicago: Chicago University Press, 1988.

Harris, David A. " 'The Elders of Zion' in Japan: What Should We Do About Japanese Anti-Semitism?" *Moment*, October 1987, pp. 32–37.

————. "Fostering Japanese-Jewish Understanding." *AJC Journal* (Summer 1989), pp. 11–12.

Havens, Thomas R. H. *Fire Across the Sea: The Vietnam War and Japan, 1965–1975*. Princeton: Princeton University Press, 1987.

————. *Valley of Darkness: The Japanese People and World War Two*. New York: Norton, 1978.

Herzog, Yaacov. *A People That Dwells Alone*. Edited by Misha Louvish. London: Weidenfeld and Nicolson, 1975.

Hijiya-Kirschnereit, Irmela. "Post-World War II Literature: The Intellectual Climate in Japan, 1945–1985." In Schlant, Ernestine and Rimer, J. Thomas, eds. *Legacies and Ambiguities: Postwar Fiction and Culture in West Germany and Japan*. Washington, D.C.: Woodrow Wilson Center Press, 1991, pp. 99–119.

Hopkins, Ellen. "Her Story." *Los Angeles Times Magazine,* June 12, 1988, pp. 18–22, 41–46.

Hori, Ichirō. "Mysterious Visitors from the Harvest to the New Year." In *Studies in Japanese Folklore*. Edited by Richard M. Dorson. New York: Arno Press, 1980, pp. 76–106.

————. *Folk Religion in Japan: Continuity and Change*. Edited by Joseph M. Kitagawa and Alan L. Miller. Chicago: University of Chicago Press, 1968.

Hoston, Germaine A. "A 'Theology' of Liberation? Socialist Revolution and Spiritual Regeneration in Chinese and Japanese Marxism." In *Ideas Across Cultures: Essays on Chinese Thought in Honor of Benjamin I. Schwartz*. Edited by Paul A. Cohen and Merle Gomand. Cambridge, Mass.: Council on East Asian Studies, Harvard University, 1990, pp. 165–221.

Huntington, Samuel P. "The Clash of Civilizations?" In *Foreign Affairs* 79, no. 3 (Summer 1993), 22–49.

Hyamson, Albert M. "Anglo-Israelism." In *Encyclopedia of Religion and Ethics*. Edited by James Hastings. New York: Scribner's, 1913, I:483–484.

Ikeda, Akifumi. "Japan's Perception of Jews and Israel," *Forum* 59. Department of Information. World Zionist Organization. (Summer 1986), 73–83.

Irokawa, Daikichi. *The Culture of the Meiji Period*. Edited by Marius B. Jansen. Princeton: Princeton University Press, 1985.

Isaac, Jules. *The Teaching of Contempt: Christian Roots of Anti-Semitism*. Translated by Helen Weaver. New York: Holt, Rinehart and Winston, 1964.

Isaacs, Jonathan. "Waking Up to the Specter of Japan's New Anti-Semitism." *Wall Street Journal*, October 5, 1987.

Iwai, Katsuhito. *Disequilibrium Dynamics*. New Haven: Yale University Press, 1981.

Jacobson, Kenneth and Hordes, Jess. "Japan and the Arab Boycott." *ADL Bulletin*. November 1986, pp. 1, 5–6.

Johnson, George. *Architects of Fear: Conspiracy Theories and Paranoia in American Politics*. Boston: Tarcher, 1983.

Johnson, Paul. *A History of Christianity*. New York: Atheneum, 1976.

———. *A History of the Jews*. New York: Harper and Row, 1988.

Johnson, Sheila K. "The Japanese and the Jews." *Japan Times Weekly*, December 12, 1992.

Katō, Shūichi. *A History of Japanese Literature: The First Thousand Years*. Translated by David Cribbett. New York: Kodansha International, 1981.

———. *A History of Japanese Literature: The Modern Years*. Translated by Don Sanderson. New York: Kodansha International, 1990.

———. "Mechanisms of Ideas: Society, Intellectuals, and Literature in the Postwar Period in Japan." In Schlant, Ernestine and Rimer, J. Thomas, eds. *Legacies and Ambiguities: Postwar Fiction and Culture in West Germany and Japan*. Washington, D.C.: Woodrow Wilson Center Press, 1991, pp. 249–59.

Keene, Donald, ed. *Modern Japanese Literature*. New York: Grove Press, 1960.

Kelly, Bill. " 'The Japanese and the Jews' Revisited." *Japan Times*, January 15, 1989.

Ketelaar, James Edward. *Of Heretics and Martyrs in Meiji Japan: Buddhism and Its Persecution*. Princeton: Princeton University Press, 1990.

Kim, Eugene C. "Education in Korea Under the Japanese Colonial Rule." In *Korea Under Japanese Colonial Rule*, edited by Andrew C. Nahm. Kalamazoo, Mich.: Center for Korean Studies, Western Michigan University, 1973, pp. 137–45.

King, Dennis. *Lyndon Larouche and the New American Fascism*. New York: Doubleday, 1989.

Kitagawa, Joseph M. *Religion in Japanese History*. New York: Columbia University Press, 1966.

Kittredge, Cherry. *Womansword: What Japanese Words Say About Women*. New York: Kodansha International, 1987.

Kohno, Tetsu. "Debates on the Jewish Question in Japan." *Bulletin of the Faculty of Liberal Arts* 46, Hōsei University (January 1983), 1–33.

————. "The Jewish Question in Japan." *Jewish Journal of Sociology* 29, no. 1, (June 1987), 37–54.

————. "Tasting a Watermelon by Its Peel—A Report on the Field Trip to the Hasidic Community in Brooklyn, New York City." *Bulletin of Faculty of Arts* 28, Hōsei University (1977), 1–21.

————. "To Be 'Alien' or 'Semi-Alien' in a Homogeneous Nation." *Bulletin of the Faculty of Liberal Arts* 66, Hōsei University (January 1988), 1–19.

Koschmann, J. Victor. "Intellectuals and Politics." In *Postwar Japan as History*. Edited by Andrew Gordon. Berkeley: University of California Press, 1993, pp. 395–423.

Kranzler, David. "How Japan Saved Jews from Hitler." *Washington Post*, November 14, 1982.

————. *Japanese, Nazis and Jews: The Jewish Refugee Community of Shanghai, 1938–1945*. New York: Yeshiva University Press, 1976.

Kuroda, Yasumasa. "Japan, the Arab World and Israel." *American-Arab Affairs* 28 (Spring 1987), 9–21.

LaFleur, William R. *The Karma of Words: Buddhism and the Literary Arts in Medieval Japan*. Berkeley: University of California Press, 1983.

Langer, Lawrence. "The Americanization of the Holocaust on Stage and Screen." In *From Hester Street to Hollywood: The Jewish-American Stage and Screen*. Edited by Sarah Blacher Cohen. Bloomington: Indiana University Press, 1983, pp. 213–30.

Langmuir, Gavin I. *History, Religion and Antisemitism*. Berkeley: University of California Press, 1990.

————. *Toward a Definition of Antisemitism*. Berkeley: University of California Press, 1991.

Lendvai, Paul. *Anti-Semitism Without Jews: Communist Eastern Europe*. New York: Doubleday, 1971.

Lerner, Michael. *The Socialism of Fools: Anti-Semitism on the Left*. Oakland, Calif.: Tikkun Books, 1992.

Levi, Primo. *Primo Levi: Collected Poems*. Translated by Ruth Feldman and Brian Swann. London: Faber and Faber, 1988.

Levin, Nora. *While Messiah Tarried: Jewish Socialist Movements, 1871–1917*. New York: Schocken, 1977.

Lewis, Bernard. *Semites and Anti-Semites*. New York: Norton, 1987.

Lewy, Guenter. *The Catholic Church and Nazi Germany*. New York: McGraw-Hill, 1964.

Lifton, Robert Jay. *Death in Life: Survivors of Hiroshima*. New York: Basic Books, 1967.

————. *The Nazi Doctors: Medical Killing and the Psychology of Genocide*. New York: Basic Books, 1986.

Lifton, Robert Jay and Markusen, Eric. *The Genocidal Mentality: Nazi Holocaust and Nuclear Threat*. New York: Basic Books, 1990.

Lifton, Robert Jay; Katō, Shūichi; and Reich, Michael R. *Six Lives, Six Deaths: Portraits from Modern Japan*. New Haven: Yale University Press, 1979.

Linton, Ralph. "Nativistic Movements." In *Reader in Comparative Religion: An Anthropological Approach*. Edited by William A. Lessa and Evon Z. Vogt, 2nd ed. New York: Harper and Row, 1965.

Lipset, Seymour Martin. *The Socialism of Fools: The Left, the Jews and Israel*. New York: Anti-Defamation League of B'nai B'rith, 1969.

Lipstadt, Deborah. *Denying the Holocaust: The Growing Assault on Truth and Memory*. New York: Free Press, 1993.

Lumer, Hyman, ed. *Lenin on the Jewish Question*. New York: International Publishers, 1974.

Makovsky, David. "Is Japan Making Amends." *Jerusalem Post*, May 24, 1991.

Marsden, George M. *Fundamentalism and American Culture: The Shaping of Twentieth-Century Evangelicalism, 1870–1925*. New York: Oxford University Press, 1980.

Maruyama, Naoki. "Japan's Middle Eastern Policy in a Dilemma." In *Bulletin of the Middle East Institute of the International University of Japan 2* (1986), 267–72.

McFarland, H. Neill. *The Rush Hour of the Gods: A Study of the New Religious Movements in Japan*. New York: Harper and Row, 1967.

Meyer, Ernie. "A Present for Purim." *Jerusalem Post*, March 12, 1982.

Miller, Judith. *One By One By One: Facing the Holocaust*. New York: Simon and Schuster, 1990.

Mintz, Alan. *Hurban: Response to Catastrophe in Hebrew Literature*. New York: Columbia University Press, 1984.

Miyazawa, Masanori. "Japanese Anti-Semitism in the Thirties." *Midstream* (March 1987), 23–27.

Morely, James W. *The Japanese Thrust into Siberia, 1918*. New York: Columbia University Press, 1957.

Morin, Edgar. *Rumour in Orléans*. Translated by Peter Green. New York: Pantheon, 1971.

Morley, John H. *Vatican Diplomacy and the Jews During the Holocaust 1939–1943*. New York: KTAV, 1980.

Morris, Benny. *The Birth of the Palestinian Refugee Problem, 1947–1949*. New York: Cambridge University Press, 1987.

•

Morris, Ivan. "The Japanese Messiah." In *The Nobility of Failure: Tragic Heroes in the History of Japan*. New York: New American Library, 1975.

Muhlen, Norbert. "The Return of Anne Frank." *ADL Bulletin*. June 1957.

Najita, Tetsuo and Koschmann, J. Victor, eds. *Conflict in Modern Japanese History: The Neglected Tradition*. Princeton: Princeton University Press, 1982.

Nolte, Ernst. "Between Myth and Revisionism: The Third Reich in the Perspective of the 1980s." In *Aspects of the Third Reich*. Edited by H. W. Koch. New York: St. Martin's Press, 1985.

Nosco, Peter. *Remembering Paradise: Nativism and Nostalgia in Eighteenth Century Japan*. Cambridge, Mass.: Council on East Asian Studies, Harvard University, 1990.

Notehelfer, F. G. *American Samurai: Captain L. L. Janes and Japan*. Princeton: Princeton University Press, 1985

Packard, George R., III. *Protest in Tokyo: The Security Treaty Crisis of 1960*. Princeton: Princeton University Press, 1966.

Peattie, Mark R. *Ishiwara Kanji and Japan's Confrontation with the West*. Princeton: Princeton University Press, 1975.

Pollack, David. *The Fracture of Meaning: Japan's Synthesis of China from the Eighth through the Eighteenth Centuries*. Princeton: Princeton University Press, 1986.

Popkin, Henry. "The Vanishing Jew of Our Popular Culture." *Commentary* 14 (July 1952), 46–55.

Pyle, Kenneth B. *The Japanese Question: Power and Purpose in a New Era*. Washington, D.C.: AEI Press, 1992.

Radtke, Kurt W. "Japan-Israel Relations in the Eighties." *Asian Survey* 28, no. 5 (May 1988), 526–40.

Raz, Jacob. *Audience and Actors: A Study of Their Interaction in the Japanese Traditional Theatre*. Leiden: E. J. Brill, 1983.

Reischauer, Edwin O. *The Japanese Today*. Cambridge, Mass.: Harvard University Press, 1988.

Rogasky, Barbara. *Smoke and Ashes: The Story of the Holocaust*. New York: Holiday House, 1988.

Rolf, Robert T. "Japanese Theatre from the 1980s: The Ludic Conspiracy." *Modern Drama*, 31, no. 1 (March 1992), 127–36.

Rosenfeld, Alvin H. "Popularization and Memory: The Case of Anne Frank." In *Lessons and Legacies: The Meaning of the Holocaust in a Changing*

World. Edited by Peter Hayes. Evanston: Northwestern University Press, 1991, pp. 243–278.

Roth, Cecil, ed. *Magna Bibliotheca Anglo-Judaica: A Bibliographical Guide to Anglo-Jewish History*. London: Jewish Historical Society of England, 1937.

Rubenstein, Richard L. *The Cunning of History: The Holocaust and the American Future*. New York: Harper and Row, 1975.

Ruether, Rosemary Radford. *Faith and Fratricide: The Theological Roots of Anti-Semitism*. New York: Seabury Press, 1974.

Said, Edward. *Orientalism*. New York: Vintage, 1979.

Sandeen, Ernest R. *The Roots of Fundamentalism: British and American Millenarianism 1800–1930*. Chicago: University of Chicago Press, 1970.

Sanford, James H.; LaFleur, William R.; and Nagatomi, Masatoshi, eds. *Flowing Traces: Buddhism in the Literary and Visual Arts of Japan*. Princeton: Princeton University Press, 1992.

Sansom, George. *Japan: A Short Cultural History*, rev. ed. New York: Appleton-Century-Crofts, 1962.

Sato, Toshihiko. "Henrik Ibsen in Japan." Ph.d. diss., University of Washington, 1966.

Scheiner, Irwin. *Christian Converts and Social Protest in Meiji Japan*. Berkeley: University of California Press, 1970.

Schlant, Ernestine and Rimer, J. Thomas, eds. *Legacies and Ambiguities: Postwar Fiction and Culture in West Germany and Japan*. Washington, D.C.: Woodrow Wilson Center Press, 1991.

Schnabel, Ernst. *Anne Frank: A Portrait in Courage*. Translated by Richard and Clara Winston. New York: Harcourt, Brace, 1958.

Schofield, John. "American Makes a Splash with Novel in Japanese." *Wall Street Journal*. October 6, 1992.

Shapiro, James. *Shakespeare and the Jews*. The Parkes Lecture. University of Southampton, 1992.

Shillony, Ben-Ami. *The Jews and the Japanese: The Successful Outsiders*. Rutland, Vt.: Tuttle, 1991.

———. *Politics and Culture in Wartime Japan*. New York: Oxford University Press, 1981.

———. "The Princess of the Dragon Palace: A New Shinto Sect is Born." *Monumenta Nipponica* 39, no. 2 (1984), 177–82.

Shulman, Frank Joseph. "Japanese-Middle Eastern Economic Relations Before the First 'Oil Shock': An Overview." Paper presented at "Japan and the Middle East in Alliance Politics" at the Woodrow

Wilson International Center for Scholars, November 16, 1984. Mimeographed.

Silverman, Cheryl A. "Jewish Emigres and Popular Images of Jews in Japan." Ph.D. diss., Columbia University, 1989.

Skloot, Robert. *The Darkness We Carry: The Drama of the Holocaust.* Madison: University of Wisconsin Press, 1988.

Smith, Henry D., III. *Japan's First Student Radicals.* Cambridge, Mass.: Harvard University Press, 1972.

Solomon, Harold. "Japan—Pro-Arab?" *Midstream* 24, no. 1 (January 1978), 14–26.

Sontag, Frederick. *Sun Myung Moon and the Unification Church.* Nashville: Abingdon, 1977.

Spector, Ronald H. *Eagle Against the Sun: The American War with Japan.* New York: Vintage, 1985.

Steiner, George. *Language and Silence: Essays, 1958–1966.* London: Faber & Faber, 1967.

Steinhoff, Patricia G. "Death by Defeatism and Other Fables: The Social Dynamics of the Rengō Sekigun Purge." In *Japanese Social Organization.* Edited by Takie Sugiyama Lebra. Honolulu: University of Hawaii Press, 1992, pp. 195–224.

———. "Hijackers, Bombers and Bank Robbers: Japanese Managerial Style in the Radical Left." Paper presented at the Association for Asian Studies annual meeting, March 25–27, 1988. Mimeographed.

———. "Portrait of a Terrorist: An Interview with Kozo Okamoto." *Asian Survey* 16, no. 9 (September 1976), 830–45.

———. "Tenkō: Ideology and Societal Integration in Prewar Japan." Ph.D. diss., Harvard University, 1969.

Stern, Willy. "David and Godzilla." *New Republic*, February 27, 1989.

———. "Japan's 'Free Traders' Boycott Israel." *Tokyo Business Today*, November 1987, pp. 26–28.

———. "Japanese Dictionaries Encourage Anti-Semitism." *Japan Times*, October 16, 1988.

Talmon, Yonina. "Millenarianism." *International Encyclopedia of the Social Sciences.* New York: Macmillan-Free Press, 1968.

Tanabe, Hajime. *Philosophy as Metanoetics.* Translated by Yoshinori Takeuchi. Berkeley: University of California Press, 1986.

Teshima, Yuroh. "What's Anti-Semitism Doing in Japan?" *Japan Times*, May 10, 1987.

Tigay, Alan M. Review of *Passover.* In *Hadassah Magazine.* April 1990, p. 44.

•

Toby, Ronald P. "Carnival of the Aliens: Korean Embassies in Edo Period Art and Popular Culture." *Monumenta Nipponica*, 41, no. 4 (Winter 1986), 415–56.

————. *State and Diplomacy in Early Modern Japan: Asia in the Development of the Tokugawa Bakufu*. Princeton: Princeton University Press, 1984.

Tokayer, Marvin and Swartz, Mary. *The Fugu Plan: The Untold Story of the Japanese and the Jews During World War II*. New York: Paddington Press, 1979.

Tsunoda, Waka. Review of *Passover*. *World Literature Today*. Autumn 1986.

Tsurumi, Shunsuke. *An Intellectual History of Wartime Japan 1931–1945*. London: KPI Limited, 1986.

Tsurumi, Yoshi. "Anti-Semitism in Japan: The Ghost that has Returned to Haunt." *Pacific Basin Quarterly* (Winter-Spring 1990), 21–22.

Vidal-Naquet, Pierre. *Assassins of Memory: Essays on the Denial of the Holocaust*. Translated by Jeffrey Mehlman. New York: Columbia University Press, 1992.

Vogel, Ezra F. *Japan as Number One: Lessons for America*. Cambridge, Mass.: Harvard University Press, 1979.

Wargo, Robert J. J. "The Jewish Conspiracy Scare: An Exercise in Paranoia." *PHP Intersect*, January 1988, pp. 30–34.

Wernick, Robert. "Don't Look Now—But All Those Plotters Might Be Hiding Under Your Bed." *Smithsonian*. March 1994, pp. 108–24.

Wetherall, William. "Pride and Sometimes Prejudice in Japan," *Far Eastern Economic Review*. October 15, 1987.

White, J. A. *The Siberian Intervention*. Princeton: Princeton University Press, 1950.

Williams, David. "Rant of Japan's Tabloids: Hysterical Anti-Semitism." *Los Angeles Times*, January 3, 1992.

Williams, Harold S. *Foreigners in Mikadoland*. Rutland, Vt.: Tuttle, 1963.

Wills, Gary. *Under God: Religion and American Politics*. New York: Simon and Schuster, 1990.

Wilson, George M. *Patriots and Redeemers in Japan: Motives in the Meiji Restoration*. Chicago: University of Chicago Press, 1992.

————. "Pursuing the Millennium in the Meiji Restoration." In Najita, Tetsuo and Koschmann, J. Victor, eds. *Conflict in Modern Japanese History: The Neglected Tradition*. Princeton: Princeton University Press, 1982, pp. 177–94.

Wistrich, Robert S. *Antisemitism: The Longest Hatred*. New York: Pantheon, 1991.

•

————. ed. *Anti-Zionism and Antisemitism in the Contemporary World*. New York: New York University Press, 1990.

————. *Hitler's Apocalypse: Jews and the Nazi Legacy*. New York: St. Martin's Press, 1985.

Yamaguchi, Masao. "Kingship, Theatricality, and Marginal Reality in Japan." In *Text and Context: The Social Anthropology of Tradition*. Edited by Ravindra K. Jain. Philadelphia: Institute for the Study of Human Issues, 1977, pp. 151–79.

Yoshida, Teigo. "The Stranger as God: The Place of the Outsider in Japanese Folk Religion." *Ethnology* 20, no. 2 (1981), 87–99.

Yoshiwara, R. See Ahlberg, Roger.

SELECTED ARTICLES IN JAPANESE

"Anne no chichi no ihin todoku" [Mementos Left by Anne's Father Arrive]. *Asahi shimbun*, August 12, 1993.

"Chinkon no shimboru heiwakan" [The Peace Memorial: Symbol of the Pacification of Souls]. *Yomiuri shimbun*, August 13, 1983.

"En: haisui no kōbō" [The Yen: Last-Ditch Defense]. *Yomiuri shimbun*. January 17, 1987.

"Erusaremu jogai no hamon kakudai" [The Impact of Excluding Jerusalem Increases]. *Chūgai nippō*, November 18, 1987.

" 'Gaikokujin oidase': tairyō no bira demawaru" ["Get Rid of Foreigners": Large Numbers of Handbills Circulated]. *Asahi shimbun*, international edition, April 7, 1993.

"Jinshu ronsō" [The Race Debate]. *Yomiuri shimbun*, November 3, 1986.

"Kifu 890-man en tsūkon no henkan" [¥8.9 Million Returned With Great Sorrow]. *Asahi shimbun*, December 18, 1993.

"Kūkyo na seremonii sekai rekishi toshi" [The World Conference of Historical Cities: An Empty Ceremony]. *Chūgai nippō*, December 7, 1987.

"Kinkyū keikoku: 'kabuka ichiman-en' de 'Yudaya shihon' ni nerawareru Nihon kigyō" [Urgent Alert: Japanese Industry Threatened by "Jewish Capital" When Stock Prices Hit ¥10,000]. *Shūkan Post*, July 10, 1992, pp. 31–35.

"Nachisu no jidai o shiru" [Learning About the Nazi Period]. *Mainichi shimbun*, March 16, 1992.

"Nosutoradamusu 'fukkatsu' " [Nostradamus "Rises Again"]. *Mainichi shimbun*, February 9, 1991.

•

" 'Seiji-teki riyū de jogai' to Imagawa shichō" [Mayor Imagawa Admits (Jerusalem) "Excluded for Political Reasons"]. *Chūgai nippō*, December 7, 1987.

"Senritsu! Kurinton o ayatsuru Yudaya shihon no tainichi senryaku" [The Ominous Strategy of the Jewish Capital that Controls Clinton]. *Shūkan gendai*, December 5, 1992, pp. 24–28.

"Shushō hatsugen ni kōgi sattō" [Deluge of Protest Over Prime Minister's Remarks]. *Yomiuri shimbun*, September 24, 1986.

" 'Wangan' o meguru shoseki shuppan no ugoki" [Trends in Book Publishing Surrounding "The Gulf"]. *Asahi shimbun*, March 24, 1991.

"Wangan sensō ga hi o tsuketa 'Yudayabon' ninki no kiken" [The Danger of the Popularity of "Jewish books" Inflamed by the Gulf War]. *Asahi Journal*, May 3–10, 1991.

SELECTED ARTICLES IN ENGLISH

"Anti-Semitic Book Ad Assailed." *Japan Times*, July 31, 1993.

"Arabs' Boycott of Israel Is Alive, But Hardly Flourishing." *New York Times*, August 23, 1987.

"Auschwitz Memorial Planned in Kurose." *Japan Times*, January 12, 1983.

"Backers, Protesters Mark Constitution's 40th Year." *Japan Times,* May 4, 1987.

"Breakdown in the Fast Lane." *Economist*, February 27, 1993.

"Chutzpah in Japanese." *Washington Jewish Week*, July 7, 1988.

"Den Fujita, Japan's Mr. Joint-Venture." *New York Times*, March 22, 1992.

"Do It My Way," *Economist*, November 24, 1990.

"Era of Radical Journalism Ends with Asahi Journal Closure." *Japan Times Weekly International Edition*, June 1–7, 1992.

"Feeling Poor in Japan." *Economist,* June 11, 1988.

"Gloom is Lifting in the U.S. and Descending on Japan." *New York Times*, December 29, 1992.

"Hiroshima and the Holocaust." *Japan Times*, February 20, 1983.

"Is Japan Making Amends?" *Jerusalem Post*, May 24, 1991.

"Israel, Japan to Sign Tax Treaty." *Jerusalem Post*, January 13, 1993.

"Issue of Japanese Racism Grows with Immigration." *Los Angeles Times*, January 1, 1990.

"Japan Apologizes for a Racial Slur." *New York Times*, August 16, 1988.

"Japan, Israel Improving Commercial Ties." *Washington Post,* August 7, 1991.

"Japan Expanding its Ties with Israel." *New York Times*, June 19, 1988.

"Japan Will Stop Supporting Arab Economic Boycott." *Jerusalem Post*, December 4, 1991.

"Japan's New Leader Pledges Sweeping Changes in Political System." *New York Times*, August 24, 1993.

"Japan's Unmelted Minority Talks Up." *New York Times*, November 5, 1986.

"Japan's Vanishing Counterculture." *Newsweek*, June 1, 1992.

"Japan, Israel Improving Commercial Ties." *Washington Post*, August 7, 1991.

"Japanese Book Praises Hitler for Politics." *New York Times*, June 8, 1994.

"Japanese Rightist Fires Shot Near Former Premier: Anger Over Apologies for Tokyo's War Role." *New York Times*, May 31, 1994.

"Japanese Start to Link Pay to Performance, Not Tenure." *New York Times*, October 2, 1993.

"Japanese to Name Park in Memory of Ambassador Who Saved Jews." *Jerusalem Post,* August 5, 1992.

"Japanese Writers Are Critical of Jews." *New York Times,* March 12, 1987.

" 'Jewish Conspiracy' a Figment of an Author's Imagination." *The East* 23, no. 2 (June 1987), 43.

"Lessons in Kyoto." *Boston Herald*, November 18, 1987.

"Losing Its Way." *Economist*, September 18, 1993.

"Minister Fired for Doubting Japan's Guilt." *New York Times*, May 8, 1994.

"Nakayama Dedicates Center at Deheishe." *Jerusalem Post,*. June 2, 1991.

"New Indignities for Refugees in Japan." *New York Times*, October 24, 1989.

"Newest Testament: Japan is the Land of the Rising Son." *Wall Street Journal*, October 1, 1993.

"Peres Calls for Greater Japanese Role in Region." *Jerusalem Post*, December 15, 1992.

"Prejudice and Black Sambo." *Time*, August 15, 1988.

"Rich Man, Poor Man in Japan: Not an Economic Party for All." *New York Times*, December 26, 1988.

"Tokyo Aide Calls 'Rape of Nanking' a Fabrication." *New York Times*, May 5, 1994.

"Toward Fellow Asians, A Lack of Fellowship." *New York Times*, January 3, 1990.

•

INDEX

About the Authors

David G. Goodman is professor of Japanese literature in the Department of East Asian Languages and Cultures at the University of Illinois at Urbana-Champaign. His books include *After Apocalypse: Four Japanese Plays of Hiroshima and Nagasaki* (1986); *Japanese Drama and Culture in the 1960s: The Return of the Gods* (1988); and *Long, Long Autumn Nights: Selected Poems of Oguma Hideo* (1989), which won the 1990 Columbia University Translation Center Award. In addition to his English publications, Goodman has written four books in Japanese, including *Isuraeru: koe to kao* [Israel: Voices and Faces, 1979].

Masanori Miyazawa is professor of history at Dōshisha Women's College in Kyoto, Japan, and former director of its Institute for Interdisciplinary Studies of Culture. He is Japan's leading authority on Japanese attitudes toward Jews and the author of pioneering studies on the subject. In addition, he has written widely on the history of modern Japanese Christianity.